Spain's
Men of the Sea

Daily Life on the Indies Fleets
in the Sixteenth Century

Pablo E. Pérez-Mallaína
Translated by Carla Rahn Phillips

The Johns Hopkins University Press ◆ Baltimore and London

Translation of this work was made possible by a grant from the Junta de Andalucía; the University of Seville; the Diputación Provincial de Sevilla; and the General Direction of Books, Archives, and Libraries of the Ministry of Culture of Spain.

This book was brought to publication with the generous assistance of the Program for Cultural Cooperation between Spain's Ministry of Culture and United States' Universities.

Originally published as *Los hombres del Océano: Vida cotidiana de los tripulantes de las flotas de Indias, Siglo XVI* by Servicio de Publicaciones de la Diputación de Sevilla, 1992.

The Johns Hopkins University Press
2715 North Charles Street
Baltimore, Maryland 21218-4363
The Johns Hopkins Press Ltd., London
www.jhu.press.edu

Library of Congress Cataloging-in-Publication Data will be found at the end of this book.
A catalog record for this book is available from the British Library.
ISBN 0-8018-5746-5

Contents

Translator's Introduction

Through much of the sixteenth century, Spanish fleets sailed back and forth across the Atlantic and around the Caribbean, largely unchallenged by European rivals. Pirates and privateers with designs on the money and goods carried by returning ships lay in wait off the Azores or hid behind promontories on the rocky Portuguese coast. Only in the late sixteenth century did marauders know enough about the Atlantic routes pioneered by the Spaniards to attack settlements and ships in the New World.

To defend the fleets, the Spanish government set up a system of convoys beginning in the 1520s, with merchant vessels sailing together under the protection of heavily armed ships. By the late sixteenth century, trade with the Indies (as Spaniards called their empire in the Western Hemisphere) had reached an impressive volume. As many as two hundred merchant vessels a year formed the great fleets of New Spain (Mexico) and Tierra Firme (South America) and their escorts. Altogether the fleets probably required between seven thousand and nine thousand mariners, most of them recruited voluntarily. The sailors who manned both merchantmen and royal escort vessels are the focus of Pablo Pérez-Mallaína's exciting study. Their labor, and the skill of their commanders, enabled Spain to maintain its empire in the face of increasing challenges from rivals elsewhere in Europe.

Pérez-Mallaína wrote this book, first published as *Los hombres del Océano*, for a Spanish-speaking audience during the quincentenary of Columbus's 1492 voyage of exploration. He assumed that his readers knew the basic facts about Spain's sixteenth-century history within the context of broader European developments. For English-speaking readers, it perhaps is useful to review that historical background.

During the sixteenth century, two great movements turned the energies of European civilization in new directions and realigned the loyalties of states and peoples. The two movements in question were the exploration of other parts of the globe, led by mariners from Iberia, and the shattering of Christian religious unity by the Protestant reformation. Spain played a key role in both movements, the first by conscious design, the second by the force of circumstance.

In 1469 Isabella of Castile married her cousin Ferdinand of Aragón. When they inherited the thrones of their respective kingdoms, Spain emerged as one of the most powerful states in Europe. Ferdinand and Isabella, the so-called Catholic Monarchs, dominated their internal rivals and waged a ten-year war against the kingdom of Granada, the last Muslim stronghold on the peninsula. Early in 1492 Granada fell into their hands, ending a Christian reconquest that had lasted eight hundred years. Immediately thereafter, the monarchs moved to enforce religious unity in their realms, expelling Jews who refused to convert to Christianity. They also agreed to sponsor Christopher Columbus's scheme to sail westward to Asia.

(viii)

The most obvious aim of Columbus's voyage was to establish direct trading links to China and Japan. The voyage also had a religious aim: to bring the message of Christianity to the peoples of Asia, fulfilling prophecy and preparing for the second coming of Christ. Many intellectuals in Europe believed that Spain had an important role to play in the unfolding of the divine plan, and Ferdinand and Isabella were keenly aware of their responsibilities in such a scenario.

In their foreign policy within Europe, the Catholic Monarchs negotiated a series of marriage alliances with other ruling dynasties. Their links with the Habsburgs of central Europe had the most far-reaching consequences, most of them unplanned. Several untimely deaths left Ferdinand and Isabella's grandson Charles, born with the century in 1500, heir to vast territories and responsibilities: Castile and Aragón in Iberia; the southern half of Italy; a collection of islands in the Mediterranean; Habsburg family lands in central Europe; the remnant of the Burgundian inheritance between France and the Germanies, including the Netherlands; and the empire that Spain was in the process of conquering and organizing in the New World.

Charles became king of Spain in 1516, ruling in his own name and in that of his mother, the mentally unstable Joanna. Elected Holy Roman Emperor in 1519 as Charles V, he immediately faced the greatest challenge to Christianity in centuries: the religious reform movement set off by Martin Luther and a sympathetic chorus of German princes chafing under the yoke of the Roman Catholic Church. Many educated observers saw Charles' imperial election as a further sign of Spain's key role in the divine plan. Almost by definition, Charles' Spanish kingdoms would occupy the front lines in the defense of Christian unity under the Roman Catholic Church.

In the first half of the sixteenth century, Charles simultaneously worked to restore unity to the fragmented Christian community and waged war against the expansionary thrusts of the Ottoman Turks. The Turks had conquered Constantinople for the Islamic world in 1453 and continued to expand into the eastern borderlands of Christian Europe. They used their powerful fleets to control the eastern Mediterranean and sponsored corsairing states in North Africa that harassed shipping and coastal communities in the western Mediterranean. Charles spent much of his life trying to contain the Turkish advance, a task made doubly difficult by the persistent rift in Christendom. Some of Charles' opponents in the Christian community, notably France, actually allied with the Turks. The enormous expense of fighting wars on several fronts depended largely on the wealth flowing into Europe from Spanish America.

During Charles' reign, Spanish adventurers conquered the Aztec and Incan empires in the Western Hemisphere. Those conquests provided new sources of wealth to fund Charles' foreign policy, at first by booty plundered from the de-   (ix)
feated empires and later by tax revenues from production, local trade, and international commerce. Even with American treasure adding 10 to 20 percent to the royal coffers, Charles ran the Spanish monarchy heavily into debt.

Spain also sponsored dozens of voyages of exploration in the early sixteenth century, including the first circumnavigation of the globe, begun in 1519 under the Portuguese Ferdinand Magellan and completed in 1521 under the Spaniard Juan Sebastián Elcano. With the Magellan-Elcano voyage, the Spanish crown gained more accurate information about the vastness of the oceans and a sense of the maritime strength that would be needed for trade and defense in its growing empire.

Religious strife and commercial rivalry in Europe continued in the reign of Philip II, Charles' son and the successor to most of his domains and titles. It was during Philip II's reign (from 1556 to 1598) that Spanish power reached its height in the early modern period. In Europe, Philip continued his father's war against the Ottoman Empire and promoted a militant Catholic response to Protestantism. In the Indies, Spain's colonial establishment confronted the persistent efforts of French, English, and Dutch pirates, privateers, and interlopers to break the Spanish monopoly. Some colonists fought the intruders, others openly collaborated with them, and even royal officials were sometimes ambivalent. The interlopers could often supply goods that the fleets could not or that would have cost much more through official channels.

Overall, however, the official monopoly held. Merchant fleets transported a vast array of goods across the Atlantic Ocean, spawning commercial fortunes all over Europe. In 1571 Spain founded Manila in the Philippine Islands, gaining an entry into the Asian trade as well. The rich mines of Potosí in South America yielded a steady flow of silver that fueled economic growth and inflation in Europe and financed trade around the world. The ancient city of Seville on the Guadalquivir River in southwestern Spain mushroomed into a bustling port. As the nerve center of imperial trade and the official gateway to the New World, Seville served as a temporary destination for tens of thousands of merchants, emigrants, and mariners plus a motley assortment of grifters, clerics, prostitutes, thieves, bureaucrats, and jobseekers.

Translator's Introduction

Pérez-Mallaína focuses his analysis on the mariners in this flood of humanity. Where did they come from, and why did they migrate to Seville? How did they fare in the dizzying atmosphere of the city? Once on board ships bound for the Indies, what did their work entail? How did they live? How much did they earn? What did they eat? How did they amuse themselves in the confining atmosphere of a ship at sea? How did officers and men interact, and how were their inevitable conflicts sorted out? How, if at all, did the men satisfy their sexual appetites on board? How did they express their religiosity? What did they think about themselves and their place in the divine plan? And what about the women and children they left behind? How did they survive while the men were at sea? What happened to them if the men never returned? By daring to ask questions that have no easy answers, Pérez-Mallaína reconstructs the lives of Spain's men of the sea in vivid detail. He relies heavily on documentation from the Archive of the Indies in Seville, using a range of materials that includes official chronicles of famous voyages as well as the legal records of obscure sailors petitioning for back pay and royal justice.

(x)

A few examples hint at the richly detailed stories unearthed by the author. Consider the case of a mulatto named Lope Martínez de Lagos, who sailed as the pilot of a dispatch boat on a voyage to the Philippines. Upon his return, he was secretly condemned to death for defrauding the royal treasury, but the crown needed his services to get the ship back to the Philippines. Unknowingly, he carried his own death sentence in a sealed envelope, which he was supposed to deliver to the governor of those islands. He somehow found out about the contents of the envelope, however, and organized a mutiny to murder all the officers on the ship. Then there was Doña Isabel de Soto y Avilés, whose husband had spent his career serving the crown. Far from enriching himself in royal service, he had even spent his wife's dowry, and she faced the prospect of a penniless widowhood. Francisco Manuel, a poor orphan boy wandering the riverbank in Seville, had much better luck. A rich shipowner named Andrés de Paz took him on as a page at the age of seven, taught him the art of navigation, and set him on the path to an important post as a ship's pilot. Stories such as these bring Spain's maritime community back to life after nearly five centuries.

In translating this important work of social history, I have tried to maintain the rhythm and flow of the author's Spanish phrasing while bringing the text into idiomatic English. For some words and phrases, I have included the Spanish original at the first mention and used English thereafter. Some of the specialized nautical vocabulary, as well as some of the imaginative invective used in shipboard brawls, have no precise English equivalents. I have translated them to preserve the spirit, rather than the letter, of the phrasing. Place names, for the most part, are left in Spanish, including accents. The notes and bibliographical citations are translated as they appear in the original, with the addition of English titles for books that were first published in that language. I hope that this English version serves as a faithful rendition of Pérez-Mallaína's rich panorama of sixteenth-century maritime life.

Translator's Introduction

ONE

The Land Environment
of the Men of the Sea

Seville, Port and Gateway to the New World

Sooner or later, any sailor who traveled to the Indies in Spanish ships made a stop in Seville, the great port on the Guadalquivir River. Many of them came from the Atlantic coast of Andalusia; quite a few originated on the Cantabrian coast in the north; some were born on the Mediterranean shores of the Iberian Peninsula; and a considerable number had arrived from distant kingdoms, from Flanders to Sicily and from Genoa to the Greek Islands. In Seville they joined with men of the sea who lived in the city's various neighborhoods, such as San Vicente, La Magdalena, De La Mar, and above all, the suburb of Triana. The Sevillian metropolis thus became the common ground on land for all the men of the sea who sailed back and forth across the Atlantic to Spain's American colonies, a trajectory known as the Carrera de Indias (the Route of the Indies). Many of them had their permanent residence in Seville. Others found themselves obliged to live in inns and lodgings in the hope of signing on for a voyage, and there they rubbed elbows with merchants, beggars, and royal functionaries, forming a human tapestry of great vitality in which the extraordinary became commonplace. An observer who was born in the middle of the sixteenth century and knew the city well captured its ambience perfectly: "Seville was well adapted to every profitable undertaking, and as much was brought there to sell as was bought, because there are merchants for everything. It is the common homeland, the endless globe, the mother of orphans, and the cloak of sinners, where everything is a necessity, and no one has it."[1]

Since 1503, when the House of Trade was established in Seville, the city was destined to direct the traffic of persons and merchandise overseas as the official port of entry and departure for ships traveling to the Indies. The wealth that flowed along the river enriched the city and enabled its population to surpass 40,000 inhabitants at the end of the fifteenth century and to arrive at about 150,000 in the last years of the sixteenth.[2]

Undeniably, the extraordinary growth of the city was a consequence of its position as a privileged port in the Atlantic commercial system; nonetheless, even before 1503 Seville was the most populous city in Castile, and an administrative, financial, commercial, and agricultural center of the first order. It was precisely for that reason that Seville was chosen as the land base for oceanic

navigation. At the end of the fifteenth century, Seville was one of the largest
cities in the Iberian Peninsula, but being chosen as the point of departure for
the Indies fleets transformed it into one of the largest metropolitan centers in
all of Europe.

Its selection was due to some obvious advantages. The route to the West
Indies followed a fixed track on the sea, defined by the constant currents and
winds in the Atlantic. The great transoceanic highway commenced in the Canary Islands and went directly to the Lesser Antilles. For that reason, the port
of departure from the peninsula had to be situated at the origin of the route toward the Canaries, that is to say, at some point on the Atlantic coast of Andalusia. Seville was far and away the most densely populated port in that region. Compared with the forty thousand inhabitants that the city had at the
end of the fifteenth century, the next largest port was Puerto de Santa María,
with sixty-five hundred inhabitants. Huelva had forty-five hundred, and similar numbers lived in Moguer, Ayamonte, and Sanlúcar de Barrameda, while
Cádiz counted only some two thousand inhabitants.[3]

Thus, the first argument in Seville's favor was its important concentration
of people, from which could be drawn the mariners necessary to crew the ships.
In addition, it had the capacity to absorb and lodge without too much difficulty the massive floating population—mariners, passengers, and merchants—
who were embarking on the fleets. A large proportion of the men who would
crew the vessels chose to reside in the suburb of Triana on the right bank of
the Guadalquivir. This neighborhood, which was the seventeenth largest urban district at the end of the fourteenth century, was among the three most
populated parishes during the sixteenth century; in 1588 it had more residents
than the district surrounding the largest church in Seville, traditionally the
most populated parish in the city.[4]

In the second place, the city was an administrative center and the ancient
headquarters of the concentrated power represented by the king. In past centuries, a dispute that pitted the monarchs against the rich and powerful lords
of lower Andalusia had represented more to the crown than a simple head-
butting contest for dominance, and it had involved more than a few setbacks.
Almost all of the important ports of Andalusia were in the hands of old aristocratic families, and for that reason the crown, engaged in turning the conquest of the Indies into an enterprise based on centralized, if not national, authority, decided to choose the river port of Seville as its headquarters. The
Catholic monarchs Ferdinand and Isabella had their castle there, the Alcázar.
Some of their ancestors resided for all eternity in the cathedral, and the city
hosted an important nucleus of royal functionaries who could be used to administer the voyages of exploration.

The royal preference for Seville was well established. Ferdinand III, the king who captured Seville from the Muslims in the thirteenth century, and his son Alfonso the Wise chose Seville as the base for the galleys that controlled the Strait of Gibraltar, and they renovated the old shipyards of the Almohad Muslims to repair ships and build new ones. Likewise, for a long time the admirals of Castile had their headquarters in Seville. In the sixteenth century, other admirals took their place, and, instead of looking only toward the Mediterranean or the Canaries, they directed their interests farther, toward the expanses of the Ocean Sea.

Finally, Seville was the economic center of the Guadalquivir valley, which, (3) because of its agricultural riches and its urban life, was the natural communications route for one of the most prosperous regions in all of western Europe. Wheat, wine, oil, and salted fish were produced in abundance there and were essential if one had plans to feed the crews on dozens of ships at a time.

To finance everything, Genoese bankers had been established in the city since the Middle Ages. These masters of loans, insurance, and letters of exchange had held a strategic position on the southwest coasts of the peninsula since the thirteenth century, when the maritime route through the Strait of Gibraltar had opened the Mediterranean to Christian powers. The initiation of maritime routes between Italy and the ports of Flanders had a decisive effect on the economy of western Europe, because it put the two most powerful industrial centers of the moment into direct contact with each other, bypassing the slow land route across the Alps. Thanks to the opening of this new route of maritime commerce, Andalusia in general, and the valley of the Guadalquivir in particular, were transformed into a transit point between east and west, which added to their traditional role as the intermediary between North Africa and the European continent.

In sum, Seville was the land base for the Indies fleets because it could supply men to sail the ships, functionaries to dispatch them, victuals to feed their mariners, a good commercial distribution network, and money to finance the expeditions. Besides all this, its position as an inland port, almost one hundred kilometers from the sea, provided protection against the assaults of all those who were tempted by the gleaming precious metals and other riches of the Indies.

But was there no defect among so many virtues? Of course there was. Seville lacked nothing in the world, but its position as a center of navigation had one great inconvenience. The city was a river port with a very limited capacity to handle large ships that were fully loaded. The tremendous development of maritime commerce in western Europe between the thirteenth and the fifteenth centuries, from which Seville had benefited so much, carried the seed that would eventually cause the decay of the port on the Guadalquivir. Eagerness to lower the costs of maritime transport led to a constant increase in ships' tonnages. Already at the end of the fifteenth century, the great Italian carracks, which frequently measured more than a thousand tons, could not even dream of crossing the dangerous sandbar at Sanlúcar at the mouth of the river, nor could they survive the river's treacherous sandbanks, even at high tide.

Fortunately for Seville, the extraordinary commercial expansion of the sixteenth century attracted many small shipbuilders who wanted to share in the bonanza. They specialized in building ships of reduced tonnage that could compete, because of their speed, with the largest and slowest merchant ships.[5] The sixteenth century was dominated by small ships measuring between one hundred and two hundred tons, which could sail up the Guadalquivir without too many problems. But time worked against the city. The average tonnage of Indies ships, which at the end of the sixteenth century was a little more than two hundred tons, was growing rapidly. If we add to this the increasing number of shipwrecks in the river, it is understandable why the Guadalquivir was losing value as a component of oceanic trade.

《 4 》

Thus, although Seville was the undisputed metropolis of the trade from a demographic, administrative, and commercial point of view, from the first it had to share with other places the role of Indies port. In fact, the great port of entry and departure for New World traffic was a complex of ports that stretched from Cádiz, through Puerto de Santa María and Sanlúcar de Barrameda, all the way to Seville. In Cádiz a delegate of the House of Trade dispatched and received ships that were incorporated into the Indies fleets, and in the port of Sanlúcar de Barrameda, situated right at the mouth of the Guadalquivir, all the convoys gathered to finish loading and to undergo their final inspections *(visitas)* before departure. Moreover, the largest of the great merchant ships and the war galleons could rarely sail the length of the river; they remained halfway up, at a place called Las Horcadas, eight leagues (some forty-four kilometers) from Seville. The rest, the great majority of ships between one hundred and three hundred tons, continued upriver until arriving at Puerto de las Muelas, which was the maritime heart of Seville, flanked on the left bank by the curtain wall of the old Almohad fortifications and on the right bank by the suburb of Triana.

The buildings in Triana extended right up to the water's edge, but on the opposite bank the shoreline had accumulated a great quantity of sand between the river and the city wall. This was the famous Arenal, or "sandy beach," of Seville, a surface some seven hundred meters long by three hundred meters wide and the center of the city's port life. There, dozens of vessels were pressed together side by side, beached perpendicular to the waterline so as not to waste even a meter of space.

Two city gates and two small doorways opened onto the Arenal. From north to south, the first was the Triana Gate, connected to that neighborhood by a bridge of boats. Practically in the center of the port was the Arenal Gate, which connected to the cathedral through the Calle de la Mar (literally, "Street of the Sea"), the heart of the original marine neighborhood where Ferdinand III and Alfonso X had located the boatswains and crews of the galleys of Castile. The Calle de la Mar continued to be an axis for mariners' lives in the sixteenth century, because it linked the port with the stone steps surrounding the patio of the old Almohad mosque, converted into the principal church of the city. These were the famous cathedral steps (Gradas de la Catedral), where mariners aspiring to crew ships or to join voyages of conquest sat and waited (5) for a ship's master or captain to sign them up. The offices of scriveners or notaries were set up in the archways surrounding the steps, so that parties to the contracts for loading, booking passage, or signing on the crew did not have to travel far to formalize the agreements.

Beyond the Arenal Gate there were two small entryways, known as the doorways of oil and charcoal. The latter had a special importance, because it provided the most direct route to the royal palace, the Alcázar, and the offices of the House of Trade, which occupied quarters that had been part of the old Muslim palace. Many riches passed through this doorway headed for the money chests of the House of Trade, so many, in fact, that popular wisdom changed its name to a grander designation, the Golden Doorway. Immediately beyond this doorway was a salient of the wall that ran to the Almohad defense bastion, the equally famous Golden Tower (Torre de Oro). To the south of this tower, the wall made a right-angle turn away from the river, marking the end of the main area of the port.

Seville did not have port installations to match the importance of its traffic, however. For example, there were no stone or wooden piers to facilitate the loading and unloading of cargo. Nonetheless, depictions of the city, and some documents, give the name "wharf" or "pier" *(muelle)* to a small cylindrical stone construction located in front of the Golden Tower, which served as a platform for the only crane in the entire port. It had been built in the fifteenth century by the cathedral chapter for unloading the large blocks of stone destined for the church's construction. It was operated by the strength of several workers, perhaps slaves, who stood in the interior of two large parallel wheels and walked on the crosspieces that united the wheels, climbing a type of endless circular staircase.[6]

Spain as a whole had very few ports endowed with features to facilitate the work of loading and unloading. Only Santander and Málaga had cranes, whereas ports as prominent as Barcelona or Bilbao had none.[7] Nonetheless, on the question of installations, the port of Seville could not compare with some of the major ports elsewhere in Europe. Antwerp, for example, was endowed with seven ample piers on the Scheldt River, where at least three great cranes operated. And there was London, where images from the second half of the sixteenth century show seven or eight cranes located on the banks of the Thames.[8]

Nor did Seville have a single dike or shipyard expressly constructed to carry out periodic careenings to repair and refurbish ships' hulls. There were some attempts to build them, but, disgracefully, the plans remained on the drawing boards.[9] Thus, the banks of the river, from Seville to Sanlúcar, served as an improvised shipyard for carrying out repairs. The method that was employed consisted of hauling the hull of the ship high and dry and pulling it over on one side in order to work on the other. Because the operation was risky and caused many accidents, many careening sites were abandoned in favor of others free of obstacles, leaving behind partly submerged hulls that further obstructed the already dangerous bed of the Guadalquivir.

But the deficiencies of technical equipment did not diminish—quite the contrary—the rich and lively human environment that developed on the Arenal, the pulsating heart that pumped the blood of the city's maritime life. The space between the river and the city wall was only partially urbanized. A pair of neighborhoods (La Cestería and La Carretería) had begun to coalesce around the waterfront warehouses and the residences of river workers such as stevedores, coopers, porters, and boatmen. Another building had jumped over the wall, so to speak, and resided at the river's edge: one of the most notable buildings in the city, the old Almohad dockyard, which was used as a jail, warehouse, and customs house. All of this was built on the sandy soil, which turned to suffocating dust in summer and mud during the winter and which was permanently crisscrossed by canals of not very clean water that were traversed by small bridges.

As if this panorama did not contribute sufficiently to the questionable hygienic and sanitary conditions of the Arenal, the inhabitants of the city were accustomed to throwing garbage over the wall, creating authentic mountains of rubbish called *muladares*. To prevent such practices, the city council eventually hired special constables, who were known by the graphic, though hardly elegant, title of the "Garbage Guards."[10]

Despite all these woes, the Arenal was a human stewpot that simmered in the midst of one of the busiest and richest ports in the world. The iconography of the sixteenth century shows us a place filled with droves of mules carrying merchandise; passengers ready to embark or preparing to cross to the other side of the river in canopied boats; duelists in the midst of combat; noble ladies transported in carriages; and caulkers filling the gaps between hulls' planking with oakum and tar.

Not surprisingly, the Arenal of Seville was one of the favorite urban haunts of the mariners in the fleets, who were protagonists in many of the scenes that occurred there. The crews waiting idly for the departure of the fleets were a constant source of problems, and the vendors who offered their products on the shore of the river or in the nearby city streets seemed to be among their favorite targets. Sometimes they were treated to nocturnal rampages that ended with the sailors throwing rocks at the street lamps and shop windows.[11] On other occasions the incidents ended in sword fights, as occurred in 1578 between the sailors and the farmers who came to sell vegetables on the banks of the Guadalquivir.[12]

A curious document from the first years of the seventeenth century depicts one of these common incidents, in which we can recognize among the contending parties and witnesses the whole small human world that populated the vicinity of the port.[13] The scene was set when three gunners from the royal armada went to buy clams from one of the innumerable fish vendors. Fish was not the only merchandise that could be acquired on the Arenal. The images of the epoch show a swarm of stalls and pushcarts protected from the sun by conical awnings, where vendors sold fruits and melons, bricks, quicklime, and all sorts of trifles.

This little market was colloquially called the "cheap junk market" *(malbaratillo)*, and its name indicates that the quality of products sold was not very high. Thus, when one of the three gunners received some rotten clams from the vendor, he had no qualms about striking and insulting her. This is the story told by "Luisa de los Reyes, a woman from Ocaña, who makes her living from sardines at the river," a friend of the clam-selling protagonist in the incident:

> This witness being at the edge of the river, she saw a man walk up to Inés Tomasina, wife of Andrés de Escobar, and he bought some clams from her, and she tossed the said clams into a handkerchief; and having eaten three or four of them, the said man . . . raised the handkerchief with the said clams and handed it back to the said Inés Tomasina and told her: "You sow, don't give me garbage!" And the said Inés Tomasina said, "Sir, I am an honorable married woman and I do not have to say a word to that." And the said man told her: "If you want something [for these clams], go ahead and ask for it, but I will leave [without paying], even if it be from hell."[14]

Thus, the irritated buyer, the gunner Juan Lázaro, with an arrogance worthy of a Don Juan Tenorio, challenged anyone to rise up in defense of the fishwife. And she, according to the testimony of her friend, demonstrated a verbal continence that was frankly incredible, given the fame for foul language that usually accompanies those of her occupation, and contented herself with calling for her husband. A scuffle ensued, and fishermen and gunners tangled with one another in a battle that ended with various knife wounds. The witnesses who came to testify in the case represented some of the types of humanity who populated the Arenal: porters and stevedores, peddlars, and a sort that was abundant in the ports, whom we have not yet mentioned: the legion of tax collectors for various imposts, whose jobs obliged them always to be on the alert, which made them wonderful witnesses.

The Arenal, like all port zones, was not known as a very safe place; some old sailors presided over inns that provided a refuge for thieves who picked pockets and cut purse strings at the gateways to the city, although the competition was very strong and varied in that occupation. By running such an inn, Hernando de Estrada, a retired gunner, eased the trials of his old age. He may well have been the model for that king of thieves, the great Monipodio imagined by Cervantes, because he protected petty thieves who came to his inn at night to amuse themselves with the street girls there.[15]

In addition to providing a place to commit evil deeds, the banks of the river also provided a showcase for demonstrating to the public how the king's justice punished delinquents. Mariners found guilty of theft were paraded on the backs of donkeys in front of the ships along the shore, with a halter around their necks and with bare shoulders, indicating to whoever wanted to know that they were going to be whipped by the public executioner.[16]

Heading for the Ports of the Indies

The Guadalquivir River was the beginning of the road toward the ports of America, which constituted a second venue in the lives of the mariners who crewed the Indies fleets. The course of the river from Seville to its mouth covered fifteen leagues, or some eighty-nine kilometers. One would think that this first stage of the Indies voyage would be rapid and present no complications; nonetheless, it was one of the slowest stages, and the one where the risk of losing a ship was most serious. It took a full week to reach the port of Sanlúcar de Barrameda, which meant that an average of only a little more than twelve kilometers was covered daily. At this speed, anyone traveling on foot would arrive in Sanlúcar long before the fastest ships in the fleet.

The reason for this slow pace was that the river was plagued by sandy shallows that posed an enormous danger for navigation. There were at least six or seven points of great risk, and in some of them the water level at low tide reached as little as four *codos* deep, each codo being equal to 574 millimeters.[17] If we take into account that a galleon of some five hundred tons had a draft of seven codos, we can understand why, for large ships of the Carrera de Indias, the adventure began at the doorstep.[18]

Because of this, only small boats left Seville with all their cargo, while those of middling and large capacity left practically empty, the better to pass over the obstacles downriver. Even so, a good number of conditions had to come together to cross a shallow point: daylight to clearly see the marks showing the depth of the water, a tide running in the right direction and providing sufficient water, and a favorable wind. Thus, it was impossible to cross more than one important shallow each day. Most of the merchandise and passengers descended at least halfway downriver on large barges; at Las Horcadas, some eight leagues from Seville, the water level made it possible to load some of the middling ships completely, and the largest could take on at least a half load.

Finally, all the ships reunited at the port of Sanlúcar de Barrameda, where they completed their loading and underwent the last inspections before departure. But one serious obstacle still remained. The sandbar at the departure point for the open sea was formed by a bottom of solid rock covered with shifting banks of sand, which ruined a happy day's journey for many a ship and converted the zone into one of the most important ships' graveyards known. The departure could be delayed for many days until the conditions of wind, daylight, and tides were propitious. Once under way, all the ships were consigned to the care of bar pilots, experienced in finding the channel that led into the Gulf of Cádiz.

Traffic toward the Indies began to be organized in convoys from the middle of the sixteenth century. The year 1543 is often cited as the date when the fleets first incorporated warships for the duration of the voyage to accompany and protect merchant vessels.[19] Nonetheless, the definitive organization of the Spanish fleet system did not occur until the 1560s. The ordinances issued on October 18, 1564, presumed the dispatch of two fleets each year. One would head for New Spain and the port on the island of San Juan de Ulúa, facing Veracruz in the Gulf of Mexico. The other would be dispatched toward Cartagena de Indias, on the Caribbean coast of what is today Colombia. From there it would sail to the north coast of Panama, to Nombre de Dios or Portobelo, where it would meet the merchants who had traveled there from Peru along the Pacific coast.

This system of fleets aimed to assure communications with the two great viceroyalties that produced precious metals, that is, New Spain (Mexico) and Peru. The rest of the American regions remained subject to a much more irregular sailing regimen. Localities in the Caribbean customarily communicated with Spain by way of vessels that left the convoy in the vicinity of each port. In order to supply zones that were distant from the habitual routes of the convoys, special permits were issued to ships that sailed independently, which were known by the name of "single registers." The Spanish crown conceded such permits with a certain stinginess, inspired by fears not only that the ships might be taken by corsairs but also that, if free from the vigilance of the generals, admirals, and overseers who traveled in the fleets, they might engage in contraband activities.

Choosing the dates when the convoys should depart was a difficult matter. The variables to consider were numerous, and many of them presented in-

The Land Environment

soluble dilemmas. To sail in winter exposed the fleets to rough seas and bad weather. In summer, the forces of nature offered a truce, but that was when corsairs gathered, trying to seize the American treasure. Besides, when it was summer in the Northern Hemisphere, it was winter on the Peruvian coasts south of the equator, and the tropical regions were in the midst of their rainy season, which precipitated epidemics that decimated the crews. It would have required a powerful computer and the aid of modern information technology to analyze so many variables and find an ideal departure date.

In general it was deemed less dangerous to confront corsairs than to expose the fleets to storms; therefore, the fleets were generally scheduled to sail in summer or in spring, especially on the return trip, when they were laden with treasure. For the expeditions to New Spain the months of April and May were most often chosen for the date of departure. The ships could then be in San Juan de Ulúa before the start of strong winds and hurricanes in the north, which tended to hit the Gulf of Mexico and the Caribbean starting at the end of summer. The expeditions to Cartagena and Panama, generically called the Tierra Firme fleets, left Seville in July or August. Thus they were sure to arrive at their destination after these two months, which coincided with the rainy season that produced devastating epidemics among the crews. But whether in the New Spain fleet or in the convoys sent to Tierra Firme, the crews faced a trip that, in most cases, would last nine or ten months before they could once again contemplate the sandy beaches at the mouth of the Guadalquivir.

The route followed by both fleets was very similar until arriving in the Antilles. Seeking the trade winds, which blew constantly in an east-west direction at latitudes of about twenty degrees, the convoys set a southwest compass direction toward the Canary Islands. Once they left the so-called Gulf of the Mares behind them, passengers and novice sailors faced their first brutal experience with the open sea. The common immediate consequence was *almadiamiento,* or seasickness. It took between seven and ten days to arrive at the Fortunate Isles (the Canaries); during the trajectory, the men got used to falling down frequently and realizing that the horizon, which they had always believed to be a firm line, could become a moving succession of curves.

The Canaries provided an opportunity to recover some of one's strength after that first contact with the ocean. There, damages occasioned in the first days of sailing could be repaired, and the food supplies could be topped off. Above all, the ships tried to fill their holds with the two items that were consumed in great quantities and whose presence was vital for the maintenance of life on board: drinking water and firewood for cooking.

They then faced the leap across the Atlantic, which, in a voyage of about a month, carried them from the island of Gomera in the Canaries to one of the islands in the arc of the Lesser Antilles, normally Dominica or Deseada (between seventeen and fifteen degrees north latitude). Crossing the Atlantic on the outbound voyage could be comfortable and placid. The winds blew constantly in the right direction, and the weather could be fine and tranquil. But toward the end of the voyage, as always happens in life, problems began to surface. The Caribbean was nearby, with apparently paradisiacal coasts that were filled with hidden dangers, which could arrive in the form of epidemics, treacherous hurricanes, or corsairs who skulked among that labyrinth of isles.

After arriving in the Antilles, the route, which up to that point had been the same for both convoys, bifurcated. The fleets that went toward New Spain followed a more northerly path, stopping at Puerto Rico to take on water and firewood. From there it took almost another month to arrive in San Juan de Ulúa. The convoy that aimed toward Tierra Firme sailed farther south and reached its initial destination in Cartagena de Indias in scarcely two weeks.

San Juan de Ulúa was a small barren island some five or six kilometers in perimeter, located off the northwest coast of the Gulf of Mexico facing Veracruz and serving as the port of entry for the huge viceroyalty of New Spain. Nonetheless, though the best port in the area, it had the fundamental inconvenience of being in an exposed position. Its advantages included water of sufficient depth that ships could sail practically up to the shore; above all, San Juan de Ulúa served as a shield against the strong winds from the north. In order to augment that protection, a large wall had been built on the southern coast of the island that was some four hundred feet long (about 111 meters), in which twenty bronze rings had been affixed so that ships could tie up. When the fleets were very large, some ships tied themselves to the sterns of others moored to the rings, and thus they took better advantage of the space. Merchandise was carried to Veracruz, situated on the mainland, by means of barges and boats of shallow draft.

For a sailor arriving in the Indies for the first time, San Juan de Ulúa did not at all suggest the tales of the grandeur and riches of the Aztec empire that he surely would have heard in Seville. At the beginning of the 1570s, the geographer López de Velasco said that, apart from the wall with the mooring rings, on one of whose extremes a fortress-like tower was just being raised, there was not another edifice of stone and mortar on the whole island. The port's only buildings were some wooden barracks with straw roofs. At the extreme north of the island during those years, some black slaves were occupied carting stones to raise the level of the land and prevent waves from washing it away during storms. On this platform of stones, a dozen huts built on wooden pilings formed a rectangular plaza with a church and some warehouses belonging to the crown. On one side of the plaza the viceroy Don Martín Enríquez had ordered a hospital built for sick mariners; like the church and the warehouse, it had wooden walls and a straw roof.[20]

The Land Environment

A sketch of San Juan de Ulúa, made by the military engineer Bautista An-tonelli, shows that at the end of the century the architectonic condition of the port had not changed much. At the left and right ends of the wall of rings two forts had been built, but the rest of the buildings were still simple barracks. Only eight or ten Spanish householders were permanent residents of San Juan de Ulúa, and the rest of its population were black slaves who worked on maintenance.[21] Sailors in the fleets were understandably frustrated when the ships' masters tried to keep them on board for the four or five months of their stay in New Spain. Their presence might be required at any moment, since, even in port, the ships were not safe when storms from the north began to blow. Trapped on the ships, or limited to the small island, the mariners did everything possible to get per-mission to go to the "other coast," that is, to the nearby locale of Veracruz. When they succeeded, many of them deserted and lost themselves in the interior of the viceroyalty in search of their private El Dorado.

Veracruz was hardly a great city during the sixteenth century, but it grew very rapidly. In 1570 it had two hundred Spanish householders. At the start of the second quarter of the seventeenth century, their number had risen to four hundred; even then, nearly all the houses were made of planks, and only a few were built of stone.[22]

In Veracruz one of the fundamental routes that linked the Iberian Penin-sula with the West Indies terminated, but at the same time the viceroyalty of New Spain served as a point of linkage with the Philippines, the most impor-tant of the Spanish possessions in the East Indies. Between the years 1519 and 1526 various armadas had been launched that attempted to link Spain direct-ly with Asia, traversing the strait that Ferdinand Magellan discovered on the first of those expeditions. Experience showed that that voyage was too long and dangerous; for that reason, communications between the Philippines and metropolitan Spain ended up going by way of Mexico. From 1565 on, the fa-mous "Manila galleons" linked Acapulco with Manila each year, on voyages that were the longest of all the Spanish routes. The return trip alone from the Philippines to New Spain took between four and five months of sailing. On that route the ships sailed to forty degrees north latitude and caught the Kuro Shivo current that carried them toward Upper California, from whence they were able to descend along the coast to Acapulco.

The other great route of the West Indies, that is, the journey of the Tierra Firme fleets, had its principal base in the city of Cartagena de Indias. This was one of the best natural ports on the whole continent, and it had been given its name because of a certain similarity with the city of Cartagena on the Mediter-ranean coast of Spain. In both cases, an island located at the mouth of a bay provided secure protection for the ships that penetrated to the interior of the port.

The island of Carex (the island of the Careyes Indians) had the port entrances called Boca Grande on one side and Boca Chica on the other. The interior of the bay is several kilometers wide and could accommodate hundreds of ships. To reach the city a ship had to pass through various straits that were made easily defensible by constructing forts on either side.

In 1574, Cartagena de Indias had a population of two hundred fifty Spanish householders in addition to several thousand black and Indian inhabitants. The houses were mostly very humble, made with reeds plastered with mud and covered with a straw roof. Nonetheless, the construction of buildings of stone and mortar occurred very rapidly. Around 1625, the population had risen to fifteen hundred Spanish householders. By then, the center of the city was nearly all built of stones and brick, and it was surrounded by a wall with forts to defend the narrows of the channel that gave access to the port.[23]

(13)

Inside the bay of Cartagena, the fleets could undergo repairs comfortably and resupply themselves with victuals brought from the interior by way of the Magdalena River, whose mouth was about one hundred kilometers north of the city. The climate, without being totally healthful, was one of the least harmful in the Caribbean, and Spanish mariners could wait there with some security for news that the ships proceeding from Peru had arrived in Panama.

One of the most notable characteristics of the Spanish system of communications in America was the fact that the outlets of the mines of Upper Peru were not on the Atlantic at Buenos Aires; instead, their silver was exported through the Peruvian ports on the Pacific. These ports, for their part, were not linked directly by sea with Spain but used the Isthmus of Panama as a place to meet up with the Tierra Firme fleet. The late founding of Buenos Aires, which did not occur definitively until 1580, the laborious trip through the desolate Chaco region, and the dangers of the maritime route through the Strait of Magellan in great part account for the characteristics of communications between the Peruvian viceroyalty and metropolitan Spain.

From the port of Callao, near Lima, a convoy was formed, which beginning in the 1580s was protected by warships and known by the poetic name of the Armada of the Southern Sea. The journey from Callao to the city of Panama ordinarily took only three weeks. From there, the silver was taken to the Atlantic coast, either on mule trains or by river. The return from the city of Panama to Callao was, however, very laborious, since just after crossing the equator, contrary winds and currents could make the voyage last for four or five months. The only advantage favoring the coastal route was that the crews could recover their strength by putting in at some of the ports along the way.[24] When news arrived in Cartagena that the armada conveying silver from Peru had arrived in Callao, the fleet got under way and sailed to the ports of Nombre de Dios or Portobelo, on the Atlantic coast of the Panamanian isthmus. Nombre de Dios was the original destination of the Tierra Firme fleet. Nonetheless, from 1584 officials considered finding another site, because the general conditions of the port were not satisfactory. The gravest problem was the climate of the place, which became a true graveyard for those mariners and merchants who were not immune to tropical diseases. In 1570, Nombre de Dios was a small town of one hundred fifty houses, all of wood and roofed with straw, and after the lively activity when the fleet was in port, the town practically died. This is not only a manner of speaking, since thousands of unfortunate mariners were buried in its graveyard, the victims of deadly epidemics.

(14)

The defenses of Nombre de Dios consisted of only six bronze cannons on top of a rampart; because of that, it was not very difficult to dismantle the town as the landfall port of the fleets.[25] In 1595, officials decided to move the commercial fairs to Portobelo, situated some five leagues west of Nombre de Dios.[26] Portobelo was a somewhat more secure port, but its climate was equally abominable; the move did not result in any special advantage for the mariners of the fleets, who wanted to stay there for the shortest possible time, perhaps to return again to Cartagena or perhaps to desert and try to find riches in the mines of Potosí.

The return of the Tierra Firme and New Spain fleets always included a landfall in Havana. From San Juan de Ulúa or Cartagena, it took two or three weeks to arrive at the Cuban port, which was the best in all of Spanish America. The entrance was formed by a narrow mouth, which customarily was closed for security with a great chain.[27] In the interior, a splendid bay opened in the shape of a cloverleaf, with water so deep that the largest ships could sail almost to the houses of the city, which was located on the right side of the entry. In 1570, Havana had only sixty householders, and it was composed of wooden huts, but already an important fort had been built, called La Fuerza. Around 1625, the population of Havana had risen rapidly and had reached twelve hundred Spanish householders, in addition to a goodly number of blacks and mulattos.[28]

The port of Havana was located at the entrance to the circuit of winds and currents that led directly back to Spain. The return trip was longer and more dangerous than the outbound voyage, however. One sailed north to a latitude of forty degrees, then turned the prow east toward the Azores. These islands usually came into sight after a month of sailing and signaled a great danger, not only because of the storms that often formed in these latitudes in spring and winter but, above all, because they were among the favorite places for corsairs to lie in wait for the treasure-laden fleets.

The trip from the Azores until sighting the mouth of the Guadalquivir generally took twenty or thirty days more; when the fleets were very close to home and it seemed that all would end happily, they still had to hazard another menacing locale. The Cape of San Vicente, in the extreme southwestern corner of the Iberian Peninsula, was an ideal place for corsairs to lay a trap for the fleets. The depth of the water where the cape met the sea allowed enemy squadrons to hide close to the land and pounce upon a convoy as it was confidently rounding the cape. Not without reason was it nicknamed the Cape of Surprises, because it provided some of the most disagreeable surprises that mariners could experience.

To avoid such occurrences, the cities of Seville and Cádiz customarily sent reconnaissance ships to the Cape of San Vicente, whose mission was to alert the fleets if they encountered enemy vessels circling in the vicinity. Once past this danger, it remained only to surmount the sandbar at the entrance of the Guadalquivir and to head slowly upriver to the port of Seville.

Returning to the City

When the ships had finished unloading, a new terrestrial chapter began in the life of the men of the sea, who spent some months at home waiting for the departure of a new voyage. What were the homes of the crews like?

If a sailor or a ship's master who had just disembarked lived in Seville, his residence was most likely in the suburb of Triana. This neighborhood had held a very modest number of inhabitants at the end of the fourteenth century, but in the course of the two following centuries it became one of the most populous neighborhoods in the city. This suggests that the Triana neighborhood had garnered a good number of the emigrants who had been attracted by the prosperity of Seville. Curiously, its identity as a habitual residence of men of the sea was a fairly recent development; until the end of the fifteenth century, the neighborhood of San Vicente, situated on the opposite bank of the river, had the largest number of householders dedicated to nautical activities.[29] Thus, it would not be outlandish to think that many of the mariners who lived in Triana during the sixteenth century had come from other parts of Spain. These persons, many of them from the maritime zones of the Cantabrian coast, would have felt comfortable in the region where the fleets departed and might have installed themselves, like other recent arrivals, in a neighborhood where immigrants were not a novelty.

The census of Seville's population in 1561 gave some information about occupational distribution and cited a total of thirty-four pilots and ships' masters.[30] This number is probably incomplete, however. According to the chronicler Juan de Mal Lara, more than one hundred fifty captains, pilots, and masters in the Carrera de Indias marched before Philip II when that monarch visited the city in 1570.[31] But the 1561 census is significant in showing the distribution of men of the sea among the city's distinct neighborhoods; of the thirty-four mariners listed, thirty-one of them resided in Triana.

The Land Environment

A document conserved in the Archive of the Indies provides a detailed view of the living quarters and household goods of some captains and ships' masters in Triana.[32] Those who held the highest positions in the maritime labor hierarchy lived on one important street (La Calle Larga) and had "substantial houses" on their properties. Still, the private buildings in the Triana neighborhood had always represented greater architectural simplicity than the rest of the neighborhoods of the city. Thus, "a substantial house" in Triana would hardly have been a palace; it was more likely to be a simple construction of brick, with one or two stories.

((16))

The listing of household goods in the census helps us understand the modesty of the buildings. The furniture was simple and very sparse: a bed and some sort of crib for the children; a table, with a bench for seating; six or seven chairs; a sideboard and a chest; and a pair of large clay jars. No adornment hung on the walls; there were no curtains or tapestries, and the only luxuries were concentrated in a few good tablecloths, various sets of sheets and pillows, and some embroidered cushions. In the case of the ship's master Francisco Hernández Moreno, we find some signs that denote a certain wealth: one black female slave, who was included in the inventory like one more object, and a silver cup and tumbler.[33]

This array of household goods, viewed with our consumers' eyes, seems very modest; nonetheless, these men of the sea were situated in the middling economic class of society, among a group who at least possessed their own house, a bed to rest in, and some tablecloths upon which a female slave served the meals. On holidays, in order to impress a friend invited to his table, perhaps the master took out his silver cup and other silver dishes and trays.

Simple sailors would not have been able to own such luxuries. The documents show us that they lived on other streets in Triana, such as Peral, Confesos, Sumidero, Victoria, Sol, or De la Cava; one suspects that they resided in some of the many *corrales,* or collective residences, that filled the city.[34] Until a very few years ago, the corrales of Triana were famous as residences of very humble people, just like the mariners of the Carrera de Indias.

The census of 1561 noted the existence of seventy-one corrales in the city as a whole, in which a total of a thousand families lived. However, other evidence indicates that some of these communal residences could hold one hundred eighteen households, with their corresponding women and children, which would considerably increase the number of inhabitants in Seville who lived in this type of shared residence.[35]

But many mariners in the Indies fleets were not residents of Seville or of Triana. In such cases, once the unloading had been finished and the ships' masters stopped giving them rations, these sailors were out of food as well as work. In the days they spent waiting for their final salary payment, and while looking for a means of transport back to their homes, they had to find lodgings in some of the numerous inns and boarding houses in Seville. They tried to limit their sojourn in the city, because the high prices there could finish off in a few months what a sailor had earned in an entire year.

When the fleets returned, there was no reason for the mariners to prolong their stay in the boarding houses, but the same logic did not apply while waiting for a new expedition to depart. Shipowners as well as the crown found it convenient to wait as long as possible before signing on crews. This meant a saving for the shipowners but ruination for the sailors from out of town who aimed to take a ship from Seville.

Some innkeepers seem to have specialized in advancing to sailors and soldiers in the fleets the cost of their bed and board and some money to buy clothes, in the hope of recovering their costs after the return voyage, when soldiers and sailors received their pay for several months of work and even had a few *reales* jingling in their purses. This was the case with the Basque innkeeper Juan de Arrieta, who had taken up residence in Seville and attracted to his inn Basque countrymen who hoped to sign up on ships in the Carrera de Indias. Around 1520, Arrieta charged three reales daily for bed and board.[36] If we take into account that in those days a sailor in the armada earned forty-four reales a month, it is easy to understand that in two weeks of living like a lord in a boardinghouse the sailor spent a whole month's wages.

Not all the sailors who came back from America were healthy. The illnesses and "fevers" contracted in the tropics could return the men to Spain half dead. In such cases, it is very possible that they were brought to the hospital for men of the sea, which the Brotherhood of Our Lady of Fair Wind (Nuestra Señora de Buen Aire) had built in Triana, on the very banks of the Guadalquivir.

The Brotherhood of Our Lady of Fair Wind was founded by about fifty ships' masters, pilots, and shipowners of the Carrera de Indias. Its rules were crafted in 1561, although they were not approved by the king until some years later. In 1562 the members also wrote the statutes of a type of professional college called the University of Seafarers (Universidad de Mareantes).[37] With these two institutions, the most prominent of the men of the sea attempted to attend to the salvation of their souls and the well-being of their bodies.

Simple sailors were excluded from the brotherhood and the University of Seafarers, but the rules established that if the cause of their illness related to their work at sea, either because they had contracted some fever during the voyage or because they had suffered an accident on board, they could be attended to in the Triana hospital.[38] If the illness ended in death, one of the principal commitments of the Brotherhood of Our Lady of Fair Wind came into play: to provide a solemn funeral and a worthy burial for their brothers and colleagues.

The Land Environment

Nonetheless, the majority of deaths on the voyages occurred in America, where the crews fell victim to virulent epidemics, shipwrecks, and the consequences of accidents at sea. Upon the return of each fleet, many sailors' wives found out that they had joined the ample ranks of the city's widows. In other cases they learned that their husbands had decided to remain in the Indies to see if fortune would be kinder to them there. This added their wives to another expanding group in the city, abandoned women.

According to Andrés Navagero, ambassador from the Republic of Venice and an avid observer of Seville at the end of the first quarter of the sixteenth century, the city itself was very nearly under the control of women.[39] Clearly, work on board ships was not the only thing that created widows or abandoned women. The expeditions of conquest, or simple emigration, contributed equally to the phenomenon. For whatever reason, in the second half of the century, 30 percent of the heads of families in the city were not men but women, most of them widowed by the sea, or by war, or by poverty.[40]

There are abundant testimonies from the wives of dead mariners who claimed the salaries that were owed to their husbands. The richest among them argued that their dowries had helped to finance the crazy dreams of their husbands, who had embarked on some maritime enterprise of discovery to which they had pledged their last *maravedí*. With allusions to their dowries, these women reminded the king that they had indirectly contributed to the financing of the fleets, and they hoped for some recompense.

This was the case with the widow of Miguel de Rodas. Her husband was one of the few survivors of the first voyage around the world. Convinced of the enormous riches of the Spice Islands, he had then invested his wife's entire dowry, some twenty-five thousand maravedís, in the expedition of Sebastian Cabot. Because that voyage was a disaster, the poor widow remained without a dowry and without a husband, and she tried to persuade the king to compensate her for some of her misfortunes.[41] In the case of Sancha de Arrieta, wife of a crewman in the expedition of García Jofre de Loaisa to the Moluccas, her husband did not personally waste her dowry, but he left so many unpaid obligations that the good Sancha had to expend her dowry to deal with his debts.[42]

One of the most dramatic testimonies of this sort was that of Ana Gómez, a Sevillian woman who in 1563 was left a widow by the royal constable Alonso González, who had embarked on the flagship commanded by General Pedro Menéndez de Avilés. In trying to demonstrate her right to receive the salary earned by her husband, she revealed that, apart from leaving no worldly goods, he had spent all of her dowry. In what followed, the widow of the constable undertook to enumerate the objects she had brought to that marriage, which, at least from an economic point of view, represented a disastrous expense.

Ana Gómez listed her belongings as a new bride: clothing of black velvet, a taffeta cloak, an orange-colored gown, a shirtwaist of black velvet, gilded clogs, a neck cloth of white silk, a hair net bordered in gold, a necklace of coral, and a gold ring, in addition to her bedclothes, sheets, cushions, embroidered cloths, and ten thousand maravedís in cash. The money had disappeared, and the clothing and household goods were presumably no longer new. That is why she asked the king for some compensation.[43]

But many other mariners' wives did not even have a dowry to reclaim. Even if the husband returned between voyages, his absences imposed a period of scarcity and privation on his family, which turned into misery if his death was confirmed. A report sent to the Council of the Indies about Juana de Durango, a householder of Seville and the wife of Juan Serrano, pilot and captain of the ship *Santiago* on Magellan's expedition, said that "at the time the fleet departed, he left his wife and daughters in the city in complete poverty and need; after that, things had gotten much worse, so that, if for the love of God some honorable persons had not given them charity, neither she nor her daughters would have been able to eat."[44] (19)

Collecting from the king the salary owed to a deceased husband took many years and hard work. That was well known to Beatriz Martín, known as La Camacha, who was not able to collect her husband's salary until 1547, though he had died on the 1519–22 expedition of Magellan and Elcano.[45] If, in addition, the widow had committed the "frivolity" of marrying again, she would almost certainly not have been able to collect even a single real. This must have been the reason why the right to her first husband's salary was denied to Isabel Rodríguez, an extremely poor woman, who "scarcely had clothes to cover herself, nor a bed in which to sleep, nor did she have belongings worth as much as four *ducados*."[46]

If the widow of a sailor wanted to ease the pain of her mourning with the bread of security, she had to keep her wits about her. In the first years of the seventeenth century, General Juan Gutiérrez de Garibay, a gentleman of the Order of Santiago and commander of the 1579 Guard Squadron of the Carrera de Indias, lay dying in his house in Seville. To reward his services, the king had conceded to him the labor services of Indians *(encomienda de indios)* in the Yucatan, worth the tidy sum of two thousand ducados in rent each year. But the general died, and the assignment of the encomienda was only for his lifetime. His wife, Doña Isabel de Soto y Avilés, was very interested in seeing that the royal concession passed to her and their daughter. That is why she did not hesitate to "convince" her husband that, even on his deathbed, he should send the king a letter with that request.

The letter is a pathetic monument to human frailty. Theoretically written by the general, it uses a baroque style, rhetorical and grandiloquent, though

A Sevillian woman
of the sixteenth century.
Drawing by Christoph
Weiditz, 1529. Biblioteca
Nacional, Madrid.

someone in those circumstances would not likely have indulged in literary flourishes. Here are some of the most interesting passages:

> My Lord. God having done me the mercy of letting me die fully aware and with my judgment intact, and knowing that I am in the last hour of my life, I wanted to acquaint your Majesty with the truth that I hope to convey to God, who cares for me in this transition from life to death. And shunning the vainglory that could result if I were to refer to my services, which all seem petty to me as they were done for such a king and lord from whom I have received so much honor and mercy, and, not being able to avoid representing to Your Majesty that . . . at the end of my life, in order to be able to live and to sustain myself, it was necessary, besides the two thousand

ducados which Your Majesty gave me for my lifetime in the province of Yucatan, to avail myself of the dowry of Doña Isabel de Soto y Avilés, my wife . . . I humbly beg . . . that you favor my wife and daughter so that they may enjoy for their lives the mercy that Your Majesty made to me of the said two thousand ducados.[47]

Following this brilliant piece of epistolary art, the signature of poor General Garibay is scarcely a scrawl. One does not need much imagination to reconstruct the scene, with the future widow dictating the letter to a scrivener, pretending it was from her spouse. It is not that General Garibay would not have agreed with the idea, which on earlier occasions he had already suggested to the monarch; but it seems certain that in his last moments, when he perhaps already had his eyes fixed on heaven, his wife had hers clearly fixed on earth.

The Land Environment

TWO

The Origin and Social Condition
of the Men of the Sea

What Made a Man Go to Sea?

That question could be answered today much as it was five hundred years ago: people go to sea only when the land denies them the means to survive. People in the twentieth century watch their contemporaries leap into the ocean in search of adventure or for the sheer joy of it. But the motivations of a recreational sailor are very different from those of a fisherman or a merchant mariner. Residents of wealthy societies love risk. They hunger for adventure to kill the boredom of their uneventful lives, whether that means climbing a mountain, crossing a desert, or sailing the ocean in a sloop. But none of these activities negates the reality that, today as yesterday, making a living at sea is difficult. These days there are well-paid jobs, honorable professions, and even good ways of doing business at sea. But if the salary were the same, how many people would permanently choose the discomforts and long absences that the seafaring life entails? Very few, surely. If that is true in the final years of the twentieth century, it was much more true at the beginning of the sixteenth, when the conditions of life on board a ship were infinitely harder than they are now.

The sixteenth-century writers who concerned themselves with life at sea generally agreed about one thing: sailing was a "desperate and fearsome business," which is to say that going to sea can only be understood as the product of desperation. Life at sea was described by such unfavorable adjectives as "cruel," "perverse," "bad," and "difficult," leading to the conclusion that it was madness to put one's life and fortune "three or four fingers away from death, which is the thickness of a ship's planking."[1] The deceitful siren's song that wafted over the waves promised untold riches, but for most people the risks were too high: the sea was "a mine where many become rich" but also a "cemetery where infinite numbers lie interred." Invariably, the certain rigors of a life at sea overshadowed the likelihood of coming out ahead. In fragments of old legends, sixteenth-century Spaniards used to say that "the sea we call 'el mar' comes from the bitterness we call 'amargura,'" noting also that it was "delightful to look at but very dangerous to sail."[2]

Other seafaring peoples had similar attitudes. The English, for example, who stubbornly challenged Spain's maritime power in the sixteenth century, had commonplace sayings contemptuous of the element in which they had developed their nautical skills. An old proverb in the British Isles said, "Those who would go to sea for pleasure would go to hell for pastime." Another no-less-expressive phrase was: "Whosoever putteth his child to get his living at sea had better a great deal bind him 'prentice to a hangman."[3]

Clearly, the men of the sixteenth century saw seafaring as an activity chosen more out of necessity than through free will. Granted, in the end there are very few things in this life that one does for pleasure, and no one could deny that maritime transport was useful and beneficial for the general well-being of society. Diego García de Palacio, a professional jurist and author of a well-known treatise on seafaring, affirmed that the peace and honor of nations depended on the efforts of mariners, and he urged them to accept the risks of their occupation with resignation, because, in the final analysis, "the worst harm it brings lasts only until death."[4]

García de Palacio could indulge in such advice because he was fundamentally an armchair sailor, but unless I am much mistaken, very few people would have been convinced by his argument. There were serious reasons why a future mariner might be obliged to abandon the land; at the same time, there were powerful forces luring him onto the bosom of the sea. Precisely for this combination of attraction and repulsion, some compare the sea to a lover: by falling into a lover's arms, one escapes and seeks comfort at the same time. Be that as it may, five hundred years ago the sea was a much more tyrannical lover than it is nowadays.[5]

A man might go to sea because he was driven out by the poverty of his home on land. That is perhaps the most obvious reason and possibly the easiest to understand. But it is not the only reason: boredom, monotony, and isolation could also drive men from home. In the twentieth century we can easily understand why many rural residents leave home in search of broader horizons, and it is even easier to explain that impulse in the sixteenth century, when the level of rural isolation was infinitely higher. Finally, we ought not forget that many people in the sixteenth century were pushed by family tradition to choose a particular occupation. Routine and inertia led many a man to take up his father's occupation, without, in many cases, having a true vocation for it.

Accident often plays a role in human lives as well, and in this light we should recognize that many men were obliged to go to sea not because of their economic circumstances but because they were literally forced to embark because of levies or because they were overpowered while in a drunken stupor. Without doubt, the most sinister and lamentable cases were those that involved the kidnapping of minors or even the actual sale of boys by their desperately poor parents.

Counterbalancing the negative factors pushing men toward the sea were positive incentives luring them outward, sometimes real and at other times no more than illusions. The dream of getting rich quick and possibly climbing up the social scale served as a powerful counterpoint to enfeebling poverty at home. Though it was difficult to get rich at sea, the life of a mariner offered more possibilities than being stuck on land as the servant of a nobleman or working at an unskilled job in a small, remote city in the hinterland. Abundant riches floated on the routes to the Indies, and even the poor devils who signed on as sailors were in a position to net some of them. By using what "remained under one's fingernails," they might begin a long process that could change their lives. A mariner could, for example, arrange to carry contraband merchandise, or he could use his natural intelligence to make himself into a pilot. Money and opportunities presented themselves more rapidly at sea than in the stable world on land, and an audacious man, with a little luck, had more options at sea than if he stayed rooted in his native soil.

But becoming a mariner was considered by many to be a transitory stage on the road to enrichment. The ship was a springboard for bounding to the Indies as an illegal immigrant. That was surely a powerful attraction for many of those who enrolled in the fleets. From the beginning, the Spanish crown imposed a goodly number of requirements for making the passage to America. A man wanting to emigrate legally had to comply with the regulations and withstand a slow bureaucratic process that also included small bribes to notaries and functionaries to speed his documents along. Besides the administrative prerequisites, he had to come up with the cost of passage and food for a voyage that could last three or four months. All of these costs assumed the equivalent of between six and twelve months' salary for an unskilled worker, and rarely did would-be emigrants have that much money saved, since poverty was often the root of their desire to go to the New World in the first place.

The crown always needed sailors to crew the Indies fleets; for that reason, many persons signed on who would have never survived the bureaucratic controls on emigration nor been able to put together sufficient money to pay the passage. Because they were advanced several months' pay when they signed on, many men enlisted as a form of emigrating without having to pay for the trip, even earning a small salary along the way. Once in America, they deserted at the first opportunity and began a new life in the Promised Land. The penalties for deserters were harsh, but the authorities' ability to capture fugitives was limited. In this manner, the great American illusion, represented by the wagonloads of Peruvian silver that the Pizarro brothers sent to Seville or the countless myths of gilded men and fabulously rich cities that circulated in the Old World, was the lure that captured these temporary mariners, who were no more than emigrants disguised as men of the sea.

But the eagerness to get rich or to emigrate to the Indies were not the only attractions of the sea. In contrast with a monotonous life where the horizons were always the same, and in an epoch when the majority of people died without seeing much farther than the panorama visible from the tower of their parish church, signing on to a ship offered a unique opportunity to see the world. An old sailor's descriptions of the transparent waters of the Caribbean, its exotic fruits, and its coppery-skinned women acted like a magnet to many souls who hungered for an earthly paradise. To travel by land in the sixteenth century meant traversing poorly paved roads in exhausting journeys on foot, in order to cover, after several weeks, a few hundred kilometers. On a ship, the most rapid means of contemporary transport, one could cover thousands of kilometers in the same amount of time and transport oneself to the ends of the earth.

(26)

In short, as Ralph Davis wrote about the English seaman, men became sailors "to see the world, to get a good rate of pay, to get a job of some sort at any price, to do what father did; these were the motives of those who went to sea; perhaps some went willy-nilly, drunk or unconscious, as the crimp made up the required crew as best he could."[6] Juan de Escalante de Mendoza knew the problems of seafarers perfectly well, since not by accident had he risen to the rank of general of the Indies fleets in the sixteenth century. He summed up in more detail the motives that impelled men toward the oceans, reducing Spanish mariners to two large groups:

> Most of the mariners who sail the sea are of two sorts. The first sort includes all those who commence to sail as a livelihood, such as poor men and sons of poor fathers. Seafaring is the most suitable occupation they can find to sustain themselves, especially for those born in ports and maritime areas. This sort is the most numerous among mariners, if we understand that, although they might want to be schooled for some other occupation, they do not have the disposition or the means to be able to do it. And also if we understand that, if some of them chance to study and become learned, they would not want to follow an occupation as dangerous and laborious as that of a mariner.
>
> The other sort from whom mariners are made consists of those whose nature inclines them toward the restlessness and the art of sailing and military occupations. Although their fathers or tutors might set them to study and give them every advantage, something else appeals to them, and they generally abandon their studies to follow their natural inclinations.[7]

To reduce the origin of marine "vocations" to this dual motivation is, of course, a simplification, but in fairness to General Escalante I must say that the documentary sources I have examined prove him right in the great majority of cases.

The sons of the poor filled the merchant ships and galleons of His Catholic Majesty. A multitude of emigrants from the rest of the country and from outside the borders of the realm flowed into Seville in the sixteenth century. The city itself was their immediate objective, but those who did not find a good place to stay or a good job had few options: either they joined forces with the abundant number of idlers, swaggerers, rogues, and truants abroad in the city, or they signed up as mariners. Of these last, there were many whose secret ambition was to desert as soon as they arrived in the Indies, which they thereby converted, in the well-known phrase of Cervantes, into "the shelter and refuge (27) of Spain's *desperados*, the church of the lawless, the safe haven of murderers, the native land and cover for cardsharps, the general lure for loose women, the common deception of many and the particular remedy of few."[8] The city of Seville and the ships that visited its port constituted their initial refuge, a kind of "first America" for those who, as we have just seen, represented a compendium of human misfortunes.

One of the most abundant human by-products in great cities has always been the children abandoned to their fate. Hundreds of them were left to run along the sandy beach of the Guadalquivir River in Seville, and their destiny would be divided between the ships of the king and the dens of thieves, like the famous patio of Monipodio that Cervantes wrote about. The best sailors had to begin their training at a very early age, because experience was the only real basis for seafaring expertise. Consequently, these children were sought after by the ships' masters, who saw them as ideal and undemanding apprentices. Rinconete and Cortadillo, the protagonists of Cervantes's novel of the same name, were between fourteen and seventeen years old, and the story ended with their entrance into the service of Monipodio, the chief of Seville's underworld.

Much younger was a real child named Francisco Manuel, a "lost orphan boy" who roamed the riverbanks of Seville and signed up as a ship's page when he was only seven years old.[9] Francisco Manuel did not even have a last name, but he certainly had good fortune. He crossed the path of one of the richest and most influential personages in the world of Seville's shipbuilders, Captain Andrés de Paz, who took him into his service and placed him on one of his ships. Francisco Manuel thus began an uninterrupted succession of voyages as a servant and apprentice mariner. When his master did not have a ship on which to send him to America, he "loaned" the boy to a colleague. In this way, Francisco Manuel rose continuously in professional standing, eventually arriving, with the support of his influential master, at the point of being examined as a pilot for the Indies fleets. Pilots had to prove their Spanish nationality, and Francisco Manuel found himself in a tight spot, because he could not say a single word about his ancestry. Instead, he relied on the testimony of witnesses who declared that, judging from the young man's good conduct, he must come from "honorable, well-born people." Besides surely being false, their supposition demonstrated that, in the sixteenth century, heritage was considered a much better guide than education in judging a person. The official inquiry into the "nature and purity of lineage of his parents and grandparents" provides an opportunity to know, from the testimony of Andrés de Paz himself, how he met the orphan.

> At the age of seven or eight years, which seemed to this witness that the said Francisco Manuel had attained, this witness received the said Francisco Manuel into his service on the riverbanks of this city as a lost boy, who could not say who his father nor his mother was, nor where he came from, and this witness, feeling sorry for him as a lost boy, and seeing that he was bonny and willing to serve, he was put on a ship belonging to this witness which was on the said river, in order to give him a place and do him a good turn, so that he would not be abandoned to his fate. . . . And he took him on the said ship to the province of Tierra Firme, and brought him back to these kingdoms, and again took him to the province of New Spain.[10]

Sons of the numerous foreign immigrants, especially Portuguese, who settled in Seville faced a situation similar to that of the abandoned children who roamed the city. One of the immigrant children called Pero Hernández had arrived when he was two years old, and at the age of ten he found himself forced to go to sea as a page. In the following twenty years he made sixteen voyages to the Indies, accumulating experience and rising in rank to become an expert mariner and to petition the House of Trade to take the pilot's examination.[11]

Pero Hernández and Francisco Manuel were lucky, or they knew how to profit from the opportunities that presented themselves. The majority of apprentice mariners were not so fortunate. Misery obliged many parents to send their sons to sea as servants of ships' officers. In this way, the boys could survive and learn a trade, but they remained subject to the arbitrariness of their masters, who paid them only their daily rations, normally adorned (by way of a tip) with thrashings if they did not discharge their duties. That is what happened to Diego Sánchez, a ships' boy whose father, a blind man burdened by a large family and earning his living playing guitar in the streets of Seville, had put him in the care of a ship's carpenter. The boy, sick of being beaten, decided to desert and disappeared without a trace; even so, his father had the nerve to present himself at the House of Trade to claim the wages his son had earned but not collected.

> I, Alonso Sánchez, blind in corporeal sight, a very poor man, say that in the ship whose master was Lázaro Gutiérrez, a son of mine called Diego

went as a ship's boy, and that the aforesaid my son, after doing the unloading of the said ship, because of the angry words and mistreatment that
they did and were doing him, giving him many beatings with ropes and
sticks, and him being a very small boy, and for the great dread that he had,
and the great fear that they would kill him on the way home, remained in
the Indies: the salary that my aforesaid son earned, I ask be ordered given
and handed over to me as his father, because I am very poor and I have extreme need in order to feed myself, my wife, and children.[12]

(29)

One of the most interesting and dramatic cases was that of the child called
Jorge Griego, who passed from hand to hand as if he were an object and was
almost hanged after finding himself involved in a mutiny. He belonged to a
poor family from Candía, the capital of Crete. His parents were not able to feed
him, and, when he was some eleven or twelve years old, they decided to commit him to the care of his uncle, who lived in Venice. The uncle, in his turn,
handed him over to a friend who signed on to a ship that was heading for Cádiz,
but the ship did not arrive at its destination, instead wrecking nearby. Jorge
Griego survived the shipwreck, and thereafter he wandered along the beaches near Cádiz doing odd jobs for mariners, until the boatswain of a Spanish
warship engaged him to carry certain earthenware jars to his ship. As recounted by Jorge Griego himself, "once there, the said boatswain by force and gag-
ging the mouth of the declarant, carried him to the said galleass."[13] The capture of boys was a common practice and a hard introduction to the career of
many mariners. Jorge Griego's bad luck continued, as the crew of the galleass
(composed mostly of foreigners) mutinied, and when the boy returned to
Cádiz, only his youth saved him from the gallows, with the death penalty com-
muted into punishment by exile.

After hearing some of these stories, which despite being true are worthy
of the pen of Charles Dickens, we cannot doubt that misery and desperation
were the source of many marine "vocations." The sons of prosperous artisans
or small shopkeepers did not consider seafaring an attractive profession, since
they could earn better salaries by practicing their father's trade. Life at sea was
the last resort for peasants who had emigrated to the coast but could not shape
a future for themselves and also for those from the most humble social strata
of the large port cities, particularly Seville.

Before resigning themselves to the sea, the pages and ships' boys, that is to
say, the apprentice mariners, generally worked at a great variety of occasional
jobs as porters, bearers, or servants. Thus, when the ship's boy called Marco
Antonio was asked about his previous work, he responded "that he is called
Marco Antonio and that he does not have any occupation, and that he lives on
this ship, he does not know where. Asked how he supported himself in the city

of Seville, he said that he worked as a lackey for Diego Núñez Royo, the over-seer of this fleet, and other persons."[14] Like Marco Antonio, many other neo-phyte mariners had no clear idea what their previous occupation had been, any more than they knew their family name.

Nevertheless, we need to add an important qualification to our discussion: jobs at sea could look attractive to the sons of pilots or masters, for example, who had been able to earn an acceptable living thanks to seafaring. For these young men, family tradition was the principal motive in explaining why they decided to follow their father's occupation. In general, this sort of mariner went to sea as a youth (between fifteen and twenty years) but not as a child. We can presume that they had received an elementary education and that, after an ap-prenticeship in the service of someone known to their family or even on the same ship as their father, they could fairly easily attain the post of pilot or mas-ter of some small ship.[15]

We should remember that one of our informants, the expert mariner Juan de Escalante de Mendoza, spoke of two large groups that produced Spain's men of the sea. The second group consisted of restless individuals who pos-sessed a certain education, but whose temperament led them to seek out the risk and adventure of a military life at sea.

The Indies fleets were protected by armed ships and galleons, that is to say, by ships built specifically for war. In command of these vessels, one found a goodly number of infantry captains expert in warfare on both land and sea as well as admirals and captains general of commercial and military fleets. These men were the supreme commanders of Spain's transatlantic convoys, and all the other captains and masters owed them obedience. Of necessity, this small but influential group had a very different origin from that of the crews (pilots and masters included) of merchant vessels. They thought of themselves fun-damentally and primarily as military men. The majority were involved in busi-ness related to maritime transport, however, and some few of them were, in ad-dition, expert in the art of navigation.

A simple glance at the names of the generals and admirals who directed the Indies fleets during the sixteenth century suggests the existence of real seafar-ing dynasties. This is evident in the repetition and intertwining of family names such as Bazán, Menéndez, Eraso, Flores, Valdés, Maldonado, Carreño, Osorio, Alcega, and Quiñones. Sometimes, a notable number of generals or admirals came from the same family group, such as the Menéndezes: Pedro, Juan, Bar-tolomé, and Pedro Menéndez Márquez. Another striking example is that of the Eraso family—Cristóbal, Miguel, Francisco, Alonso, Gonzalo, and others. Like-wise, the same family names were often combined by marriage: Diego de Flo-res Valdés, Álvaro Flores Quiñones, Pedro Menéndez Valdés, and so on.

All these families had a sort of patriarch who began the tradition and upon

(30)

whom the other family members were generally dependent. That was the case with Álvaro de Bazán Sr., Pedro Menéndez de Avilés, Cristóbal de Eraso, and Diego de Flores Valdés. The patriarchs were customarily knights of the military orders, that is to say, members of the lower nobility, and they normally inherited a middling amount of wealth, which they supplemented by business dealings as shipbuilders, corsairs, and even merchants.[16] In those days, the lower nobility provided some of the best warriors for the Spanish monarchy, since the old military nobility, loaded down with titles and riches, was no longer disposed to risk their lives and fortunes for the benefit of the crown. Minor noblemen often began their careers as pages or gentlemen attendants of members of the royal family, whom they accompanied on voyages and other travels, thereby establishing strong links with those in power.

Frequently, they also had some protector in the court who occupied himself with directing their professional development. The Eraso family, for example, counted on Francisco de Eraso, the secretary for marine affairs under King Philip II. The heads of these family groups, when they acceded to the command of fleets and armadas, never arrived alone but were surrounded by a coterie of sons, relatives, friends, and hometown acquaintances. Thus, the network of noble dependence that began with the protector resident at court and continued with the head of the family clan in command of a fleet extended to a small circle of friends and relatives who soon came to occupy posts as captains of various warships or admirals of segments of the fleet. The youngest and least experienced members of the clan were named ensigns or gentlemen attendants of the generals. These young pups of the lower military nobility dedicated themselves to practicing the duties of command so that later they would be able to succeed their fathers, older brothers, or other relatives.

No one looked unfavorably on this evident nepotism, and the king himself had no qualms about recommending young gentlemen to the generals of fleets, so that they would be given favored treatment. Royal letters of recommendation are extremely common in the archives of the epoch. There was no better school in which to learn the art of seaborne warfare, and practical experience in military matters was the only way to shape good captains. In our times, the repetition of family names in public administration can lead to scandal (though this does not prevent its happening), but in the sixteenth century it could be considered meritorious to have generation after generation serving the king in the same job. The cult of the individual, so well developed in our society, was not as strong then, and the worth of a person, his honor and his strength, were linked with belonging to a group. Little confidence was placed in the impersonal functioning of the machinery of state, and only the support of a countryman, or of a relative, was considered an effective aid in difficult times. That is why when personages such as Pedro Menéndez de Avilés or

Origin and Social Condition

Cristóbal de Eraso wanted to recount the services they had rendered to the crown, they listed all in their clan who had put themselves under the king's command.

Some of these patriarchs were real masters in the art of placing their offspring, countrymen, and friends. Especially noteworthy were the aforementioned Pedro Menéndez de Avilés and Cristóbal de Eraso, who were, successively, captains general of the Guard Squadron of the Indies Fleets, that is to say, supreme commanders of the forces defending Spain's Atlantic routes.

Pedro Menéndez de Avilés was, without doubt, one of the best mariners of the sixteenth century. The hero of many famous victories at sea, he was also the man responsible for filling the Indies fleets with his countrymen from Asturias. Beginning with his immediate relatives, he made admirals of his son Juan, his brother Bartolomé, and his nephew Pedro Menéndez Márquez. He also sponsored various future ships' captains, admirals, generals, and even captains general: Diego de Flores Valdés and Álvaro de Flores Valdés, natives of Sumiedo in Asturias, Gregorio de las Alas and Esteban de las Alas, natives of Avilés, Álvaro de Valdés, and so on. Of this group, those who did not bear the family name of the head of the clan were still directly or indirectly related to the Menéndezes. For example, the last of the men cited, Álvaro de Valdés, was the son of Diego Menéndez,[17] and Esteban de las Alas was married to a Valdés.[18] Apart from these higher officers, a mere glance at the intermediary posts in the mid-sixteenth-century fleets shows them filled with Asturians, old comrades in arms of Pedro Menéndez de Avilés.[19]

Even more accomplished at placing his relatives was Don Cristóbal de Eraso. When Pedro Menéndez de Avilés died in 1574, Diego de Flores Valdés succeeded him until 1576, when Cristóbal de Eraso was named captain general of the Guard Squadron of the Indies Fleets. Although originally Basque, the family settled in the city of Écija, in the rich countryside near Seville. Very soon the armada was filled with members of the lower nobility from Écija, together with the numerous sons, brothers, cousins, and nephews of the captain general. Cristóbal de Eraso had been a Gentleman of the King's Household, and because of that he enjoyed the personal and direct confidence of the monarch. As if that were not enough, another Eraso, Francisco, was the royal secretary for marine affairs. With this network of support, no one could stop Don Cristóbal from employing (at the same time) four of his sons, a brother, a cousin, and various nephews in different posts in the armada. One would think, in order to observe the proprieties, that Don Cristóbal might have placed his relatives in intermediate posts; but nothing could have been further from his intentions. The captain general practiced his nepotism without any self-doubt, and at one point his brother Miguel was lieutenant general, his sons Alonso and Francisco were admirals, and another of his sons, called Gonzalo, was captain of the ship bearing the fleet's insignia. Don Cristóbal's behavior can serve as a perfect example of how to solve the employment problems of an entire family.[20]

At times, Don Cristóbal's zealous favoritism toward his relatives brought him into compromising situations, but they were customarily resolved without changing a single detail of his policy. In 1578 Captain Gregorio López Polanco was presented with a royal patent to command one of the galleons of the armada. Unfortunately for Polanco, the only vacant post was occupied provisionally by Don Gonzalo de Eraso, son of the captain general. As a result, despite his royal commission, Polanco found himself unable to take command. He protested to the king and received new orders, but he gained his objective only by pure chance. Alonso de Eraso, another son of Don Cristóbal who served as an admiral, died in Havana; his brother Gonzalo took over the job and thereby opened a path for the valiant and long-suffering Polanco.[21]

The actions of Cristóbal de Eraso or Pedro Menéndez de Avilés were not exceptional; thus it should not surprise us that some fleets and armadas to the Indies carried generals and admirals with the same last names.[22] It is also evident that the solicitude in taking care of one's relatives, countrymen, and friends served as a magnet to attract to the sea young noblemen who wanted to carve out a brilliant career for themselves as warriors embarked in the king's service.

So far I have discussed the most frequent reasons people made the daring decision to enlist on ships for the Indies. We also ought to leave room for cases that did not correspond to these common denominators but, instead, represented personal circumstances or attitudes that can be classified as marginal. Within the variety of situations that explains the behavior of this last group of individuals, there was one common element: the sense of not feeling at ease in the community where they lived. All those who considered themselves discriminated against, rejected, oppressed, or persecuted saw life at sea as a form of escape, if only temporarily, from an insufferable situation. On board a ship, working conditions were, of course, rigidly disciplined, but traditional norms of social control were relaxed because of the distance from the centers of power and because of the solidarity among men who dared to confront the unleashed force of nature.

The sea has always been, and continues to be, a good refuge for the marginalized. It can shelter not only the venturesome but also fugitives from justice, seducers of trusting maidens, those fleeing from overly possessive wives, or, simply, those incapable of dealing with a poisonous family situation. One of the best examples of social and cultural marginalization is represented by homosexuality. Various documents in the Archive of the Indies mention the presence of homosexuality on the ships of Spain's Atlantic routes, and I refer to them in more detail later, when I speak about daily shipboard life. Here, I merely discuss why homosexuality, like other behavior usually considered marginal, could explain why many individuals chose the rigors of a life at sea.

In *Sodomy and the Perception of Evil* (1983), B. R. Burg tried to prove that the possibility of practicing homosexuality in a predominantly male atmosphere was one of the most powerful attractions of seafaring, at least on the ships of His Britannic Majesty. According to Burg, "The all-male atmosphere was the very feature of Royal Navy life that brought a portion of each ship's crew into His Majesty's service."[23] The author emphasized that homosexuality was discouraged but not harshly punished in seventeenth-century England. This permissiveness encouraged many homosexuals to choose a life at sea to be able to develop their sexual appetites in a propitious milieu. But Burg went even further in affirming that, despite the importance normally given to economic motivations, there were other, more decisive reasons why men went to sea, and the ease of developing homosexual relations would occupy a prominent place among them. To demonstrate this thesis, the author pointed out that there was always a shortage of men to serve on the ships, despite salaries that were quite high in peacetime and even higher in wartime.

From my point of view, this thesis is difficult to accept in its entirety. In particular, the main argument employed to justify it instead provides a contradiction. If economic reasons had a clearly secondary character, it would make no sense that salaries rose in wartime. Moreover, if the eagerness for adventure or the desire to free oneself from repression had been the predominant motives for choosing a life at sea, crew members would never have been scarce. As we have seen, the question was not so simple, because a variety of factors entered into the decision to become a mariner, stemming as much from the repulsion of the terrestrial milieu as from the attraction of the maritime world.

Burg's study refers specifically to groups of men at sea in the total absence of women, either because of the duration of their passage or because of some peculiarity in the type of ship on which they traveled: pirate ships, warships, or those that served routes to the Far East. It is also well known that fierce warriors in ancient times, and in the present, have often been fond of maintaining relations with young boys. Stories immediately come to mind of the feared warriors of ancient Sparta and their affection for boys in the bloom of youth, to whom they taught as much about the arts of love as those of war. Given all that, it is no wonder that dashing buccaneers in the old movies of our childhood were less given to carrying away beautiful women than we have been led to believe and that, when they did so, they may have been bedazzled more by the potential ransom money than by the beauty of their hostages.

Spain's transatlantic communications presented a different panorama from the picture painted by Burg. Early on, the routes had relatively fixed sailing times and itineraries that were not too long; above all, the voyages mixed passenger and freight traffic. In the ships of the Indies run, one could not escape female passengers and servants, who were often charitable souls disposed to dispel the boredom of the crew.

Even with all these qualifications, however, Burg's thesis opens our eyes in a very important sense. Explanations of why men went to sea that are based on grand theories, especially economic theories, provide an overall vision of human behavior, but they are not inclusive. Thus, one can reasonably accept the notion that many men approached a life at sea looking for a sexually propitious atmosphere. The same thing happened in military camps and monasteries, that is, in other places with an exclusively masculine environment. Therefore, though homosexual motives would not have been the major reason for going to sea, there is no doubt that they would explain some behavior. At the moment of embarkation, men were pursuing a thousand and one dreams: "Aboard these ships there would be no home in the traditional sense, no family, and no women."[24]

Prestige and Dishonor for Maritime Occupations

Among the crew members on the ships of the Carrera de Indias a social barrier existed that was practically insurmountable. On one side were the military chiefs of the galleons and war fleets, with their entourages of gentlemen, relatives, and hangers-on. The great majority of them belonged to the lower nobility; to serve on a ship was a matter of happenstance for many, because they could equally have begun their careers in the armies of Flanders, and it was not uncommon for them to end up commanding a unit in one of the king's land armies. Between these men and the apprentice seamen, sailors, masters' assistants, pilots, and ships' masters on different ships opened the decisive frontier that separated the nobility, however low in that hierarchy, from the common people in society. For this reason I emphasize that basic classification, and we begin by studying the social sectors considered less prestigious.

The Social Condition of Sailors and Officers

The term *marine officer* was thought to distinguish those who had begun their careers as simple apprentice seamen from those others who had begun as gentlemen or adjutants of fleet commanders and who, finally, arrived at positions in command as so-called officers of sea and war. In the sixteenth century, the majority of persons who occupied a responsible position on a merchant ship had begun their careers when they were children, as pages or apprentices.

To be a pilot meant to have risen to the summit of success as a specialized worker. The House of Trade offered brief courses and gave examinations for pilots; but the fundamental work of the crown was not the training of pilots but the certification, in the form of an official stamp of approval, of the sailing abilities and experiences that had already been obtained by an aspiring pilot.

The next step—becoming a ship's master—was the most difficult to climb, since the master of a ship was its economic administrator and, normally, part owner of the vessel. Only a chosen few could cross over that economic frontier and, with luck, become a shipowner, that is to say, a "lord of ships." Of course, in the sixteenth century there were noble gentlemen and rich merchants who were also owners of ships, but, as we shall see, it was still very common for the owners who personally ran their ships to have sprung from the humble lineage of pilots and even from simple sailors.

Between a poor apprentice and a rich "lord of ships," the economic difference would be considerable, but the social difference was not so great. In this manner, the rich shipbuilder who came from a family of mariners still carried the ignominious brand of his obscure origins as a manual laborer, practicing one of the "mechanical occupations" of low social prestige. However rich he was, if a shipowner had callused hands from having hauled on thick fiber cables and his face was tanned by the sun and full of wrinkles, his social position would never be excessively prestigious.

For a long time, work at sea was considered dishonorable, and a gentleman could lose his nobility by choosing this occupation. If a poor gentleman wanted to initiate a military career to escape his misery, no one would look askance if he signed up as a simple soldier in the company of a countryman, trying to succeed, through his valor, in rising even to the rank of general. To do the same thing beginning as a mariner was inconceivable. Specifically, at the start of the seventeenth century, when King Philip III wished to give some privileges to the men of the sea due to the scarcity of Spanish mariners, he had to stipulate that from then on, "those who were of the lower nobility, not only would suffer no prejudice to their nobility . . . to have served me on the said armadas and fleets as a sailor, or in other posts that the said men of the sea are accustomed to serve on the ships . . . but that the fact of having done so was of the most honored quality and esteem of their persons."[25] But this formal declaration of the monarch probably did not change things much, and there would be few members of the lower nobility who would let themselves be seduced into climbing barefoot into the rigging of a ship, skinning their hands rowing a ship's boat, or working at the bilge pump to clear the bottom of the hold of rotten and putrefied water.

It was clear that, while the smell of dust could be a motive for pride, the smell of tar did not ennoble anyone in the slightest. Thus, it is truly amusing to see the efforts made by the well-known writer of naval treatises, the jurist Diego García de Palacio, to convince his readers of the honorable origins of some of the earliest navigators. Was Noah not a sailor, the man whose ark was designed by God the Father himself? Were the apostles not fishermen, and thus men of the sea, with whom Jesus Christ himself embarked on a multitude of occasions? Without navigation, how would Christianity have been spread, and how would King Solomon have been able to transport the rich materials to build the great temple of Jerusalem? Even so, despite his invocation of such illustrious ancestors, García de Palacio was not able to persuade his contemporaries of the honor implied in being a sailor; he himself was not fully convinced, since in the same paragraphs he affirms that sailors and pilots were "mostly ignorant and unlettered people."[26]

The society of this time did not forgive men of the sea who came from very poor families for earning their bread with physical force. It would seem as if the sweat generated by muscular activity during work produced a sort of social allergy, which irritated those who considered themselves the descendants of the Cid, who would certainly have done his share of sweating inside the breastplates and chain mail of his armor in the blazing sun of Castile.

If this were not so, one could not well understand the mean treatment accorded to Gonzalo Gómez de Espinosa, one of the few survivors of the Magellan expedition. Gómez de Espinosa was a semiliterate man who departed Seville in 1519, exercising the job of constable *(alguacil)* of the fleet, charged with maintaining order and other policing functions. After the assassination of Magellan and his principal captains, Gómez de Espinosa was named by the survivors as captain general of the small fleet, which had been reduced to the two ships *Trinidad* and *Victoria.* Unfortunately for him, the *Trinidad* could not make it home, and the glory of being the first to sail around the world fell to his subordinate Juan Sebastián Elcano. Gómez de Espinosa had to suffer several years as a prisoner of the Portuguese, and when at last he succeeded in returning to Spain, the king's attorney denied him the salary of captain general, alleging that someone named as a constable could not have the ability or the dignity necessary to exercise supreme command in a fleet "because the said office [of constable] for which he was chosen requires bodily force and work, rather than the personal eminence and education of those who govern and command."[27] For this reason Gómez de Espinosa was not fully compensated for his almost ten years of sacrifice in the Moluccas, and, possibly, the coarseness of his person and of the office he initially held was the determining cause of that fact.

Evidently, the men of the sea were not all equal. There existed a certain scale of prestige, or, better said, of social prestige. The least favored were those who carried out work that was purely manual—pages, apprentices, and sailors, including also the lowest grades of officers, such as guardianes, stewards, or masters' assistants, who were no more than old experienced sailors.

We are already familiar with the humble origins of a large portion of the mariners. Not only were they from a "lowly cradle," but many of them had nowhere to fall after leaving the arms of their mothers. Then, after choosing and practicing navigation, they continued to be surrounded by individuals who occupied the lowest sectors of the social scale. Studying the legal cases in which mariners became involved and the witnesses who testified for them, we can learn the identities of their neighbors, their relatives, and their friends. Very few of the said witnesses were farmers, which leads one to think that the first generations of emigrants from rural areas did not easily choose the profession of mariner, since the change of element would have been too abrupt for a man stuck in the soil. On the contrary, we can see that the working and social milieu of the men of the sea was formed by urban laborers, who made their living practicing mechanical trades.

(38)

One example of this is the case of the sailor Juan Hidalgo, a native of Huelva, who was killed in 1588 by some Gypsies near the town of Manzanilla. When his relatives petitioned the House of Trade for the salary he was owed, the witnesses were three illiterate persons: a nephew of the deceased, who was a tailor, and two neighbors who were, respectively, a shoemaker and a tailor.[28] Besides these occupations, in other legal cases heard before the House of Trade the persons linked to the mariners by ties of neighborhood, family, or friendship worked as servants, porters, boatmen, coopers, barbers, fish sellers on the Arenal of the Guadalquivir, women who sold artichokes in the plazas of Seville, rope makers, makers of hempen sandals, and so on. In many cases, the mariners themselves had done similar work before going to sea.

Though all manual work had scant social prestige, the occupations cited above occupied the lowest places. These were not even artisanal activities that enjoyed a certain distinction and good wages, as did silversmiths, printers, or apothecaries. To Iñigo de Lecoya, who was a captain of sea and war, the mariners and soldiers who served in the fleets had inferior origins, since "almost all of them are lackeys, tailors, jacket makers, shoemakers, and exercise other low occupations."[29]

The lowliness of jobs at sea can be well appreciated by noting that many posts of apprentices and sailors were occupied by blacks and mulattos. Some of them were free men, but others were slaves who worked on the ships in order to hand their wages over to their owners. Looking at the lists of crewmen on the armadas and merchant fleets, we find cases like that of the sailor "Diego Fernández, a native of Pontevedra, black in color, [who] was a slave of Gonzalo Barbeto, a native of Pontevedra; he is free and showed proof of his freedom and he is forty years old."[30] On some galleons there were veritable families of slaves or ex-slaves. Thus, for example, one sailor and three apprentices from the Chávez family, "black-skinned," sailed on the galleon *San Martín* in 1579.[31]

There is no doubt that the slaves, or freed slaves, of the black race constituted the lowest rung on the social ladder of the times. The fact that they frequently performed the work of sailors leaves no doubt about the social consideration that such an occupation had for their contemporaries. That black men would exercise the office of judge, or notary, was absolutely inconceivable, but no one was astonished that they were on ships serving as sailors. Moreover, a modest man of the sea could come to consider one of these descendants of slaves as his friend. An incident that proves this point occurred in 1583 on board the flagship of the New Spain fleet. On board, for a matter of no importance, two sailors got into a fight. One of the contenders was a free black from Triana who was called Juan de Ribera. The other, also illiterate and somewhat younger, was called Domingo López. A witness who was there told what had happened. "There were angry words; the witness did not know what they were about, but he saw the said Domingo López tell the said Juan de Ribera that he was a black dog and he took a stick of wood that was there on the ground and he hit him with it, and then Juan de Ribera, black, went for the said Domingo López and grappled with him and with a knife that he had in his hand he gave him a stab wound in the ribs on the right side."[32]

Up to this point we have a violent incident, like many that happened on board ships, and we can even see hints of racial prejudice on the part of the white sailor, who insulted his comrade by calling him a "black dog." The curious thing about the incident happened afterward, when the victim, who had suffered a dangerous wound "next to the kidneys," said that they had made their peace and that he was a friend of his aggressor, so he forgave the incident and ended the quarrel.

The office of pilot occupied the highest rung on the occupational ladder that a worker at sea could attain, and for that reason the job carried somewhat more prestige. Nonetheless, we are dealing with a very small ladder, since no one forgot the obscure origins of the majority of the pilots, who all came from the ranks of the able-bodied sailors and whose only difference rested in having an elementary education, which enabled them to pass the examinations of the House of Trade. But the instruction of the pilot was nothing unusual; as proof of this it is sufficient to note that most authors of nautical books written in the sixteenth century saw their books as a way to lessen the ignorance of pilots, who were generally described as "coarse," "ill-bred" *(tosco),* "rude," "lacking in understanding," and other pretty phrases of that ilk.[33]

It is possible that there were pilots who possessed social and occupational origins somewhat more elevated than those of simple sailors. We know some cases in which the pilots were the sons of specialized and well-paid artisans, normally linked to work related to the refitting of ships, such as river carpenters, caulkers, or coopers.[34] They tried to distance themselves from the inferior groups in society; thus, for example, the pilot of the Carrera de Indias Alonso de Zapata complained that, by means of bribes, mulattos, Moriscos (converted Muslims), and shoemakers were being admitted to pilots' exami-

Black slaves filling water barrels during a stop in port. Drawing by Christoph Weiditz, 1529. Biblioteca Nacional, Madrid.

nations, though such men were unworthy of piloting a ship.[35] As we can see, yesterday, like today, people very soon forgot their own origins and tried to hide them by criticizing those of others. But that was difficult to do, because the office of pilot could also be occupied by persons who had carried the infamous stigma of slavery. Although they were much less numerous than ordinary sailors and apprentices, there were some examples of black and mulatto pilots in the Carrera de Indias.

One of them was the mulatto Lope Martínez de Lagos, pilot of a dispatch boat in Miguel López de Legazpi's expedition to the Philippines. Secretly condemned to death for defrauding the royal treasury, he returned to the Philippines with his death sentence written in a closed and sealed envelope, which he was supposed to deliver to the governor of those islands. But Lope, the mulatto, found out about the contents of the envelope and led a bloody mutiny that ended the lives of the officers on his ship, an act that makes him a true "Lope de Aguirre" of the Pacific.[36] Another case, one that sounds much less like a novel, is that of the pilot Manuel Luis, a householder from Tavira in Portugal, a man "black in color with a large body," who rose to the rank of pilot on the galleon *San Pedro* in the royal Guard Squadron of the Carrera de Indias.[37]

Above the pilot, and at the summit of authority on merchant vessels, was the ship's master, who acted as its economic administrator and was often part (41) owner of the vessel. The passage from pilot to master signified a very important qualitative change: ceasing to be exclusively a salaried employee and converting oneself into an owner. A hard-working master with a good business sense could become majority owner of a vessel and transform himself into a rich "ship lord." Nonetheless, although some masters and ship lords came to possess fortunes measured in thousands of ducats, that did not erase their origins. Masters were often subjected to small and large public humiliations calculated to remind them that, not long ago, they, or their fathers or grandfathers, had arrived on a ship's deck to sign on as simple apprentices, with the stigma of hunger or their status as bastards or orphans reflected in their faces.

In the eyes of government officials, the social condition of a simple sailor did not differ much from that of a master, since both were subject to the same ignominious punishments when they failed to comply with the ordinances of the House of Trade. The infractions of apprentices and sailors could be punished by public flogging, in which the miscreant not only was cruelly punished but was also subjected to the vexation of being paraded through the Arenal of the Guadalquivir, riding on the back of an ass and exposed to the jests of the curious throngs that circulated there. For the masters, the sanctions generally consisted of heavy fines, but if they did not have the means to pay them, they too were subjected to the infamy and torment of receiving one hundred lashes.[38] The masters complained bitterly about this lack of consideration, and judging by the tone in which they expressed themselves, it seems that they feared the affront as much as the lash of the public executioner:

> The instructions assign to the masters penalties of one hundred lashes, and in this we are affronted and aggrieved, given that we are the lords and masters of ships, very honorable and rich and wealthy persons, and that when we do things that we ought not do, our resources will pay for it . . . and to assign to persons such as we are penalties of blows of the lash is to affront our persons and our reputations.[39]

I do not know if masters were ever flogged, but very frequently, in the case of any infraction of the ordinances, they ended up laden with chains and shackles in the jail of the House of Trade, without being given any special treatment because of their wealth. Besides these notorious humiliations, some of the most prominent among the shipowners and shipbuilders in Seville in the sixteenth century had to put up with small vexations in their everyday treatment by local authorities, always designed to remind them of their modest origins.

In the society of the time, the prestige of each person was measured externally by a series of tiny details, which appeared in the eyes of contemporaries as pillars that sustained their honor. Whether one remained seated or standing, head covered or with hat in hand, at the head or at the sides of a table, to the right or to the left of the altar during the mass were fundamental elements marking a person's prestige. Precisely for that reason, the representatives of the Sevillian shipowners and masters felt themselves slighted when the officials of the House of Trade received them seated and made them remain standing while conducting their business. Because they knew that the representatives of the merchants were offered seats, their humiliation was all the greater, and for this reason they decided to mount an official protest:

> On the 27th of January of 1582, being in our council [of the University of Seafarers] . . . the matter was dealt with that . . . the current president of the House of Trade should offer chairs to the deputies and other officials of this University, when they are called before it, or go to report on matters pertaining to His Majesty's service inside the House of Trade, as they are accustomed to give to the priors and consuls [of the Consulate of Indies Shippers], as this is a University founded by His Majesty.[40]

Undoubtedly, on the question of honor the seafarers of Seville would think that the office of merchant was not very far removed from that of maritime transporter. Moreover, perhaps they found it difficult to accept that transatlantic commerce produced such high profits that it was capable of covering up even the most humble of lineages and of placing a secure patch over any holes in one's honor.

Possibly, the real problem for masters and ship lords was that they never succeeded in becoming as rich as the merchants, at least not rich enough to make others forget their modest origins. Thus, in 1584 when the king summoned four of the richest ship lords in Seville to serve in the royal armadas, he offered them positions that they considered dishonorable: to be "masters of rations," in other words, to act as superintendents of the ships, keeping the accounts of the rations distributed. Among those called was Andrés de Paz, the richest shipowner in Seville, who at the time presided over the association of Sevillian seafarers.[41] For men who owned oceangoing ships and houses in the city, serving as simple distributors of rations would seem of very little importance. They aspired to be named generals and admirals, but the normal thing was to give them secondary posts, related to seafaring but not to warfare. Men of the sea with many years of experience and who owned large ships, men such as Cosme Buitrón, had to content themselves with serving as "pilots major" under the orders of generals and admirals who usually knew little about the art of sailing but who, on the other hand, belonged to families of the lower nobility traditionally dedicated to military service.[42]

It was very clear, then, that the social disrespect for the men of the sea, albeit with some notable shadings, extended from the apprentice seaman to the lord of the ship. Precisely for that reason, all who dedicated themselves to maritime affairs tried to better their positions by receiving small privileges from the crown, which could distinguish them from the common herd. In a society where human inequality before the law was a basic principle, any social group that wanted to rise in status and gain the respect of others had to be endowed with differentiating prerogatives.

Naturally, the most powerful among the men of the sea were the first to try to endow themselves with special concessions. This was one of the motives that led to the formation of the dual framework of associations that has already been mentioned: the Brotherhood of Our Lady of Fair Wind and the University of Seafarers. When these associations were created in the middle of the sixteenth century, the pilots, masters, and ship lords of the Carrera de Indias had two main objectives: on the one hand, to be able to count on an association for mutual aid to help members of the group in need; and, on the other hand, to build a group capable of defending its professional rights and to elevate the prestige of maritime occupations in the eyes of the rest of society.

That the acquisition of prestige and honor was a central proposition of these institutions can be seen clearly in the very memorandum in which they presented themselves to the king. Juan Rodríguez de Noriega, in the name of his colleagues, expressed his desire that, through the association, the monarch could easily identify "honorable men and natives of these kingdoms," in order to maintain in perpetuity "this bridge by which one passes to the New World."[43] In addition, the memorandum revealed the ambition for honors among those who felt themselves unjustly undervalued: "That the privileges and liberties that the men of the sea enjoy in this city of Seville not only are not observed, but we are aggrieved, vexed, and bothered by many things that are worth being remedied."[44]

The concrete forms of elevating one's prestige varied. In the first place, the institutions would have representative buildings, capable of showing the whole city the physical existence of the group. In the second place, members of the brotherhood would undertake to surround themselves with complicated ceremonials filled with pomp, canticles, and candlelit processions for the key moments in the lives, or the deaths, of members of the association, showing outsiders the dignity of their association. Finally, they would try to get the king to endow the group with special favors that would place the seafarers among the privileged sectors of society. Possibly, in the minds of the masters and pilots was the image of the University of Merchants of the Carrera de Indias, gathered together around the Consulate of Indies Shippers of Seville and which had already been functioning for more than thirty years.

But the seafarers also tried to separate themselves from the undifferentiated mass of the common people. The really interesting thing is the speed with which these men, who not so long before had used their callused hands to push the bars on the capstan, thought about excluding from their association the sons and sons-in-law of members who worked at "mechanical jobs." In the same way, some pilots, many of whom had not known their fathers or even heard about them, took it upon themselves to prohibit illegitimate sons from acceding to an office in their brotherhood.[45] It would seem that there are few things as fragile as human memory when it comes to remembering a humiliating past.

Unfortunately for the Sevillian seafarers, the king, having consulted the House of Trade, did not agree to grant one of their fundamental requests. Article 23 of the proposed ordinances of the Brotherhood of Our Lady of Fair Wind said that the members should act as a tribunal in differences that arose among the members. To accede to this point, an apparently innocuous concession, would have meant giving the seafarers a tribunal with special jurisdiction and thus confirming their position as a privileged group. The crown ordered, instead, that any differences among the members be resolved in the tribunals of the House of Trade. In this, the men of the sea failed to achieve the same privileges as the merchants, whose consulate acted as a special tribunal in mercantile matters.[46] Thus, their attempts to equate themselves with the powerful group of merchants in the Carrera de Indias proved futile, even though they were the richest of Sevillian seafarers.

More modest men of the sea, such as sailors and gunners on ships of the Carrera de Indias, also struggled to obtain privileges. The first to acquire a formal declaration of prerogatives from the king were the naval gunners, who constituted a professional group much in demand by Spanish war fleets. Once the crown became aware of the lack of Spanish gunners, it had to provide incentives for the profession, and in 1595, it conceded important rights to them. The gunners of the Carrera de Indias could bear arms; in the case of a lawsuit for debt, their salary could not be embargoed, nor could a basic set of household goods composed of personal clothing and bedclothes; they and their wives would not be obligated to house soldiers or public functionaries; and, finally, they would be judged exclusively by generals of the armada or, if they were on land, by the House of Trade. This last concession included the added benefit of not having to lay their bones in the terrible royal jail in Seville, a veritable hell on earth, exchanging their place of incarceration for the House of Trade's own jail, which might as well have been a palace in comparison with the public prison.[47] Simple sailors had to wait for their privileges a bit longer, but by a royal decision of 1606, they ended up having privileges similar to those of the gunners; to this was added the privilege of being able to wear certain sorts of clothing, which for the times would have been considered elegant: Walloon-style shirts, suede doublets, and so on.[48]

《 45 》

The Level of Prestige of the Naval High Command

The warships that protected the fleets were commanded by men who possessed a social prestige far superior to that of the officers and sailors of the merchant ships. The generals and admirals of the armadas, the captains of the galleons, and a whole series of adjutants who customarily accompanied them in the hope of occupying their posts in the future were ordinarily members of the lower nobility. The best known among the admirals and generals could sport, as we have already indicated, the uniform of a gentleman of one of the many Spanish military orders: Pedro Menéndez de Avilés was a knight commander of Santa Cruz de la Zarza; Diego de Flores Valdés, Cristóbal de Eraso, and Pedro de Valdés were knights of Santiago.[49]

These persons, who acted as patriarchs of great dynasties of military professionals at sea, could include rich and powerful people. The case of Pedro Menéndez de Avilés is significant, as he possessed abundant rural properties in his native Asturias. Granted, the rest belonged to a group that was socially prestigious but without many economic resources. Any of the great "plebeian" shipowners of Seville, such as Andrés de Paz or Cosme Buitrón, doubtless had more money than the great majority of hidalgos who commanded galleons in the Carrera de Indias, but these latter retained the arrogance of men who belonged to a group chosen from the old military nobility.

There are good examples of ruined hidalgos who desired to achieve fame and fortune through the gratitude and favors of the king. One such case was Toribio Alonso de Salazar, an hidalgo who rose to lead the expedition sent to the Moluccas, initially under Commander Loaisa. Salazar was no more fortunate than Loaisa, and he also perished during the voyage. Thanks to his will, we know that he was burdened by debts. He was the second son in his family, and the only paternal inheritance he had was a property in Santander province, worth so little that he did not even charge rent to his tenants. Besides that, the only thing he had was his salary from the expedition, from which we must discount a substantial portion because of the loans he had received before departing. The most valuable part of his patrimony was not economically quan-

Origin and Social Condition

tifiable and might be described as the glory of having served with Gonzalo Fernández de Córdoba in the wars against France. But it was well known that the "Great Captain," as Fernández de Córdoba was known, had a peculiar way of settling his accounts, and poor Salazar must have been one of those prejudiced by this, because he also owed money for his participation in the wars in Italy that had made Fernández de Córdoba famous. He had no other solution than to pawn some of his weapons, as he acknowledged having pawned a broadsword in Valladolid for a ducat. What could a warrior do who had come to the hard pass of pawning his weapons? Possibly what Alonso de Salazar did: embark on an almost suicidal expedition searching desperately for a way to better his precarious economic situation.[50]

(46)

A similar case might be that of the admiral Álvaro de Valdés, a member of an hidalgo clan from Asturias, with very good family connections but also with too many children to feed. In order to try his hand at a military career, Álvaro de Valdés entered the service of Pedro Menéndez de Avilés and fought at his side in numerous battles. Nonetheless, fortune was not his ally, and shortly after obtaining command of a galleon, he was captured by some Barbary corsairs, having to pay the ransom with his own funds. When he died in America serving as admiral of the Tierra Firme fleet, he left two thousand ducats in debts and a family that bitterly claimed some gift from the crown to sustain themselves, in recognition of his services.[51]

From these two examples we can infer that the hidalgos who directed the fleets were not especially rich, nor was the attainment of money the exclusive objective of their lives. For a nobleman, more important than knowing how to accumulate ducats was knowing how to spend them elegantly. Therefore, there existed numerous generals and admirals who, when the monarch was slow in rewarding their services, had no qualms about simply taking their recompense directly at the crown's expense. But, however they acquired them, they happily spent many of the riches obtained, behaving like lords. Noblemen, like Caesar's wife, not only had to be what they were but also had to seem to be what they were, and there was no better way of keeping up appearances than spending money in an extravagant manner within a circle of friends.

That is why, in the petitions that such a person filed in search of royal favors, he would customarily complain of being ruined for having spent his fortune in sustaining a small court of servants and friends, nobles like himself, maintaining them at his table so that they could continue exercising the art of combat. Every gentleman needed his small court, and only in its midst could he demonstrate his noble condition, which he accomplished through largesse, generosity, and a capacity for showing his lack of attachment to money. The maintenance of these little entourages was expensive, but we ought to consider them as a sumptuary expense, providing evidence of the social importance of those who sustained them. The only thing asked of the members of the group in exchange was their loyalty, since every one had to be disposed to serve his lord and friend in any circumstance. Such behavior demonstrated that an admiral could not have the same interest in accumulating riches, nor would he spend money in the same way as the men of low birth who earned their living in the carrying trade.

Some paragraphs taken from the petitions cited above can be very illuminating. Thus, Captain Hernando de Lierno, who rose to be the admiral on the Pacific coast of Tierra Firme, said he was "an illustrious man and an hidalgo (47) and as such he had always behaved honorably and generously, sustaining at his table many soldiers."[52] For his part, when Pedro Menéndez de Avilés was accused of engaging in contraband and of increasing his fortune at the expense of the royal treasury, the witnesses presented in his defense insisted that the general had impoverished himself serving the king and that "all that the said general has earned and earns in salary and expenses for his voyages and ships, he has spent and spends in sustaining and bringing into his company illustrious men such as knights and hidalgos, and in other expenses in His Majesty's service."[53]

Thus, at the side of each important personage in the royal fleets there was a small entourage of gentlemen or "expectant" knights, so called because they were waiting for the moment in which they would accede to a responsible post. Sebastian Cabot, sent in 1526 as captain general of a royal fleet to the Far East, carried an escort of twelve "gentlemen of honor," while the generals of the Guard Squadron of the Carrera de Indias had the right to carry six gentlemen.[54] Some of these were paid by the king, but the majority were friends and relatives attracted by the promise of finding suitable employment. Naturally, the members of these small courts engaged in an intense contraband trade in order to earn some money while they waited to receive a suitable post in the king's employ. This fact was widely known, but the fiscal authorities in American ports encountered many difficulties in inspecting warships. The generals, in reciprocating the loyalty of their entourage, were bound to prevent the functionaries from bothering their friends.

Thus, when royal officials on the island of Cuba tried to inspect the armada commanded by Diego de Flores Valdés, they did not succeed, not even by carrying in their hands a royal order signed by the king. The general kissed the royal order, bowed, and pressed it to his forehead in a show of respect, but he did not comply with it, and to justify himself he said:

> If I were to permit the officials to enter the fleet, the men on board would be scandalized . . . because in the said armada there are many illustrious people, gentlemen and hidalgos, who are serving His Majesty, with-

out thought of financial gain, spending their wealth and patrimonies, suffering very great and excessive trials, and if any judge [but the general] were allowed to enter the fleet, they would go away and abandon the fleet.[55]

The crown was responsible for this situation, since the very same king sent individuals who had been recommended to him to the armadas, so that the generals would find posts for them. We cite the case of Captain Francisco de Salazar, who, according to the royal order recommending him, merited a good post "for always having behaved with much nobility and generosity, in accordance with his quality, and because he had been given neither advantages nor rewards, he was poor and indebted."[56] Thus, the quality of a person required a proportional expense, and it is not difficult to understand how these ruined military men not only "polished" their own honor but also contributed to "cleaning" the royal treasury.

In order to feel superior, one always ought to find someone to look down upon, so the military men of the Carrera de Indias customarily unloaded their disdain on the masters of the merchant ships. The situation was made particularly delicate when a young military officer was sent out to a merchant ship whose master had been provisionally named captain. Conflict could then erupt very easily, especially if the master tried to impose his authority on the ship, and the proud pup of a warrior reminded him of his low condition as a transporter of hides and other such merchandise.[57]

Self-affirmation could also play itself out within the same social group, and, as if economic capacity were not an adequate marker of hierarchy for an hidalgo, some of them showed themselves to be tremendously punctilious over questions of preeminence. Thus, for example, the simple matter of who ought to initiate a salute could unleash a storm based on honor besmirched. All the captains and admirals of the armada's ships wanted to be recognized as authentic knights, and if anyone's action cast doubt on this fact, conflict was assured.

A demonstration of this type of confrontation was the incident between the captain of a frigate of the Guard Squadron of the Carrera de Indias, Gregorio de Polanco, and the admiral of the said armada, Francisco Carreño. The customs of men of the sea, reflected in royal ordinances, signaled the precise forms in which ships ought to approach one another and, of course, the manner of exchanging salutes. The simple fact of exchanging a few words on the high seas had to be regulated by a precise ritual, one that clearly marked which of the two ships was commanded by an officer of greater prestige. The ship commanded by a captain of minor rank always had to approach from leeward and to initiate the salute. This consisted of a shout or a "salute" from the crew directed by the whistle of the boatswain. "God save you [Dios os salve], Lord Ad-

(48)

miral," or phrases of that ilk, constituted the vocal salute. The salute could also be given with cannon fire, but in order not to waste powder, this type of courtesy was reserved for special occasions. The matter of approaching to leeward was not by accident, since, because this position signified a disadvantage in combat, it was a form of expressing submission, which brings to mind the attitude of animals who present their throat to the victor in a fight as a sign of surrender.

Both Captain Polanco and Admiral Carreño were hidalgos who took great care in small matters of honor. Polanco, in the lawsuit filed against him for showing disrespect, presented a patent of his nobility that ran to fifty folios. Carreño, for his part, was a member of the prestigious municipal council of Seville, to which he would not have been admitted without being able to prove he was an hidalgo. For some time the two men had had disagreements in the matter of salutes, since the admiral demanded not only to be saluted first but also to receive an extra salute *(salva de más)*, which Polanco refused to do. Finally, the dispute forged ahead under full sail with a strong verbal confrontation between the two military officials. When the admiral demanded an extra salute, Polanco indicated that he did not mean to dishonor anyone but only to comply with the ordinances and responded without vacillating that

《 49 》

> his honor would not bow to anyone's, since he was as much a noble as any other in the said armada . . . because, apart from the favor of being the admiral of this armada, I was as much a noble knight as were all the captains of the armada . . . because, although my ship was not as large as those of the others, it belonged to His Majesty and to the fleet, to which [the admiral] replied that he would make me pay for these words back on land.[58]

It was evident that Captain Polanco felt humiliated because his ship was the smallest in the armada, and he tried to make himself feel better by his disrespectful behavior. But these sorts of incidents were so frequent that they cannot be blamed only on the personal frustrations of individuals. Nor do I believe that the problem was restricted to the past, since even in the final years of the twentieth century similar conflicts continue. Nonetheless, it seems that today, as then, such encounters were more frequent between persons who belong to groups in which power is not measured exclusively by economic status. Perhaps that is why we witness in historical politics disputes as puerile as those between Captain Polanco and Admiral Carreño.

The Number and Geographical Origin of Crews
on the Indies Route

The maintenance of communications between Spain and its overseas possessions during the sixteenth century presupposed a tremendous organizational effort, which was even more notable if we take into account that there were no precedents from which to learn. In order to maintain yearly contact between Spain and its American possessions, it was crucial to accumulate money, arms, foodstuffs, and, of course, thousands of men capable of handling the hundreds of ships that served as mobile bridges between the continents. The question is: How many sailors and officers had to be mobilized for the functioning of Spain's fleets? Above all, it would be of interest to evaluate the magnitude of the effort, and thus it seems especially interesting to quantify the maximum number of crewmen necessary to keep the system of fleets functioning.

(50)

It is evident that, for the century as a whole, there were very important variations in the volume of naval traffic, due to economic cycles and political and military contingencies. These themes have been described elsewhere, and this is not the place to revisit them. We know that from the mid-sixteenth century there was a rapid increase in transatlantic commerce, which reached its zenith in the first decade of the seventeenth century. That level of exchange would not be repeated until well into the eighteenth century. For this reason I center my analysis on the last two decades of the sixteenth century, though penetrating also into the first years of the seventeenth century, when the largest fleets were sent across the ocean.

The final objective is to estimate the largest contingent of sailors that had to be gathered annually to crew the convoys and individual ships that linked the metropolis with its overseas colonies. Nonetheless, however many sailors were sent to America, they constituted only one part of Spain's naval force, because in those years Spanish ships not only crossed the Atlantic but also traversed the Mediterranean and the Channel and sailed the Pacific from north to south and from east to west.

Because carrying out a complete statistical study would be very laborious, I have instead localized some of the lists of crews that the House of Trade sent to the Council of the Indies. These sources provide information about more than twenty thousand mariners sent to sea, in purely military expeditions (armadas) and in merchant convoys (flotas) protected by a pair of warships. With these data I have established the average number of men per ship, distinguishing between armadas and merchant fleets, since the ships on combat missions always left with proportionally more numerous crews.[59] The results obtained are summarized in tables 2.1 and 2.2.

With these data I calculate that the average number of crewmen on armada ships was sixty-nine. In merchant fleets, the number was forty-three men per ship. Taking into account the list, found in Pierre Chaunu's classic work, of the number of ships that left Spain annually for the Indies, I can estimate the total number of crewmen that would have been necessary. The two years with the highest number of departures in the sixteenth century were 1594 and 1596,

2.1 Composition of Armadas, 1579–1602

Year	General in Command	Ships (no.)	Mariners (no.)
1579	Don Cristóbal de Eraso	8	393
1592	Luis Alfonso Flores	8	530
1592	Juan de Uribe Apallúa	21	1,349
1593	Don Francisco de Coloma	16	1,405
1594	Don Francisco de Coloma	20	1,559
1597	Juan Gutiérrez Garibay	9	562
1598	Don Luis Fajardo	21	1,370
1598	Pedro Cobiaux	13	810
1599	Don Francisco de Coloma	17	1,201
1600	Marcos de Aramburu	13	839
1602	Luis Fernández de Córdoba	11	783
Total		157	10,801

(51)

Source: Data from AGI, Indiferente General 1095, 1102, 1104, 1113–16, 1118.

2.2 Composition of Merchant Fleets, 1587–1594

Year	General in Command	Destination	Ships (no.)	Mariners (no.)
1587	Don Miguel de Eraso	Tierra Firme	32	1,535
1588	——	New Spain (?)	36	1,510
1589	Diego de Ribera	Tierra Firme	29	1,414
1590	Antonio Navarro	New Spain	81	3,319
1593	Marcos de Aramburu	New Spain	53	2,310
1594	Sancho Pardo Osorio	Tierra Firme	29	1,148
Total			260	11,236

Source: Data from AGI, Patronato 25, no. 2, general 2, ramo 1; Indiferente General 1099, 1100; Contratación 1099–1108.

with 150 and 151 ships respectively.[60] The armada that left in 1594 under the command of Don Francisco de Coloma included twenty ships with a total of 1,559 persons, between officers and men. Applying the average of forty-three crewmen to the remaining 130 ships yields a total of 5,590 men. Thus, for the year 1594 there is a total of 7,149 crewmen. In the first decade of the seventeenth century, the total of 150 ships was surpassed only in 1608. In that year a record number of 202 ships left for America. Applying the same method used above, I estimate that the ships in the Carrera de Indias in 1608 would have required somewhat more than 9,000 crewmen.[61]

The numbers that I have just given are the product of an estimation, but I believe that if one carried out more detailed statistical studies, the numbers would not vary much. The important thing to know is that, in the final years of the sixteenth century and the first years of the seventeenth, Spain needed between seven thousand and nine thousand men, including officers, gunners, sailors, and apprentices, to crew the ships that linked Spain with the New World. This number does not include the soldiers, nor the passengers, who completed the variegated human landscape of the ships in the Carrera de Indias.

Of this ample number only a few occupied the superior posts of captain, pilot, and master. In the first third of the century, Hernando Colón, son of the discoverer, owned a book in which he had noted the names of more than 150 pilots.[62] The founding members of the Brotherhood of Our Lady of Fair Wind and the University of Seafarers of Seville, which included pilots, masters, and shipowners, numbered only fifty-seven men,[63] but evidently not all the seafarers of Seville belonged to such associations. When King Philip II visited the city, the chronicler Juan de Mal Lara described a procession past the monarch including "more than 150 captains, masters, and pilots of the Carrera de Indias."[64] In the final years of the century, the increase in maritime traffic led to a considerable increase in the number of pilots; between 1577 and 1600 there were 418 examinations of new pilots by the House of Trade.[65]

These numbers would not tell us much if they did not appear within a comparative framework. Parallelism can be established with relation to the number of sailors in various areas with a great maritime tradition. A document in the Archive of the Indies in Seville, written around 1572, calculated the number of sea captains and experienced sailors in the eastern ports of Spain's Cantabrian coast, from Fuenterrabía to Laredo, at something less than three thousand persons.[66] Extending the comparison beyond the frontiers of the Spanish monarchy, we find that in 1582 the sailors in London numbered 3,086,[67] and the English "royal Navy" was crewed by 5,534 persons in 1603.[68] A final example can be taken as definitive: mariners recruited in 1588 for the Great Armada sent against England numbered 8,050 men.[69]

With this comparative information, the importance of the number of men of the sea employed in the Carrera de Indias can be better appreciated. It is certain that seven thousand or nine thousand men were the absolute maximum, but from the 1580s annual departures toward America frequently surpassed one hundred ships, and that meant contingents of mariners of around five thousand men. If we are impressed by the organizational effort required to crew a great invasion squadron, such as the one recruited in 1588 against the British Isles, think what it meant to contract each year for the thousands of mariners that manned the Indies fleets.

The preparation of large armed fleets represented the most complex task that states could face in those times, and one of the most problematic parts of that task was to unite expert crewmen in sufficient numbers. One must recognize that sailors were free wage laborers with a high degree of specialization; bringing together large contingents of this type of worker was not easy at a (53) time in which the tradition of seigneurial labor systems continued to have great power. I do not think that present-day Spain has any single enterprise that would have to recruit such a quantity of manual labor, and only the mobilization of great armies could surpass the concentrated numbers of men of the sea required in the sixteenth century.

As evidence for that claim, it is sufficient to make a comparison with one of the most massive building projects in that epoch. Even today, popular speech makes reference to "the building of the Escorial" to signal some enterprise of larger than normal size. However, the contingents of workers required for the construction of the combined monastery, church, and palace of the Escorial, ordered by Philip II, were notably smaller than the contingents of mariners for any one year's traffic with America. Father Sigüenza, a contemporary of the Escorial's construction and one of its first librarians, commented on the gala celebration that took place in 1575 to inaugurate the building of the monastery church that was to be part of the complex. The combination of all the workers who participated in that phase of the work did not reach one thousand persons.

> His Majesty determined . . . that the site should be chosen and the work commenced in a great hurry. . . . Friar Antonio de Villacastín, the principal overseer of the work, secretly arranged a delightful entertainment, although he is a man of few jokes and festivities; all the foreigners, master workmen, foremen, day laborers, and workmen—they would have been few less than a thousand persons—put on costumes [and] formed a handsome parade and military review; in the vanguard the day laborers came, and, instead of pikes and lances, they brought the tools of their trades and offices: picks, stonecutters' hammers, shovels, spades, bricklayers' beaters, and hoes, with the men wearing strange masks.[70]

This make-believe army of workmen who constructed the edifice with the largest floor plan in Spain, one that would cost a fortune of six million ducats, would have been greatly outnumbered if they had had to confront the ships' crews of the Carrera de Indias. That is why, even in a city such as Seville, with its 130,000 inhabitants at the end of the century forming the largest city in the kingdom and one of the largest in Europe, the presence of this enormous mass of mariners would have had a tremendous impact. Certainly, a great proportion of the mariners of the fleets were householders of the city, but many others came from outside and formed part of its floating population, which gave the city an unequaled vitality but also created many problems.

《 54 》 I have not made a detailed statistical study of the regional origins of Spanish mariners in the Carrera de Indias, but my soundings in the documents strongly corroborate some hypotheses and suggest that they pertain to the evidence as a whole. Ninety percent of the Spanish crews came from Andalusia and the Cantabrian coast. The remaining 10 percent were distributed throughout the interior of the peninsula, including the Kingdom of Aragón. Nor is it surprising to find a certain regional specialization among them. The armadas, that is to say, the expeditions composed exclusively of warships, were crewed for the most part by Cantabrian men, especially by Basques ("Vizcayans," as they were known at the time).[71] The fleets, on the other hand, composed essentially of merchant ships, generally had crews that were mostly Andalusian.[72] This pattern did not diverge much from the tendency begun in the Middle Ages, when Castile's seaborne war efforts were formed around the magnificent mariners of the northern coast. Thanks to the actions of Basque and *montañés* corsairs (the latter from the Santander area), Castile defeated England's attempt to dominate the Channel and remained free to send her shipments of wool and iron to Flanders during the Hundred Years' War. Even in the sixteenth century, in the popular imagination, one of the basic activities of the *vizcaínos* was maritime warfare. When Friar Bartolomé de las Casas summarized the aptitudes of his opponent, the all-powerful bishop and royal minister for Indian Affairs, Juan Rodríguez de Fonseca, he commented ironically that Fonseca was very able at organizing armadas, although that was "more an occupation for a vizcaíno than a bishop."

The participation of foreigners in the crews of the Carrera de Indias is a subject that is much less known, and for that reason it seems useful to analyze it at some length. In this respect, reality surpassed any preconceptions or suspicions I might have had, enabling me to conclude that the proportion of foreigners in the fleets and armadas to the Indies reached very high percentages.

Moreover, the phenomenon was present from the first. Columbus himself, once he had discovered the Indies and become the first viceroy of the new lands, transported a good number of Genoese to Hispaniola; they were so numerous that Franciscan friars on the island went so far as to complain of an invasion.[73] We are not certain whether the admiral's countrymen worked as mariners, but we do know that foreigners played a fundamental role in the crews of the great voyages to the Far East, above all on voyages in which the commander in chief was not a Spaniard.

Using the data collected by Fernández Navarrete about the geographic origin of crews on Magellan's expedition, we see that at least 90 of the 265 men, somewhat more than 35 percent, were foreigners.[74] They came from almost everywhere in western Europe. Above all they were Portuguese, but also very many were Italians; there were also "levantiscos," that is, Greeks and inhabitants of the Venetian colonies and the eastern Mediterranean, Flemings, Germans, French, Irish, and at least one Englishman. Nonetheless, the proportion of foreigners on this voyage was perhaps even higher than Fernández Navarrete calculated. A document preserved in the Archive of the Indies points out that some of the mariners who officially passed for Spaniards were, in reality, camouflaged foreigners. Unfortunately, the document only includes data about 107 crew members, but forty-eight of those were foreigners, which would raise the percentage to about 45 percent.[75] This fact became so notorious that Magellan felt obliged to swear before a notary that he had tried to assemble Spanish mariners but, not obtaining satisfactory results, he was forced to resort to foreigners:

> I ordered a public announcement made throughout the city of Seville and in the plazas and markets and customary gathering places, and along the banks of the river of this city, saying that all persons, including sailors, apprentices, carpenters, and caulkers and other workmen who wanted to go on the said armada, should come to me, the said captain. . . . [But] even with all these efforts, and with many others that were made, I could not crew the ships of the said armada with the natives of these kingdoms, and not finding them, I ordered the said masters to receive foreigners who seemed to be qualified for the said armada.[76]

Something very similar happened with the expedition that Sebastian Cabot, pilot major of the House of Trade, directed in 1526 trying to find the mythical countries from which the biblical Queen of Sheba had extracted her riches. The crown had given him permission to include foreigners as one-fifth of the crews. Then it agreed to increase the proportion to a third; finally, it had to recognize that even this sizable proportion had been superseded. A letter from the Council of the Indies recognized the fact in these terms: "Sir captain . . . [we] are informed that there are very few [Spanish] men in the armada . . . and that most of the sailors that it carries are foreigners to these kingdoms . . . and, in this situation it seems to us that it would be convenient to have more [Spanish] men . . . and that foreigners be no more than one third of the crew."[77] In the end, the percentage of foreigners who traveled in the expedition must have come to around half, since, in a petition for salaries filed by fifty survivors

Origin and Social Condition

of the crew in 1531, twenty-one of them were not Spaniards, which meant the crew was composed of 42 percent foreigners.[78]

One might think it natural that these expeditions, sent to the other side of the world with tremendously uncertain outcomes and commanded by foreigners, would attract few Spaniards. Yet a foreign presence was not lacking in enterprises with much closer and more attractive objectives. For example, after the discovery of the Southern Sea off the Pacific coast of South America by Balboa, this vigorous leader, who had to justify himself for having taken command by force, represented the recently discovered lands as a prodigious source of riches. Present-day Panama was officially designated "Golden Castile," a name that reflected dreams and ambitions and hid a much harsher reality. But the sailors and other members of the expedition did not know this when, in 1513, they fought to enlist in Seville to travel to those lands. Among the sailors on the expedition to Golden Castile led by Pedro Arias de Ávila, almost 15 percent were foreigners.[79]

Once the discovery phase ended and the phase of exploitation and defense of the American commercial routes began, foreign sailors continued forming an important part of Spanish armadas and fleets. The presence of these men on warships could lead to dangerous situations, as Pedro Menéndez de Avilés learned when he lost his flagship, the galleass *San Pelayo*, because of a mutiny provoked by foreign crewmen, who formed a majority on the ship.

In 1565, the galleass disembarked its troops, who went off to demolish the settlements of French Huguenots in Florida, and sailed toward Hispaniola seeking shelter from a storm. Its crew was composed of some twenty Spaniards and thirty foreigners. These latter were mostly levantiscos and Flemings, but there were also on board, as prisoners, two French sailors, who had passed themselves off as Catalans, and a levantisco boatswain accused of homosexuality. These three initiated the mutiny and convinced the rest of the foreigners to overcome the Spaniards. Afterward, events unfolded in a manner worthy of a novel. Among the mutineers, some wanted to become pirates, and others wanted to head toward France or England and use the ship to fight against Spain. After indulging in various brawls and murders among themselves, the rebels headed toward France, but they did not know enough to find the correct route, and the ship sank on the coast of Denmark.[80]

To avoid a repetition of this sort of incident, in 1568 the House of Trade wrote some instructions prohibiting the presence of foreign boatswains on the Carrera de Indias. The number of non-Spanish sailors was limited to a maximum of six per ship, and carrying even this number was contingent upon obtaining a license in advance.[81] The mere presence of six foreign sailors could mean on average between 12 and 15 percent of the crew, but this limitation was rarely complied with. An analysis of 4,839 officers, gunners, and sailors on different armadas and fleets in the last quarter of the sixteenth century produced a total of 981 foreign crewmen, which equals 20.27 percent. This means that, according to official figures extracted from the registers of the House of Trade, one in five crewmen was not Spanish.[82]

Among the nationalities represented, the Portuguese made up 50 percent of the foreigners, followed by the Italians, who represented 25 percent. The remaining 25 percent were divided almost in equal parts between levantiscos, Flemings, and Germans. The presence of English or French sailors was rare, as they were subjects of nations that were traditional enemies of Spain in the sixteenth century. With respect to the professional distribution of the foreigners, their presence was especially strong among the naval gunners. Practically one in every three gunners was Flemish, German, or Italian, which constituted one of the principal disadvantages of the Spanish navy. Although my study did not include an investigation of the infantry on board, it is interesting to note that, among the soldiers, the proportion of foreigners did not reach 4 percent.[83] In sum, one could say that in the Spanish fleets of the sixteenth century, Spanish soldiers were plentiful, there were commonly problems in filling out the crews with Spaniards alone, and there was a grave lack of Spaniards expert in naval gunnery.

If the official registries of the House of Trade indicate a foreign presence of 20 percent among the men of the sea, the reality would no doubt have amply surpassed this percentage. For officials to recognize the truth of these numbers meant accepting the futility of limiting the number of foreigners, and when an official admitted a failure, it was generally always of greater magnitude than what was admitted publicly. The questions that immediately arise are: How were the restrictions imposed by the House of Trade flouted? And why were there so many foreigners among the mariners on Spanish fleets?

One universal form of scaling bureaucratic barriers has been, and will always be, bribery. Practically from the start of navigation to the Indies, obtaining a license to exercise the two highest posts on merchant ships, that is, master and pilot, was conditional upon passing an examination and proving oneself to be Spanish by birth or by naturalization. Nonetheless, the pilots and cosmographers charged with evaluating such proofs were very badly paid, and one can easily believe the frequent accusations that, in exchange for some ducats, the officials would be less than punctilious in the examinations and proofs.

In 1551, Alonso de Zapata, pilot on the Carrera de Indias, wrote a memorandum in which he accused various cosmographers of the House of Trade of letting themselves be bribed in the examinations. He presented some pilots as witnesses, and among those presumed to be implicated were personages as well known as the cosmographers Pedro de Medina, Alonso de Chaves, and Diego

Origin and Social Condition

Gutiérrez, besides the pilot major, Diego Sánchez Colchero. According to Zapata, in three years they had approved thirty or forty persons who had not complied with the requirements, and among them were various foreigners, Greeks and Portuguese, who had paid some twenty ducats each to grease the administrative wheels at the House of Trade. The Portuguese, due to their status as neighbors, found it easiest to camouflage their condition as foreigners. This was the road followed by various of the aspiring pilots, according to Alonso de Zapata:

> As many Portuguese have arrived who want to be examined, they send their wives to the town of Ayamonte, just over the border into Spain, and they make a false declaration saying that they are resident in the town of Ayamonte, and with the said declaration, the men come to the city of Seville to Diego Gutiérrez, cosmographer, so that he will serve as an advocate for them and say that they are natives, giving him a sum of money, and after the pilot has made the grade, they return to take their wives back to where they are natives.[84]

If it was possible for a foreign pilot to pass himself off as a Spaniard, it was much easier for a simple foreign sailor to camouflage himself from the regulation-loving functionaries of the House of Trade. The master who wanted to contract with a Portuguese, or an Italian, had in his favor the difficulties of tracking down an individual in that time. To be a pretender or an imposter was much simpler in the sixteenth century than it is today, although there will always be confidence artists of this kind. Neither photographs nor methods of fingerprint identification existed in the sixteenth century. Nor did documents of personal or fiscal identity exist; nor, of course, were there computers and other instruments to classify the long-suffering citizenry and track their whereabouts. The men of the sixteenth century had to put up with difficult living conditions, but, on the other hand, they had many more opportunities to flout the control of the state. If they had escaped the misfortune of having some prominent physical deformity or other unmistakable personal mark, it was relatively simple for people to pass for others on official lists and during inspections. Nor was a signature a good indication of identity, because two thirds of the mariners were illiterate.

Dozens of persons were capable of passing for a sailor described as having "middling stature, a sound body, and a black beard." One common type of fraud consisted of contracting Sevillian sailors to carry out the loading of a ship and undergoing the inspections. Then, at the last minute, they were replaced with foreigners, while the Spaniards remained on land. The presence of these local sailors, who worked as day laborers with the promise of not being obliged to sail to the Indies, is amply documented. For example, the practice is mentioned in a long report edited by the constable Juan de Melgarejo, who had accompanied the inspectors of the House of Trade on their rounds for many years: "Some sailors work, and have worked, on the ships for a certain sum each day, without wanting to nor having the intention of going to the Indies, although they are sailors . . . and it is with the agreement of the masters that they sign up as sailors and are entered in the register, although they do not have to go."[85]

Another helpful factor for the master desirous of contracting foreigners was the regional and linguistic variety of Spain. Many men from Galicia, Catalonia, and the Basque country scarcely knew the Castilian language, and when they spoke it they had a very strong accent. This cultural plurality of Spain, which even today is clearly perceptible, had much more intense shadings in the sixteenth century, when the distinct human communities were much less interconnected. Well aware of this, the ships' masters became veritable alchemists of nationalities, but, instead of transforming stones into gold, they were capable of transforming foreigners into natives. To pass a Portuguese off as a Galician was child's play; Italians and Frenchmen could be confused with Catalans. One would think, given the strong philological personality of the Basque language, that any foreigner speaking a non-Romance language, whether Greek or Hungarian, would have been able to pass for Basque; however, the abundance of Basque sailors in the armadas and fleets meant that such stratagems were not easy. This is how Melgarejo the constable described the masters' ability to interchange the nationalities of their sailors: "Other levantiscos, Portuguese, and Flemings, forbidden to emigrate to the Indies, worked on the ships with promises from the masters to take them to the Indies, and thus many Portuguese passed the inspections, saying they were Galicians, and other foreigners saying that they were Catalans."[86]

Despite all these tricks, the inspectors of the House of Trade unmasked many foreigners, but the masters still held the possibility of pretending that a Spanish sailor had fled at the last minute and had to be replaced quickly so as not to delay the fleet's departure. The generals, who carried out inspections en route, were normally less demanding in these matters and worried only about whether the ships had the necessary men:

> When the general makes his inspection at sea . . . in arriving at the name of a sailor who had conspired to remain behind and who was included for the sole purpose of complying with the rules . . . —when his name is called—the master says that So-and-So Sailor fled in Sanlúcar and that he took in his place Such-and-Such Sailor, whom he presented at musters, and if he was a foreigner . . . the master warned him to say that he was from whatever part of Spain he could fake best.[87]

With these subterfuges abounding, it is no surprise that on many lists of sailors names appear that seem to be completely Hispanic, such as Andrés

Hernández, with the notation that he is from Cyprus; a Tomás Rivas and a Martín Hernández, natives of Genoa; or a Pero Díaz, who later is said to be Flemish *(flamenco)*, meaning not that he was fond of fandango dancers but that he was born in Bruges or Antwerp.[88] The Hispanicizing of their last names on the part of many foreigners proves that Spain, thanks to its hegemonic position in sixteenth-century Europe, was the focus of a welcomed immigration that tried to integrate itself as much as possible into the life of the country. That fact affected not only sailors; Alejo Fernández, the artist of the famous "Virgin of the Seafarers" from the chapel of the House of Trade, was, despite his Castilianized name, German.

(60)

What justified the presence of so many foreigners on Spain's maritime routes? The explanations are wide ranging. In the first place, the very characteristics of maritime labor favored the internationality of the occupation. Ports everywhere in the world are veritable Towers of Babel, a summation and living reflection of the variety of the human species. The mobility inherent in the job took care of the rest. In addition, all the great maritime powers in the world, as long as they remained at their peak, could not fully satisfy their demand for sailors. In England, for example, "even though the Navigation Acts had required that three out of four seamen on English ships be subjects of the crown, such requirements were rarely enforced, especially in times of war and labor scarcity, when even the British state admitted that half or more of ships' crews could be foreign."[89]

Turning to reasons that were specifically Spanish, the presence of foreigners on the great voyages of discovery often was due to the fact that the captain general was also foreign. It was natural that, in order to enlist on a dangerous and uncertain expedition, the men had to know and have confidence in their leader. All that came about more easily through a sense of belonging to the same homeland, one of the few feelings capable of holding together the people from the isolated societies of the sixteenth century. At the same time, the leader felt strengthened if he had countrymen among those who supported him and with whom he could face down the frequent attempts at mutinies and revolts.

Once the routes of communication between Spain and America were formalized in the mid-sixteenth century, the presence of some foreigners was due to their precise technical knowledge. This was the case for some naval officers and, above all, for gunners. Nonetheless, naval gunners were a minority among the totality of the crews. The majority of foreign mariners who sailed on Spanish ships were contracted because they constituted a source of docile and cheap manual labor. For their part, they were looking for a way to flout the House of Trade's controls on migration.

For someone who had not been born in Spain, it was almost impossible to get a license to emigrate to the Indies. To be accepted on a ship as an apprentice was much simpler, and the only thing that remained was to desert upon arriving in the Indies. The Spanish shipmasters knew about, and even encouraged, these activities, because they could exploit the work of these men, paying them ridiculously low wages. Protest was unthinkable, since the threat of being denounced to the authorities always weighed on the foreigner. If upon arriving in America the man deserted, the damage for the master was not very great, because the cargo on return trips was always much reduced, and so was the need for hands to work the ships.

As we know, the exploitation of one man by another is as old as the world itself, and abuses were simple enough to perpetrate with emigrants who left their country looking for new promised lands. This was well understood by Captain Iñigo de Lecoya, who wrote in 1575:

> It would be fitting if Your Majesty would once again order that no master be authorized to carry any foreigner as an officer or sailor on his ship, especially Portuguese, whom they bring to the coasts of the Indies, because more of them make the passage than natives, and the masters do this because these foreigners, as they cannot make a living in their countries, are accustomed to so much misery and bad fortune that they are satisfied to sail with these masters for a bit of biscuit and a sardine and a little watered vinegar that they give them as a ration, and they are content with thirty ducats, of the hundred that the master receives for their salary. . . . And so, the masters arrange in many instances to carry them in their ships, and they do not want to carry men who know how to ask for the food and wages that are their due, so that they do not want to carry any good man in their company as a sailor, nor does anyone who is a good sailor want to go with them.[90]

The consequences of the presence of so many foreigners on Spanish fleets were summed up very well by Captain Lecoya. In the first place, the unfair competition from this cheap source of manual labor discouraged many Basque sailors, who before had been "the prime sailors in the world." Between the fear awakened by the military campaigns in the seas around Flanders and the scant salary that was offered them in the Indies fleets, most of the young men in the Basque ports preferred to dedicate themselves to fishing rather than enlisting on the king's ships.

In the second place, the supposed barriers to migration raised by the House of Trade had the same success in stopping the passage of foreigners as a spiderweb would have had in stopping an ox. According to Iñigo de Lecoya, in every fleet no fewer than three hundred Portuguese and Italians made the passage to the Indies, of whom scarcely fifty returned. The foreign sailors were welcomed on the ships that carried out local trade among the American ports, and, according to our informant, "all the Indies are filled with Portuguese, Italians, and other nationals, and it is a marvel to find there a boatman, small innkeeper, grocer, doctor, or apothecary who is not Portuguese."[91] There is no doubt that, in the clandestine traffic of foreigners, signing up as a mariner on the ships of the Carrera de Indias was one of the most secure and well-traveled ways to make the passage.

The Ship as a Place of Work

Handling the Most Complex Machine of the Epoch

A multidecked ship in the sixteenth century formed a floating collection of the incredible successes achieved by human ingenuity to that time. Precisely because it had to conquer the immense desolate oceans and be subject to their menacing isolation, it constituted a small universe endowed with the highest possible degree of self-sufficiency. Ships that left Iberian ports for the East and West Indies were veritable showcases of the technological developments of western Europe. They were the most complex machines of the epoch, but they were something more. Each one carried within its hull a great quantity of specialized mechanisms that combined to carry out the ultimate task of the vessel: conquering the vast emptiness of the oceans and thus reaching out to the diversity of humanity that inhabited the planet.

What other machine of the times could compare with a great ship of the Carrera de Indias? Perhaps the pulleys and cranes destined to raise stones for large construction projects? Perhaps the powerful bronze cannons, the culmination of military technology, formed in the foundries filled with furnaces and powerful bellows? Perhaps the iron springs and harnesses of the fastest carriages? Or could they be compared with sophisticated apparatuses for astronomical observation, used by sages to scrutinize the heavens and extract the secrets of the universe? One might judge hastily that, in effect, any of the artifacts cited could compare in complexity and efficacy to an oceangoing ship. Nonetheless, one would soon realize that a single ship could bring together within its hull a substantial part of the most effective and sophisticated mechanical inventions of the time.

The quintessential machine called a ship was filled with devices of very diverse type. Hundreds of sets of pulleys served to raise the yards and the sails; in the eyes of someone unaccustomed to it, a ship would appear to be a labyrinth of cables, a forest of fixed and moveable rigging that, respectively, held up the masts and positioned the sails. The capstan served to move great weights, turned by the levers extending out from it like spokes, where a good part of the crew could concentrate their efforts without occupying more than a minimum of space on the ship. Another vital mechanism was the transmission system that allowed the helm to shift the rudder from port to starboard

The most complex machine
of its time. *Architectura
Navalis*, 1629. Biblioteca
Nacional, Madrid.

without requiring the helmsman to move out of sight of the compass. This was accomplished thanks to the *pinzote*, or whipstaff, a vertical lever endowed with a knee joint to facilitate its turning, which passed through the deck and was fastened to the helm of the rudder. This combined apparatus set a precedent for the future helmsman's wheel, which would not make its appearance until the eighteenth century.

But that hardly completes this summary relation of the mechanisms that made up a ship. In the space between decks, dozens of cannons were lined up, representing the most powerful war machines of their time. Of course, warships were better armed than other vessels, but no merchant ship could do without artillery, because in those dangerous times ships had to be prepared to defend themselves to stay afloat. In the belly of the ship the bilge pumps worked continually, filling sleeves and sluiceways with water, an activity fundamental to the ship's integrity. The levers that operated the plungers in the bilge pumps defined one of the work stations that the sailors feared most, though the life of everyone on board depended on them. Finally, and not to draw this discussion out excessively, were the precision instruments that the pilot used: the astrolabe, the quadrant, and the cross-staff, which were essentially devices to measure the angles formed by certain stars over the horizon, measurements that helped to fix the position of the ship on the limitless expanse of the oceans. (65)

Besides all that, there was no other vehicle in the sixteenth century that could surpass the ship in average velocity or carrying capacity. Even in the eighteenth century, Adam Smith could affirm that a ship crewed by a dozen men could do the same work as fifty large carts driven by a hundred coachmen and pulled by four hundred horses. The pride that people feel at the end of the twentieth century about the machines they have created may prevent them from fully appreciating the instruments built by their ancestors five hundred years ago. Nonetheless, they were as proud of their ships as we are about a spaceship, and they were not too shy to rank them in complexity with some of the creations of God himself. There were those who compared a ship to the human body, a living mechanism that, even today, and until and unless some extraterrestrial surprise makes us change our minds, we continue to judge pretentiously as the pinnacle of creation. Diego García de Palacio wrote the following in 1587:

> To use an example that each one of us can see, this machine or labyrinth that we know of as a ship . . . seems to me the perfect semblance of a man, whom Your Grace wishes to compare to a ship . . . because its hull is like the body: the rigging and cords, like the nerves; the sails, like the many little flaps of skin and tendons in the body; the main hatch like the mouth. The ship also has a belly and related organs to purge and clean itself, like those a man has; the people [on board] are like the soul, the principal officers are like the governing faculties [of the soul].[1]

These few examples, and there are many more, demonstrate that a ship was a very complex machine, endowed internally with diverse mechanisms that had to be worked by diverse specialists, who were assigned very different jobs. A ship was, in the first place, a warehouse of merchandise that had to be loaded and unloaded. But it was a mobile warehouse that had to be steered across the ocean. En route, it had to guard against the dangers not only of nature but also of men, and on many occasions the ship had to convert itself into a castle for defense or attack. The men who crewed these warehouse-vehicle-fortresses had to perform very different tasks.

The Ship as a Place of Work

The first obligation of the crew was to load the ship with provisions for their survival and with merchandise to transport. This first task required them to handle hundreds of large barrels, heavy boxes, and voluminous bundles. All this labor had to be carried out using the elements on board: fundamentally the muscular force of the sailors and apprentices, with the help of pulleys fixed on the yards and hauled with the capstan as a last resort if the weight was excessive. Cranes were almost nonexistent in the ports; as we know, the port of Seville had a single crane, popularly called "the engine."

The most common container on ships of the epoch was the *pipa,* a cask *(tonel)* with a capacity of about 443.5 liters.[2] The space occupied by two of these casks served to define the basic unit of capacity on the ships: two toneles equaled one *tonelada.* There was a somewhat larger cask called a *bota,* with a capacity of 532.2 liters. Five of these botas equaled three toneladas. The smallest barrels were the ones called *quintaleños,* which held approximately 64.52 liters. An even smaller container was the *botija,* a type of large bottle or demijohn of almost spherical form and with a wide mouth. Constructed of clay, the botija was protected by a wicker basket. The volume of botijas varied, but normally they held between 20 and 30 liters.

The rest of the merchandise was transported in bales and crates of various dimensions. According to José de Veitia, the celebrated seventeenth-century author of treatises, the largest crates were 1.89 meters long by 0.84 meters wide by 0.63 meters tall. The smallest crates were 1.15 meters in length and 0.42 meters in width and height.

In order to provide an idea of the volume of merchandise and provisions that had to be stored by the crew on a ship of the Carrera de Indias, I have estimated the carrying capacity for a ship of three hundred toneladas (which could be considered a middling to large-sized merchant vessel at the end of the sixteenth century) with fifty men in the crew on a voyage from Seville to the Indies.[3]

The first work that the crew had to confront was loading and distributing a volume of merchandise and provisions for a ship of some three hundred toneladas, which would have included more or less what is listed in table 3.1. The weight, the value, the form of its packaging, and the possibility that a piece of merchandise might be damaged by contact with water determined its position in the ship. The least valuable and heaviest objects were located in the lowest and most central parts of the hold. The delicate and high-priced items of merchandise, such as fine cloth, were placed below decks, arranged so that nothing heavy was placed on top that might damage them. The crates and bales were stacked on top of one another, whereas the barrels were always placed on their sides, following the curves of the hull and in various layers, with the first layer resting directly on the ballast. The spaces left between the different sorts of packaging were filled with

3.1 Provisions and Cargo on a Ship with a Capacity of 300 Toneladas

Item	Amount

Provisions for Fifty Persons for Three Months, Occupying 45 Toneladas of Capacity

Item	Amount
Biscuit	20 sacks of 100 kilograms each
Wine	15 pipas of 443.5 liters each
Oil	6 botijas of 19 liters each
Vinegar	4 botijas of 24 liters each
Water	30 pipas of 443.5 liters each
Salt meat	3 botas of 532.2 cubic decimeters each
Salt fish	3 botas of 535.2 cubic decimeters each
Broad beans, garbanzos, rice	3 botas of 532.2 cubic decimeters each
Salt	100 kilograms
Cheeses	3 dozen
Firewood	450 sacks of 100 kilograms each

Estimated Cargo for the Outbound Voyage, Occupying Some 250 Toneladas of Capacity

Item	Amount
Wine	52 pipas of 443.5 liters each
	40 botas of 532.2 liters each
Oil	200 botijas of 19 liters each
Mercury	28 barrels of 7 liters, or 95 kilograms, each
Nails	25 barrels of 507 kilograms each
Iron in bars	26 crates of $70 \times 30 \times 30$ centimeters, or 500 kilograms, each
Bales of cloth	150 cubic bales of 60 centimeters on a side
Bales of cloth	100 cubic bales of 1 meter on a side
Crates of fine cloth	80 of $1.5 \times 0.5 \times 0.5$ meters each
Vinegar	147 botijas of 20 liters each
Olives	45 barrels of 65 cubic decimeters each
Almonds	45 barrels of 65 cubic decimeters each
Wax	6 crates of $1.5 \times 0.5 \times 0.5$ meters each
Soap	6 crates of $1.5 \times 0.5 \times 0.5$ meters each
Glassware	6 crates of $1.5 \times 0.5 \times 0.5$ meters each
Books	6 crates of $1.5 \times 0.5 \times 0.5$ meters each
Weaponry	4 crates of $1.66 \times 0.63 \times 0.63$ meters each

(67)

Loading ships was carried
out, fundamentally, by the
force of human muscles.
Drawing by Christoph
Weiditz, 1529. Biblioteca
Nacional, Madrid.

low-quality cloth or smaller bundles to serve as chocks. A perfectly stowed ship was far less likely to experience a dangerous shifting of the load.

To the effort needed to load and stow the merchandise would be added that of loading the artillery, because the cannons were customarily kept in warehouses during the winter to prevent their deterioration. If the ship had not secured sufficient cargo to fill its hold completely, that still did not free the sailors from hard work, since a ship could not sail without having its hold well ballasted. Because of this, if a ship was unable to contract for a cargo of heavy iron bars, it had to fill the hold with stones, whose transport supposed a certain measure of frustration, above all for the sailors who were going to be paid with a percentage of the freight charges.

Once the floating warehouse had been filled, the crew had to begin sailing it toward its destination. Their first task consisted of untying the mooring ropes, or raising the anchors if the ship was anchored in a bay like that of Cádiz or if it was waiting at the mouth of the Guadalquivir for the rest of the fleet. In order to raise the anchors from the bottom, the capstan had to be brought into play, since the weight of the largest anchors ranged between five hundred and seven hundred kilograms for ships between two hundred and four hundred toneladas. The thick cables of hemp that held the anchors weighed as much as the anchors themselves, which doubled the force needed to raise them.[4] After collecting the anchors and the ship's boat, which normally would have helped in weighing the anchor, the yards were hoisted, the sails were unfurled, and the ship got under way. This is how the veteran mariner Juan de Escalante de Mendoza described the departure of a ship for the Indies:

> When the hour had arrived in which they had to make sail . . . the pilot ordered the men to raise all but one of the anchors and to attach the cable on the last anchor to the capstan . . . and with the yards and sails aloft, he ordered two apprentices to climb the foremast and stand ready to unfurl the sails when and as they were ordered and directed. And if the special pilot for the sandbar [of Sanlúcar de Barrameda] said that it was time to make sail, the ship's pilot would call out the following to the two men aloft on the yard: "Ease the rope of the foresail, in the name of the Holy Trinity, Father, and Son, and Holy Spirit, three persons in one single true God, that they may be with us and give us a good and safe voyage, and carry us and return us safely to our homes!"[5]

At that point the crew's work began in maneuvering the ship on the open ocean. Their labors were directed by the officers from a covered area on the poop deck, where the pilot or the master paced about, giving orders. The sailors scurried around the upper decks, fastening or loosening ropes and sheets, climbing to the yards by the shrouds, hoisting sails, or tightening rigging. Because men doing these jobs had to move rapidly from the forecastle to the aftcastle, it was common to suspend between these two elevated parts of the ship some passageways, formed at the base by a network of wood or well-tightened cords (the *jareta,* or harpings). These passageways bypassed the intermediate zone of the main deck, which therefore appeared as if it were sunken (hence its name, the *pozo,* or well of the ship) between the elevations of poop deck and prow. As shown in some of the extant engravings of shipboard work, the harpings were the place where the sailors carried out most of their work; García de Palacio himself confirms this when he says that it was the part of the ships "from which the sailors set the sails and work them, and beneath it are the passengers or the soldiers."[6]

The Ship as a Place of Work

Once the ship had been positioned on course, and if favorable winds prevailed, the sailors could dedicate themselves to more routine activities, such as repairing the rigging, sewing up holes in the sails, greasing the mechanisms on board, or simply arranging the cargo and cleaning the decks. They were blessed with such periods of tranquility once they reached the route of the trade winds, which blew in a constant and favorable manner, creating a true marine superhighway. Then they could pass entire days without having to change the set of the sails, and their work was limited to guiding the rudder or carrying out preventive maintenance on the mast tops and yards. Only if a sudden change in the force of the wind obliged them to shorten or lengthen sails was the majority of the crew obliged to leave the monotonous work of repair, cleaning, and inspection of the cargo.

With the arrival of night, and above all if land was already close, the sensation of insecurity became more evident, and precautions were increased. When the sun set, and after reciting the evening prayers, the crew divided into three groups that stood guard one after another. The nighttime was divided into three approximately equal periods, which were expressively called the "first watch," the "sleepy watch," and the "dawn watch." Naturally, the "sleepy watch" was the worst, because it broke the night into two parts, preventing an uninterrupted rest. With a rotating schedule, everyone took a turn at the awkward middle watch, in which drowsiness overcame even the most vigilant of mariners. In the eighteenth century, when ships cut costs by reducing personnel, the crews were assigned to only two watches, which made each watch more efficient but at the expense of the men, who lost half a night's sleep instead of just a third.

Each segment of the watch was commanded by one of the highest officers on the ship, that is to say, the captain, the master, or the pilot. If the captain was a military professional without nautical experience, his post was occupied by the *contramaestre*, the master's assistant or boatswain. In any case, the officer of the guard had to check carefully to see that the cooking fires had been put out at nightfall and that no fires were lighted on board except the few lanterns located in strategic places, with the flames protected by glass lenses. Fire was a terrible enemy of ships, and the fear was that passengers and mariners would secretly ignite a flame that could start a fatal fire. Blankets were carried as a preventative; in case of emergency they were soaked in water or even in urine, which gave rise to coarse jokes, but it was very effective in suffocating a would-be fire.[7]

One of the greatest dangers of sailing at night was the chance of coming upon a coastline unexpectedly and destroying the ship against the rocks. In order to avoid such an occurrence, vigilance was increased, the anchors and pumps were poised to go into action, and a sailor kept the sounding line in his hand all night long, checking to find out if the draft had decreased suddenly and dangerously. Along with these precautions, designed to protect the physical security of all on board, there were other advisable methods to protect their economic health. For the latter reason, the pilot major of the House of Trade, Alonso de Chaves, advised that a ship should sail in maximum silence at night, since the cloaking hours of darkness were the ones most favored by the friends of impropriety to unlock a chest or by thirsty sailors to drill into a cask and withdraw a free ration of wine.[8] In short, the hours of darkness brought an increase in dangers and in the measures designed to thwart them. Thus, Juan de Escalante observed that "for the good sailor the night was the day and the day had to serve as the night to get some indispensable and necessary sleep."[9]

Of course no work, night or day, carried out under normal conditions could compare to what had to be done when the ship faced a storm. The forces unleashed by nature did not respect the sailors' need for rest. In the middle of the night, even those who were not on guard were awakened and ordered to climb the masts to gather the sails. Half naked, without having had time to put on shoes, they had to climb up damp and slippery ladders to the masts that were balanced dangerously between sea and sky. In the dark of night they could not see one another nor even hear one another, due to the clamor of the storm, which sounded, in the expressive phrase of a seventeenth-century English sailor, like millstones rolling downhill.[10]

But if work in the rigging during a storm was risky, on the decks below, the rest of the men carried out an exhausting task: pumping water out of the ship to keep it from sinking. Storms often broke through the structure of the hull and created enormous openings for water to flow in. Everyone's life depended on extended days working the levers of the pump. A line drawn with chalk on the inside of the ship's hull set the maximum level that the water could rise; if it passed beyond that level, death was certain.[11] Because of the dual psychological and physical pressure that working the bilge pumps entailed, sixteenth-century Spanish sailors normally remembered this as a terrible experience. We have frightful testimonies about it, above all on the long and hard Pacific crossings. For example, Vincenzo de Nápoles, a sailor on the expedition that Álvaro de Saavedra commanded from Mexico to the Moluccas, recounted how the crew of the flagship spent two and a half months combating a leak that was discovered shortly after departure.[12] Andrés de Urdaneta, one of the few survivors of the expedition under Commander Loaisa, described the efforts of sailors struggling at the pumps for their survival in the middle of the largest ocean on the planet:

And with the high seas we experienced, the ship opened up in many places. As it was so stormy, we took on so much water that even with two pumps

---

The Ship as a Place of Work

worked with hard labor we were not able to accomplish much, and each day we thought we were going to drown. . . . If we went two hours without working [the pumps], we spent another two hours working them, and we were also hard pressed by the sea and by the scant and spoiled rations and little water, and many died from overwork.[13]

If the pumps could not overcome the entry of the water, then all that could be considered excessive weight had to be thrown into the sea. The ballast was the first to go, followed by the least valuable merchandise and the sea chests of sailors and passengers. If that was not sufficient, the cannons went into the sea, the superstructures were cut down, and the masts were felled to keep them from completely breaking open the hull. Some texts recount that as a last resort the crew could try to girdle the hull with the anchor cables, knotting them as if the ship were a bale of merchandise, to try to keep the waves from breaking it apart. With all that, even in the midst of danger, the human affinity for silver and valuable merchandise made these the last to be thrown overboard. The story told by the pilot and shipowner Juan Rodríguez de Noriega, about a serious crisis suffered in 1560 in the middle of the Atlantic, shows that half the ship was thrown into the water, but the cargo and the silver were untouched. They were retained and finally placed in safety on another ship that came to the rescue:

> We got into a really furious storm . . . and the storm opened up the ship in such a way that with two pumps we could not overcome the water that the ship collected. We cut the mainmast because it was destroying the ship with its lashing back and forth; we razed and took apart the bridge and lightened the ballast and girdled the ship with cables and tried all the other remedies that are in the hands of man. . . . We continued trying to contain the water . . . with the ship completely opened up . . . and thus we held on for three more days.[14]

If luck was with them and the ship was saved, once the storm let up the damage had to be repaired. Often this task had to be undertaken in the middle of the ocean, so ships had to carry all the resources of a town with them to repair the damages. This was another difficult and dangerous task in which all the members of the crew had to participate, especially the carpenters and caulkers. The ship's boat was put into the water, and men began the task of covering the breaches situated above the waterline with planks of wood or sheets of lead. The largest ships could afford to carry a diver, who was simply a good swimmer accustomed to going underwater to repair damage to the "live work" of the hull below the waterline. If a ship did not have such a specialist aboard, someone else had to take the risk. There is little need to insist on the enormous risk and difficulty of trying to nail a sheet of lead around the keel of a ship at

(72)

Sailors hauling on a cable.
Drawing by Christoph
Weiditz, 1529. Biblioteca
Nacional, Madrid.

sea; nonetheless, there were men who seem to have done it with great perfection:

> The said Pero Díaz stripped himself down to his skin and began to swim toward the ship of the said Pero Milanés, which came as the flagship . . . and the said Pero Díaz searched underneath the water for the hole in the said ship of the said Pero Milanés, and he found it, and he stopped it up and nailed a sheet of lead over it. . . . Afterward he went to the ship of the said Luis Rizo, which was also sinking, and he swam underneath the water, looked for the place where the water was getting into the said ship, and found it in three or four places, and he nailed his lead sheets so that he stopped the leaks.[15]

The Ship as a Place of Work

One last type of work could await a sailor, which would transform him into a soldier or gunner. If a corsair attacked, everybody had to participate in the defense, helping to reset and reload the cannons, raising the yards in order to sail against the enemy, or defending the decks against an attempted boarding. To the degree that protecting the merchant fleets was commended to the warships that accompanied them, defensive tasks fell to the escort galleons, but one could never be sure of not becoming separated from the convoy and needing to defend one's ship unaided.

In short, handling the most complex machine of the epoch involved a goodly number of distinct tasks. But all the sailors' work had some things in common. First, it was hard. Work at sea was, in general, a young man's job, and few of them succeeded in growing old on the job. But even these young men paid dearly with their own flesh in the form of injuries from the many on-the-job accidents to which they were exposed. Without referring for the moment to injuries that had mortal consequences, there were many others that left men marked forever: fingers crushed from moving the cargo, wounds produced by falling pieces of the masts or the rigging, splinters embedded in their faces, and so on. These marks were very important for the functionaries of the Carrera de Indias, because they provided a way of identifying individual sailors. In the registers of the House of Trade, officials carefully noted any mark or bodily detail, especially the scars of old wounds. Of course, these were not all due to accidents while working. Violence among members of the crews, especially knife fights, were the order of the day; that is why establishing the origins of the scars is difficult. The registers often signaled which scars were the product of knife wounds, knowing that these were the least serious. In any case, the number of sailors whose faces or hands were crisscrossed by deep suture scars was very high, indicating the degree of violence as well as the danger of working aboard ships. In a study of the registry of two thousand sailors, half of them showed the mark of some old wound on their bodies.[16]

Another characteristic common to sailors' work in the sixteenth century was the complete lack of stability in the labor force. All the members of the crew, from the master to the least apprentice, were contracted only for the period of the voyage. Once the ship arrived in port and the unloading terminated, they remained without work for several months. Only a small crew of some few men remained on board to guard the ship during the winter layover. On the armada ships belonging to the king, something similar happened. Only the generals and admirals of the Guard Squadron for the Carrera de Indias, and a few captains of other galleons, were excluded from the misfortune of losing their salary as soon as they arrived on land. Not even the generals and admirals of the merchant convoys enjoyed the privilege of continued pay; their appointments lasted only as long as it took for each fleet to make the return voyage. Still, once the rhythm of navigation to and from America reached a high degree of regularity, the sailors could at least count on working for some eight or nine months out of the year, while knowing that they would be disembarked and deprived of salary for the remaining three or four months.[17] From this point of view, their position was much more regular than that of a goodly number of rural and urban day laborers.

One final requirement of maritime labor was being constantly on call for the duration of the voyage. Sundays and holidays that would mark a break from work on land made no difference for mariners. Nature did not understand such lulls and unleashed its hurricanes against the ships without respect for the calendar. Nor could the sailors fix one schedule for work and another for rest. An agricultural day laborer, who had to withstand working from sun to sun without any other limit but the presence of daylight, had the night to rest. A sailor going to sleep was never sure of not having to spring into action in case of emergency. That is why, as Juan de Escalante quite accurately wrote, "in sailing one cannot make a certain rule nor a limited term, because ships sail in conformity to the winds and weather they find . . . which gave birth to the old proverb that says: 'workdays at sea are not for counting.'"[18]

The Division of Labor on a Ship
Pages, Apprentices, and Sailors

Pages were the youngest members of the crews. They entered into service at sea when they were still children, between eight and ten years old. If they were not very clever or diligent, they could remain on this first rung of the ladder until they were up to seventeen or eighteen years old, although the average age was about fifteen years.[19] The pages were similar to apprentices in their least experienced versions, and the majority of them arrived fleeing from orphanhood or poverty. Nonetheless, no sooner had they embarked than they learned one of the first and hardest lessons that life could give them: that we are not all equal. In fact, there existed two well-differentiated types of pages. The first were those who enjoyed ties of friendship or family with one of the higher officers of the ship (captain, master, pilot, or boatswain), and under his protection they began an apprenticeship to prepare them to achieve positions of responsibility in the future. But the majority of the pages could not count on the protection of anyone, and they were at the service of everyone. They were the so-called ship's pages, and upon them fell, like the August sun in Seville, the not-always-well-intentioned authority of any member of the crew.

The page who had a protector on board had as his exclusive mission to serve his master; however hard his apprenticeship on the sea was, being the nephew, relative, or simply the son of a friend of one of the authorities on the ship freed him from many discomforts. The rest, that is to say the ship's pages,

Sailors working from a
platform of rope harpings.
On the aft castle, the
pilot measures the angle
of the sun.

had to carry out the least specialized tasks: to scrub and clean the ship, to prepare the distribution of the provisions, to call the crew to meals, and to put
away the table after the meal. The two most specific obligations of the pages
were referred to as keeping vigilant during the night watches and maintaining
a certain ritual for religious observances. The pages were the ones charged with
keeping track of the time by turning the *ampolletas,* or sand clocks—the only
time-keeping instruments capable of functioning correctly on the unstable
bridges of ships—every half hour. Each turning of the glass had to be accompanied by the recitation of psalms or litanies filled with religious invocations.
These were answered in chorus and let the officers of the guard know that
drowsiness had not conquered the young crewmen and that the time contin-

ued to be measured correctly. When the night was over, the "Good Day" *(Buenos Días)* chanted by the pages began each day of life on board.

Besides watching the sand clock, the pages also watched over the divine cult on board, because at the end of the afternoon they recited the tenets and principal prayers of the Christian faith. Their youth required religious formation, and their almost infantile innocence was considered a better vehicle for the transmission of prayers to the Lord than the crudeness of the veteran sailors, who moreover were not generally very careful in complying with religious precepts.

Finally, the ship's pages had to take orders from all the sailors and apprentices on the ship and help them with whatever they needed. In cases of disobedience, standing orders said that only the boatswain could mete out corporal punishment to them. As a general rule their youth saved the pages from most of the blows due them, but corporal punishment fell with full force on the backs of the apprentices.

The apprentices were, simply, young sailors who still had not achieved their maximum professional experience. Their ages varied between seventeen and twenty years, and the mean was around eighteen and a half. The agility and strength that their youth afforded them constituted their best armament and determined their principal roles on board. Climbing to the yards to furl the sails in the middle of a storm or leaping from the gunwale to a ship's boat in the middle of the ocean were tasks specific to the agile and flexible bodies of the apprentices. It was they who served as lookouts on the mast tops or who pulled the oars of the ship's boats and launches, but they also employed their stamina in carrying out the hard tasks of loading and unloading merchandise as well as firewood, water, and ballast.

The apprentices had to obey the sailors and officers in matters pertaining to the handling of the ship, but theoretically they were not obliged to render personal services. Nonetheless, custom established that many officers used some apprentices as servants, apart from their assigned work on the ship. In this sense, there were frequent cases of apprentices who made the beds or cooked the meals of an older crewman in exchange for some gift or, simply, in order to seek his protection. In some cases, the documents indicate that the work done by the apprentice could become more personal: for example, to shave the legs or clean the toenails of their "masters." In such extreme cases it is no wonder that many of these connections involved homosexual relations, which sometimes came to light, to the disgrace of those accused and the great scandal of everyone on board.[20]

Finally, another of the roles of the apprentice was to serve as an outlet for the frustration of many members of the crew; apprentices were used as veritable punching bags in many instances, receiving the majority of whacks ad-

---

The Ship as a Place of Work

ministered on a ship. Naturally, that mission was totally involuntary on the part of the long-suffering apprentices, who had to put up with more than the lash of a whip wielded by an officer or a sailor exasperated by their slowness in following an order. The maltreatment of apprentices was officially prohibited, but in those times pedagogical principles based on the use of the stick were considered absolutely necessary for a boy's proper formation. Unfortunately for the apprentices, the pages were too young to be whipped and the sailors were too old, but no one found it strange that an apprentice received his proper formation at the end of a thick cable expertly wielded by the *guardián*, or boatswain's helper.

(78)

On attaining twenty years of age, more or less, and after having accumulated experience on the job, the apprentice received a document signed by the master, the pilot, the boatswain, and the notary of the ship certifying him as a sailor.[21] A professional career then opened before him, which, if he did not suffer an accident or find a way to rise in rank, could last some twenty years, even beyond the age of forty. The mean age of sailors in the sixteenth century was around twenty-eight or twenty-nine years, and in general a sailor between thirty-five and forty years of age was already considered somewhat old for the job. Nevertheless, I have found some cases of sailors on active duty who were fifty years old.[22] Taking into account the life expectancy of the time and the hard work required of a sailor, this assumed that he was already an old man.

Sailors had to take on missions that required more dexterity, which was only acquired through many years of experience. Perhaps the most characteristic task of this type was handling the helm. This was not simple on ships where the wheel had not yet been invented. The sailor who set the course had to station himself at the poop deck, under the awning-covered aftcastle, with his eyes fixed simultaneously on the compass and the position of the sails and his ears attentive to the orders given him by the pilot above him on the poop deck. Another delicate mission was handling the sounding line, because the speed and precision displayed when determining the water's depth and the type of bottom could save the ship—or cause its destruction. Sailors handled the rigging during the most complicated maneuvers and also knew how to fix or splice a cable, being artists when it came to uniting two cables by means of complex knots. In difficult circumstances the good sailor stood out, capable of threading a cable through the anchor ring and leaving it ready to be launched into the sea or of deploying an auxiliary sail in a full storm.

If a sailor had native intelligence and the will to advance in his job, he could ask the pilot to teach him the art of marking charts, calculating the angle of the sun and the pole star and using declination tables to calculate the ship's position. If he also knew how to read and write and had some savings so that he could spend the months out of work in attending classes at the House of Trade in Seville, he could perhaps become a pilot himself in the Carrera de Indias. This step, however, was reserved for very few. The great barrier was that the pilot needed a minimal theoretical formation, however little it may seem to us today, which was far beyond the reach of the rude schooling of the majority of sailors. Hence, with experience on the job and after gaining the confidence of some of the higher officers on the ship, a sailor could climb the occupational ladder and become a gunner or, even better, ascend to the post of a "sea officer."

Gunners and Officers

The barrier separating the sailors from the gunners and officers was marked by a specialization in certain tasks, some of which involved the exercise of an important package of authority over the whole company of mariners. The gunners were the specialists nearest to the common sailors. According to the precepts of the Spanish authorities, good gunners (called *lombarderos* in the beginning) should be expert sailors who also know how to make a cannon function. Of course, this latter job was not easy. Artillery was the most complex weaponry of the period, and a good gunner needed to master many different skills. He had to know how to make and refine gunpowder, fill grenades, select various types of projectiles for use (against the hull, the masts and rigging, enemy crews, and so on), load the cannon with the exact measure of powder, take aim, maintain the gun in a serviceable condition and free from the deterioration it could suffer through inclement weather and saltpeter, and, finally, secure the cannon to keep it from moving at sea and know how to maneuver it quickly for reloading during battle.

The official in charge of the artillery was called the *condestable,* or sergeant. The proportion of foreigners among the sergeants and gunners in Spanish fleets was very large. Above all we encounter Germans, Flemings, and Italians occupying these posts. The crown made serious efforts to increase the presence of Spaniards as gunners, and by the end of the century the proportion of Basque and Andalusian gunners in the Carrera de Indias seems to have increased notably.

The House of Trade employed a chief gunner, who gave instruction in cannon handling and carried out gunnery practice outside the city, in the vicinity of the Butcher's Gate (Puerta de la Carne) on a small hill called La Goleta.[23] Preparing for a gunner's examination was not easy. The course was expensive, since the aspirants had to pay for the cost of the gunpowder and munitions that they used in practice. At least the House of Trade provided the cannons! Then there was the payment of fees to the chief gunner, who was not satisfied with the salary that he received from the state and obliged his students to collaborate in supporting him. Finally, the aspirant had to demonstrate his experience

The Ship as a Place of Work

as a sailor on a voyage to the Indies. In order to be exempted from this last prerequisite, he had to demonstrate that he had formerly exercised the job of carpenter, mason, ironsmith, sword maker, or stonecutter, which demonstrated that he had a certain manual dexterity.[24]

The lists of ships' crews in the Carrera de Indias included under the heading of "officers" jobs with very diverse requirements. Nonetheless, they could be divided into two major groups, according to whether or not they exercised authority over the crew as a whole. Thus, the first group of officers comprised specialists with precise and important commissions for the functioning of the ship but who neither needed nor received authority to give orders to the crew as a whole.

The three most common offices were those of carpenter, caulker, and scribe, and on the largest ships there could also be a barber-surgeon, a cooper, a diver, and even a chaplain. If we examine these jobs, we realize that many of them were not specifically related to the sea, with the exception of the diver and perhaps the caulker.

The carpenter, caulker, and diver formed the repair team, which on modern ships is generally assigned to internal security. The carpenter was possibly one of the most indispensable specialists on board a ship and, at the same time, the oldest. The hull, the masts, and the pulleys were all made of wood, and for the duration of a voyage, there were a thousand and one possibilities for mishaps that would require repairs. A good ship's carpenter not only had to be able to cap a breach in the hull but also had to know how to use a lathe to make a pulley, create a cabin out of wood paneling for an illustrious passenger, and, should the need arise, even be capable of building a launch. The caulker was charged with maintaining the hull in sound condition, putting oakum and tar between the junctures of the hull planking and the deck. An especially delicate mission in his charge was the care of the bilge pumps, an indispensable element for the integrity of the ship. If the efforts of the carpenter and the caulker did not succeed in plugging a leak or freeing a blocked rudder, the diver had to attempt it, going into the water in midocean or upon arriving at the first port.

If the carpenter and the caulker were responsible for maintaining the ship's machinery in good condition, other specialists occupied themselves with its contents. The scrivener registered the cargo, verifying the marks on each bale or box, to certify that it would be delivered without error to its legal owners upon arrival at its destination. In addition, he was occupied in writing wills and recording any judicial proceedings that might occur on board before the ship's officers. The cooper repaired the containers on board, especially the barrels that carried the wine, water, and a goodly part of the salted provisions that were consumed.

Finally, the barber-surgeon and the chaplain were charged with the health

The caulker filled the joints between the planks with tarred oakum. Drawing by Christoph Weiditz, 1529. Biblioteca Nacional, Madrid.

of bodies and souls, very arduous enterprises on ships where the conditions of health and hygiene were horrendous and where superstitions and a lack of compliance with religious precepts were habitual. One office that Spanish ships in the sixteenth century systematically lacked was that of cook. If a person wanted to eat something hot, he had to attend personally to the cookstove or pay someone for the service. In general, culinary activity was considered demeaning, and to complain to someone in the vicinity that he still carried the smell of smoke from the cookstove in his beard was usually a good excuse for a fight.

The officers who did have authority over all the crew, the "commanders," as Juan de Escalante called them, were the *despensero,* or steward, the boatswain and his helper, the boatswain's mate, or guardián, and, of course, the trio of supreme authority on a ship: the pilot, the master, and the captain. The steward was the least prestigious of the officers in command. His mission was, obviously, to guard the store of food and to dispense and give rations to the crew. At first glance, one might think he did not need much authority to do his job. Nonetheless, there was no occasion on board as propitious for the development of quarrels and mutinies as the distribution of the daily rations. That is why the steward had to be invested with sufficient authority to stifle grumblings about the low quality and quantity of the rations as well as to punish those involved in the frequent attempts to steal food. In addition, the crew was under his orders for moving provisions around in the interior of the ship as well as during the resupply operations necessary upon arriving in ports.

The symbol of the steward's position was the keys to the food storage areas, from which he was never separated. His power was rooted in the fact that to secure his friendship or to incur his wrath meant the difference between eating and not eating. On the other hand, stewards, like the majority of those in charge of administration, found themselves in an ideal situation to traffic in the common stores for their own benefit. This is a temptation that seems unstoppable in the human species, and many stewards fell wholeheartedly into the practice. Precisely for this reason, the figure of the steward did not awaken any sympathy on board. Some English sketches from the eighteenth century show naval stewards as portly personages whose prominent and well-fed stomachs seem to have been filled with what they skimmed from the sailors' rations. Retired stewards were normally considered thieves, enriched through the suffering of others.[25]

The boatswain was the direct executor of the orders transmitted by the pilot and the master, that is, all the orders that focused on steering a course and keeping the cargo in good shape. Acting as an authentic courier, he was charged with seeing that the sailors carried out orders punctually and precisely. The first mission of the boatswain was to accomplish a good stowage of the cargo and to see that it did not shift (which could put the ship in danger of sinking) or deteriorate during the voyage. Second, he was a sort of orchestral conductor directing the maneuvers on board, the handling of the anchors, yards, sails, and whatever type of equipment. If the keys were the symbol of the steward, the whistle was the symbol of the boatswain. Its piercing sound served to coordinate the movements of all the crew and to direct their energies toward a common goal. Finally, the boatswain was the one in charge of maintaining all the mechanisms of the ship in good condition and of ordering necessary repairs.

The guardián, while he was on board, was the boatswain's helper. Normally he directed the work at the prow, while the boatswain remained on the poop to be able to hear the orders transmitted by the pilot. Nonetheless, the guardián became autonomous from the moment in which the ship's boat was put into the water. This was his principal mission: to be the commander of the auxiliary craft. The tasks of the ship's boat were quite varied: to load and unload the ship, since good loading docks were not abundant; to use the oarsmen on the boat to tow the ship through narrow passages and on calm days; to go in front of the ship taking soundings in order to avoid shallows, and so on. The guardián was also in charge of maintaining discipline among the apprentices and pages, the youngest, and therefore potentially the most turbulent, members of the crew.

The minimum age for rising from a sailor to an officer generally was around twenty-five years, and once a man had risen to such a post, his professional career was likely to be extended by several years, because the officers did not have to expend as much physical energy, and it was not too unusual to reach the age of forty-eight years on active service. In spite of everything, the mean age of officers and gunners did not exceed thirty-two years.

Theoretically, any sailor could rise in rank. For that to happen he needed only two things: to demonstrate his knowledge and to earn the confidence of his superiors. Both requirements were achieved only with practice, as there was no school in the world where a young man could be taught the office of boatswain, or of guardián, other than on the wet and unstable deck of a ship at sea.

Pilots, Masters, and Captains

Pilot, master, and captain constituted the pinnacle of power on a ship in the Carrera de Indias.[26] Each of them was in charge of a fundamental aspect of the good running of the ship. The pilot was occupied with purely nautical matters, being the one charged with guiding the ship from its port of departure to its destination by the proper route, keeping it safe from storms and accidents at sea. The master was the economic administrator of the ship and the person responsible for its loading. The captain was the figure with exclusively military competence, and for that reason on a merchant ship, where there was always a pilot and master, there might not be a captain. Still, when attack was feared, a person might be chosen to act as captain and to coordinate and direct the ship's defense.

The condition of the highest officers was reflected in a series of traditions that defined the daily life of the ships. In the first place, their prestige had a purely spatial dimension, since they were the only persons authorized, together with distinguished passengers, to have their lodgings at the poop deck. The master, the captain, and sometimes the pilot had individual cabins at their disposal, each served by a page, which was another distinction of great importance. The rest of the officers and the crew normally resided at the prow, or wherever they could find a free space to place their little sleeping pad to pass the night. Also, at mealtimes, captain, master, and pilot gathered at a separate table from the rest of the crew, to which they invited from time to time distinguished passengers and the surgeon or the chaplain, if the ship had them. But leaving aside their common condition as superior officers, the actual work that each of these three high personages carried out on board was very different.

The office of pilot presented a novelty that distinguished him from all the others discussed until now: to achieve this great distinction took more than just years of experience at sea and the assimilation of the wisdom transmitted by old practitioners of the office. Separating the office of pilot from the rest was the barrier that separated experience from science or, what amounts to the same thing, separated the knowledge acquired through experience alone from knowledge that required a certain theoretical depth.

This does not mean that knowledge transmitted orally from generation to generation and personal experience ceased to have importance. As a vital instrument of his office, a pilot had to recognize each bay, each cove, each reef, along a coastline where he had to sail and through which he had to guide his ship. At the same time, he had to be capable of predicting a storm simply by observing the color of the seas, the disposition of the clouds, or the direction of a flight of sea birds. A good pilot should be able to receive the impressions transmitted by the sea, by its winds, its creatures, its colors, and even its smells, and to glean useful information from all of it. With a single glance at the wake of his ship or the way in which the prow broke the waves, an expert pilot should be able to calculate the speed of the ship.

But besides all that, nautical science for the duration of the late Middle Ages was incorporating much other knowledge. First came navigation, with its magnetic compasses and its *portulan* charts, which linked ports with fine lines that followed the rhumb lines of the wind rose; the compass dividers for marking "the point" or position of the ship on a chart; and finally, the abacus, to carry out small arithmetical operations more easily. Then pilots learned to calculate latitude by measuring the angle that the sun formed with the horizon at midday (the "altitude of the sun"). This was the most revolutionary technique employed in the Renaissance, but it obliged pilots to learn how to use instruments such as the astrolabe or the cross-staff and to correct the measured angle against published tables of solar declination. They then had to carry out a series of small mathematical calculations to obtain the latitude at their location. For men of little schooling, such as the majority of men of the sea, even the simplest computation that included formulas, arithmetical operations, and the use of printed tables presented no small difficulty.

Thus, a pilot in the sixteenth century had to carry his saddlebags filled as

A pilot trying to calculate the position of the ship by using an astrolabe.

much with science as with experience, but I would venture to say that, for the length of that century, the bag containing traditional knowledge still weighed a bit more. Nautical science was not very sophisticated, and the measuring instruments were not very precise. For this reason the barrier that separated science from experience was permeable. That is how totally illiterate mariners could become pilots: their natural intelligence and their many years of practical experience compensated for their lack of theoretical training. This occurred not only in Spain but in other maritime countries, such as England, where many merchants still complained in the seventeenth century of illiterates being in command of ships.[27] Nonetheless, time was running out for these autodidacts. As early as the eighteenth century, the perfection of navigational knowledge

The Ship as a Place of Work

converted the barrier between science and experience into a frontier that could not be crossed by an illiterate.

Granted, in the sixteenth century one could still find situations where some high armada officers valued above all other merits in their pilots a perfect familiarity with the coasts along which they had to sail. Don Cristóbal de Eraso expressed it thus, while explaining to the president of the Council of the Indies why four ships in the New Spain fleet had sunk in 1578:

> I found myself very confused on this voyage, because, although the pilot brought along was the oldest and most experienced on this route and dealt properly with the matters related to charting the course and calculating the latitude, he and all the others were not very experienced in the knowledge of this coast, which is what really mattered . . . and it is important that Your Lordship and the Royal Council order . . . that no pilot be examined without first-hand knowledge of all the coast and without having seen and taken soundings of it himself . . . because all the pilots, when faced with a disorienting storm, get perturbed and do not know what to do.[28]

For the crew and passengers, a good pilot was a man with many years of experience, able to take advantage of a good wind and to follow the rhumb line of the compass; who slept during the day and stayed awake at night; who was capable of recognizing any coast without making mistakes; who was agile minded so that he could remember by heart all the rocky shallows and difficult passages, but whose prudence made him conscientiously use the sounding line so as not to find himself surprised. If he was also a master at calculating the latitude with an astrolabe, so much the better, but in general one can detect in the documentation a certain lack of confidence on the part of contemporaries about the precision of the positions calculated by the pilots. In the consultations that took place in the fleets, presided over by the pilot major, very frequently there were as many different positions calculated as there were pilots on the ships.

One aspiring admiral of the fleet, Esteban de las Alas "the younger," who was stating his merits as a navigator, commented that on many occasions he had gone on the fleets "comparing notes" with the other pilots about the position of the ship, and that he often succeeded in "approximating" the correct position.[29] As one can see, the determinations seemed more akin to a game of dice than to a true science. For that reason, and to prevent his imprecision from being discovered, the pilot customarily surrounded his calculations with an atmosphere of secrecy that made the determination of the ship's latitude into an arcane ceremony comprehensible only to a chosen few. A passenger endowed with a good sense of humor, such as Eugenio de Salazar, thought he had discovered the motives for this pose:

At such times it is something to see the pilot calculate the Pole Star's position . . . and finally, to throw in his own minimal judgments as to the altitude of the sun . . . and above all it made me tired to see how the pilots wanted to keep secret from the passengers the degree or point that they calculated, and the leagues that it seemed to them that the ship had sailed on its course, although afterward I understood the cause, which is that they never hit the mark nor understand what they are doing . . . because they take the altitude as a little more or less, so that a space no bigger than the head of a pin on their instrument will cause them to make more than five hundred leagues of error in their estimate.[30]

But if science was not very precise, the pilot had recourse to his experience, and we already know that this was acquired with age. That is why the pilots had the highest average age of all the officers in the Carrera de Indias, forty and a half years. Among some eighty pilots, of the ones whose ages I have been able to ascertain, only five were younger than thirty, and there were several who would remain in service after the age of fifty. Of course everyone had a limit, and at times the pilot found himself obliged to carry out tasks that were not very appropriate for an older man. This happened when he had to quickly identify some point along the coast. Then there was no alternative to climbing to a spar, and no one could do this work except the pilot. An error could lure the ship toward a nonexistent anchorage, so that, instead of being the door to salvation, the chosen route would lead directly to the gates of hell. A pilot whose years had allowed him to put on too much weight or to acquire too many aches and pains could be a danger for everybody. This brought disaster to the *almiranta* of the New Spain fleet of 1582, whose pilot had to give orders from his bed because he was "overweight and ill" and "old and walking with difficulty."[31]

The master without doubt was a key personage in the maritime business of the epoch. For that reason it is no wonder that the majority of masters had already reached a certain maturity, and their average age was about thirty-two years. Their mission was easy to define but difficult to carry out: to see that the ship had all the material and human resources necessary to arrive at its destination and that the passengers and the cargo were delivered in perfect condition, after having paid all their taxes. But the master not only carried out important missions on board; he also had to certify to the owners of the ship, the owners of the cargo, and the royal functionaries that everything had been done in conformity with what had been contracted and legislated. In short, the master was the administrator of the ship and the person responsible to the financial and governmental authorities for everything that happened on board.

His first commission consisted in acquiring a license from the authorities

The Ship as a Place of Work

of the House of Trade to sail to the Indies. The master then had to arm himself with patience in order to fight the bureaucracy and to use the subtle arts of bribery, applying adequate grease to unblock procedures that had been stalled by functionaries worried about the welfare of their own families.

Once the permit had been secured, and while taking care that the ship went through its required inspections, the master had to employ another virtue: his status as a man who was on good terms with, and well connected in, the world of maritime business, since he was the person in charge of finding merchants ((88)) to consign goods to the ship, for both the outbound and the return voyages. To succeed, he had to know the maritime and commercial ambience of sixteenth-century Seville like the palm of his hand. The steps of the cathedral and the vicinity of that centrally important church were the financial heart of the city. Through that district passed the merchants carrying on their business, and the master had to find them and offer them the services of his ship. The Arenal near the river, the area called Altozano in Triana, and the plaza and courtyard of the House of Trade, not very far from the cathedral, were other habitual places where the master cast the net of his personal connections in search of clients. The most famous taverns in those parts of the city rounded out the geographical setting for developing his preliminary but vital work of assuring the success of the voyage.

At the same time that he acquired a cargo, the master had to form a crew. Normally a master resided in the maritime neighborhood of Triana, so it did not take much effort to make the rounds of the inns, taverns, and even the very residences of the mariners. This task did not even need to be done personally; contacting a boatswain or guardián who had traveled with him on earlier expeditions, the master would commission him to recruit a crew for the ship.

Then began the work of rigging the ship and providing it with all the equipment, provisions, and arms required by official ordinances. Another task in which the good master demonstrated his abilities was bargaining with the purveyors in search of the best quality at the lowest prices. Finally, he had to be vigilant to see that everything was put on board and that the sailors received some advance on their salaries.

Everything was then ready: the cargo could be received, and the names of its recipients noted. The last moments before sailing saw the most frenetic activity; Juan de Escalante presents the master as a man who arrived at the ship quarreling with everybody, complaining about how badly everything had been done in his absence, and spending several sleepless nights before departure arranging everything, with the help of the boatswain.

Once the voyage began, the master saw that all the sailors did their jobs and that the cargo was in good condition. If a storm made it necessary to jettison part of the cargo, he made the final decision. If the ship did not travel in convoy, the master decided about changes in the route and determined layovers in ports along the way. Only questions that were purely technical in matters of navigation remained reserved for the pilot, while the real capacity to make general decisions about the destination of the ship remained in the hands of the master, who was the supreme authority on board. Good masters also understood navigation and customarily were capable of substituting for the pilot. The ordinances of the House of Trade stipulated that each master pass a nautical examination proving that he would be able to guide the ship in an emergency.

Upon arriving at the port of destination, the master was the person responsible for paying royal taxes on the cargo, which fees he would collect, in turn, from the receivers of the merchandise. Once having completed official requirements, he would proceed to hand the cargo over to its owners and to collect the corresponding freight charges, in cash, in kind, or in letters of exchange. With the unloading finished, he began his efforts anew to find cargo for the return voyage, and a new cycle of responsibilities began that would not end until arriving in Seville. Once the inspections by the House of Trade had finished and the men had been paid their salaries, the only thing that remained was to present his accounts to the owners of the ship, who, if they were satisfied, signed a final receipt and paid the salary for his labors.

As we see, the virtues of a good master were extremely varied, as were the multitude of tasks that he had to perform. He needed patience in dealing with the bureaucracy and a liberal hand to bribe corrupt functionaries; he had to have many friends and hundreds of personal connections to obtain and load the cargo and choose the crew members; he had to be a hard bargainer to acquire good and cheap supplies; he had to have the gift of command and the organizational capacity to guide the ship; he had to possess a business sense to collect debts, pay taxes, and issue or accept letters of exchange. Above all, his great virtue consisted in knowing how to earn the confidence of others. A contemporary, Diego García de Palacio, summarized the characteristics of a good master in a very expressive paragraph: "The master . . . ought to be a man who is able and diligent and a man of business, known to merchants and enjoying good fame and reputation, such that all have confidence in him because of his good qualities . . . and he has to know well how to load merchandise and to secure the cargo and to order everything put in its place: a peaceable man and well prepared for his job."[32]

The master's good reputation and the confidence that he could inspire were the principal qualities that persuaded others to entrust great quantities of wealth to his hands. Maritime commerce has always presented the owners of capital with the terrible uncertainty of having to entrust strangers with transporting their riches to far distant regions. At times, their worst fears have been realized. Oceangoing trade has produced, and continues to produce, some of the most successful examples of great thefts in human history: cargos that disappear without a trace; false sinkings and ships that are supposedly lost, only to reappear with another name and under another flag; and so on. All these intrigues are made possible by the mobility of the ships, and the potential conflict of diverse national jurisdictions impedes the resolution of any problem that arises, even when the causes and the authors of the crime are known.

For all those reasons, more than for anything except his ability the master was appreciated for his honesty or, better said, for the loyalty that he displayed toward his clients, which did not exclude his doing business at the margins of the law for their mutual benefit. An extreme situation, such as the death of a master during a voyage, could throw into relief the relations maintained by these personages within the world of mercantile affairs in the Carrera de Indias. When the master Pedro de Mata died in Cartagena de Indias in 1562, his testament showed that, besides the official registers of merchandise, he carried "a small book one-fourth the size of a folio sheet" with twenty-nine entries of merchandise carried "in confidence," which had not passed through any customs inspection. Upon the book's return to Spain, its contents were read at Sunday mass in Seville's principal parishes and repeated by town criers in the busiest public places.[33]

As human ingenuity has always shown itself to be especially imaginative when it comes to avoiding the payment of taxes, the Spanish crown worked hard to find a candidate to hold personally responsible for royal tax collection. The master of each ship seemed an ideal candidate for this task. Instead of requiring payments from each one of the thousands of proprietors of the cargo, the officials of the king collected only from the master of the ship, and that simplified the process. But the state also charged him with impeding the passage of illegal emigrants and the desertion of mariners in America, converting masters in fact into the executors of its migration policies. In general, one could say that the House of Trade considered the masters responsible for any infraction of the ordinances that occurred on board the ships.[34] One long series of documentation conserved in the Archive of the Indies shows the legal actions that masters faced as soon as they arrived in Seville after the return voyage, which generally began with their immediate incarceration if any irregularity was suspected.[35]

But a master could be jailed only if he returned to Seville. What would happen if he decided to flee with the ship or with the money to an enemy nation, betraying all the confidence placed in him? This occurrence was not infrequent, and as an example we cite the case of Juan Sánchez de Vizcaya, master of the merchant ship *La Magdalena*, who fled to Portugal with half a million maravedís belonging to one of the brothers of Francisco Pizarro, the conqueror of Peru.[36]

285

This is how masters and ship lords might have dressed at the end of the sixteenth century. Cesare Vecillio, *Degli abiti antichi e moderni di diverse parti del mondo*. First ed., Venice, 1590. Biblioteca Nacional, Madrid.

It could also happen that the master returned to Spain after having sold the cargo and then bankrupting himself, or he could try to cheat his patrons by falsifying the accounts. In order to avoid all these unfortunate possibilities, and demonstrating that in the business world, even the strictest confidence ought to be accompanied by guarantees, masters were obliged to present guarantors who would vouch for them.

But the master was not the only potential instigator of chicanery. The owners of ships could also play tricks on their administrators. One technique consisted of placing a "false master" in charge of the ship, who would serve as a screen for the owner to carry out all sorts of fraudulent dealings.[37] The game was complex and began with the initial appearance of a master with good credit who was held in full confidence. He was charged with securing the license to travel to America and initiating the process of readying the ship. Almost at the last minute, the first master would feign illness and leave his charge, being replaced by a master who was totally insolvent. This was the "false master," someone ruined and in need of money, who hired himself out as a cover for the owner, in exchange for the chance to earn some ducats and the promise that the owner would use his influence to get him out of jail when the time came. Once the "false master" was placed on the ship, the owner could sell part of the cargo, carry illegal immigrants, or take merchants to the Indies disguised as sailors. The master was held responsible for all this, and he would have to answer to the authorities of the House of Trade.

Because of this practice, and in order to avoid becoming the honest dupe of tainted owners, the masters customarily included clauses in their contracts where they stated that, although they (the masters) signed receipts and promised to pay salaries to the sailors, the shipowners had the final responsibility for those expenses.[38] The one who went to jail was the master, but he could be freed if the owner complied with the payment of the debt. Such situations were part of the burdens peculiar to the office of master.

The post of captain completed the central triumvirate of authority on a sixteenth-century merchant ship. In the majority of cases this charge was more or less honorific, and the onboard activity of the captain consisted in nothing more than directing the defense of the ship in case of enemy attack. In this situation, however, the captain held all the authority on board, and the pilot as well as the master were under his command. Otherwise, he ought not, nor did he have any reason to, interfere in the nautical or commercial decisions on the ship. Besides, although he may have wanted to intervene, he would have been unable to do anything, because normally he was completely ignorant in maritime matters. In order to understand what this post was like on a merchant ship of the Carrera de Indias, it is sufficient to note that the generals of armadas could choose as a captain a distinguished gentleman who traveled on board like a passenger, by which they intended to do him honor but not to assign him to a post with real authority. The situation changed if the shipowner traveled on board and was named a captain by the general of the fleet. Then the post of captain was filled with substance and authority, beyond simple military questions, not because of the office itself but because of the person who occupied it.

The "Ship Lords"

A ship lord, according to the terminology of the epoch, was the owner of a ship, and during the sixteenth century many ship lords sailed on board their vessels, personally directing what went on in them. These days this seems somewhat strange, as it is perfectly normal for the majority stockholders in large shipping companies never to have set foot on the bridge of a ship. Instead of handling ships confronting storms, they settle for directing them from their offices in the great financial centers of the world, where storms sometimes form as well, provoked not by raging gales but by swift declines in the stock market. In the twentieth century a shipowner surely defines himself not as a "man of the sea" but more as a capitalist specializing in the business of maritime transport. In the sixteenth century, a shipowner was in many cases a true "man of the sea."

(93)

We know the names of some of the most influential and the richest proprietors of ships in sixteenth-century Seville, and we have the documentary certainty that a good part of their wealth, which could amount to tens of thousands of ducats, was earned by personally directing their business on the decks of their ships. Thus, for example, Juan Rodríguez de Noriega, who was the principal promotor of the creation of a University of Seafarers in Seville, sailed in 1560 on a ship he owned, the *Concepción*, of which he was "lord and pilot."[39] In the inspections of the 1573 and 1577 fleets, we find that two of the most powerful Sevillian shipowners, Cristóbal de Monte Bernardo and Andrés de Paz, sailed on board their ships as captains.[40] The latter personage, an old acquaintance of ours, became the most prominent and richest figure in the University of Seafarers by the end of the century. In spite of that he continued, until a very advanced age, directly commanding his own ships. One last example of the owner-sailor is offered by Cosme Buitrón, another eminent figure in the maritime traffic of Seville, who acquired a great fortune without renouncing his status as a simple pilot, eventually serving as chief pilot on several Indies fleets.[41]

Alongside these rich magnates were modest proprietors, owners of a small ship or part of a larger ship, who also traveled on board personally watching over their interests. The existence of this type of "ship lord" was favored by the relatively small average tonnage of ships in the sixteenth century. As Fernand Braudel noted, "In the sixteenth century small ships went everywhere, children of the evident expansion of commercial activities."[42] A ship of lesser tonnage (the average was about one hundred toneladas during the first half of the century, rising to something more than two hundred at the end of the century) was not as expensive as the great carracks of over a thousand toneladas that had plied the seas in the previous century. Thus, in the documents of the Archive of the Indies, cases appear with a certain frequency of simple pilots who had become the total or partial proprietor of a *nao* of one hundred toneladas. That was the case with Alonso Martín, a Sevillian thirty-three years old, who was a pilot and lord of a ship of that size.[43] One way of obtaining a type of official subsidy was to commit to make a first voyage as a *navío de aviso* (dispatch ship) in royal service, for which the king provided a sizable sum of money that helped to pay for the ship's construction.[44]

Without carrying out a detailed statistical study, it is difficult to say how many ships of the Carrera de Indias carried their owners on board during the sixteenth century. Nonetheless, based on partial data, I would say that the proportion hovered between 40 and 50 percent. Thus, for example, of 330 ships inspected in Veracruz by the Inquisition between the years 1572 and 1600, on 154 of them (46.6 percent) the ship lord formed part of the crew.[45] It is also significant to note the professions of the forty-eight "men of the sea" who supported the creation of the University of Seafarers in Seville: exactly half of them said they were "lords of ships," of whom thirteen added that they were also pilots, masters, or captains.[46]

When the owner of a ship traveled on board, he normally also occupied one of the three commanding offices of the ship. Some went as pilots, although it was more common for them to serve as masters or captains. If as captains, they reserved the honorary command of the ship for themselves and had at their side a master who carried out the administrative work under their supervision. But whether or not the owner exercised an actual charge, when he traveled on board he inevitably made important decisions, because he had the authority to open or close the tap from whence flowed the daily wages. The proprietor had an added advantage: he could hold the master or pilot responsible for any accident or disaster that occurred.

It is interesting to note that over time the trend seems to have been against owners' being present on their own ships. The founding documents of the University of Seafarers complained that there were fewer and fewer "important men" who sailed in the last quarter of the sixteenth century,[47] and the studies done on English seafaring in the seventeenth and eighteenth centuries show that the ownership of vessels fell progressively into the hands of commercial capitalists.[48] On the Carrera de Indias during the sixteenth century many merchants were also owners of ships. Sevillian families dedicated to a variety of mercantile activities had invested in ships. Even some members of the noble town council of Seville, the famous "Gentlemen Twenty-Four," did not consider it beneath them to devote themselves to lucrative investments and had entered into maritime commerce.[49] Still, it would be difficult to claim that mercantile capital controlled maritime commerce in that century; there remained a sizable number of shipowners whose background and specialization were fundamentally nautical. And in the sessions of the University of Seafarers, at least, we can clearly see that merchants were perceived by shipowners as competitors. The merchants' guild strove for cheap freight rates for the largest possible amount of merchandise—exactly the opposite of what the seafarers wanted.

(94)

The passage of time seemed to work against the men of the sea, however, and it is very probable that in the Carrera de Indias, as in England, commercial capital ended up controlling the shipping business. The shipowners had to contend with ever more difficult conditions as Spanish military power crumbled: more and more ships were seized by enemy powers, and the king of Spain, not having sufficient ships of his own, requisitioned the best merchant ships in order to employ them in his armadas. The deterioration of Spanish maritime and commercial traffic furthered the concentration of capital in the hands of the richest, who were the only ones able to withstand the growing difficulties. Those who gained the most benefits were, almost always, the great privileged members of the Consulate of Indies Shippers. It is very possible that they ended up controlling maritime commerce.

(95)

Another circumstance made it increasingly unlikely that men of modest means, who had begun their careers as wage earners, spending their time as pilots or masters, would own small ships. The average size of ships continued to grow throughout the early modern period, and it became more and more difficult for an old "man of the sea" to put together the huge sums of money necessary to buy a substantial part of the ownership of such a vessel.

Superior Officers in the Navy

On warships dedicated to the protection of commercial traffic, in addition to the officers serving on merchant ships, others appeared who were specific to the armadas. First were the constables (*alguaciles*) charged with maintaining order on royal ships. The constable major of the armada exercised the functions of a chief of police on board: he intervened in quarrels, prevented prohibited gaming, and, if the need arose, put unruly persons in the stocks. A figure peculiar to warships was the water constable, who was charged specifically with seeing that the rations of that vital liquid were delivered to all members of the crew without any wastage occasioned by theft.

Another group, endowed with greater prestige than the constables, was composed of the high officials charged with the overseeing of the interests of state. These were the *veedores*, or inspectors, purveyors, accountants, and treasurers of the armadas. They guarded and administered the money, a role that conferred great power upon them. Their intervention was necessary to acquire supplies and provisions, to incur any type of expense, and to pay salaries. They were also charged with keeping the accounts and presenting the final reports of the income and expenses of each armada's money.

The superior officers on warships were the so-called captains of sea and war, professional military men who retained, without discussion or limitation, the highest authority on the ships, in a role completely different from that of the shipowners or distinguished passengers who served as captains on

The Ship as a Place of Work

merchant ships. The armadas overall had two superior officers: the admiral, or second-in-command, and the general, who had supreme command over the entire squadron. Each convoy sent to Tierra Firme or New Spain was under the command of a general and an admiral of the fleet, who flew their insignias on private ships that had been rented by the king and armed especially for the occasion. When, from 1568 on, the so-called Guard Squadron of the Carrera de Indias was organized, composed of galleons belonging to the crown, the generals and admirals of this armada constituted the supreme Spanish authorities on all the seas in the Western Hemisphere, to whom even the general and admirals of the merchant fleets owed obedience.

In the sixteenth century, the captains of sea and war, like the admirals and generals, as has been said, were professional military men. Nonetheless, there was a great distance between the professional careers of those men and of the actual fighting men on board ships. In the twentieth century, the commander of an aircraft carrier is a professional who has been schooled from his youth uniquely and exclusively to command a ship. In reality, he is a public functionary who is financially dependent, like a mailman or a university professor, on his monthly pay.

The formation of an admiral of the Carrera de Indias during the sixteenth century was fundamentally military, but it did not have to be specifically naval. He could have begun his career as a soldier in a company of infantry commanded by a captain who was a family friend; then he might become an ensign *(alférez)* and, finally, accede to the command of his own company. At some determined moment he might go to sea to defend a galleon and, after specializing for some years in maritime warfare, be given command of a squadron. Naturally, the sooner he began his connection with life at sea, the better his qualifications to become a good admiral. The great Spanish mariners of the sixteenth century were military men who had wielded their weapons on board ships from the start of their careers, such as Pedro Menéndez de Avilés and Álvaro de Bazán. Nonetheless, other personages, such as Cristóbal de Eraso, who commanded many fleets and became a general in the Guard Squadron of the Carrera de Indias, did not have a naval education from his youth. In official reports he is characterized as a good military man, but with the indication in the margin that "he was not a sailor."[50] In similar fashion, a military man who had exercised the post of admiral could afterward command a cavalry unit or become the governor of a frontier region in the Indies.[51] In sum, the supreme chiefs of the armadas of the Indies in the sixteenth century were, in the great majority, multifaceted military men without a specialization in naval matters.

Moreover, one could not say that they were public functionaries in the modern sense, since they lacked a condition that is fundamental today in defining such a position: stability of employment. In effect, the generals and admirals of the fleet were selected for each expedition from among the many candidates who aspired to the post. The choice was at first made by the House of Trade and then came to depend directly on the monarch and his Council of the Indies.[52] After the return of each fleet, even the fleet's general remained without further secure employment or salary. Only the posts of general and admiral of the Guard Squadron of the Carrera de Indias had a certain continuity, but that was an exception to the rule.

Although this was not the only reason, the unstable employment of the armadas' high command was one reason its members sought income beyond their official salaries. Many generals and admirals owned the ships on which they sailed, which had been leased by the king to serve as escorts for the merchant fleets. This did not occur only with rich and powerful personages, such as Pedro Menéndez de Avilés or Don Álvaro de Bazán, but also with less well known figures, such as, for example, Juan de Alcega, general of the New Spain fleet of 1572, a man of the sea who sailed "in ships of his own."[53] The possession of a galleon signified an investment of thousands of ducats, and as the king tended to pay late for the rentals, the owner had to take out loans as well as advance significant sums of money on his own account. Such activities converted these mariners into authentic businessmen. It is no wonder that on many occasions it was impossible to prevent their sense of personal profit from bankrupting the Royal Treasury. Consider, carrying this situation to our times, what it would mean if the commander of an aircraft carrier owned the ship and leased it to the state. How many deals would have to be arranged in order to finance and maintain the ship? Then take into account that galleons were the capital ships of the naval strategy of the sixteenth century, occupying the position that aircraft carriers hold in the twentieth century.

Finally, admirals in the sixteenth century did not restrict their sphere of influence to the simple military command of their armadas. Because they would be out of touch with any other authority during their voyages, admirals constituted the supreme judges of all crimes that were committed on board; they had the power to open legal proceedings, to punish the guilty with torture, and even to condemn them to death. Moreover, because in that period the governance of bodies was not well distinguished from that of souls, generals were also charged with the maintenance of "good customs." Thus, a general was as responsible for seeing that lechery did not erupt on board ship as he was for seeing that the cannons were always ready to launch their projectiles; he had to put the same ardor into extinguishing the fires of prohibited love as he applied in putting out real fires. Thus, it is no wonder that when General Diego de Flores Valdés underwent inspection after his arrival in Seville, the inspec-

The Ship as a Place of Work

tors were interested, among other questions, in asking witnesses the following:

> If they know if the said Diego Flores Valdés and the said admirals endeavored and saw to it that everyone on the said armada . . . traveled in peace and concord, and reconciled the ones with the others and saw that they lived honestly and pacifically, without there being among them tumults nor disputes, nor disturbances, nor gaming, nor love affairs, nor other scandalous and public sins, and that those that came to his notice were punished, corrected, and reformed, and regarding this that they rendered justice.[54]

The Pay for One's Effort
Types of Salaries on the Indies Route

The crew members of ships that departed for the Indies did not all collect their wages in the same manner. The different forms of salary emerged from a combination of two variables: (a) the type of remuneration was not always the same: one could collect in money, in kind, or in space; and (b) the extent to which the worker at sea participated in the risks of the enterprise determined the diverse forms of payment, which ranged from a share of the profits earned by the ship to a salary fixed at a specific amount.

Payment in money (normally silver reales) constituted part of the salary of all the sailors and officers of the Carrera de Indias. It was also common to receive a salary in silver bars, a mode that we could consider as intermediate between payment in kind and in money. An ingot of silver was commonly accepted as a means of payment, and knowing its weight one could very easily figure out its equivalence in currency, since the silver peso (literally, "weight") was the monetary unit of the Spanish Indies.

All members of the crews had the right to receive food and drink as part of their salary, and provisions for the men of the sea always ran on the account of the shipowner. In the Middle Ages, payment in kind had a rather more ample meaning, going much further than the simple distribution of food to which it had been reduced in the sixteenth century. Some documents in the Archive of Simancas show that the crews of the Cantabrian galleys that fought in the Hundred Years' War received, besides money, arms (coats of mail, crossbows, helmets), pieces of cloth ("English cloth," "London cloth," "cloth of gold"), and above all, clothing (doublets, stockings, waistcoats, girdles, and so on).[55] Even in the sixteenth century, some reminders of these old customs remained. Thus, for example, masters generally collected a supplement to their salary in money for what was called "the master's stockings," evidently an allusion to a time when they were really given this type of garment as part of their salary. Another form of payment in kind that continued in the sixteenth century was characteristic of slave ships, in which some of the officers were paid with part of the merchandise, that is to say, with the right of sale or ownership of various of the slaves transported.[56]

In the sixteenth century, some of the sailors and officers still earned part of their remuneration in the form of cargo space on the ship, which they could use to their profit. This concession was usually called the *quintalada*, because normally the sailor transported *quintales* (hundredweights, each forty-six kilograms) of merchandise, returning home with the value of its sale in cash or in some exotic goods that could fetch a high price in Europe. When the sailor had no capital to invest in merchandise, he could simply rent the space to a merchant and receive the corresponding freight charge. This was a very old system of remuneration, existing in maritime-commercial legal codes of the Middle Ages, such as the famous Rôles d'Oléron of the thirteenth century.[57]

On large Spanish expeditions to the Pacific, the quintaladas constituted the most interesting and valuable part of the crewmen's salaries. Nonetheless, during the sixteenth century crew members in the Carrera de Indias more often collected quintaladas as a simple monetary addition to their salaries.

At the beginning of the century, the most common salary formula treated the crew members of merchant ships as coparticipants in the risks of the shipowner; because of that, their salary was a share of the profits obtained on the voyage. The sailors who were paid according to this system said that they sailed "with the luck *[ventura]* of the ship," "with the value *[monto]* of the freight," or simply "with the third *[tercio]*," to indicate that the crew as a whole received a third of the net proceeds from the freight charges. The system included payment in cash, in kind (the food ration), and in cargo space (although, as mentioned above, the quintalada had been reduced to a cash addition to salary).

When a ship arrived in port with crew members who had shared the risk of the shipowner, the value of the freight charge was then calculated. In earlier times it is very possible that the profits, perhaps the product of wartime booty or bartered merchandise, were heaped up in one place near the dock or on the ship itself. This custom of forming a heap *(montón* or *monto)* with the profits gave a name to the system; it clearly figured in the procedure for distributing booty from the expeditions of conquest in the Indies. Bernal Díaz del Castillo tells us in much detail about the distribution of the montón that was formed with booty from the conquest of Mexico.[58] Like the *conquistadores*, the sailors formed a "company," and the profits were shared among all of them as a function of their support for the common enterprise.

Bernal Díaz del Castillo commented that Hernán Cortés first paid the expenses incurred for the benefit of the enterprise as a whole out of the montón from the conquest of Mexico. The same thing happened on the ships. The master, in the name of the owner, had the right to deduct a small portion of the profits in order to make necessary repairs.[59] Then he subtracted all the money spent in paying the bureaucratic fees necessary to ready the ship for embarkation. He also took out the wages for skilled laborers in port, stevedores, and the hiring of auxiliary craft that had collaborated in the loading and unloading. Also included were the common expenses for ordinary alms to the ship's saint-protectors or extraordinary alms promised in the teeth of a storm, as well as contributions destined for the sustenance of charitable brotherhoods and guild associations. The deductions from the monto that the sailors watched with the greatest discontent were those compensating for damages to the cargo that the master ascribed to careless handling on the part of the crew.

It is curious that the common expenses also included the salary of the ship's pilot, who in a certain sense was considered apart from the rest of the crew. The explanation for this is very clear: high-seas pilots were a relatively recent novelty on ships, a fruit of the development of oceanic navigation. (Medieval law codes such as the Rôles d'Oléron made reference to pilots who were experienced with a particular coast or port but not to pilots who were expert in navigational techniques and sailed for the whole voyage.)[60] Besides high-seas pilots, there were other positions that had relatively recently become habitual on a ship. Their salaries were also taken out of the monto. Among these were the gunners, the scrivener, and even the captain, as a specialist and the chief of military defense, who was not always present on a merchant ship.

Once the deductions for common expenses were taken, another 10 percent was deducted from what remained of the monto. Of this sum, three-fourths went to the master under the heading of "stockings" and the remaining fourth constituted the quintaladas to be shared among all the crew. Once all these sums had been deducted, the remaining income from the freight charges was divided into three parts. Two parts went to the owner, or owners, of the ship, and the remaining third (tercio) went to the ship's company, that is to say, the traditional components of the ship's crew.

The specific form of dividing the tercio of the freight charges and the quintaladas among the company differed in different periods and according to the customs of each ship. In general, we can say that each sailor received a share, called a *soldada*, that served as the unit of distribution. The apprentices earned three-fourths of a soldada and the pages earned half a soldada. The officers earned two soldadas. In order to calculate the value of a soldada, it sufficed to divide the value of the quintaladas and of the tercio of the freight charges by the total number of shares represented by the crew.[61]

The second form of payment used on merchant ships separated the crews from the outcome of the enterprise and obliged the shipowners to pay a fixed amount for each round-trip voyage. This system was described by phrases such as "so much fixed [tanto fijo]" or "a certain amount [partida cierta]." It included only the salary in cash and the food and drink ration, but it did not give the crew the right to receive quintaladas or the master the right to collect for his "stockings." As a first step before enrolling a crewman under this system, a brief contract, or concierto, between the owners, normally represented by the master, and the worker had to be signed. This form of payment was not as common as the other at the start of the sixteenth century, but it gained ground as the century advanced and in subsequent centuries came to be the most usual form.

A variant of the system just described consisted in the payment of a fixed quantity per month. During the sixteenth century, this formula was used only on warships or on ships in service to the crown. In the majority of cases it included only the cash salary and daily rations, but in the first years of the century, and above all on the great expeditions of discovery in search of the Spice Islands, the payment of the quintaladas was a very important part of the total salaries received by the officers and sailors.

The Spanish expeditions to the Pacific were collaborative financial enterprises involving the state and a goodly number of private partners. The distant destination and the uncertain future of the crews, who knew that many were condemned not to return alive, obliged the shipowners and the crown to provide special incentives for men to enroll. That is why considerable amounts of space on the ship were conceded to them in the form of quintaladas, to which was added the right to carry one or more "boxes," theoretically with personal objects but which in reality were also used to transport merchandise. If the said space was used to bring back to Spain a cargo of spices, a crewman could earn a small fortune that made the monthly salary for which he had enrolled look minuscule.

On the voyage of Magellan and Elcano, the captain general could bring 82 quintales; each captain, treasurer, or accountant, 59; the scribes, 25; the masters and pilots, 17; the boatswains, 13; and thus on down to the simple sailors, who were authorized to transport 3.5 quintales. Taking into account that on the return voyage a quintal, or hundredweight, of spices sold for forty-two ducats (one ducat was valued at 375 maravedís), the sailors on the expedition obtained 39,520 maravedís for their total monthly salary payments over three years and 44,493 maravedís for the sale of spices that they had brought under the quintaladas, once taxes and alms had been deducted. That means that the sale of a small sack of spices of one quintal (forty-six kilograms) was worth approximately the same as a full year's salary for a working sailor. Juan Sebastián Elcano himself had the right to 104,535 maravedís for his monthly salary and 508,720 maravedís for the sale of his quintaladas.[62]

It should not surprise us, then, that when the expedition of Sebastian Cabot to the Moluccas was organized, the crews held heated discussions with the shipowners and the crown, not about monthly salaries but about the number of quintaladas they would be assigned.[63] After the failure of the expedition, which, as is well known, remained in the Río de la Plata and never reached the Spice Islands, some of the survivors bitterly lamented the economic failure of the enterprise and recognized that "the principal end for which we went on this voyage was for the quintaladas that we hoped to bring back if the voyage had taken place."[64]

To the degree that sailing routes became more secure, it was less necessary to provide incentives for the enlistment of sailors; nor did their professional zeal need to be enhanced by making them coparticipants in the profits. For this reason, shipowners were increasingly reluctant to share their business profits with the crews, and the quintaladas ended up being converted into a simple supplement to the salary. One wise Burgalese man of business, Cristóbal de Haro, who participated actively in the financing and organizing of the armadas to the Moluccas, had already suggested depriving the sailors of their traditional right to use space on the ships, substituting a fixed sum of money.[65]

Terms and Conditions for Receiving a Salary

Before leaving on long transoceanic voyages, the crews received an advance on their salary. The amount usually varied quite noticeably according to the circumstances, but in general one can say that the more uncomfortable or long the voyage was predicted to be the higher the advance. Thus, for example, when the authorities were trying to carry out a draft for the king's armadas in wartime, several months' advance salary was offered as an inducement. On the armada organized to populate the desolate region near the Strait of Magellan after Drake had passed through those waters, the crown had to offer four months' payment in advance.[66] On early expeditions to the Moluccas, similar advances were given, and, because classes have always existed, the officers customarily received much more money than the sailors, as much as six months or even a year of salary before departure. On ordinary voyages, the sailors of royal armadas collected two months' salary in advance, and sailors on merchant ships received between 10 and 20 percent of the predicted salary.

These quantities were essentially for the families of the men of the sea, since that would be the only money to enter the household for many months. With it, debts could be paid and new credit could be advanced, awaiting the return of the fleet. Another very common use of the advance payments was for clothing purchases. In many cases the masters acknowledged giving some money to the crewmen because they "arrived broke," that is to say, with their clothing full of holes as big as fists. The famous engraving of Hoefnagel that depicts the payment of salary advances prior to embarkation for the Indies shows barefoot sailors with their breeches and shirts in shreds. But surely there would have been many others, less careful about their appearance and their families, who would dedicate their money to celebrating their last days on shore as raucously and enjoyably as possible.

The remainder of the salary would be paid after the voyage was completed. On merchant ships paying "by the third of the freight," the principal payment would be made on the return trip after leaving the Bahama Channel. There the freight charges earned on the outbound voyage would be distributed; these were always the most important, since on the return trip the cargo was generally much reduced. Payment was not made upon arrival in America but later, and in the middle of the Atlantic, in an attempt to keep the sailors from deserting and leaving the ship without a crew as soon as they had money in their hands. Sailors on royal armadas and those who sailed for a fixed amount received their salary upon returning to Spain, once the unloading was finished.

The payments made to crews on warships were carefully detailed in the documents. Normally they were made at the House of Trade itself, where an official judge and various scribes called out to the mariners who anxiously surrounded the table where silver coins were stacked up. The identity of the sailor was proved by the personal characteristics that had been noted in the register, and if there was any confusion, as, for example, having a scar on the right cheek when the annotation noted it on the left, the sailor could have serious problems in collecting. If things went well, the sailor received a good fistful of silver coins that he customarily carried in his hat.

The sum that the crew member finally received had been diminished by deductions for alms, damage to the cargo, and so on. On the other hand, the mariners' salaries were exempt from royal taxes, which alleviated the burden. Nonetheless, the sailor had to be very alert so as not to suffer another type of "discount," this one much more dangerous. A cluster of the most notorious members of the Sevillian underworld swarmed around the men who had received their pay, ready to use every means at their disposal to see that the sailors did not arrive home with all their money. A man who had spent various months, perhaps years, at sea would surely have been predisposed to celebrate his arrival on land by getting drunk in the taverns of the city; there he would show off the silver pesos that filled his purse or his hat. In such cases, he would become easy prey for gamblers, cardsharps, thieves, and other components of the dishonorable "university of friends of marginal behavior."

One of these miscreants, who, judging from the lack of skill he displayed, must not have mastered his trade, was caught with his hand in the cookie jar (in this case, in the silver reales) in the midst of the tumult that formed in the House of Trade at the hour of payment. When the factor of the House of Trade proceeded to pay the crew of one of the fleets recently arrived in Seville, a man dressed in a "friar's sackcloth" to gain the confidence of the sailors approached those who had received their money and asked them for alms. The false friar pretended to be helping the proceedings along, repeating in a loud voice the name of the man called to collect, and he even—height of amiability—offered to help convey the coins from the factor's table to the mariner's hat. Predictably, not all the coins arrived at their destination, but various of them remained stuck in the hand of the solicitous apprentice-thief; I say apprentice, because his work was not executed cleanly, and he was discovered and seized. This is what a witness recounted: "I saw that at the time they paid the boy who was called Lorenzo, a native of Sanlúcar, who sailed as a page on the said flagship, the said man (dressed like a friar) put the money with his hand into the boy's hat and he took four reales, which remained in the palm of his hand. It is not known whether they were stuck with tar or turpentine; then he dropped them into his pocket."[67]

When a merchant voyage ended happily, the sailor had the right to collect his salary. On the other hand, if the ship was lost with all its cargo, although the sailor had been able to save his life he had no right to collect his salary. As a well-known British scholar wrote, "Freight is the mother of wages." If the sinking had disadvantaged the owners of the cargo and the shipowners, they would ensure that the sailors would not be the only ones to gain.[68] Granted, if part of the cargo were saved and the freight charges were collected, the mariners' right to collect their salary had a higher priority than any claims of the shipowners or merchants. On military expeditions, even if the mariners who were victims of a shipwreck were picked up by another ship in the armada and continued working on it until arriving in port, they had no right to collect a salary. If a rescued sailor asked for some type of remuneration, normally the response was that he had been paid enough by having consumed part of the water and food rations belonging to the crew of the ship that had saved him.

It could also happen that a sailor failed to finish a voyage because of sickness or death. In that case, the destiny of his pay depended on the form in which he had signed up. If it had been for a "fixed sum," the shipowner considered that the crew had excluded him voluntarily from continuing to benefit from the luck or the disgrace of the enterprise; because of that he was obligated to pay only that part of the salary effectively earned. The principle was expressed with clarity in the saying "A dead man earns no salary." Nor did anyone earn a salary who remained behind ill in an American port.

By contrast, if a sailor had signed up for the "third of the freight," that is, following the "luck of the ship," custom established that even if he died at the beginning of the voyage, his heirs received his entire wage. It seems, nonetheless, that to receive the quintaladas the sailor had to be personally present at the sale of his merchandise. If he was not and no companion offered to negotiate in his name, his heirs had no right to claim anything for the quintalada. At least, this was the custom followed on Spanish expeditions to the Pacific.

Bonuses at the Margins of the Law: Contraband, Bribery, and Other Ruses

For some men who were normally poor, such as the majority of men of the sea, it would have been an irresistible temptation to see and touch the dazzling riches of the colonial trade. For that reason, it is no wonder that sailors and officers on ships of the Carrera de Indias tried by every means possible to snare even a minuscule part of those riches. The most basic procedure was to transport a small load of merchandise to sell in the Indies; to maximize profits, it was better to do it completely outside the official registers, that is, transporting the merchandise and the silver obtained from its sale as contraband.

The most common way that men of the sea earned a bonus on their salary was to buy articles of clothing in Spain and sell them in the Indies, where European textiles were much in demand. Many crewmen carried small cargoes of clothing, according to their economic situation. Thus, for example, the pilot Juan Sánchez transported "four dozen pair of short hose, seven doublets, and some full stockings."[69] A simple sailor, such as Juan Rodríguez, a Sevillian householder from the neighborhood of La Cestería, contented himself with having sold "a loose coat, a black cape, and some shirts."[70] To Rodríguez' disgrace, a constable found the silver produced by his little overseas business, which, moreover, he carried *sin quintar,* that is, without paying the taxes due to the crown. From the questioning to which he was subjected, we gather that the sale of those few articles of clothing raised an amount of money equivalent to half his salary as a sailor. As the sum was not really very large and because Rodríguez swore that he had only sold his own clothes, driven by the need for money, he was fined only 25 percent of the confiscated silver.

Clearly, there were other cases in which it was very difficult to allege innocence. This happened when three individuals, leading a horse loaded with silver in the middle of the night, were detained in Tomares, a tiny town on the right bank of the Guadalquivir. The case involved the master, the pilot, and a sailor of the ship *Santa Ana,* recently arrived from New Spain in the 1567 fleet. The men were on their way to hide the proceeds of their dealings in the New World in a safe place. Their situation was most compromising, but despite this, the three mariners decided to resort to the old ploy of denying even the most obvious crimes. They said their intention was to lighten the ship's load so that it could more easily pass through the shallows in the river, and that, of course, they were carrying the silver to the House of Trade. Not surprisingly, the justice of the peace of the Holy Brotherhood—a rural police force—who caught

The Ship as a Place of Work

them did not believe their story, given that Seville was on the other side of the river from where they were apprehended.[71]

Other sailors earned a bonus by practicing an activity that was legal but frankly macabre: they bought the clothing of mariners who died during the voyage in order to resell them in the Indies.[72] Public auctions of the belongings of the deceased were run by the constable of the armada, who earned a percentage of the sale price. However, the constables earned greater profits by the sale of playing cards, although gaming was theoretically prohibited in the fleets. Experience had shown that if the authorities provided the decks, they at least would not be marked, and conflicts arising from the games would be minimized. Another common form of profiting from the misfortunes of others consisted in taking advantage of the anguish of passengers during storms, who were willing to pay large sums of money to ensure themselves a secure place on the boats if they had to abandon ship.

This was how the crew profited in a tragicomic incident on the ship *Santiago*, in the New Spain fleet in 1562, commanded by Don Álvaro Flores Quiñones. The whole convoy found itself in a serious crisis when, not very far from Veracruz, a strong north wind caught them unawares and pushed them against the coast. The ship that was second in rank (the almiranta) sank, and the general ordered all the ships to send their boats to rescue the shipwrecked passengers and the cargo. Despite this order, he was able to prove that the boat of the *Santiago* did not go but instead headed for land, transporting various passengers. Not even cannon shots fired at the boat could stop it from continuing on its undeviating route. The later investigation showed that the passengers taken to land had offered the boat's crew six thousand ducats—a fortune!—if they would deposit them on land safe and sound. In the face of this tempting offer, not even cannon balls from the flagship could intimidate the sailors. This is how a witness described the offer made by Antonio de los Cobos in the name of the other passengers: "Where do you want to take us to drown? We are going to land. We want to save our lives. And he said: 'Sir mariners, I ask you for God's sake, who I believe we will serve in the next life, that if we go to land I will give you six thousand ducats: two thousand from me and two thousand from Francisco de Estrada and two thousand from Martín Alonso de Flandes, for all of you.'"[73]

The case against the crew of the ship *Santiago* for their disobedience and lack of collective responsibility took on the aspect of an authentic farce. The master, who in reality was the one who gave the order to carry the passengers to land, threw the blame on the pilot, the pilot blamed the guardián, and he blamed the apprentices who pulled the oars. For their part, the apprentices declared that the passengers threatened them with their daggers, in a clear demonstration of how money can make gold doubloons be mistaken for steel daggers.

When the general asked for explanations from the spokesman of the passengers, he responded that his desire to reach land was influenced not by fear but by his wish to resolve as soon as possible a matter of honor in the house of his father-in-law, in which the honor of a young lady in the family had been besmirched. The agitated passenger had thought that resolving the problem dry was more salutary than confronting someone wet, and, because in this epoch a duel of honor could not be renounced, that seemed to him to be a good excuse to abandon ship, leaving aside whether or not his story was credible.

Another of the most common forms of obtaining supplementary income was pure and simple theft of part of the cargo or of the equipment on board. The majority of the boatswains trafficked in hempen ropes and cordage, the carpenter in wood, the constable in metalwork and weapons, the steward in provisions. And the master could defraud the owners merely by manipulating the accounts of his administration.[74]

Some offices on board were especially well situated to generate juicy bonuses. The scriveners, for example, collected fees for the many procedures that they ought to have done free of charge, and they even invented unnecessary paperwork whose only real purpose was to provide them with new sources of income. One clever scrivener on the New Spain fleet of 1574 had mounted an ingenious business, counting, of course, on the support of the general of the fleet. He would not permit any passenger to come on board who did not present a certificate, created by the scrivener, of having sworn not to leave the ship until the inspectors of the House of Trade in Seville had given their permission. This was a totally unnecessary bureaucratic redundancy, since this order had been given many years before and the obligation to comply with it was known to everyone. In spite of that, the testimonies given upon arrival in Seville by those affected made clear that the scrivener had set up a stall in the main plaza of Veracruz, where he collected a peso from every passenger in the fleet for creating their passport to embark.[75] With such goings-on it is no wonder that the office of scrivener, which was effectively sold to the highest bidder by the authorities of the Consulate of Indies Shippers in Seville, always had candidates desirous of exercising it. Nor is it surprising that the office of scrivener seldom inspired admiration. As Miguel de Cervantes said of them, with his devastating irony: "There are very many good, faithful, and legal scriveners, and . . . not all of them feed upon lawsuits, nor advise all opposing parties, nor do all of them exact excessive fees for their services, nor do all of them go snooping into other people's lives in order to bring them to law, nor do all of them consort with the judge."[76]

But the salaried mariners were not the only ones capable of earning income at the margin of the law. The shipowners also knew how to make a living by these means. Some decided, in the middle of the ocean, to increase the fees they

The Ship as a Place of Work

charged the passengers, when the passengers had little option to abandon ship. Others, when they realized that their ship was old and almost unserviceable, could try to have it collide along the way with another ship in order to make the other ship's owner pay damages, just as some citizens do today with their unserviceable motor vehicles.[77] There were also some who specialized in obtaining large loans, pledging their own ship and its cargo as collateral. If the owner was able, he could even get various advances whose total value surpassed that of the ship, and then it only remained for him to see that the ship sank in order not to have to repay his financial obligations. One interesting report conserved in the Archive of the Indies made clear that the presence of rogues in the world of insurance and marine loans is not just today's news.[78]

Until now we have seen how practically all the crewmen on merchant ships had small or large opportunities to obtain some extra income. Nonetheless, no one enjoyed a more favorable position than the supreme commanders of the great convoys sent to the Indies, that is, the generals and admirals of the various fleets and armadas. A general with ambitions of becoming rich could let himself be corrupted for hundreds of motives. Just think that the sailing date of the fleet depended on his will and that the delay or advance of the departure date could mean the ruin or the enrichment of many merchants. Generally speaking, European merchants were interested in the fleet's remaining in port in America as long as possible, to be able to sell their cargo at a good price. To the merchants based in America, a rapid turnaround of the fleet suited them better, as it forced the merchants on the fleet to lower the price of their merchandise for fear of returning to Spain without having sold it. Some thousands of pesos spent at an opportune moment could help the generals and admirals make a decision one way or another. But besides this, gold could cloud the vision of the commanders of armadas and prevent them from seeing that their ships were loaded with illegal passengers or help them make a hoped-for decision when choosing a replacement for a vacant post, and so on.

From the last quarter of the sixteenth century, careful inspections (visitas) were made of the fleets that returned from America, and thus the procedures used by some superior officials of the armadas came to light. As an example, one could take the inspection of the Tierra Firme fleet of 1576 and 1577 that sailed under the command of General Francisco de Luján and Admiral Rodrigo de Vargas.[79] The general was found guilty of carrying a sizable cargo of botijas of wine and accepting at least one bribe for naming a master to replace another who died on the voyage. The admiral was condemned for carrying merchandise and above all for accepting bribes so that some persons could travel on his ship who had not passed through the official procedures for emigration.

The investigation showed that all of the bribes were made through third persons who served as intermediaries. In the case of naming the replacement master, it was shown that the ensign of the nao acting as flagship received, in the name of the general, a bar of silver worth 257 pesos, sent by the candidate who wanted to occupy the vacant post. The ensign tried to exculpate the general by presenting himself as the only one responsible: "The said Cristóbal Sánchez graciously gave me the said bar of silver for the intercession that I made with the said captain general, so that he would give him the job of master that he wanted, and for other causes that moved him, and the said bar remained in my power and I benefited from it as a thing of my own."[80] The guilty plea of the faithful ensign was useless, as many others directly accused the general. The bribes received by the admiral Rodrigo de Vargas are also very interesting, because they show how some persons who wanted to emigrate to the Indies could do so without passing through any of the controls established by the Spanish crown.

Bartolomé Sánchez, an artisan who earned his living making quilts and coverlets in a small workshop in the neighborhood of La Magdalena, intended for one of his sons to go to the Indies and there exercise the office of coverlet maker, which, according to him, had a great future in the New World. We do not know the motives that induced him to evade the legal procedures for emigration; perhaps he was a New Christian or had some matter pending with the Inquisition. The fact is that he decided instead to bribe Bartolomé Guzmán, a servant of the factor of the House of Trade. He would be the person charged with delivering three hundred reales to the admiral Rodrigo de Vargas so that he would permit the son of the coverlet maker to travel on his ship, masquerading as a sailor. The documents make clear that the servants and hangers-on of the high functionaries of the House of Trade had a perfectly arranged business, and, due to their humble personal condition and their familiarity with the functionaries of the House of Trade, they were ideal intermediaries. So secure did they feel in their office that they even sent receipts for the bribes they passed along, for which they received a commission and which, according to them, allowed them to buy certain articles of clothing ("for stockings"). We see how the artisan Bartolomé Sánchez described the steps he took to send his son to the Indies:

> And when this occurred, in the courtyard of the House of Trade, the same [admiral] Rodrigo Vargas happened to be coming out of the rooms of the factor . . . and the said Guzmán pointed him out to this witness with his finger and told him that was the one who would transport [his son] . . . to the Indies. And this witness told the same Guzmán: "Well, speak to his grace." He then went over to talk to him briefly in private . . . with which this witness assumed the business had been done.[81]

The Ship as a Place of Work

Admiral Rodrigo de Vargas was accused of carrying eight illegal passengers disguised as sailors, for each one of whom he collected between thirty and forty ducats. It is no wonder that when a tailor, who was traveling as a false sailor, was accused by the rest of the crew of not attending to his work, he responded with all naturalness "that his money had bought [his passage] and they should talk to the admiral."[82]

It is not easy to say with certainty how many generals and admirals of the Carrera de Indias accepted bribes, but one can be sure that practically all of them carried merchandise of their own on their warships to sell in the Indies. As this practice was prohibited, it is natural that the said merchandise went without being registered, constituting, purely and simply, contraband cargo. One of the very rare exceptions must have been the general Don Antonio de Osorio, whose nomination to lead the Tierra Firme fleet in 1584 explained it thus:

> Because the king wants the generals not to carry cargo on the ships, though everyone does, he named Don Antonio Osorio on this occasion, without having consulted the Council of the Indies . . . and because of not having loaded nor carried on that voyage more benefit than that of his salary, which was then four ducats each day, he arrived owing two thousand ducats, as is well known; and understanding this, the king our lord . . . ordered . . . that the said Don Antonio be employed in the best post available in the Indies.[83]

That many of the great figures of Spain's seaborne military in the sixteenth century were linked to mercantile enterprise and maritime transport is indisputable. Thus, for example, Don Álvaro de Bazán, "the elder," was paid for his military service to the crown, and especially for the construction of great galleons, with the concession of special privileges, so that these same vessels could also make voyages as simple merchant ships, without having to wait for the formation of convoys. Protests from the merchants' and shipowners' guilds of Seville about the advantages conceded to Bazán occasioned more than one lawsuit before the authorities at the royal court.[84]

Far more problems were caused by the mercantile activities of Pedro Menéndez de Avilés, one of the most prominent figures of all time in Spanish maritime history, who was jailed for several months, accused of carrying contraband on the ships under his command. One must take into account that this person was at the same time a soldier under orders from the king and a private shipowner, the proprietor, for example, of the largest ship sailing to the Indies in the 1560s.[85] One can understand that it was difficult to separate his mercantile activities from his military activities, and when he returned to Spain in command of the New Spain fleet in 1563, functionaries of the House of Trade arrested him at the dockyards of Seville under serious charges. He was accused of accepting bribes from the merchants for delaying the departure of the fleet; of detaining the convoy so that his own ships had time to join it; of not following orders to come straight back to Seville, instead making a stop in the Azores; of carrying merchandise and treasure without registering it; and of not letting the galleons that he owned be inspected by officials of the House of Trade. Menéndez de Avilés defended himself. He showed the falseness of some of the accusations and the bad faith of many functionaries envious of his position, but that did not prevent him from being condemned for transporting unregistered cargo. He tried to excuse himself by affirming that his galleons only carried some few goods as a form of ballast, but his excuse served for nothing when it was discovered that the cargo was composed principally of a dyestuff of exceptionally high value: *grana*, or cochineal. To ballast a ship with grana was the equivalent of ballasting it with gold, and Menéndez de Avilés could not prevent himself being found guilty of trafficking in contraband.[86] (111)

One of the most notable scandals regarding contraband on warships involved Don Cristóbal de Eraso, who substituted for Pedro Menéndez de Avilés on the main flagship of the Royal Guard Squadron of the Carrera de Indias. At the end of autumn in 1579, the *licenciado* Martín de Espinosa, judge of the court of appeals in Seville, kept dozens of constables on alert, patrolling the shores at the mouth of the Guadalquivir on foot and on horseback, awaiting the arrival of the fleets coming from the Indies. That hyperactivity had been caused by a royal order naming Espinosa as inspector of the armada, in which the king notified him that "we are informed that the warships and frigates of our Royal Armada . . . of which Don Cristóbal de Eraso is our captain general, were so loaded with merchandise, belonging to the said general and his sons, as well as other persons, that, having been presented with some occasions to fight with enemy vessels, not only could they not do it, but they were at risk of receiving much damage."[87]

Slowly the various ships of the armada began to appear, many of which were under the command of relatives of Don Cristóbal de Eraso. Also arriving in the expedition was Don Diego Maldonado, who had sailed as general on the last convoy of merchant ships sent to Tierra Firme. One of the last ships to arrive was the galleass *San Cristóbal*, where the captain general himself flew his insignia. The inspectors of the House of Trade made the crewmen and passengers declare all the objects they had brought without registration, and many of them, frightened by the deployment of police, were taking out jewels, strips of gold, silver ingots, and purses filled with coins. The defrauders represented all sorts and conditions of humanity, from simple trumpeters in the armada to ensigns, pilots, and masters. Even various of the beatific religious on board, who traveled as passengers, did not deprive themselves of bringing their little

The Ship as a Place of Work

sack of coins or their strips of gold sewn to their clothing. We may wish to believe that these good friars were going to employ their riches for the benefit of their religious order, but, after all, they had taken a vow of poverty!

When the voluntary declarations ended, the inspectors went straight to the personal sea chests of the crewmen and looked into the storerooms and holds of the ships. Then it was as if the depths of each ship spewed forth fantastic fountains of silver. Under the sacks of biscuit, scrambled with the black powder, placed inside the ballast, or hidden in the interior of water and wine barrels, they discovered and began to take out ingots and round plates of silver, coins, and jewels. From the belongings of the general of the Tierra Firme fleet, Don Diego Maldonado, they confiscated jewels worth 16,000 ducats, but much more productive was the inspection carried out on Captain General Don Cristóbal de Eraso, his children, and relatives. If we accept completely the enormous judicial record of the inspection, which occupies eleven full bundles in the Archive of the Indies, Don Cristóbal de Eraso transported more than 150,000 ducats worth of contraband.[88] It is difficult to know the exact sum, but we certainly can document that the captain general personally carried hidden in his cabin various small sacks of coins with a value of around 8,000 ducats. These were the "sacks of the general" that appear among diverse lists detailing the defrauders of the king's treasury and which were found hidden in such a manner that they left no doubt about Don Cristóbal's intention to defraud.

> This said day [November 17, 1579], the said sir judges having issued many warnings and proclamations for individuals to declare the items that they brought without registration, and not having anyone else who wanted to declare . . . we broke a water jug that was in the chamber at the rear of the ship where General Don Cristóbal de Eraso had traveled, which was locked with a key, and inside of it, in the said water, were found six large sacks with reales in them, which were put under guard.[89]

There is not the least doubt, then, that the great mariners of the sixteenth century engaged in contraband trafficking and brought their galleons filled with silver derived from private business dealings. Nonetheless, the most surprising thing of all is that a king such as Philip II, who was so strict in many respects, was content with punishing this conduct with relatively small fines. Even Pedro Menéndez de Avilés, as well as Cristóbal de Eraso, recovered royal favor and the command of other armadas. Thus, Menéndez de Avilés was put in charge, after his jailing, of destroying the French settlements in Florida, a task that he did with uncommon efficacy. Eraso, for his part, also after suffering a legal prosecution for engaging in contraband, was named second-in-command to Don Álvaro de Bazán, and the two of them obtained the celebrated victory in the Azores in 1581 against a Franco-British armada.[90]

There is no doubt that the king had no choice but to treat as small sins the economic transgressions of men who, when the moment came to fight, threw themselves into it body and soul and with notable success. And this not only happened with figures as well known as Pedro Menéndez de Avilés or Cristóbal de Eraso. Some pages back we related the accusations against General Francisco de Luján and his admiral Rodrigo de Vargas for accepting bribes. Luján was the mariner who, in 1568 in the port of Veracruz, had inflicted a crushing defeat on John Hawkins and Francis Drake, forcing them to withdraw, leaving the English flagship in Spanish hands.[91] Admiral Vargas, for his part, served under Don Álvaro de Bazán in the Battle of the Azores, and his heroic service merited a eulogizing letter of recommendation to the king from Bazán, who considered him appropriate to command any fleet.[92]

Much has been written blaming corruption as one of the fundamental causes of Spanish decadence. Nonetheless, the deeds of these mariners seem to teach us that, although there were important instances of corruption in the gilded splendor of the sixteenth century, Spanish power continued to be a force in the world. Of course, everything is a question of degree, but I believe that one perhaps ought to start considering these types of phenomena more as symptoms than as determining causes of profound historical changes.

Finally, in favor of the defrauders of the royal treasury, one should say that the state favored many of these activities, since its constant economic difficulties led it to rely on the private patrimonies of its generals and admirals. We have already seen that many of them were proprietors of the ships that served in royal armadas. Others found themselves obliged to advance the payments to the crews under their command from their own purses. It is no wonder that a certain confusion arose between public and private money and that many commanders of the fleets thought that their business dealings were no more than the collection of old debts that the crown had contracted with them. The justifications that Don Cristóbal de Eraso gave for the accusations of contraband are representative of this manner of thinking. He was certainly guilty of favoring his own enrichment and that of his relatives, but it was also evident that his whole family were in the king's service, and many of them ended up losing their lives in the bargain. That is why, when he was accused of filling his flagship with bars of silver and gold, Eraso answered: "The real bars of gold that I brought on this last voyage from the Indies, of which Your Majesty put me in command, were the most valuable items I had in my lineage: the bones of Don Alonso de Eraso, my eldest son, admiral for Your Majesty in this armada under my command, and the bones of Don Gonzalo de Eraso, my nephew, the son of my brother Don Miguel de Eraso."[93]

Don Cristóbal de Eraso thus reminded the monarch that if on one side of the scale with which he was being judged were put the unregistered gold bars,

The Ship as a Place of Work

then on the other one had to place the bones of his firstborn son, who died in America in service to the king. How much were the bones of a firstborn son worth? A complex question to ponder, but Philip II, who also suffered because of the loss of his eldest son, ought to have understood and pardoned his captain general. Don Cristóbal de Eraso showed with his defense that he was of equal stature to another well-known military man. I refer to Gonzalo Fernández de Córdoba, who also was in the habit of squaring his accounts by adding values that were difficult to quantify. Where these two personages were equal was in their dialectic and not in its efficacy, since, whereas Fernández de Córdoba, "The Great Captain," used the corpses of his enemies to argue in his favor, Cristóbal de Eraso was obliged to resort to those of his own family.

The Economic Stature of the Men of the Sea
The Buying Power of Mariners

During the sixteenth century, the lowest salaries in the Carrera de Indias were earned on warships. Royal functionaries were accustomed to using the full coercive powers of the state to fill out the crews, whereas private shipowners compensated for shortages by offering better pay. The more strongly military the character of an expedition, the lower the pay. Thus, until 1578, the sailors who served on the *capitanas* and *almirantas*, the first and second ships in a fleet (normally merchant ships leased and heavily armed, which accompanied convoys for the whole voyage), earned a ducat more per month than their counterparts on the Guard Squadron of the Carrera de Indias, a squadron with an exclusively military character, formed principally by ships that were built for warfare.[94]

Table 3.2 summarizes the evolution of salaries for sailors on armadas and compares them with those of other workers in different regions of Spain. This is expressed in *jornales*, that is, daily wages, and in the case of the sailors the monetary value of the daily rations has been incorporated.[95] The lowest salaries earned by the sailors on armadas in the first third of the sixteenth century were on the order of 750 maravedís per month, which is 25 maravedís per day, to which 10 maravedís would be added for rations. From the beginning of the last third of the century, the salary stabilized at 1,500 maravedís per month (50 maravedís per day). The rations were valued at 34 maravedís daily in 1566 and had risen to 50 maravedís in 1600.

Only the salaries of the sailors are included in the table, but from them we can deduce those of the other men of the sea. The value of a daily ration was always the same for all, from the page to the boatswain. Regarding the payment in money, the pages earned half what a sailor earned, and the apprentices earned two-thirds what a sailor earned. The gunners, by contrast, earned one-quarter more than the sailors, and the officers, leaving aside the pilot and the master, ordinarily earned one and two-thirds more than a sailor.

Sailors raising an anchor with the help of the ship's boat. Tapestries of the conquest of Tunis. Reales Alcázares, Seville.

Upon leaving for the Indies, the sailors received several months' wages in advance. Engraving by Georg Hoefnagel, *Civitates Orbis Terrarum* (1599).

A Spanish fleet in the first half of the sixteenth century. Tapestries of the conquest of Tunis. Reales Alcázares, Seville.

Portrait of Don Álvaro
de Bazán, Marquis
of Santa Cruz. Museo
Naval, Madrid.

Bars of gold from the
salvage of a Spanish
galleon, recently
auctioned by Christie's,
New York.

Two ways to enliven
life on board: drinking
and making love. Water-
color by Hans Holbein,
the Younger. Städelsches
Kunstinstitut, Frankfurt.

Spanish galleon in a
military action near
Pernambuco, Brazil, 1635.
Oil painting by Juan de
la Corte. Museo Naval,
Madrid.

The terrible torment
of the *garrucha* was a
common punishment on
ships on the Indies route.
Fresco in the church
of San Pietro in Gessate,
Milan.

English edition of the
Dutch book of naviga-
tion *Spieghel der Zeevaerdt*
(Leiden, 1584). One can
see a varied array of
nautical instruments on
the cover.

Cover of one of the
great Spanish nautical
treatises of the sixteenth
century, Pedro de
Medina's *Regimiento de
navegación* (Seville, 1561).
Biblioteca del Palacio
Real de Madrid.

Men of the sea believed
in the ghostly apparitions
of saints-protectors.
Oil painting by Giovanni
di Paolo, in the collection
of the Museum of Art,
Philadelphia.

The life of a man of
the sea was at the mercy
of the unleashed forces
of Nature. Anonymous
Flemish painting of the
sixteenth century, detail.

3.2 Comparison of Daily Wages (in maravedís)

	Armada Sailors (wages + rations)	Carpenters, Caulkers and Masons in Seville	Day Laborers in Castile
1500–33	35–45	55–85	22–35
1534–66	45–65	85–204	35–68
1567–1600	65–100	204–306	68–85

Comparing the salary of a sailor with that of a specialized worker in Seville shows that the latter were much better paid and that the difference in salary was growing over the course of the sixteenth century. At the end of the century, a river carpenter who worked on repairing ships in the Guadalquivir earned three times more than a sailor. Clearly this artisan would not have worked every day of the year, but neither did the sailors, who only received pay for the eight or nine months that expeditions to the Indies lasted.

In the sixteenth century, when prices in Andalusia quintupled, sailors' salaries only tripled, which indicates that at the end of the century their buying power was much lower than at the beginning. Naturally, no worker with a certain level of specialization was tempted to sign up as a sailor, unless he intended to use the job to emigrate illegally to the New World. Perhaps life at sea was not economically profitable, even for the unskilled workers of Seville, since the city had one of the highest salary levels in Spain.

Only the day laborers from the interior of Castile earned salaries lower than those of sailors. One can imagine that many of the emigrants who came down from the central plains, attracted by the riches of the Andalusian metropolis, ended up enrolling on ships in the armadas if they did not quickly find good jobs in the city. Even so, the salaries of day laborers grew more rapidly than those of sailors, and in midcentury they momentarily came to equal them, only to fall behind again after a significant rise in maritime wages authorized by the king.

Now then, what could a sailor buy with a salary between twenty-five and fifty maravedís a day? We know of an interesting list of prices extracted from the archives of notarial protocols, corresponding to the expenses realized between 1544 and 1545 by the Sevillian canon Juan de Herrera, during the illness that ended up sending him to the grave.[96] In those days, sailors' wages had fallen to their lowest levels in the whole century. For example, on the carrack *La María*, sent in 1543 to pursue French corsairs, sailors earned twenty-five maravedís per day, plus rations.[97] Table 3.3 presents the quantity of food that could be bought with an armada sailor's daily wage of twenty-five maravedís.

While he was on board, the sailor received his daily ration of provisions,

The Ship as a Place of Work

3.3 Buying Power of the Daily Wage of an Armada Sailor, 1543–1545

Product	Price in Maravedís	Quantity Acquired with a Day's Wages
1 kilogram veal	30.43	822 grams
1 kilogram beef	22.82	1 kilogram and 96 grams
1 kilogram pork	30.43	822 grams
1 kilogram beef tripes	15.21	1 kilogram and 644 grams
1 chicken	20	1¼ chickens
1 partridge	25	1 partridge
1 dozen eggs	24	1 dozen eggs
1 kilogram fish (cod?)	24.7–28.26	885 grams–1 kilogram
1 kilogram flounder	21.7	1 kilogram and 152 grams
1 kilogram *pargo* (red snapper)	16.3	1 kilogram and 534 grams
1 kilogram sea-bream	18.47	1 kilogram and 354 grams
100 sardines	7–25	100–357 sardines
10 loaves of bread	25	10 loaves of bread
1 liter milk	5	5 liters milk
1 kilogram sugar	73.9–95.6	261–338 grams
1 liter cooking oil	14–16	1.6–1.8 liters
1 head of lettuce	1–2	12.5–25 heads of lettuce
1 squash	1–2	12.5–25 squash
1 kilogram apples	10.86–26	1–2.3 kilograms
1 kilogram pears	21.7	1 kilogram and 152 grams
1 melon	2–6	4–12 melons
1 kilogram grapes	2.17–3.2	7.8–11.5 kilograms
1 kilogram pear preserves	73.9–110.86	225–338 grams
1 kilogram marzipan	69.56	359 grams
1 small box quince preserves	30–38	658–833 grams
1 liter white wine	6	4.2 liters
1 liter red wine	10	2.5 liters
1 liter sweet wine	8	3.1 liters
1 liter distilled spirits	40–50	0.5–0.6 liters
1 kilogram charcoal	3.2–6.5	3.8–7.8 kilograms
1 kilogram soap	13–18.4	1.4–1.9 kilograms

and he could save his pay completely if he did not dedicate himself to wagering it in gaming with his companions. If he was a bachelor and worked for eight or nine months each year (which was the normal duration of a voyage to the Indies), during the winter he could eat his fill. However, if he had to maintain a family or did not manage to enlist in a continuous manner, his savings were not going to last long. As we can see from the data in table 3.3, a family of four or five members, who also needed to clothe themselves and pay for housing, would be able to eat only bread and water if the daily earning were twenty-five maravedís a day. A single person, on the other hand, could eat a balanced diet, thanks to the cheapness of certain fruits, vegetables, and fish. He would even have access to the good local wines that not only provided food value but also provided a certain glow and helped to cushion life's displeasures. Meat continued being prohibitively expensive and was destined only for the tables of the rich. The poor had to content themselves, as in much else, with eating the refuse from slaughtered beasts, fundamentally the tripes, which popular cookery had to turn into palatable food. Nor were sweets accessible to a sailor, since sugar, an essential component of such delicacies, was a very scarce commodity that had not yet lost its initial designation as a medicine for the sick and a gastronomic privilege for the powerful.

A sailor could not let himself fall ill, because medical treatment was almost as high in price as it was ineffective. The care received by the Sevillian canon who serves as a point of reference for us cost 2,872 maravedís, equal to almost four-months' salary for a sailor. Table 3.4 provides some details.

The clothing that covered the sailors' nakedness immediately marked them as members of the least-favored groups economically, since their salaries did not allow them—far from it—to wear the rich clothes of a gentleman. In the second great Spanish expedition to the Moluccas, led by Commander Loaisa in 1526, the majority of the superior officers perished. One of them was the royal accountant Iñigo Cortés Perea, whose clothes, which suited the dignity of his office, were auctioned on board, according to the custom of the men of the sea. The result of the auction shows us that the apparel, constituting a complete wardrobe suitable for an hidalgo, sold for 14,984 maravedís.[98] Perhaps, on such a long expedition, the price of the clothing was overvalued, but the salaries on expeditions to the Far East were also much higher than normal. The sailors on Loaisa's expedition earned 1,125 maravedís a month (13,500 a year), which meant that the price of a gentleman's wardrobe, sword included, was equivalent to something more than a year's salary for a sailor (see table 3.5).

Armada sailors were a minority of the total men of the sea who served in the Carrera de Indias. On the hundreds of merchant ships that crossed the ocean, the salaries were higher, but at the cost of running a certain risk. As we know, the salaries that private shipowners paid consisted, besides the rations,

Medicines and Services	Price in Maravedís	Days of a Sailor's Work to Pay for It
1 ounce (28.75 grams) salve	25	1.0
4 ounces medicinal oils	24	1.0
1 ounce "manus cristi" tablets	51	2.0
1 liter orange flower water	68	2.7
Powders made of sandalwood, emeralds, and coral for strengthening broths	714	28.6
1 doctor's visit	136	5.4
1 nurse's visit	204	8.2
1 purge	340	13.6
Help to urinate	204	8.2
Extract a molar	34	1.4
Shave	34	1.4
1 mass said in the house	34	1.4
Testament and powers of attorney by notary	822	32.9

(118)

in a share of the profits from the freight charges or in a fixed quantity of the income from the voyage. In both cases the sailor could face disagreeable surprises: either the profits from the freight charges were not very great, or delays in the expeditions lengthened the voyage without augmenting the fixed salary agreed upon beforehand. Luckily for the men of the sea, the Spanish fleet system functioned with a notable regularity in the sixteenth century, and the volume of business steadily increased. For these reasons, we can understand why the general of the Guard Squadron of the Carrera, our old acquaintance Cristóbal de Eraso, advised the king in 1576 to raise the salaries paid on warships, since it was practically impossible to find men who would serve voluntarily in the armadas.[99]

Making a reliable estimate of the salary level of merchant mariners is much more complicated, since salaries varied from ship to ship according to the value of the freight charges or the content of the accords signed before departure, in which the wage was fixed as a function of the law of supply and demand for manual labor. As a general rule, one can say that those sailing "with the value of the freight" on large ships could earn more money, since there were fewer sailors per tonelada. For those enlisting at "so much fixed," the salary varied according to whether the contract was made in Spain or in America. In the Indies, manual labor by white workers with a certain degree of specialization was very scarce, and for that reason very expensive. Also, because a large part of the

3.5 The Cost of Dressing Like a Gentleman

Type of Article	Price in Maravedís	Days of a Sailor's Work to Pay for It
Stockings	272	7.3
Shoes	153	4.1
Shirt	510	13.7
Waistcoat	1,870	50.5
Loose coat	4,688	126.6
Cloak	4,500	121.6
Cap	1,122	30.3
Sword	1,870	50.5
Total	14,985	404.6

Note: Figures represent prices at auction for the belongings of Iñigo Cortés, accountant on Loaisa's expedition, August 3, 1526.

3.6 Salaries on Merchant Ships, Last Third of the Sixteenth Century

Destination	Spain to America to Spain	America to Spain Only
New Spain	50–60 ducats (18,750–22,500 maravedís)	25–65 ducats (9,375–24,375 maravedís)
Tierra Firme	50–104 ducats (18,750–39,000 maravedís)	40–60 ducats (15,000–22,500 maravedís)

Note: Salaries are based on freightage and for a fixed sum and do not include the value of the daily food ration.

crews deserted in America, the masters were obliged to contract with sailors for very high prices. There were cases in which they paid as much for a return trip to Spain as for a round-trip voyage.

Table 3.6 presents a summary of the range for wages of merchant mariners in the last third of the sixteenth century. As in the case of the armada sailors, these quantities can also be used to calculate the salaries of pages and apprentices (who earned half and two-thirds of a sailor's wage, respectively), and of the officers (who received, with the exception of pilots and masters, twice that of a sailor).[100]

The table shows the maximum and minimum values for the salaries, although in general terms we could say that the standard wage for a transoceanic round-trip voyage hovered around sixty ducats, or 22,500 maravedís. As the average voyage lasted eight months, a sailor on a merchant ship earned some 2,800 maravedís per month, compared to the 1,500 maravedís (four ducats) that his comrades on armadas earned, that is to say, 86.7 percent more.

Nonetheless, there were exceptional situations in which the crews of merchant ships earned salary payments that were much higher. The voyages to Tierra Firme paid somewhat better, possibly because abundant silver from the rich Peruvian mines had made wages rise. To be precise, the highest salary that I have been able to discover was paid to the sailor Andrés Sánchez, who sailed to Tierra Firme in 1581 on the merchant ship *Trinidad* and received somewhat more than 104 ducats. I do not know exactly how many months the ship took to go and return, but if the trip had an average duration, Andrés Sánchez would have earned thirteen ducats a month, that is to say, three and a quarter times more than if he had sailed on a warship.[101] One could also earn high wages when the enlistment took place in an American port. For example, the sailor Pedro Ortiz signed up in 1597 to go from San Juan de Ulúa to Seville for seventy-five ducats. Taking into account that this trip only lasted between four and five months, Pedro Ortiz could have earned fourteen and a half ducats a month.[102]

Clearly, there were also situations in which the advantages of a small but secure salary were preferable to a higher but riskier salary, although those situations were less numerous. The apprentice Gonzalo Pérez must have thought about this when the voyage he had contracted for in 1589 to go to Tierra Firme took three years in returning, because of various mishaps. In this same period, had he been a sailor on an armada, the delay would not have affected the three ducats that he earned a month, and at the end of the time he would have collected 108 ducats.[103]

Now then, we might ask if the fifty or sixty ducats a year, which merchant mariners earned on average during the last quarter of the century, was sufficient to maintain a family with ease. The great historian Fernand Braudel wrote that, for the whole of the Mediterranean world during the reign of Philip II, "for the active members of the population . . . an income below 20 ducats a year is miserable; from 20 to 40 ducats, small; and from 40 to 150 ducats, reasonable."[104] Following this classification, the wages of mariners would fall between the categories of small and reasonable. This same author mentioned that, in the interior of Castile between 1576 and 1578, the average income for a family was some forty-four ducats.[105]

Clearly, to have an income slightly above the statistical average did not mean that one could enjoy an existence filled with comfort; this is certainly true in our time, and it was much more so in the sixteenth century, when the average living conditions were appalling. If we add to this the fact that Seville, where a goodly part of the crews of the Indies fleets lived, was one of the most expensive cities in the world, we will understand that the life of sailors could not have been surrounded with comforts. Moreover, if a sailor had a wife and five children, as was the case with Pedro Rabí, who died in San Juan de Ulúa in 1562, it is no wonder that he left only debts in his testament, and his only estate was the money that remained to be collected for his wages.[106]

In general, the testaments that we have from sailors are dramatic expressions of poverty, because practically the only goods that they possessed were wages and some few articles of clothing that was of low quality and worn out from use. A document from the Archive of the Indies summarizes the value of goods left by 413 crewmen who died during voyages between 1569 and 1576. In all, the average value per person was 59.7 ducats, and the largest part of this quantity came from the wages that remained to be collected.[107] I have not been able to find evidence of landed property in any of the sailors' testaments, and the value of the personal objects, when they had any value, generally did not surpass 10 ducats.[108]

(121)

Many testaments of sailors consist of a single sheet of paper on which, in a very simple manner, the man of the sea recorded his small debts and asked that his salary and his few personal effects be sent to his family. A sailor from Galicia might leave "a bagpipe, some knives, and some short stockings."[109] Another was worried about recovering some very humble articles of clothing that he had loaned to a comrade: "Ask from whoever has the sea chest of Frasquito, the page who died, a change of dirty clothes and some clean trousers."[110] In any case, the destiny of these few personal effects was to be auctioned off among the rest of the crew: "Pedro de Mazueco, sailor on the said galleon *Santiago el Menor*, native of the port of Santoña. He died in Cartagena [de Indias] on the first of September, and his goods, so that they would not rot, were sold on the galleon on credit, for the accounts of which, ask the master."[111] They must have been goods of inferior quality if they were susceptible to rotting, and the dead man's companions must have had few economic resources if they had to buy them on credit!

Some historians have pointed out that, despite the general poverty of the men of the sea, their occupation offered some opportunities to better their economic position.[112] At least a sailor always had more hope of rising in the ranks than a peasant attached to the land, and he could supplement his salary with small licit or illicit business deals. To become a guardián was easy. To become a boatswain was not too complicated. With much effort and a bit of luck, he could become a pilot. A pilot who saved some of his income, although this was very difficult to do, could enter into the sparse group of people who possessed and administered capital. However, if the goddess of fortune did not cooperate, the destiny of a man of the sea could be very sad. The diary of a British sailor described the situation of someone who had been surprised by old age without rising through the ranks: "Always in need and enduring all manner of misery and hardship, going with many a hungry belly and wet back, and being always called —old dog—, and —old rogue—, and —son of a whore—, and such like terms, which is a common use among seamen, and that would be a great grief for an aged man."[113]

The Difficult Leap toward Middling Status: Pilots and Masters

(122) Pilots on the high seas, capable of guiding ships through immense oceanic spaces, had an advantage that they learned to use to their benefit. The techniques of transoceanic navigation were relatively recent and were not employed effectively before the fifteenth century. On the other hand, the knowledge that pilots possessed was undergoing an intense process of improvement. Guiding a great oceangoing ship was ceasing to be an activity based solely on experience and was adapting to the much more complex techniques of celestial navigation. The knowledge of sailors or boatswains had not changed much between the thirteenth and the sixteenth centuries, but the same thing could not be said of pilots; these highly qualified specialists knew they were increasingly indispensable, and they made that fact pay. Over the course of the sixteenth century, people still joked about the lack of certainty in the pilots' calculations, but the dexterity and precision of those calculations could only increase, and that was a trump card that they knew how to play skillfully.

At the start of the sixteenth century, not even the best pilots contracted by the House of Trade, which included the pilot major himself, received salaries that distinguished them economically from the most prosperous artisans in the city. In the first decades of the century, Amerigo Vespucci, the first pilot major, earned 75,000 maravedís a year (200 ducats; 1 ducat is the equivalent of 375 maravedís), but when Sebastian Cabot succeeded him, the salary had been reduced to 50,000 maravedís a year. The rest of the pilots contracted by the House of Trade earned between 20,000 and 40,000 maravedís a year.[114]

A salary of fifty thousand maravedís a year had been promised to the pilot Miguel de Rodas as a reward for being one of the few survivors of Magellan's expedition; he returned with Elcano on the nao *Victoria*. From his testament we know that his financial situation was not very secure, among other things because the crown had not paid him regularly, and he had been obliged to spend his wife's dowry of twenty-five thousand maravedís.[115] The value of the dowry can serve to measure the prosperity of a prominent pilot in the first half of the sixteenth century. According to the work of Ruth Pike, the sum that artisans of Seville provided for their daughters' dowries ranged between twenty thousand and eighty thousand maravedís; to provide less than twenty thousand maravedís meant brushing up against the poverty line, and there were rich businessmen in midcentury who provided dowries for their daughters of four hundred thousand maravedís.[116]

But the pilots were determined to escape from circumstances that placed them at the level of modest artisans. The progression of their salaries was swifter than that of other crewmen, and the crown even found it necessary to set a ceiling on their wages. Ordinances promulgated in 1536 stated that one could collect between 115 and 130 ducats (43,125 to 48,750 maravedís) for directing a fleet to Tierra Firme or New Spain.[117] In that same epoch, the magistrates of the appeals court in Seville earned 400 ducats a year.[118] The pilots of the Carrera de Indias protested and explained that they were not rich persons. Sebastian Cabot, as pilot major, reported that "in every occupation there are rich men, but among pilots there is no one who is rich."[119] For his part, the cosmographer Diego Gutiérrez stated that pilots lived from day to day and that to suffer financial reverses or illness during a voyage could lead to ruin:

> When a pilot is delayed on his voyage or some illness strikes him, he spends all that he earns, because most of the pilots are married and they have a house and a wife and children and family, and it takes everything they earn to provide for them; when they are delayed, they have expenses here and there and they spend everything they earn, especially when some illness strikes them, which is a very common thing; and this witness knows most of the Indies pilots, and there is none of them who is rich from his pilot's salary, and they can do no more than live day to day on it.[120]

But, despite their complaints, the pilots recognized that the ordinance had never been obeyed and that their salaries were much higher than those fixed by the king. In the second half of the century, the wages of pilots continued growing, and remunerations between three hundred and four hundred ducats for a round-trip voyage were completely normal in the Carrera de Indias.[121] It is difficult to say if these salaries permitted a pilot to save, since the rise in prices throughout the century would have used up an important part of the increment in their salaries. Nonetheless, there were many pilots who became owners of small dispatch boats or who were part owners of larger ships. Moreover, true opportunity could arrive for them if they acceded to the position of master.

During the course of a voyage carried out by the Tierra Firme fleet in 1576, the master of the nao *San Juan Bautista* died. The pilot of the ship, Cristóbal Sánchez, saw his opportunity to occupy the vacant post, and in order to secure it he had no qualms about bribing the general of the armada with a bar of silver worth 257 pesos (186.9 ducats).[122] The size of the bribe shows the worth that he attached to becoming a ship's master. Could the promotion have meant a rise in salary? In reality, that was not the main desideratum. Masters earned salaries similar to those of pilots, but, in addition, they had access to a much

The Ship as a Place of Work

more attractive source of income. A master was the administrator of all the economic resources on board the ship, and that gave him extra income, difficult to quantify but much more appealing than the collection of a simple salary. Whoever acceded to the charge of master crossed the frontier that separated salaried workers from those who handled and administered capital; in that sense, they found themselves in an unsurpassed position to turn themselves into capitalists.

Clearly, there were many sorts of masters. Some were in charge of the administration of ships smaller than one hundred toneladas, and others directed great galleons of close to a thousand toneladas. Some never succeeded in enriching themselves, because success depended fundamentally on ability, luck, and the scruples of each master. Thus, there were cases of masters such as the captain Pedro de Mata, who, upon dying in Cartagena de Indias in 1562, left a small fortune calculated at some five thousand ducats.[123] In contrast, there were examples such as that of Juan de la Vega, whom the University of Seafarers accepted as a brother in 1598, exempting him from paying the entrance fee because of his poverty and giving him alms of twenty ducats so that he could buy the navigational instruments necessary to practice his profession.[124]

The truly interesting thing about the office of master was that it provided the opportunity to prosper and to enter into the middling economic level of society, although, naturally, not everyone knew how to take advantage of the occasion. As Ralph Davis wrote: "The advance from chief mate to master of a ship effected for the individual concerned a transformation in status and a trebling of income and opened the way to much greater prizes. It took the lucky individual firmly into the middle class and offered him the possibility of saving for old age or of turning into a merchant; it put a fortunate few on the road to real wealth."[125]

The Richest Men: The "Ship Lords"

Shipowners were members of the most powerful economic groups in society. Ships were expensive, so much so that ownership was frequently shared among a considerable number of partners. That is why the large shipowners who possessed several vessels could clearly consider themselves wealthy individuals.

In the first decades of the sixteenth century a caravel of between sixty and seventy toneles cost around five hundred ducats.[126] A nao of something more than one hundred toneles, which was the most common, was worth between six hundred and seven hundred ducats.[127] But as time went on, the average size and price of ships rose notably. During the last quarter of the century, a ship of 140 toneladas could cost fourteen hundred ducats, and large ships could cost between seven thousand and ten thousand ducats.[128]

These quantities of money supposed authentic fortunes that were within the reach of very few. Only men such as Andrés de Paz or Cristóbal de Monte Bernardo, who confessed to having personal wealth between thirty thousand and forty thousand ducats, could be the exclusive owners of a large ship, and the common practice was to share the risk with a colleague, to avoid investing such a high percentage of one's fortune in a single enterprise.[129]

The shipping business could be very productive, but it also demanded increasing investments and enormous risks. These consisted not only in facing enemy cannons or the unleashed forces of nature; on many occasions, the only thing unleashed was the crown's urgent need for ships in the royal armadas, and the best galleons were embargoed to carry out escort missions. The king paid a rental fee per tonelada, but the fee grew very slowly over the century, while the costs of salaries and of maintenance for the ships were unstoppable due to strong inflationary pressures.

That happened, for example, to the Sevillian shipowner Cosme Buitrón. He had bought the galleon *Los Tres Reyes*, of six hundred toneladas, for 7,000 ducats; he intended to send it as a merchant ship in the fleet of 1557, but it was requisitioned by the king. According to Buitrón, if the ship had been loaded with merchandise, the freight charges would have generated 14,500 ducats. If we discount the salaries of the crew, the supplies, and the cost of careening and getting the ship in shape, he still would have cleared some 6,000 ducats. By contrast, as the king paid something less than half a ducat per tonelada per month, the rental of his galleon for a year only earned him some 3,250 ducats.[130]

As we see by the data Buitrón provided, a voyage to the Indies that ended happily, and with the ship fully laden, could almost amortize the cost of the ship, and the next voyage involved nothing but net profits. Nonetheless, completing two trips to America without encountering some type of misfortune was not simple, and the likelihood of misfortune is what caused the high risks run by the great shipowners. The already mentioned Andrés de Paz had to suffer in his own flesh, almost more than in his doubloons, from the requisitioning of his galleass *San Cristóbal*. He had bought the ship from the king himself for seventy-seven hundred ducats, a higher price than normal given the condition of the ship, which had just returned from an expedition to the Strait of Magellan. Nonetheless, the shipowner decided to make the purchase, since he had obtained assurances that he could travel to the Indies without the ship being embargoed. Preparations for the Great Armada to invade England made the authorities forget this promise, and Don Álvaro de Bazán requisitioned the ship in 1587. But the misfortunes did not end there: the following year the galleass was lost in Lisbon in an accident. That set of events was ruinous for one great Sevillian shipowner, and the lawsuit he filed against the crown to recover his damages was still going on in 1617.[131]

The Ship as a Place of Work

The most important ship lords were, of course, rich individuals, but compared with the large merchants specializing in transatlantic trade, their fortunes appear modest. The most powerful and influential members of the Consulate of Indies Shippers had fortunes between two hundred thousand and four hundred thousand ducats, and those of lesser importance had between one hundred thousand and two hundred thousand ducats.[132] For that reason, the thirty thousand or forty thousand ducats of an Andrés de Paz placed him at the end of the line among the powerful members of the consulate. In other words, the richest of the shipowners could only compare with the least favored of the great merchants of the Carrera de Indias.

Gentlemen Who Were Not Always Powerful: Generals and Admirals
of Armadas and Merchant Fleets

The supreme military commanders of the Carrera de Indias always received the highest salaries, though this did not mean that they were the richest men in the Carrera. As we know, to make a fortune through a fixed wage, however high it was, was impossible. To become rich they had to dedicate themselves to buying and selling or let themselves be bribed, but naturally the latter was not included in the pay that they officially received.

Among the highest wages paid in the first half of the century, the most prominent were the eight ducats a day (2,920 per year) paid to the commander García Jofre de Loaisa, who in 1526 led the second great Spanish armada sent to the Moluccas. From the middle of the century, a general of a fleet earned four ducats a day (1,460 per year), and an admiral earned half that. These salaries remained unchanged until the end of the century, when the generals of fleets began to earn two hundred ducats a month (2,400 a year).[133]

The absolute military command of the seas in the Indies fell to the general of the Guard Squadron of the Carrera de Indias. Pedro Menéndez de Avilés, who was the first to hold this post, earned two thousand ducats a year in 1566. Don Cristóbal de Eraso, who succeeded him in the charge in 1576, made his connections at court pay and collected six thousand ducats a year. That, as we know, did not stop him from actively dedicating himself to contraband trade, and the king must have thought that, since the generals busied themselves with looking for ways to increment their bonuses, their official salary ought to be reduced. At the end of the century, the general of the Guard Squadron earned three thousand ducats. The admirals of this same force were not so lucky and collected only as much as the admirals of the merchant fleets, that is, two ducats a day.[134]

These wages, if we compare them with what a sailor earned, and even a pilot, can seem very high, but those who received them considered them entirely inadequate. When a general or an admiral was surprised in flagrante delicto with contraband, his excuses were generally always of the same type: the honor of fighting for the king, the dignity of the charge, and the honor of their persons, obliged them to make up from their own purse for the chronic delays of the public treasury. On many occasions, they had to advance money to pay the crews or to repair ships that were sometimes also owned by them. Moreover, they felt obliged to support groups of friends and relatives who came to serve the king under their protection and for whom they felt responsible according to old codes of seigneurial fidelity. All of this caused them extraordinary expenses that were not compensated by their official wages.   (127)

Pedro Menéndez de Avilés, upon being tried in 1563, defended himself by saying that, because of entering the king's service, bringing two galleons of his own with him, and paying a great amount for his entourage out of his own pocket, his private fortunes had been seriously affected, forcing him to sell a good part of the landed estates inherited from his parents. One of the questions posed to the witnesses presented in his defense was worded thus:

> If they know that the said general Pedro Menéndez, after leaving on the said voyage and the Carrera de Indias . . . had now less wealth and is poorer than when he began, because of bringing his ships and armament in good condition, and bringing top-notch men who were very adept to serve His Majesty as he pleased, and he has spent his salary and the fees for his ships . . . and has sold his belongings; and thus it is notorious . . . that he has much less wealth than when he began the said voyage.[135]

Don Antonio de Osorio, general of the Tierra Firme fleet of 1584, who wanted to be known as an honorable man and who at least was sincere, wrote in relating his merits and services that, because he had not brought contraband merchandise to sell and had relied only upon his wages of four ducats a day, he had become indebted to the sum of more than two thousand ducats.[136]

It is very likely that the generals exaggerated their economic afflictions, but the truth is that many of them, after having served at sea for some years, preferred to retire to other posts, possibly more lucrative and surely more tranquil. I have uncovered various cases of experienced mariners who ended up asking the king to name them to a military or municipal post in the Indies. Thus, for example, the aforementioned Antonio de Osorio became the king's representative *(corregidor)* in Cuzco from 1539 on.[137] Esteban de las Alas "the younger," who had served as captain of a galleon with his countryman Pedro Menéndez de Avilés and then in 1581 sailed in an armada to the Strait of Magellan, seems to have tired of the hazards of life at sea. When he petitioned the king for a new post, he at first asked to be named general of a fleet; having thought further about it, he remembered the hardships he had suffered amid the ice in the Southern Sea and scratched out his first request, substituting instead his desire for "a good governorship or a good posting as a corregidor in those parts [the Indies]."[138]

To a twentieth-century observer, the attitude of these military men who complained continually about their salaries, despite earning the best wages at sea, might seem to be simply a question of social egoism. However, one should say in their favor that an admiral who earned a salary of two ducats a day had to live with the humiliating knowledge that in the brothels of Seville, "the young prostitutes of good appearance . . . took in from four to five ducats a day."[139] We can well imagine the shamed blush that would color the honor of an hidalgo, who would surely be familiar with the going rate, when he realized that a fine whore could earn twice what he did, without having to use weapons as sharp as his Toledo sword. Nor would it be pleasing to see that the hangmen who tortured homosexuals discovered on board were paid three ducats for their minimal labors.[140] Possibly he would be consoled thinking that the offices of prostitute or hangman were certainly uncomfortable (in the second case, above all, for the "client"). If this reflection did not fully satisfy him, he might conclude that it was not possible to become rich following an honorable path, and on his next trip to the Indies he might dedicate himself to filling his ship with contraband for the return voyage.

The Ship as a Place of Life
and Death

An Oppressive Living Space

At the beginning of autumn in 1571, various crewmen of the flagship commanded by General Cristóbal de Eraso were condemned to remain for a month
"imprisoned with their feet in the stocks." Their crime, although common
enough, was considered grave in those times, since they had dared to embell-
ish their discussions with a sonorous "For the life of God and his Holy Mother." A phrase such as that, which today would seem almost a profession of profound religious faith, was considered blasphemy in the sixteenth century, above
all after Moses had written on his tablets that "to take the name of God in vain"
was a hideous sin. Those condemned denied the accusation and asked for a less
severe imprisonment with these expressive words: "Thus we say that we have
been imprisoned in the stocks on the mandate of Your Grace, for a reason that
we oppose, and if . . . someone said a blasphemy, it was not us . . . ; the prison
that the law allows for similar offenses is to be behind iron grills *[grilletes]* . . .
and not the stocks, *especially on a ship that is already jail enough by itself.*"[1]

These afflicted blasphemers thought, no doubt with reason, that being on
a ship was in itself a hard punishment. But they were not the only ones to equate
being on a ship with being imprisoned. In this, even the venerable and ener-
getic missionary friars were in agreement with the blaspheming sinners. Friar
Tomás de la Torre, who accompanied Friar Bartolomé de las Casas on a difficult sea voyage in the middle of the century, wrote: "The ship is a very confining and powerful jail from whence no one can flee, although it has no grilles
or chains, and it is so cruel that there is no difference between prisoners and
the rest, who are equally ill treated and confined."[2]

As we can see, the good friar complained not only about the confinement
but also about the fact that its democratic distribution erased any distinction
and rank. The similarity between a ship and a prison was widely recognized
and acknowledged, with some English men of the sea stating that jail possessed
certain advantages: at least in a cell one did not run the risk of drowning in the
middle of the ocean. Moreover, a man would have more physical space in jail,
and better food, and there were no notable differences regarding the honor of
the company.[3] It is perhaps difficult to agree that a man ate better in prison and
enjoyed better society there than on a ship, but at least one ought to accept as

an indisputable truth that, regarding living space, someone in jail had no reason to envy a sailor or a passenger on a ship in the Carrera de Indias.

At the beginning of the sixteenth century, the majority of ships that traveled to the Indies were small. Caravels generally had between 60 and 80 toneladas of capacity, and the naos around 100 toneladas. According to the ordinances of the House of Trade, a nao of 106 toneladas ought to have approximately the following dimensions: 18 meters of maximum length *(eslora)*, 5 meters of maximum breadth or beam *(manga)*, and 2.5 meters of depth in the hold *(puntal)*, measured from the lowest planked deck to the keel.[4]

At that time naos had a single planked deck, although certain superstructures were built above it to protect the passengers and crew from bad weather. From the mainmast to the far end of the poop deck a raised structure supported on both sides reminded the crewmen of being under a bridge; for that reason, it was known by the generic name, "the bridge." This part of the ship was also known as "the awning" *(tolda)*, in reference to the fact that some makeshift structures not long before had been simple awnings stretched between the two sides. Regional diversity provided two more names for this space. To the people from the Cantabrian coast, the well-being that obtained there reminded them of the warmth of the great hearths at home, and they called it the "chimney." The Andalusians preferred to focus on its character as the highest place on the ship, and they gave it the sonorous name of the "castle," or *alcázar*, a word of clearly Arabic roots. Above the "awning," "chimney," or "castle" could be raised another structure of much more reduced proportions, called the *toldilla*. Beneath the toldilla there was an enclosed chamber, or *camarote*, designated for the use of the highest-ranking person on board. At the prow, supported on the gunwales and extending to the foremast, another small superstructure formed the forecastle *(castillo)*.

In these reduced spaces dozens of persons were crammed together for weeks without touching land. To give an idea of the degree of crowding, two concrete examples should suffice. On the expedition directed by Pedrarías Dávila for the conquest of Castilla del Oro (today, Panama), a caravel of something more than 80 toneladas carried sixty passengers and fifteen crewmen, while a nao of 110 toneladas transported a hundred passengers and more than twenty crewmen.[5] Moreover, these cases were not exceptional, since in ordinances issued in 1534, the Council of the Indies tried to stop masters from stuffing their ships with people and limited the number of passengers to sixty for every 100 toneladas. If this was what the law mandated, what must the reality have been![6]

To better evaluate these figures, consider this: according to the dimensions for a ship of 106 toneladas, and counting as habitable space the surface of the main deck plus the tolda, toldilla, and castle, those on board enjoyed a habit-

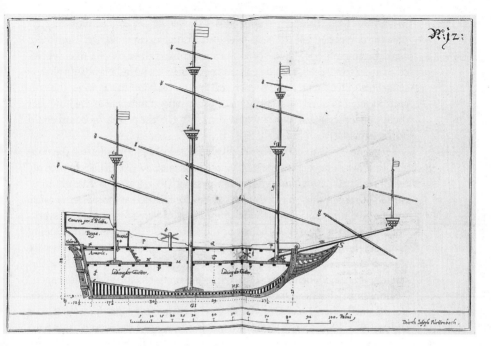

able space of between 150 and 180 square meters, that is to say, the surface area
of what we would consider a good-sized urban apartment. Into that space between 100 and 120 persons crowded together for months at a time, without using water for anything but drinking! With this fact alone, I think someone in
the twentieth century can gain a general impression of the conditions in which
his ancestors customarily traveled.

Each of the persons on board was afforded, on average, 1.5 square meters
of space. A study directed by Philippe Ariès about daily life in Europe during
the Renaissance found that in the rural milieu of France and England "a family of five or six persons had an interior living space of scarcely thirty-five square
meters."[7] What luxury that would have been for a sailor in the Carrera de

---

The Ship as a Place of Life and Death

Indias! Of course some readers will recall that peasants customarily shared their houses with their farm animals. But the sailors and passengers were also obliged to share their scarce living space with all sorts of animals, some of them carried voluntarily but most of them involuntarily.

In effect, the ships' crews faced serious competitors in the struggle to find a free space. Some competitors were inanimate objects, since boxes and chests with clothing and personal effects were customarily placed on the decks, plus the passengers' food, which could not be kept in the storerooms below deck. In addition were the nautical apparatuses stowed on the bridge, plus the capstan, the cookstove, and even the masts; all of these occupied space. Then there were the animals carried on board. A caravel of sixty-five toneles that departed in 1507 toward Hispaniola carried, besides its crew and eighty-three passengers, eighteen mares and twelve yearling calves.[8] On this voyage, the animals traveled as cargo, and surely space was arranged for them in the hold, but there were other animals from whose direct contact the people on board could not free themselves.

Passengers customarily carried live animals to slaughter during the voyage, in order to have fresh meat. The most common were chickens, which after all are small beasts, but some passengers, with foresight or simple gluttony, carried dozens of these birds. One passenger complained to the master because some of the fifty chickens he had brought aboard had been stolen.[9] If everyone had acted as he did, the ships of the Carrera de Indias, instead of being simple merchant vessels, would have been more like chicken coops with sails. Pigs were also commonly carried under the label of live provisions; one frequently finds evidence of masters' acknowledging receipt of the passengers' "various pigs," to be slaughtered during the voyage.[10] We have testimonies that these animals shared places on the deck with owners who did not want to lose sight of them, lest they fall into the hands of someone determined to have a feast at their expense. An English sailor commented that, despite the danger unleashed by a tremendous storm, no one could resist smiling at the sight of seasick pigs staggering around the decks vomiting.[11]

But along with the chickens, pigs, sheep, and goats carried as food, there were other "passengers" who had not been invited to climb on board. The mice and rats formed authentic legions, and since the cat, an animal of Oriental origins, was still fairly rare in Europe, crew members had to organize "hunting parties" to chase the rodents. On some fleets, plagues of rats developed, and eventually thousands of them were killed.[12] Then there were the insects, which infested bodies, clothing, and the chinks between the planking: cockroaches, bedbugs, and lice formed a discomfiting but abundant and loyal marine company. As one contemporary said, any crewman surely would have had more lice in his waistcoat than coins in his purse.[13] The great traveling wit

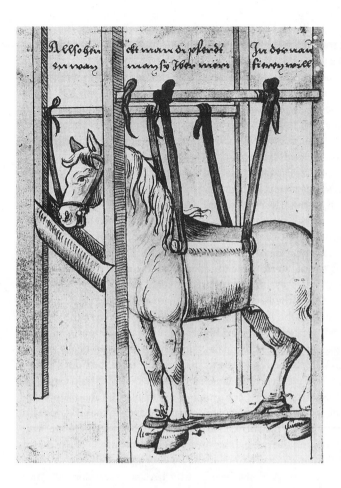

System for transporting horses on a ship. Drawing by Christoph Weiditz, 1529. Biblioteca Nacional, Madrid.

Eugenio de Salazar described, with as much humor as exaggeration, the abundance and voracity of these unwelcome traveling companions: "There are also . . . lice so large that some of them get seasick and vomit up pieces of flesh from apprentice seamen. . . . [The ship] has an enormous profusion of game birds—cockroaches—which are called "curianas" here, and a great abundance of game—rats—many of which will turn and challenge their hunters like wild boars."[14]

   In summary, adding to all the irrational animals those that were pleased to call themselves rational, traveling on a ship must have been one of the most uncomfortable and oppressive experiences in the world; that is why Miguel de Cervantes, who knew the medium well, complained about "the strange life in

The Ship as a Place of Life and Death

those floating dwellings, where most of the time the bedbugs mistreat you, the galley slaves rob you, the sailors offend you, the rats destroy you, and the motion of the sea wears you out."[15]

For the whole of the sixteenth century, ships' tonnage was increasing. At the same time, shipowners were trying to augment the usable space by adding full decks and even cargo platforms made with wooden lattices *(jaretas)* or thick braided hempen cords, which weighed less, to the highest parts of the superstructures. One document from the Archive of the Indies describes the form and interior and exterior spaces of a galleon of 550 toneladas, which was a ship of above-average size capable of being used as much for trade as for warfare.[16]

The ship was 25 meters in length overall by 9 meters in beam and 4.5 meters in depth in the hold, from the second deck to the keel. The first deck would have been located half a meter below the waterline, and beneath it would have been the majority of the cargo and the storerooms for provisions, equipment, gunpowder, and munitions. In its military version it would have carried four great cannons, two at the prow and the other two at the poop, mounted on platforms and great wheels so that the gun ports could remain above water. This artillery would be of the largest caliber on board and would be designed to pierce enemy ships at the waterline with its cannon balls. Between the first deck and the second, located 1.75 meters higher (creating a space more than sufficient for the average size of individuals of the time), a "between-decks" opened up. If the ship sailed armed for war, this space would lodge the troops and the crew, but if the ship were used as a merchantman, it would also hold cargo. The majority of the ship's artillery, consisting of ten or twelve cannons per side, traveled on the second deck, which remained partly open to the air. Above that deck were built the two half-decks: the tolda, which extended from the mainmast to the poop, and the castle, from the foremast to the prow. The platforms above the tolda and the castle were joined by a wooden gridwork, leaving a space in the middle called "the well," partly because water sluiced into it through the openings in the gridwork.

Beneath the castle, protected from inclement weather, the two cookstoves *(fogones)* of the ship were located, one on each side, built of firebricks and separated from the deck with sand in order to prevent the fire from spreading. Beneath the tolda was the capstan, and above it was the toldilla, the back of which enclosed the principal cabin on the galleon. The front part of the toldilla formed a covered space where the pilot or the captain guided the ship. In good weather, the upper part of the toldilla, which constituted the highest part of the ship, served as an observation platform for the officers. On top of the wooden gridwork and supported by the toldilla and the masts, networks of thick hempen cords might be stretched, reinforced with chains.

Thanks to the proliferation of decks, superstructures (tolda, toldilla, and castle), and networks of wood and rope, the habitable space of one of these galleons was notably increased and could reach eight hundred square meters. But the number of crewmen and passengers also increased, and the usable surface area per person was not much greater than in the cases we have already mentioned. The size of the crew of a galleon of 550 toneladas was proportionally somewhat less than that of a ship of 100 toneladas, but even so it numbered between sixty and seventy persons. If the ship were armed for war, serving as the flagship (capitana) or its second-in-command (almiranta), it had to carry the general staff and one or two companies of soldiers, which meant between 120 and 150 more men. Of course, the number of passengers ultimately determined the real conditions of habitability on board ships. As the galleons were generally the largest and best-armed ships in a fleet, passengers preferred them and stuffed them with their persons, baggage, and provisions.

With everything said thus far, it is not difficult to agree that whoever traveled on a ship in the Carrera de Indies entered into a type of hell. As in Dante's *Divine Comedy*, where a sign warned those entering hell to abandon all hope, anyone who boarded a ship knew instantly that within its confines he would have to renounce the pleasure of any type of comfort, intimacy, or hygiene. The only thing that really distinguished a ship from hell itself was that at least the people on board could eventually hope to leave.

The discomforts began with the realization that furniture was a luxury permitted only to the highest members of the ship's hierarchy. The chairs on board could be counted on the fingers of two hands. Only the pilot or the master had the right to "stand" watch seated on a large chair located on the tolda. Apart from that, inside the principal chamber there was a table and some other chairs, and that was all.

The most common article of furniture on board was the sea chest that each member of the crew carried to hold his clothes and personal effects. They were generally made of wood and capable of resisting bad weather, since, as the hold was filled with cargo and the majority of covered space at the poop was occupied by the passengers, the sea chests of the sailors were tied down on the decks or on the grillwork, in the open air. The sea chest was a multipurpose instrument; besides being a trunk, it served as table, chair, and, if it was on the large side, even as a bed. Card games were organized with the players seated on their sea chests and using the chest of a companion as a table. In the same fashion, any conversational group was formed by a chorus of crewmen resting their weary buttocks on their sea chests.

No sooner had they got under way than a new discomfort assaulted the people on board: seasickness, or *almadiamiento* (literally, "fainting-spell"), as it was called then. From this ailment, according to Escalante, almost no one escaped, not even experienced sailors: "It is very common for men to get seasick

---

every time they go back to sea, even though they be very old sailors, some more than others, according to their natural constitution."[17] Escalante went on to say that each man had a greater or lesser propensity for seasickness, according to his nature. Anyone could accept this affirmation. Nonetheless, our good mariner went on to give other explanations that were somewhat stranger, as he argued that sexual activity increased the likelihood of seasickness. According to him, "recently married men" or those who had "recently behaved as such" fell seasick like overbalanced spinning tops. Seasickness also plagued the friars who accompanied Bartolomé de las Casas when he went to take possession of his bishopric in the Indies, although the cause for the ills that these religious men suffered must have been different from those of the men singled out by Escalante:

> Soon the sea made us understand that it was not a fit place for human beings; all fell seasick like dead men, and nothing in the world could make us move from one place; the only ones who remained standing were the father vicar and three others; but those three were in such bad shape that they could not do anything, and the father vicar served us all and brought us chamber pots and basins for vomiting, which we could not handle or manage by ourselves.[18]

Once delivered from the peril of seasickness, which, like any other complaint, man can get used to, the difficulties of making do with minimal living space became more evident. As in other aspects of life, one's relative social, economic, and occupational rank determined the place one would occupy on board. In general, from the mainmast toward the poop was considered a prestigious zone, the prime residential neighborhood of each vessel, whereas the area toward the prow was the place for the mariners, that is to say, something like the suburbs of the ship. Beneath the tolda and the chambers on the toldilla resided the captain, the master, the pilot, and the rich and distinguished passengers. The rest of the officers could seek out accommodations under the forecastle, and the mariners and poor passengers situated themselves wherever they could.

Initially one might think that, if the ship had two decks, the space between them would be the most comfortable lodging. Nonetheless, the between-decks was generally filled with cargo, and, in any case, the passengers and crewmen chose better-ventilated spaces. The available testimonies agree that people preferred to put up with inclement weather rather than the nauseatingly pestilential smell that wafted up from the interior of the hold and easily reached the between-decks. Besides, because Spanish fleets generally sailed in summer and, once they reached the Canaries, traveled through the warmer latitudes, the discomfort of sleeping in cold weather could be lessened with a simple blanket, and squalls could be combated by taking shelter under a tarred awning. The tremendous heat of the tropics, which could melt the tar that made the planking waterproof, was a more feared enemy than the cold. The interior of the ship became a veritable oven, where the sticky mixture called *alquitrán* (usually pitch, tar, and grease) in the ship's seams slowly melted. Besides this, continuous squalls could rot the rigging and undermine the morale and the health of the crews.

With the arrival of nightfall the problems of space increased, because lying down occupied more space on deck than standing up. Easing things a bit was the fact that one-third of the crew had to remain on guard, which left some space free. On oared galleys, a type of vessel where human density was even more oppressive, and which on various occasions crossed the Atlantic in the fleets, a witness noted that it was physically impossible to find sufficient space to extend a sleeping pad:

> It is sound advice that the uncommon or delicate passenger provide himself with some little narrow cushion, a folded sheet, a small blanket, and no more than a small pillow; the thought that anyone would think of carrying a large full bed on a galley would make some people jeer and others laugh, because by day there is no place to keep it, much less any place to stretch it out by night. . . . It is sound advice at the hour of embarking on a galley to importune the captain . . . so that . . . he will let you lodge in some chamber . . . because if you are careless or lax in this, it will be said and done that you will not find anywhere to sit during the day, much less anywhere to sleep by night.[19]

To sleep in a bed or a cot was a luxury permitted only to the superior officers and, perhaps, to some distinguished passenger. A good bed had such value that Commander García Jofre de Loaisa bequeathed as one of his most prized possessions his "campaign bed with a red coverlet."[20] The majority of the crew sought out a level place on the decks, which was not always easy, and there they extended their sleeping pads, which in many cases were simple sacks filled with straw, and covered them with good blankets. There was not even a fixed place to sleep; if during the night the position of the sails had to be changed and some sailor had found a place to sleep that got in the way of the maneuver, the unhappy sleeper was awakened without a thought and obliged to look for better accommodations.[21]

It is worth mentioning that, though the Spaniards had direct contact with natives of the Caribbean who slept in hammocks, they did not adopt this system on their ships during the sixteenth century. Hammocks can save space, hanging one under the other in the between-decks; they are comfortable, cool in warm climates, and easily rolled up and stored during the day. For all these

---

The Ship as a Place of Life and Death

reasons, they eventually were put into use on the majority of navies and merchant marines and were quite common from the eighteenth century. Nonetheless, I have only encountered one testimony to the use of a hammock on a ship in the Carrera de Indias, compared with dozens of references to the use of mattresses and cots to rest during the night.[22] Perhaps custom or the lack of space and hygienic conditions in the between-decks made Spanish mariners prefer a small mattress to lie on and, in many cases, only the night sky as a roof for their dreams.

(138)   If finding a good place to sleep was a blessing from heaven, to sleep without being observed by everyone else was an authentic miracle, the type of feat that could only be achieved with money. Privacy was a commodity within reach of only the richest people on board, who paid dearly for the construction of little chambers under the tolda, formed from panels nailed together by the ship's carpenter. The master and the pilot had the right to use the chambers in the toldilla, but many found it more profitable to rent them out and earn a considerable supplement to their wages. The rest of the officers and ordinary passengers had to content themselves with hanging some sort of curtain, so as to gain at least a certain appearance of privacy.

The greed of ships' masters converted the interior of the hulls into a real labyrinth of rooms and chambers built in precarious fashion, where the passengers pressed themselves in with their families and their provisions, because the master was only obliged to give them a daily ration of water, firewood, and salt.[23] Juan de Melgarejo acted as a constable during inspections made of ships before departure. He denounced this widespread custom in a memorandum directed to the king:

> All the masters of the ships that go to the Indies make many chambers on their ships in the castle, and beneath the tolda, that the passengers rent . . . so that the whole of the castle is occupied, which leaves only a very narrow place through which a person can pass. . . . They carry in the said chambers large earthen jars, and many jugs and barrels of water and wine and vinegar and oil and olives, and they put in many encumbrances and heavy things, which is very prejudicial, because that is where the artillery goes. . . . Nor can the gunners pass through nor reach the gun to which they are assigned, for the same reason that the ships travel overly loaded. Neither the bronze nor the iron artillery can be lifted into place, and therefore they dismount the guns from their carriages, axles, and wheels and put them below on the ballast.[24]

Obviously, greed for rental fees from the chambers was detrimental to the defensive capacity of the vessels and even to their fitness to sail, since excess weight in the superstructures robbed the ships of much of their stability. Inspectors from the House of Trade regularly ordered the dismantling of many of these chambers; they even ordered the harpings eliminated, to prevent their being used as extra cargo platforms. Nonetheless, once the inspectors had left, the ships' carpenters raised the chambers again, rendering the inspection useless. One of the inspectors reported that the nao *San Vicente*, which belonged to the Tierra Firme fleet of 1582, ignored orders to remove the harpings and the chambers. Just after leaving the sandbar at Sanlúcar, with the wind only a little stronger than normal, it began to roll dangerously, which forced the crew to throw the superfluous weight into the water. As the ship sailed away, it left (139) behind a wake of wooden chicken coops, beds, and pieces of paneling from the chambers built for the passengers.[25]

The well-known expression "Make ready for combat" *(zafarrancho de combate)* signaled the act of putting the ship in a battle-ready condition. If we pay attention to its etymology, the phrase means nothing other than to make free or unencumbered *(zafos)* the *ranchos,* or lodgings on board, so that the ship's defenders could move about easily. This operation was difficult to carry out on the merchant ships of the Carrera de Indias. If they did not travel with an armed escort, they were ideal prizes for a corsair, as an experienced mariner of the time pointed out:

> All the ships loaded with merchandise for the Indies travel . . . so encumbered inside with chambers, chests, and other things that the men have nowhere to put themselves, so that if by chance they run into corsairs and are assaulted, they would not be able to mount a defense in time. Although some will say that in emergencies they can dismantle the chambers and ready the ships, that cannot be done, because dismantling half a chamber on these ships and throwing it into the sea would take four hours; in a full day, even if the enemy did not come, they could not disencumber the ship.[26]

For common sailors, the only way to secure a private space was to delimit it with their sea chests or "coffers." Thus the sailors formed small ranchos or *camaradas* for a group of crewmen who customarily ate together and set up common living arrangements. During the long months of sailing, a sailor's only authentically private space was that occupied by his sea chest, where he stored some personal items that linked him to life outside the ship. Miguel de Cervantes commented in his novel *El Licenciado Vidriera* that, for a sailor, "his God was his sea chest and his rancho." Thus, it is no wonder that the displacement of one of these chests occasioned strong disputes; it was not rare that men ended up with daggers drawn in a ferocious struggle to acquire some few square centimeters of private space.

On board ship there was not much place to hide intimate matters. If the mariners ingested their food in view of everyone, the moment that each one confronted the imperious necessities imposed by nature after digestion was also public and notorious. The latrines of the mariners were located at the prow, on a wooden grating jutting out directly over the sea.[27] There, each morning, a picturesque line formed, where each one carried his pants in his hand and resigned his soul to recognize one of the clearest demonstrations of human weakness. But in this as in everything else, there were distinctions. The officers and rich passengers had access to latrines at the poop deck, located on the corridors that girdled the outside chambers, and which, surely as an attempt to mask their real purpose, carried the name of "gardens."

But the gardens were not alone in giving off pungent smells. Taking into account the conditions of hygiene of the passengers and crewmen, the presence on board of chickens and pigs, the heat, and the scarcity of fresh water, it is no wonder that contemporaries complained openly about the odors and the lack of hygiene on board. These complaints are even more impressive considering that the sanitary conditions of cities in the sixteenth century were nothing to marvel at. Thus, if a man of that time tells us that the ships were dirty, we should have no doubt that they were truly filthy.[28]

The moment most dreaded by all on board was when the bilge pumps were engaged to extract water that had filtered down to the bottom of the ship. Totally corrupted, it came out "fuming like hell and reeking like the devil."[29] The usual thing was to wait for arrival at the first port to wash one's accumulated dirty clothes, thus at least improving one's personal hygiene. But there were some cleaner individuals who could not wait that long and who used seawater to wash their clothes. Normally it was enough to soap them and throw them into the ocean firmly tied to a cable, for the waves to make a primitive but effective washing machine.[30] Nonetheless, being so clean also had its inconveniences:

> If someone felt the need to heat water, take out bleach, make a bucking solution, or soap a shirt, he had better not do it if he did not want to provide the occasion for some to laugh and others to jeer ... but if some favored and fastidious passenger did soap some rag ... , because seawater makes you itch and causes a rash, the captain would give him permission, and the galley's boatswain would make room so that he could scratch his back on the mast or find an oarsman who would scratch it for him.[31]

Meals and Clothing

No ship on the Carrera de Indias earned fame for its culinary delights. The noble art of fine dining was too far removed from the mariners' cookstoves. However, albeit without gastronomic sophistication, at least on the ships one ate regularly. This was still a novelty and a luxury in a time when misery abounded even in the most powerful countries on earth. Many men were disposed to sell not only their rights of primogeniture but also their muscles, their entire bodies, and even their immortal souls for something like a plate of lentils.

Today we have accurate knowledge about the usual type of provisions carried on the transoceanic routes. With minor variations, the menus on board followed patterns fixed for centuries on land and adapted to the limitations occasioned by long sea voyages. These limitations centered on the need to use provisions capable of lasting longer, either because of their natures or because they could be preserved in salt, which was the most widely used and the cheapest preservative of the epoch. As an example, although there were others that were practically identical, I am going to discuss the daily rations per person for crews on the armada captained by Pedro Menéndez de Avilés in 1568.[32]

(141)

Mondays, Wednesdays, Fridays, and Saturdays: a pound and a half (690 grams) of biscuit, one liter of water, one liter of wine, half a peck of a mixture *(menestra)* of horse beans and chickpeas for each twelve persons (150 grams per person), and one pound of salted fish for each three persons (153.3 grams per person).

Tuesdays: a pound and a half (690 grams) of biscuit, one liter of water, one liter of wine, one pound of mixed rice and oil for each ten persons (46 grams per person), and half a pound (230 grams) of salt pork.

Sundays and Thursdays: a pound and a half (690 grams) of biscuit, one liter of water, one liter of wine, one pound (460 grams) of salted meat, two ounces (57.5 grams) of cheese.

Each month: One liter of oil and something more than a half liter of vinegar per person.[33]

As can be observed, biscuit, water, and wine constituted staple elements of the diet and the most ample. "Biscuit," also called *galleta*, had nothing in common with the foods that we know by such names today, one of whose fundamental ingredients is sugar. Ship's biscuit (from the Latin *bis*, twice, and *coctus*, cooked) was an unleavened bread subjected to a double process of cooking, which preserved it from deterioration for a long time. In order to be able to eat it, one had to soak it for several minutes, either in water or in wine, which no doubt enhanced its acceptance by the crew. Some mariners of the period justified their great affection for wine by saying that men accustomed to travel surrounded by water had a natural inclination to ingest liquids.[34] Although that ingenious excuse was hardly convincing, one must concede that alcohol was a doubly necessary part of the rations. Not only did it provide calories, but it was the only component of the menu capable of making one momentarily forget the hardships of life on board ship. For that reason, and because water customarily had a bad taste and a worse smell after being kept for many weeks

The Ship as a Place of Life and Death

in old barrels, wine was everybody's favorite drink, by a wide margin. Nonetheless, many sailors sacrificed their fleeting pleasure and saved their wine ration to sell in America, where cheap Andalusian wines fetched high prices.

During the voyage the travelers ate salted meat, which was eaten stewed. In American ports, to the degree that the rapid extension of herding made it possible, fresh meat was used. As meat was considered a luxurious and highly nutritious food, a small piece of cheese was all that was needed to fill out the ration on meat days. Cheese constituted the only complement to biscuit when storms or the presence of enemy vessels made it inadvisable to light the cookstove. In other words, rations during storms and battles were formed exclusively of bread, cheese, and wine.

The menestras, that is to say, mixtures of rice, horse beans, or chickpeas, were normally accompanied with salted fish and sometimes with salt pork. The fish most frequently served was probably *tollo*, the name by which they knew *cazón* (dogfish), and which even today is common and relatively cheap in Andalusian coastal towns. In addition, they used *pargo* (red snapper) and sardines, found in abundance on Spanish coasts, but they also carried provisions of salted cod from northern European waters.[35] Stews made with a base of legumes and fish continued to form part of the gastronomic heritage of southern Spanish coasts. Chickpeas with cod constituted, until very recently, a veritable institution during the vigils before religious holidays. For all these reasons, it is no wonder that the pilot who served as protagonist in the book by Juan de Escalante invited his interlocutor to come "eat our fish and chickpeas, since the table is set and they are calling us to eat."[36]

In books on the art of sailing written in the sixteenth century, references are made to how the mariners went "to the table" or "to table," but that was a figure of speech rather than an indication that meals were taken at a table with a tablecloth and the assembled company comfortably seated in chairs.[37] Only the master, the pilot, and the captain, if there was one, dined in this way. These three persons ate apart in their chamber, at times inviting the surgeon or the scrivener and some of the distinguished passengers to join them.

At the master's table they served higher-priced foods. Instead of dark biscuit, which today we would call *integral* (whole grain), they ate white biscuit, which was then considered of higher quality. This last detail makes clear that the groups in power in the sixteenth century had not suffered, as ours have, the healthy but somewhat fastidious natural diet so much in vogue at the end of the twentieth century in opulent industrialized societies. Perhaps they had a better memory of what hunger was, and they were too close to life in the countryside to waste time in such sophistications. Their wine was certainly better than the cheap watered-down variety that was offered to the sailors. From time to time the superior officers could indulge themselves with a roasted chicken, and they regularly ate dried fruits and delicacies for dessert: preserved quince, fruit conserved in syrup, figs and raisins, and so on.

The other men of the sea ate under the watchful eye of the boatswain. The sea chests or coffers of the sailors, covered by some sort of cloth, made up the table, but there were no seats available other than the planks on the deck.[38] In order to convey the edibles to one's mouth, besides the hands that God gave them, the sailors used only their knives. There were not enough plates for everyone, and the meat was served on large platters of clay or wood, from which a group or rancho of mariners ate communally.[39] This is how a passenger, with a bitter irony that foreshadowed Quevedo's humor, described a meal on board ship in midocean.

(143)

> With the sun already on high, I saw two of the said pages bring from below deck a certain bundle that they called tablecloths, arranging them in the waist of the ship . . . ; then they heaped on this table some small mountains of ruined biscuit, so that the biscuits on the tablecloths looked like heaps of dung in a farmer's field. . . . After this they put three or four large wooden platters on the table, filled with stringy beef joints, dressed with some badly cooked tendons. . . . In the twinkling of an eye, all the mariners arrived, saying "Amen," and seated themselves on the ground . . . one with his legs behind him, another sticking his legs forward; this one squatting; that one reclining . . . And without waiting for grace to be said, they took out their knives . . . of diverse fashions, some made to kill pigs, others to flay lambs, others to cut purses, and they grabbed the poor bones in their hands, separating them from their nerves and sinews.[40]

The ration had to be divided among the three daily meals. Breakfast consisted of some of the biscuit and wine accompanied by a bit of salt pork or a few sardines. Lunch occurred at eleven in the morning (twelve noon or one in the afternoon according to today's reckoning, which is an hour or two different from the solar schedule of hours), and that was the main meal. Dinner always took place before the sun set, with a quantity of food that was approximately half of what was consumed at midday.[41]

Various modern researchers have tried to quantify the caloric and nutritional value of this type of diet for the work that the men of the sea had to accomplish. All of these studies agree that the caloric content, estimated at between thirty-five hundred and forty-two hundred calories per person per day, was sufficient for the effort required.[42] Proteins accounted for 13 percent of the total, which would also be within the levels recommended today by the World Health Organization for the maintenance of a balanced diet.[43] The most important deficiency was, without doubt, the lack of vitamins found in fresh fruits and vegetables, which did not form part of the diet of the crews.

The Ship as a Place of Life and Death

The terrible scourge of scurvy commenced approximately six weeks after not consuming fresh foods, but on Spain's transatlantic routes the existence of intermediate stops such as the Canaries, Puerto Rico, Havana, or the Azores meant that the periods of sailing without touching land rarely surpassed a month. This, unfortunately, did not entirely solve the problem, since the medical theories of the day had not assimilated the practical experience that witnessed prodigious cures after ingesting the juice of some types of fresh fruits.[44] Because of the difficulty of conserving fruits and vegetables and the lack of appreciation for these foods in the gastronomic culture of the times, scurvy was always a latent menace on long transpacific routes.

《 144 》

Another important deficiency was in the water consumed, which was totally insufficient for men who carried out hard physical labor in some of the hottest regions on the planet. Even adding a liter of wine to the liter of water provided in the rations, this quantity was small. A man of some seventy kilograms who consumes around thirty-five hundred calories a day should normally ingest between two and three liters of water; in tropical climes, where the production of sweat can cause the loss of a liter of moisture an hour, he ought to consume ten liters a day.[45]

In the sixteenth century there was no possibility of desalinating water from the sea; for that reason, all the potable water had to be transported in barrels that occupied a considerable portion of the hold. The masters were not interested in carrying too much water for their sailors, since that was directly detrimental to the space destined for cargo and, therefore, freight charges. To make matters worse, and as if it were part of some biblical punishment, the crews consumed a great quantity of salty foods. Like a modernized version of the punishment imposed on Tantalus by the gods (in the matter of imposing punishments, the divinities on Mount Olympus were worthy competitors of those on Mount Sinai), the sailors could die of thirst with water all around them. No wonder that the most frequent complaint on board ships was the lack of something to drink. We already know that the military authorities took a lack of discipline very seriously and that religious authorities were always vigilant in defense of the faith. That is why one poor soldier on the armada of General Sancho de Arciniega faced legal proceedings because "lying on his bed he said for the life of the Son of God, that he was dying of thirst."[46]

But perhaps the greatest difficulty with the rations was not their deficiencies in vitamins, water, or calories but that they were almost never completely distributed. The smallest setback in the course of a voyage could serve as a pretext for diminishing the rations. A period of calm, or storms whose contrary winds blew the ship off course, put the crews on half rations. We have already mentioned the bad reputation of the stewards, who were accused of keeping part of the mariners' food for their own benefit. In this task the steward could be abetted by the owner or the master, who saw in it a way to lower the costs of manual labor. The business could come full circle if what was kept back from the rations was sold in the informal shops on board and deducted from the sailors' salaries. This type of abuse indebted the mariners before they arrived in port and forced them to return to sea. It occurred frequently in regions where the mariners were most scarce, as for example in the Spanish armadas organized in Peru, but similar methods were also followed in the navies of other countries.[47]

Another abuse committed at the expense of the sailors and their rations was providing food that was low in quality or spoiled. As an English man of the sea commented in the seventeenth century, "a warm country, rotten meat, wormy bread, and the fetid and poisonous stink of the water in the bilge have made many brave English mariners food for sharks and crabs."[48] On Spanish armadas there were also consummate artists in the widespread art of substituting cat for hare, as the saying went. Most of the time their skills were hidden by a thick curtain of vested interests, but on some occasions they came to light. That happened with one of the stewards of the armada that went to Florida in 1566. This august person turned out to be a real genius in chemistry, ambitious to show that miracles did not happen only at the wedding at Cana; he was tried for mixing one jug of vinegar with two of water, converting them into three jugs of "wine"![49]

Only one recourse remained for sailors to compensate for short rations: to exploit the great storehouse of food represented by the ocean. We can be certain that, among his belongings, a mariner almost never omitted a fishing line and some fishhooks, so that he could dedicate himself to fishing in some of his free time. The available texts also make plain that from the ship's boats, and with the help of harpoons, the men fished for sharks and other large fish, which provided a considerable reinforcement of fresh food.[50] Necessity converted the sailor into a master of survival; it is no coincidence that a Scottish sailor, Alexander Selkirk, provided the inspiration for Daniel Defoe's well-known character, Robinson Crusoe.[51]

Regarding the clothing of the men of the sea, one can say that clothes did not make a good sailor, any more than they made a good monk, but they did contribute to making his work easier. They also served to let contemporaries know at a glance the profession of anyone who wore such clothes. In the same way that it is possible nowadays to dress oneself, or disguise oneself, as a sailor, in the sixteenth century also there were distinctive articles of apparel for the profession, although they were very different from those current now.

Five hundred years ago, masculine fashion imposed models of dress that girded the body and tried to hold it rigid, with the head erect, in an attempt to give the figure an air of dignified elegance.[52] Nonetheless, fashion dictated from

Sailors wore loose, comfortable clothes. Drawing by Christoph Weiditz, 1529. Biblioteca Nacional, Madrid.

the parliament, or Cortes, which was convenient for reinforcing the majesty of princes and lords, was not very useful for climbing on the rigging of a ship; that is why the first characteristic that distinguished sailors' clothing was its amplitude. Men of the sea wore loose clothing that did not slow down their movements and that did not have too many adornments in the form of pleats or decorative slashes, which were susceptible to getting caught or ripping.

The waistcoat *(jubón)* was the garment that elegant people wore over their shirt, covering the body down to the belt and forming a type of fitted shirtwaist with sleeves. Sailors preferred more roomy clothing for work. Normally they wore blouses with a hood, or directly over the shirt they wore a woolen jacket called a *sayuelo*, that is, a type of short gown with skirts that they tied at the waist and under which they wore their pants. One of the most characteristic articles of clothing for ships' crews was the wide pants that fell from the waist to the knees and bore the name of *zaragüelles* (literally, "drawers" or "breeches"). It was very rare not to encounter this article of clothing among the belongings of the men of the sea, from the simplest apprentices to the ships' masters and right up to the highest functionaries on the royal armadas, such as treasurers or accountants. The simplest were made of *anjeo*, a coarse linen that took its name from the French region of Anjou. But there were some made of fine woolen cloth, and some officers even wore zaragüelles made of heavy silk taffeta.   (147)

Zaragüelles were the maritime counterpart of breeches or trousers. Trousers covered the body from the waist to the lower legs, and their use by gentlemen and monied people made them much more aristocratic than the humble zaragüelles. Breeches were a type of voluminous pantaloon that extended to the knees, made of vertical strips of cloth over a taffeta lining. This part of the breeches was known generically as the "legs," and the garment continued with fitted "stockings" down to the feet.[53]

If waistcoats and breeches were distinctive of economically powerful urban groups, the loose blouses and zaragüelles were distinctive of the rural milieu and of manual laborers. Although farmers, shepherds, and many other workers wore zaragüelles, they ended up being almost exclusively associated with laborers at sea.[54] Although they could be made in rich cloths such as taffeta, their form distinguished them as clothing proper to mariners. Thus, the gallant gentleman Loaysa, who tried to woo the beautiful and innocent Leonora in the novel *El Celoso Extremeño* by Cervantes, dressed himself "in ample breeches of tawny-colored taffeta in the mariners' style."[55]

The next characteristic common to the apparel of men of the sea was some sort of covering against bad weather. Even when the ship was sailing through warm seas, the wind, rain, and long nights on guard made it essential to have adequate protection. For that purpose, mariners used generous capes, which in the inventories of their belongings were usually denominated as "sea capes" *(capotes de la mar)*. Juan de Escalante related the way that the general of an armada, Don Francisco de Mendoza, carried out his guard duty: "On that voyage he customarily stood the first quarter of the first watch; covered with his great cape, which he had provided for that purpose, he sat aft of the mainmast, and thus he spent the whole night watching over his ship."[56]

Because one's head was not protected by the cape, mariners wore woolen caps called *bonetes*, whose form approximately coincided with that of the well-known Catalan caps called *barretinas*. The bonete was another distinctive symbol of mariners, but at the same time it marked whoever wore it as being excluded from the narrow circle of distinguished and elegant people. Among the articles of clothing that covered the head, as with apparel that covered other

---

The Ship as a Place of Life and Death

Nothing better than a good long cape to cover yourself during the night watches. Drawing by Christoph Weiditz, 1529. Biblioteca Nacional, Madrid.

parts of the body, some had a more distinguished lineage than others. Caps of velvet or silk were symbols of elegance, and broad-brimmed and other hats shared this honor. By contrast, the simple woolen caps worn by sailors were no more than practical garments to keep out the cold. Their use on the Indies routes was documented as early as the first voyage of Columbus; the admiral mentioned in his diary, around October 15, 1492, that he tried to ingratiate himself with one of the local inhabitants by giving him a red bonete.[57]

Finally, color also served to distinguish sailors. The bonetes were almost always red, and they struck a brilliant note in the sailor's garb, which normally was dark: black, and above all, blue. Blue was the color *por excelencia* for mariners, especially in outer garments; in the auctions of the goods of deceased sailors, capes or capotes of "sea-blue" were common. That is why, when Juan de Escalante de Mendoza introduced the pilot who was the spokesman of his work, he wrote: "Look over there, sir, where that old man is coming dressed in blue," indicating in the margin that "the color blue is good for the sea."[58] In the same way, when in 1567 a constable of the Holy Brotherhood arrested several men as contrabandists in the vicinity of Seville, he rapidly distinguished them as mariners because they were dressed in clothing of that color.[59]

We might think that the choice of blue had a mimetic explanation, in which the sailor tended to dress himself with the predominant color of the medium in which he worked. Nonetheless, the mimicry served to hide or obscure someone's presence, and on a ship that does not seem to make much sense. If a sailor fell into the water, he would have a greater possibility of being found and rescued if he were dressed in orange, or yellow, which are colors that can be seen better in the sea. On the other hand, blue was a more durable color that would better hide stains, which was no small boon to people who had few changes of clothing. Also there was the problem of cost and the difficulty of finding some dyes. From that point of view, blue was a color that was easy enough to obtain and that customarily served as a base to achieve other colors. Thus, in contrast to the distinction carried by textiles treated with red or purple dye, blue cloth had a much more plebian character.[60]

Although the apparel of the men of the sea had certain common characteristics, and some garments were worn as often by apprentices as by masters, there was, of course, a great difference in the quality, the quantity, and the diversity of the wardrobe of the different members of the crew. Sailors kept very few clothes in their sea chests, and what they had was almost always old and worn. A pair of shirts and pants, a large jacket and a small jacket *(chaquetilla),* together with a sea cape, or *capote de mar,* customarily was their entire wardrobe. At times, a woolen waistcoat and a nicer small cape were included. The sailor wore the only shoes he had, and his head was covered with a bonete. For the rest, in the sea chests of the sailors there were neither bedclothes nor pieces of dishware for his individual use. Each group of crew members had their communal trenchers made of clay or wood and handed out by the master. Besides being used for meals, they were among the objects commonly thrown in fights, as a way of supporting each combatant's opinion with something that would have an impact.[61] When a disagreement escalated, the sailors used the knives that they always carried in their belts and which served as defensive weapons as well as tools for work and eating utensils. One article that was rarely missing in a sailor's belongings was a jug to receive his wine ration, since that was a liquid that was too valuable to risk sharing from a common cup. Equipment for fishing and a musical instrument complemented the modest possessions of pages, apprentices, sailors, and even minor officers. As an example, I summa-

The Ship as a Place of Life and Death

rize the contents of the sea chest of Antonio González, a twenty-six-year-old illiterate sailor from Triana, who traveled to New Spain in 1571.[62]

- Two old linen shirts, and one other that is old and torn
- An old linen waistcoat
- Three old zaragüelles, one of linen, another of coarser linen, and another of black woolen cloth
- Two short, loose linen jackets *(chamarretas)* of coarse linen
- One old jacket of blue wool
- Two old jackets of dark woolen cloth
- One old cape of black woolen cloth
- One large German cape made of blue woolen cloth, with front panels of turquoise taffeta
- One clay jar
- Fishing lines

The superior officers had more items of apparel, of better quality and more variety. Mainly, they combined the typical garments of the sea with more distinguished touches: shirts, waistcoats, and pants made of fine cloths such as satin, taffeta, velvet, fine linen from Rouen, and so on. Even so, once embarked, their customary outfit consisted of a shirt and waistcoat and, over both of them, a wide loose coat with skirts called a *sayo*, tied at the waist. Normally, instead of fitted breeches they wore loose trousers or zaragüelles, which were much more comfortable on board. Such an outfit greatly resembled that of simple mariners and was distinguished only by the quality of the cloth. A sketch made by a German traveler in the first third of the sixteenth century defined the image of a ship's master; the sketch lets us visually recreate the typical garb of rich men of the sea at the beginning of the century, which, besides the loose coat (sayo) and trousers included pointed shoes and a cap of woolen cloth.[63]

In the middle of the sixteenth century, the apparel of masters and pilots remained essentially unchanged, consisting fundamentally of an ample coat and trousers. This is proven by the inventory of goods of Pedro de Mata, captain, master, and shipowner, who died in Cartagena de Indias. His wardrobe can be considered archetypal, as much in the type of clothing as in its color, since among his clothing were found: "a loose coat, some stockings, and some zaragüelles, all in blue woolen cloth ... and a large cape in sea blue."[64] Nonetheless, as the century advanced, the wide coat was being replaced by other, shorter, garments of military origin, which were worn over a waistcoat and breeches.[65] These were the *cueras* and *coletos*, types of sleeveless jackets, initially made of leather and later made of various cloths. The owners, masters, and pilots of ships seem eventually to have adopted this fashion; when Philip II

The admiral Andrea Doria
(left) and the owner of a
ship (right). Drawing by
Christoph Weiditz, 1529.
Biblioteca Nacional,
Madrid.

visited Seville in 1570, 150 of them filed before the monarch dressed in the following manner:

> And coming almost in front of the Jerez Gate, the judges and officials of the
> House of Trade arrived, accompanied by more than 150 captains, masters, and
> pilots of the Carrera de Indias, all expensively dressed, because they wore waist-
> coats of white satin, decoratively stitched and pricked, breeches of velvet and
> white satin with silver cords, sleeveless jackets of black velvet, and German-
> style wide cloaks of damask with many buttons of gold and pearls and adorn-
> ments. They had caps of black velvet richly adorned and embellished with
> many pieces of gold, gilded swords ... and all wearing a gold chain.[66]

The Ship as a Place of Life and Death

The captains and military commanders of royal armadas, apart from wearing typical military apparel, such as sleeveless jackets, broad-brimmed taffeta hats, and leather boots, were distinguished by their *bizarría*, a term used initially to define persons dressed in colorful clothing. Because such clothing was a flamboyant affectation of military men, the term ended up signifying the notion of bravura, which was precisely what the soldiers wanted to convey with their attention-getting outfits.[67] It is not rare to find garments inventoried that were silver in color, or tawny, red, violet, or yellow. The generals of armadas and their sons might even sport a whole array of jewels to adorn and distinguish their persons: gold chains, buttons encrusted with pearls and diamonds, emerald rings, and so on.[68]

In the final years of the century, fashion imposed a new garment among the nautical and military commanders of the Indies fleets. These were the *gregüescos*, or Greek-style, wide breeches, which possibly constituted an evolution of the old zaragüelles, except that this new type of garment presented exaggeratedly swollen forms. The Japanese screen paintings of the arrival of Portuguese mariners at the end of the sixteenth century contain near caricatures of the gregüescos worn by Portuguese mariners, who seem to be walking around wearing inflated pantaloons.[69]

The belongings that masters, pilots, and generals carried on board were not limited to their personal wardrobes. Besides the weapons and instruments of their office, the sea chests of these personages held articles that brought a certain comfort to important activities such as sleeping and eating. Their bedclothes consisted of various sets of sheets, pillows, blankets, coverlets, and, of course, one or two mattresses. These comforts were supplemented with carpets to place next to the bed, and some sybarites even carried copper urinals, to avoid finding themselves in the uncomfortable dilemma of having to go on deck on a cold night; instead, they could relieve themselves in the warmth of their own chamber.[70] During the day, possession of a humble utensil of that kind could guarantee the dignity of a royal treasurer or even of an admiral. Thanks to it, they did not have to let their subordinates know the hour that Mother Nature forced them to yield to the weakness of the human condition.

The officers customarily carried a series of cooking implements such as pots, roasting spits, and frying pans, which their servants used to prepare their food. They also had tablecloths and dishes. The captain and master Pedro de Mata had a basket with porcelain plates and Triana pottery, and he drank from a gilded silver cup.[71] More common were plates and jars of metal, either tin, copper, or pewter (an alloy of zinc, lead, and tin). Thus, for example, Juan Sebastián Elcano carried the following pieces of dishware and cooking equipment on his second expedition to the Moluccas: three copper kettles, a tin pot *(puchero)*, four tripods to support earthen pots over the fire, a grill, three iron frying pans, eight tin plates, one jar, two large cups, and three spoons.[72] But without a doubt, the prize for refinement goes to one of the sons of Captain General Cristóbal de Eraso, named Francisco de Eraso, who compensated for the lack of culinary delicacies on board by eating his food with a golden spoon.[73]

Ways to Spend Free Time: Games and Diversions

Sea voyages customarily combined exhausting times when the men had to struggle day and night against pirates, storms, and rough seas with other times in which the changing of the guard, the call to meals, or the recitation of daily prayers by the apprentices at sunset were the only events that broke the monotony for crews and passengers. Once the ships left the Canary Islands behind and held the trade winds in their sails, a routine and tranquil round of activities took over. A month of sailing lay ahead until the first of the Antilles would be sighted, during which, barring unforeseen events, much time remained free to dedicate to leisure activities. Thereafter came the interminable waits in American ports, where the masters, in order to impede desertions, generally required the mariners to remain on board. The return voyage was always more "entertaining." In the first place, the Atlantic crossing was made in latitudes near forty degrees, which have always been propitious for the formation of squalls and storms. And to keep the sailors from becoming bored, corsairs combined with the forces of nature, harassing the ships that returned laden with treasure. There is no doubt that these attacks provided plenty of entertainment for Spanish crews, although the spectacle could be disagreeable and quite costly. Even so, after leaving the dangerous passage between Florida and the Bahamas, there was a certain tranquility until sighting the Azores.

How did ships' crews occupy their free time? Friar Antonio de Guevara commented that at sea there were three principal entertainments: "gaming, talking, and reading."[74] Another traveling cleric, Friar Tomás de la Torre, added the pastime of singing songs to the sound of a guitar.[75] Of course there were some crewmen who employed their leisure in less honest diversions, such as lightening the purses of the passengers, sneaking food from the steward, or dedicating themselves to wooing the female passengers and, in more than one case, the young pages and apprentices in the crew. Of these last two forms of passing the time, our two religious informants say nothing at all. Perhaps they did not see it, or they did not want to tell about it, but the documents contain irrefutable testimony about similar activities. Certainly, the two friars would never have considered erotic entertainments as "diversions." For that reason, to respect (without sharing) the spirit of the epoch, we will not mix oil with water and will leave for a while later these "dishonest" pleasures.

The Ship as a Place of Life and Death

Playing games, chatting and telling stories, singing songs, and reading were possibly, and in that order, the most common diversions. One could add fishing, but this last activity had a larger component of vital necessity than of pure entertainment. Everyone played games of chance on board ships, and everyone knew that it was prohibited by royal ordinances. Some instructions issued in 1535 by the officials of the House of Trade ordered the masters "not to consent to cursing, nor blaspheming, nor to playing games of chance, unless the wagers be for pieces of fruit in order to pass the time."[76] If the functionaries of the House of Trade truly believed that their orders were going to be obeyed, they surely earned a place among the most naive men on earth. Imagining a band of dirty, bearded sailors sitting around on their sea chests playing amicably for so many walnuts and chestnuts, without launching imprecations, and addressing one another as "Your Grace," is the same as imagining the snow burning or oxen flying. I would rather believe that the royal bureaucrats knew beforehand how faintly their dispositions would echo, and, like Pontius Pilate, they simply washed their hands of the matter after having put the rules in writing.

The rules prohibiting gaming with dice and cards were always maintained but impossible to enforce. As often happens in such cases, the situation gave way to tolerated transgressions and more than a few dissimulations. Juan de Escalante de Mendoza, when he rose to be a general commanding fleets, was responsible for maintaining discipline. In his book on life at sea, he referred only to the honest and intellectual game of chess, and other generals did the same when they received routine inspections upon arriving in port.[77] Nonetheless, if royal officials probed a little deeper in their investigation, they found that not even the generals themselves, theoretically charged with preventing gaming, avoided accusations of playing a few hands with their friends. Thus, for example, Francisco de Luján, who commanded the New Spain fleet in 1574 and who issued various orders that the soldiers and sailors not gamble, personally participated in various games of cards: "I saw that the said general Francisco de Luján, being on the island of San Juan de Ulúa with the ships and people of the said fleet and armada, played for amusement at very low stakes games such as 'triunfo del basto,' 'malilla,' 'cientos,' and other trifling games of cards, and this witness understood that the soldiers and sailors of the said armada also would play."[78]

But our surprise could be writ even larger by showing that the royal constables of each armada, who were directly responsible for maintaining discipline on the ships by orders of the general and who were supposed to prevent gambling as one of their principal duties, were actually the ones who distributed decks of cards. Some constables would claim that, given the scant salary paid by the king, their office would not yield sufficient income without the profits they earned selling—or renting, really—playing cards. The investigation carried out on the New Spain fleet of 1573, commanded by General Juan de Alcega, could be taken as an example of how the lack of compliance with the ordinances was as obvious as it was unpunished. The testimony of the scrivener who kept track of the rations is very expressive:

> This witness saw how, on the ship that was head of the fleet, the men played games of cards and dice publicly for the money each one wanted to wager, without there being any limitation. . . . The man who distributed the cards . . . was Juan Vázquez de Olivera, the royal constable of the said fleet and armada, in conformity with what is done on similar fleets and armadas, because this is the preeminence of the office of constable, which would not be worth anything if not for the price of the cards, which are generally sold by the deck for each game. . . . And they asked for the *barato*, according to whether the quantity of money wagered was a large or small sum, and that was customarily eight reales per deck.[79]

As we see, the constables astutely did not collect for the decks of cards beforehand; instead, they waited for the euphoria of the winner and then asked him for *barato*, that is, the tip that everyone who is lucky in a game customarily leaves for the onlookers. In this way, the losers were not obliged to pay for the instrument of their disgrace, and it did not matter much to the winner, because, after all, he paid with other peoples' money. In this case, the constable defended himself saying that he acted according to established custom and that, thanks to his supplying the decks, the games were not played with marked cards, nor were great sums of money wagered. Evidently, this was considered a minor evil; in a voyage that lasted more than four months from departing San Juan de Ulúa until arriving at Sanlúcar de Barrameda, "one cannot avoid the fact that the crew did not have any entertainment on the way and the voyage was so long."[80] The judges of the House of Trade accepted this reasoning and preferred to have the constable distribute cards rather than have the sailors placate their boredom and tensions by exchanging blows.

Unfortunately, the constables' claim that, thanks to their vigilance, prohibited games were not played, nor excessive wagers made, was totally false. The certainty is that all sorts of gaming took place on the ships, including some with stakes high enough to ruin the greatest potentates on earth. The phrase "losing everything, including your shirt" was not merely a metaphor among the sailors, who did not have much more to wager. Generals and admirals issued orders prohibiting sailors and soldiers from gambling their clothing and weapons, but many such orders fell on deaf ears. Thus, in the armada that Sancho de Arciniega led to Florida in 1566, two crew members were jailed for swearing and blaspheming after a game of cards. The problem arose

---

The Ship as a Place of Life and Death

when one of the players, after having lost his pants and shirt, tried to recover them:

> One day Juan Martínez the soldier and Ayala were gambling, and the latter having won some pants and some shirts and monies, . . . Juan Martínez said:—"Go to the Devil!—because we aren't on land (I can't make you return it to me)"—. . . . And then he again asked Ayala to give him back his shirt for the love of God, and Ayala responded: "I would do many things for the love of God, but since you wagered it, ask me to lend it to you some day, and I'll give it to you so that you can change that other shirt you brought."[81]

(156)

Naturally, after the loser's fruitless petition, they both hurled blows and blasphemies at one another and found themselves placed in the stocks, not for gambling but for cursing and blaspheming. Gambling was a permanent source of conflict, and problems could arise among the simple onlookers as well, since they waited for the game to end so that they could ask for the barato from the winner. On one occasion, an insistent importuner made excessive demands and tried to wheedle "a real for the money-box of Our Lady of the Barato," making a dangerous comparison between the abundant poor boxes that the friars put on board ship and his own coffer.[82] Needless to say, the rash sailor paid for his offensive comparison, and for a blow he had landed in a prior scuffle, with a few days' confinement.

I have not found many penalties for gambling, only some fines, and only in exceptional cases. One of them was the case of Toribio de Lara, captain of a ship that returned from Tierra Firme in 1543, who, instead of setting a good example for his men, spent the voyage gambling and winning large sums of money from the passengers. The case brought against Toribio de Lara shows the amount of money that could change hands during a single voyage. Diverse witnesses acknowledged having lost more than one thousand gold pesos, besides individual pieces of silver dishware and some "sticks and bars" of silver and gold. The fine, consisting of 130 ducats, was minor compared with the winnings obtained by the accomplished captain.[83]

Thus, it was not "pieces of fruit" that changed hands on the improvised gaming tables on board, as the House of Trade claimed, but bars of gold and "pieces of eight." Moreover, the men customarily played games that were prohibited. Among the most common were "parar" and "treinta por fuerza." In the first, each player received a card, and thereafter the rest of the cards were dealt until someone received another card with the same number: then, the one who had "paired" *(paraba* or *pareaba)* won the game and the stakes. The game of "treinta por fuerza" was a variant of the modern and well-known game of "siete y media" (literally, "seven and a half"), but where the winning point was thirty.

The fact that these games were normally played by professional gamblers and lowlifes is shown by Cervantes in his "Rinconete y Cortadillo"; in the story, Pedro del Rincón relates how he had traveled from Madrid earning his living from inn to inn "playing 'twenty-one' . . . and besides, I was a master at the game of 'parar,' which they also call 'el andaboba' [the fool's walk], which proves, as Your Grace can see in the focus of your eyeglasses, that I can be a master in the boorish sciences."[84] Sailors practiced in real life the arts described by Cervantes's roguish characters, and like them, they knew how to work together to fleece the incautious passengers who dared ask for a place in the game. According to Friar Antonio de Guevara, on the king's galleys this refined fleecing technique was called "the game of playing one against all the others," and more than one unhappy passenger suffered its consequences.[85]

(157)

One has the impression that card games were more popular than dice in the sixteenth century. Card games started in Italy in the fourteenth century, but their beginnings were marked by difficulties caused by the high price of the decks of cards. With the diffusion of woodblock printing from the start of the fifteenth century, cards became increasingly cheaper and began to compete with dice.[86] With regard to the ships of the Carrera de Indias, the documents tell us many more names for games of cards than for games of dice. Besides the two cited, these others were also normally played on board ships: "el triunfo del basto," "el chilindrón," "la malilla," "los cientos," "el rentoy," "la primera," and so forth.[87]

A more peaceful activity consisted in practicing the tranquil art of conversation. Nonetheless, we know already that boredom is a bad counselor, and to enliven a chat, the best approach was to talk about others. In this way the comrades who decided "to tell stories, speak of vain things, brag about themselves, and praise their hometowns" to pass the time ended up by "talking about other people's lives."[88] In other words, they succumbed to the sweet temptation of criticizing their fellow creatures. Once they arrived at this point, chatting was sometimes not such a peaceful activity, especially if some of those present on the ship felt the allusions aimed at them. Then, what had been an innocent and peaceful gathering could end with blows, which is what happened on a hulk in the armada of Sancho de Arciniega, where the author of the comments tried to show his innocence in these terms:

Being on the said hulk talking with a soldier from Galicia about things to pass the time, especially dealing with the genealogy of good people, as the saying goes, in prejudice to no one, a soldier from the same company, who was named Antonio López, challenged this witness, and asked him why he dealt with other people's lives and said that it was very bad to say what he had said; and this witness responded to him that he was not discussing

---

The Ship as a Place of Life and Death

the lives of anyone on board, but of lineages and of towns that were far away; and to this López said that it was very badly spoken and thus he launched an attack against this witness.[89]

Reading was the most peaceful entertainment of all, but, although it seems strange, it was still subject to certain risks, since the Inquisition in the Americas reviewed the books handed around during the voyage to see if they might represent some danger for morals, religious doctrine, or good customs. However, in a twist of fate, the records of inspections by the Holy Office of the Inquisition permit one to know today which books were brought on board for reading, as distinct from those that were transported as merchandise to sell on the American market.[90]

In fact, the difficulties in dedicating oneself to reading were numerous. In the first place were the bothers that the inquisitors could cause, since no one liked to raise suspicions by bringing some book along that was prohibited or considered inappropriate. The functionaries of the Holy Office, secure in their power, were punctilious in maintaining their authority, and they lost patience easily. That was a lesson learned very well by the master of the ship *Trinidad* in the 1585 fleet, who, in order not to interrupt a game of cards, kept the inquisitors waiting; in retaliation they put him in prison, where he remained all week for his insolence.[91]

But there were more inconveniences: books were expensive, and the level of illiteracy among the mariners was very high. That is why the form of reading was not individual but collective, with listeners gathered around a reader who recited aloud the passages of the chosen book. A cultured passenger might lend himself to this labor, such as happened on the ship *Santa María de Arratia*, of the 1582 fleet, in which "the passenger Alonso Almaraz one day was reading the legend of the life of San Luis, and from then on the sailors had him read to them."[92] Finally, reading could be done only during the day, since as soon as the sun went down there remained only a few lights on board (for fear of fire), and the bridges of the ships were filled with an almost total darkness.[93]

Despite all these limitations, it was a rare ship in which there were not at least a few books to be used as reading material during the voyage. Of the 330 ships reviewed by the Mexican Inquisition between 1572 and 1600, there is evidence of books on 326, and on 198 the literary genres and some of the concrete titles were specified.[94]

Books with a religious content were the most numerous on the ships. Of the 198 ships for which we possess data about titles and genres, "devotional books" were found on 156 (78.8 percent). The contents were varied, but books of hours predominated—in other words, types of manuals that marked the prayers appropriate for each phase of the day (matins, vespers, complin, and so

(158)

the lives of anyone on board, but of lineages and of towns that were far away; and to this López said that it was very badly spoken and thus he launched an attack against this witness.[89]

on). Then came the lives of the saints, histories of the popes, tales of miracles, moral advice, and a large variety of other devotional literature.

In second place, and very close behind the pious books, came a very different genre: adventure stories and books of chivalry written as much in verse as in prose. On 121 ships (61 percent) there were examples of the melodramatic adventures of valiant knights and beautiful damsels that so inflamed the imagination of our ancestors. Among the most popular were *Orlando Furioso, Amadís de Gaula, El Caballero de Febo, Palmerín*, and *Oliveros de Castilla*.

Thereafter, although at a greater distance, came the collections of romances, verses, and songbooks, which had the advantage of being able to be recited and sung to the sound of guitars. History was also popular, above all history with a high epic content, which related tales of battles and heroic deeds. There were three favorite historical moments among the men of the sea: the splendor of the Roman Empire, the reconquest of the Iberian Peninsula from the Muslims, and the conquest of America. In this way, stories on the ships of the Carrera celebrated the deeds of Julius Caesar, "El Cid" Ruy Díaz, Hernán Cortés, or Francisco Pizarro. Along with them appeared a hero native to the New World: the Araucanian chieftain Caupolicán, immortalized in *La Araucana* by Alonso de Ercilla. (159)

Another level of literary tastes on the ships favored books that related tales of voyages and exotic countries and customs. Descriptions of Jerusalem, of the African continent, or of Japan provided entertainment during the leisure hours on board. Voyagers were also interested in much more recent events, such as the reception given to King Philip II by the city of Seville in 1570, which was a social event of extraordinary proportions and whose brilliance impressed the sailors as much as the marvels of the Orient.

Novels about subjects other than chivalry, and poetry, had a modest representation on the ships. In the first category, pastoral themes stood out above all, but there were a few ships where *La Celestina* and the *Aventuras y vida de Guzmán de Alfarache* also were read. The diffusion of that great picaresque novel by Mateo Alemán seems especially rapid and significant, as its first part was published in 1599 and two examples of the work already appeared on ships inspected by the Inquisition in the following year. Among the most frequently read poets were Lope de Vega, Boscán, Petrarch, and some of the classical writers such as Virgil and Ovid.

Apart from books of devotion and entertainment, there were also some volumes employed by the professionals on board in the dispatch of their offices: books of navigation, collections of legal dispositions (for example, the *Repertorio de Chaves)*, books about weaponry, and even various treatises that were carried by a conscientious and educated barber-surgeon on the almiranta in the 1582 fleet. Finally, I want to mention a very unusual work, a manual regarding

Books of chivalry enthused
the men of the sea.
Illustration by Gustave
Doré for an edition of
Orlando Furioso.

the learning of seven languages, brought by a Fleming—we do not know
whether he was a sailor or a passenger—on the flyboat *Nuestra Señora del Rosario*,
in the 1595 fleet.[95]

Naturally, people tried to diversify the themes of reading material carried
on each ship. At least they customarily carried books both of religion and of
chivalry, which served as literary ambassadors for the sacred and the profane.
But they also added some other genre to increase the possibilities for diversion. One example comes from the merchant ship *Santa Elvira*, which arrived
in Veracruz in the last year of the century and whose master acknowledged that
on his ship they read "books of romance, chivalry, history, and devotion."[96]

Nonetheless, there were cases of ships on which there was very little from which to choose. On twenty-five ships, all the books had a religious content. These ships of almost monastic character made up 12.6 percent of the total, which is not a negligible percentage. But even more ships did not have even a single religious book. There were forty-two (21.2 percent) ships that carried only books of entertainment, and among them, ten carried only books of chivalry. Despite the importance of texts on pious themes, this gives the impression that the men of the sea preferred diversion to devotion, at least when they had to choose between the two extremes.

Until now, we have discussed the literary genres and the general typology of the books preferred by the men of the sea. But it is also interesting to know the authors and the specific titles that appeared with most frequency on the ships of the Carrera de Indias. To that end, one can put together the following list of the top ten books, which are followed by the number of ships on which the work could be found.[97]

(161)

- *Libro de la Oración y la Meditación* and other works of Friar Luis de Granada (37)
- *Flos Sanctorum*, by Alonso de Villegas (36)
- *Orlando Furioso*, by Ludovico Ariosto (29)
- *Historia Pontifical*, by Gonzalo de Illescas (19)
- *Amadis de Gaula* (Anonymous) (10)
- *La Araucana*, by Alonso de Ercilla (9)
- *Oratorio Espiritual* (9)
- *Repertorio de Chaves*, by Alonso de Chaves (9)
- *La Diana*, by Jorge de Montemayor (7)
- *El Cancionero de Guzmán* (7)

As we can see, on this list the predominant works are prayer manuals: the *Oratorio Espiritual* and also the *Libro de la Oración y la Meditación* by Friar Luis de Granada, which was considered the most read book in Spain and Spanish America during the sixteenth and seventeenth centuries.[98] Along with these, there were two more works of religious content: the histories of the saints in the *Flos Sanctorum* and the histories of other personages who were not so saintly—the popes of the *Historia Pontifical*. There is also a book of legal instruments: the *Repertorio de Chaves*, a compilation of medieval and modern laws. And, finally, five works of pure entertainment appeared on the list: *La Araucana*, an epic poem idealizing the military deeds of Caupolicán, historical chieftain of the Araucanian Indians; *El Cancionero de Guzmán*, a collection of traditional tunes; *La Diana*, a pastoral novel; and *Orlando Furioso* and *Amadis de Gaula*, the two most famous books of chivalry of the times.

The preference for these books showed that the most important interests of the men of the sea related, on the one hand, to the eternal salvation of their souls and, on the other, to escaping the realities of their hard daily lives. Both interests had in common a certain denial of the here and now, of the routine that bound their lives and made them yearn for the celestial paradise promised by religion and the fantastic worlds of poetic and novelistic imagination.

The pastoral songs and stories transported them to a world charged with lyricism. In particular, *La Diana* presented an idealized vision of country life. Shepherds with such un-Spanish names as Sireno, Silvano, Selvática, and Felismenia tripped through leafy and fragrant meadows and gathered together near a grove of green willow trees to discuss the metaphysics of platonic love. Reading this, of course, was a way of obliterating the rude reality of men who, instead of strolling up gentle hills, had to shinny up to the rough spars of ships and, instead of smelling aromatic flowers, had to put up with the pestilential stench of the bilge or the rancid odor of fish grease and tar.

Given that the number of ships on which pastoral novels appeared was not very large, it seems that the majority of men of the sea preferred another type of escape, where action superseded contemplation and passions overcame platonic love. For that reason, the most popular book of fiction on the ships was the famous epic poem of chivalric themes by Ludovico Ariosto. Moreover, these preferences would have been in accord with the origins, cultural formation, and activities that had produced the men of the sea, who would have identified more easily with epic fantasies than with the metaphysical and intellectualized lucubrations of pastoral novels.

Orlando Furioso by Ariosto had all the necessary components to make it a tale of fantastic adventure that could satisfy a wide range of individual tastes. That is why it could interest even illiterate men who were used to enjoying the epic narrations that jugglers and blind storytellers had spread through towns and villages during the Middle Ages. The beginning of Ariosto's work left no doubt about the themes it was going to treat: "I sing of ladies and gentlemen, weaponry and love affairs, gallantry and the daring enterprises, from the time when the Moors of Africa went to sea. . . . At the same time I will tell of Roland what has never before been said in prose or in verse: how, because of love, that man became raging mad, though beforehand he had been the model of prudence."[99]

The themes are so universal that one cannot doubt their appeal: love capable of unchaining madness; violence and heroic actions; exotic places; magic and fantasy; monsters who devour damsels; and voyages through space on winged horses or in chariots of fire capable of transporting the heroes to the Moon. And everything was bathed in hints of a hidden eroticism that clearly went beyond the purely platonic. In sum: love, sex, violence, fantasy, and heroism. Regardless of its superior literary virtues, Ariosto's work grabbed attention with the same devices used by recent movies such as *Star Wars*,

which delighted young and old, bringing together huge masses of a public theoretically, at least, much more enlightened than the sailors of the sixteenth century.

One must suppose that the crew would listen with rapt attention when a passenger or one of their comrades recited the deeds of Roland. It is quite probable that they particularly enjoyed the passage where the knight named Anglante skewered six enemies on his lance at once, and "because it was not long enough to accommodate the body of another man at the tip, the seventh remained apart, but so badly wounded that he did not take long to succumb."[100] Nonetheless, surely their interest would have taken on a higher tone when the author described how the knight Ruggiero saved the beautiful An-

The Ship as a Place of Life and Death

gelica, mounted on his winged horse; although, reading that passage one would hope that, had there been some moralistic friar on board, he had gone to take a nap:

> That fierce people, inhospitable and barbarous, had exposed the most beautiful of women to the voracity of the monster at the shoreline. She was completely nude and as nature had made her, without even a veil to hide the white lilies and the glowing scattered roses of her delicate members. . . . Ruggiero might have believed that she was a marble statue . . . had he not clearly seen the tears that ran down her fresh pink cheeks and moistened her heaving breasts.[101]

((164))

The Risky Search for Pleasure: Sexuality on Board

To the misfortune of the men of the sea, any kind of sexual relation that they tried to carry out on board was considered a sin, or even a crime. The situation thus made it difficult to alleviate carnal tensions. Because sailors could not bring their wives with them, heterosexual relations on board always had an illegitimate character, as much for married men as for bachelors. Thus, the crewmen were condemned (in a manner of speaking) to maintain sexual relations with women who would have, at best, the status of lovers (*mancebas* was the sonorous term employed then) and, at worst, that of prostitutes.

If, on the contrary, a sailor swooned for beautiful young men, things were much worse, because homosexuality was considered the "nefarious" sin, which is the same as saying "repugnant" or "filthy." To practice "sodomy" (a term also very common in the period) was considered a sin worse than robbery and even worse than murder. Cervantes, reflecting the popular mentality, put a curious valuation of crimes and malefactors into the mouth of one of the thieves who gathered in the patio owned by Monipodio. Perhaps—the great thief said, denying the serious wrongdoing of his profession—"it is worse to be a heretic or a renegade, or to kill your father and mother, or to be a 'solomico' [for *sodomito*]."[102]

In other words, the two sexual options at the disposal of the men of the sea had an immoral quality: either fornication or sodomy, and both were condemned by the church and punished by the civil authorities. Thus, for example, there was a curious case in which the judges of the House of Trade punished a ship's master as much for carrying contraband as for relieving the boredom of the long voyage in the arms of a widowed passenger: "Also, adding one crime to another [that of contraband], the said Felipe Boquín, carrying in his ship as a passenger a widow woman who was called Catalina, he got together with her and they became lovers, eating and drinking together in one bed, which he did with little fear of God."[103]

This close identity of sin and crime was due not only to the existing collaboration between church and state but also to the widespread opinion that whoever contravened one part of the moral norms was potentially suspected of noncompliance with any sort of law. This monolithic conception of morality, which can still destroy the careers of politicians in Anglo-Saxon cultures who are caught in sexual transgressions, already had its adherents in the sixteenth century. One example of this is in the accusations against Diego Gutiérrez and Pedro de Medina, two great cosmographers of the House of Trade. A pilot of the Carrera de Indias, Alonso de Zapata, denounced them for accepting bribes in the examinations of new pilots. According to Zapata, it should have surprised no one that they had done these things, because they had demonstrated their lack of scruples by living in permanent concubinage:

(165)

> He [Diego Gutiérrez] was predestined for this moral blindness, or better said, this evil [of accepting bribes]. I do not marvel that he does not see the blindness, because for more than thirty years he has been lovers with a woman besides the one whom God gave him to care for, and with this woman he is loaded down with children and lives most of the time in mortal sin, maintaining the law of the Moors with two women.[104]

Clearly the punishment was very different according to the crime. If a romantic relationship were discovered on a ship, the guilty parties might be admonished, fined, separated, or, in the worst cases, abandoned ashore, though with each one in a different port so as not to favor the work of the Devil. The sodomite, however, was subjected to torture, and, if his guilt was proved, he was very likely to go to the stake as if he were a heretic. Precisely because the treatment of the two sexual transgressions was so different, we discuss them separately, beginning with the most common "vice": the well-developed fondness of many mariners to "converse carnally," according to the graceful euphemism of the epoch, with women who were not their legitimate spouses.

While at sea, the generals of the armadas, as the supreme civil and military power, were in charge of repressing this type of conduct, and appeals to their rulings were heard in the law court *(audiencia)* of the House of Trade. In other words, the curious circumstance arose that a general was as obliged to keep his subordinates apart from their compliant mistresses as he was to keep the convoy together. As an example, one can point to the instructions received by Sebastian Cabot, which, besides a good number of recommendations of a military and administrative type, said that "if after the departure of the said ships you find a woman on board, whoever brought her on board should be punished as you see fit, and she should be put ashore at the first land arrived at that is populated by Christians."[105]

In other words, the presence of women capable of using their charms to entertain the sailors was considered supremely inconvenient. Alonso de Chaves, who was pilot major of the House of Trade and wrote one of the best nautical treatises of the sixteenth century, undertook to enumerate all that was necessary to carry on a ship, but he also related some things that ought to be left in port. Among these last he cited rancor among the crew members; sins, which ought to be confessed before departure; and, of course, prostitutes: "The captain or the master . . . ought not allow public women to travel on the ship, because that is a matter of great prejudice for all the people on board."[106]

If the generals did not play the role of sexual repressor, the authorities of the House of Trade could review their records and punish them for noncompliance with their instructions. The witnesses of the "visitas y residencias" (visits and inspections) to which the commanders of the armadas were subjected upon arrival were asked if commanders had been able to maintain sexual order. Thus, a general such as Diego de Flores Valdés found himself obliged to prove that, having discovered the existence of a pair of lovers, he had separated them, leaving one in Nombre de Dios and the other in Puerto Rico.[107]

But as temptation is the constant companion of the human species, and as the sin was presumed serious but the punishment not so serious, even the very generals and admirals charged with repressing others succumbed to love's charms! They even provided cases demonstrating the true spirit of camaraderie among comrades in arms: On the Tierra Firme fleet of 1576, the intermingling was so close among the fleet's two highest commanders that when General Francisco de Luján turned command over to his admiral Rodrigo de Vargas, he also turned over his lover. The woman in question was a mulatta named María Coto, whom we can suppose was beautiful, since she was capable of dazzling such illustrious personages. Specifically, the admiral established her in a house in Nombre de Dios, and on the return voyage he ordered a private cabin built for her under the tolda, where he made amorous visits to her. In his explanation, Rodrigo de Vargas admitted that the mulatta had sailed to Tierra Firme "with the said captain general Francisco de Luján, serving him and regaling him," and that on the return voyage it seemed normal that she do the same for him. However, he denied that any "dishonest conversation" was included among the "gifts" (regalos) provided by María Coto. Naturally, the authorities of the House of Trade did not believe him, and the admiral was fined the equivalent of ten-days' salary. After all was said and done, Vargas must have thought that neither the risk nor the punishment was excessive for having enjoyed such agreeable company.[108]

Who were these women, such as the mulatta María Coto, who gladdened the loneliness of the men of the sea? In some cases sailors more or less secretly embarked their lovers, who surfaced as stowaways (llovidos; literally, "raindrops") once the ship was at sea. Mulattas seem to have been especially attractive for the men of the sea, and there is other evidence of their sudden appearance on the ships.[109] Other cases deal with lovers with white skin but much darker reputations, since, as Friar Antonio de Guevara commented, women who dared to come on board the ships were generally "more familiar with charity than with honesty," since they charitably distributed their favors among all who needed them.[110]

But the ships of the Carrera de Indias also carried female passengers who, though they were not very numerous, potentially at least were a source of sexual contacts for the crews. One can assume that married women traveled closely watched by their husbands. Widows have always provided a morbid temptation, but there were not too many of them. Thus, the most appropriate candidates were, without doubt, the many female servants who accompanied passengers of a certain rank. Cervantes may have been referring to these servants when he said that the Indies, besides providing a refuge for those who had lost hope in Spain, served as "a general lure for loose women."[111] The unattached women who went to America attracted by its riches were not straitlaced ladies, nor were they as restricted by the rigid sexual repression that bound the privileged sectors of society; for that reason, they constituted appropriate aspirants to share a fleeting love affair with members of the crew.

Unmarried women were seen by some passengers as a danger to the virtue of their daughters, since the example set by some of them was not generally very edifying. For that reason, Iñigo de Lecoya, a prudent captain of the Carrera de Indias, devised a brilliant solution that could simultaneously put an end to various problems on board ship, whether those problems were moral or hygienic! When male and female passengers were mixed together, it could damage not only the honor of some but the sense of smell of all, since, faced with a natural reluctance to denude oneself in front of persons of the opposite sex, no one washed. That is why Lecoya thought the best solution was for all the women to be lodged in the chambers at the poop, leaving the men to their own modest intimacy. Lecoya described his project in these words:

> Every merchant ship should have a chamber, if there are not already two on the upper and lower poop deck, in which, or in each one of them, all of the women on each ship can travel; there they would travel better and more securely from people's gossip. And if some people wish to say that the women and their young daughters do not want to be mixed in with the unmarried women, one can respond that they travel much better than if each one traveled by herself and more secure from the inconveniences that can occur; and thus all the male passengers could sleep in the forecastle more relaxed and seemly and with more cleanliness.[112]

No one doubts that being virtuous is an arduous task, and in order to preserve one's purity in the compromising space of a ship, the best solution was to undergo the penance of being closed in. At least, that is what a thirty-year-old widow named Leonor de Cárdenas had to do, after she suffered the amorous importuning of Francisco de Espínola, the owner of a ship traveling to New Spain. The resistance of the lady in question was meritorious, but various friars on board came to the aid of her virtue, and they were responsible for bringing the rumors about Espínola's intentions to the attention of the general of the fleet. He ordered an investigation into the conduct of the lecherous pretender:

> the priest Father Dionisio told this witness that the said Francisco Espínola had importuned Leonor de Cárdenas, a passenger on the said ship, to give him her body. . . . Many times the said Francisco de Espínola intruded into the cabin of the said Leonor de Cárdenas, with half his body inside the cabin and the other half outside . . . and along the same lines, this witness one night heard the said Leonor de Cárdenas complaining and crying loudly that she wanted to be a good woman and she did not want to do what Francisco de Espínola had asked.[113]

In order to avoid greater evils, Leonor de Cárdenas decided to shut herself in her cabin and not leave again for the duration of the voyage. On other occasions, however, female passengers were much more agreeable and bestowed their favors without any limitation. Then, the only ones who protested were those who were deprived of such attentions. That happened, to his disgrace, to Cristóbal de Maldonado, a passenger on the ship *Santiago* in 1571, who, annoyed at not getting what all the common sailors could get, relieved his frustration by launching "ugly and injurious words against the honor of the female passengers who traveled on that ship." Maldonado's accusations were quite direct, since "he claimed that all of the women who traveled on the said ship were fornicating even with the apprentice seamen." Confronted with such rudeness, the captain of the ship ordered Maldonado to remain confined below decks.[114]

The punishment was actually worse than it sounds; after spending weeks at sea, and just when their approach to the Caribbean made the nights warm, the ardent Maldonado was forbidden to go on deck, which is where the type of diversion that interested him was concentrated. Because of that, when the captain of the ship asked that he remain closed in, Maldonado's laments from the hold recalled the lament of Sigismund enchained in his tower: "Now sir, am I some heretic or some evil man that I cannot come out where the other passengers sleep because it is so hot? . . . Since they are all screwing one another, allow us to look out for ourselves. . . . Since [the women passengers] parade around from poop to prow brushing against everybody, allow us to parade around where we can find them."[115]

The laments of the unhappy Maldonado provide evidence of the dissimulation that crew members and passengers practiced in order to give slack rein to their passions in a reduced space crammed with people. He referred on various occasions to the fact that "the women who traveled on the said ship brushed against everyone on the said ship,"[116] and, although he did not describe this technique with precision, I do not believe it takes much acuity to imagine it. However, we should not lose sight of the fact that the concept of privacy has changed a great deal. People in the sixteenth century were accustomed to living heaped together, and it was normal that parents shared a single room with their children, the grandparents, and perhaps another relative. For this same reason, sexual contacts were not as restricted as they are today to the interior of alcoves; the crew members on board would have enjoyed ample instruction in these tussles, which enabled them to take advantage of any opportunities that arose.[117]

However, although there were some ships where the female passengers proved to be especially accessible, one must suppose that the majority of sailors would not have had opportunities to establish heterosexual relationships for the duration of the voyage. The proportion of female emigrants was frankly a small minority; even at the end of the sixteenth century, women accounted for only 30 percent of the white inhabitants of the American continent. On any given fleet, the number of women was not very high. As an example we can examine the case of the fleet that went to New Spain in 1594; from a total of 398 officially registered passengers, there were thirty-six married women who traveled with their husbands, five widows, and twenty-eight unmarried women.[118] Of course, the real number of emigrants would be much higher on board this fleet, and as on any fleet, there would have been a sizable contingent of illegal female passengers. But despite this, in those days it was a rare convoy that did not have from fifteen hundred to two thousand sailors, who would have had to compete for women with the male passengers, many of them bachelors who had more freedom of action than the men of the sea. However large the number of llovidas (female stowaways), a sailor in the Carrera de Indias had to be a real Don Juan, with luck on his side, to obtain the gift of some welcoming female arms.

Thus, during the voyage the scant number of candidates for female sexual partners, and the moral authority of the generals, made heterosexual relationships difficult for the sailors to arrange. However, upon arrival in port, it was much harder to exercise control over the mariners, which led to the logical consequence of their repressed desires.[119] Some of these desires were relieved through prostitution, but on other occasions, pure sexual violence was unleashed on the unhappy inhabitants of the ports. Thus, for example, General Cristóbal de Eraso had to sit in judgment on some officers and sailors who had dedicated themselves to robbery in Cuba and Veracruz, raping Indian and Negro women in the process.[120]

The Ship as a Place of Life and Death

Acquiring a female partner on a ship was difficult, but it carried a limited risk. Candidates for a homosexual relationship were many, but if the matter was discovered, it carried a real danger of ending up in the hands of the hangman. The question immediately arises as to the level of homosexuality on the ships of the Carrera de Indias. Naturally, there is nothing resembling statistics on this subject, but certain legal cases regarding sodomy do exist among the documents in the Archive of the Indies. I have been able to find half a dozen specific references to such cases between 1519 and 1606, and surely many more exist among the documentation.

At first glance that does not seem like many. However, given that much homosexual conduct remains hidden even now, despite the fact that it is not considered a crime, it is perfectly understandable that in the sixteenth century, when homosexuals could end up at the stake, people used all their discretion in trying to keep such behavior hidden from the world. Even in those relationships that were discovered, we know for certain that they had been kept secret for months and were brought to light only by unforeseen circumstances.

There is a theory that the special conditions of isolation and the predominantly masculine component of the crews converted the workplace on long transoceanic voyages into a situation especially favorable to the development of homosexuality. Similar circumstances obtained among the fierce pirates that infested the Caribbean, who, like other groups of warriors, lived together for long periods removed from the rest of society. According to this theory, sexual relations among persons of the same sex constituted one of the most common and secret traditions of the men of the sea.[121]

On the other hand, some recent ethnohistorical studies point to the existence of a certain misogynist tradition among mariners. A woman on board was seen not only as a disturbance but even as a source of disgrace and bad luck. Those who espouse this theory argue that the only woman for whom many sailors felt real respect was their own mother, while the well-known stereotype of a sailor with a girlfriend in every port was only a symbol of Don Juanism, that is, of immaturity and a fear of establishing a stable relationship.[122]

From my point of view, the existence of a certain depreciation of things feminine could be explained by the common human tendency to devalue what one is not in a condition to possess; in any case, such sentiments did not necessarily lead to permanent homosexual relationships. The real and persistent problem in determining the degree of homosexuality among the crews of oceangoing ships is the lack of statistics. To compensate for this lack, some scholars have drawn parallels to homosexuality in current prison situations, which are thought to reproduce the conditions on board ships—authentic "wooden jails."[123] In any case, despite the force of such arguments, little more than conjectures can result from this type of comparison.

Regarding the Spanish seaborne routes in particular, we have already seen that women were always on board, and for that reason, the ambience of the ships of the Carrera de Indias was never exclusively masculine. Moreover, we know that in the city of Seville, there was an average of three executions a year for sodomy over a period of thirty-eight years.[124] Taking this last piece of information into account, and even without conducting a systematic investigation of the thousands of legal cases heard by the House of Trade, it is difficult to accept that homosexuality was more common on board ships than in the streets of a great port city. Nonetheless, there is no doubt that the phenomenon existed on board Spanish ships. We know perfectly well the forms and circumstances under which it occurred, the tremendous punishments meted out, and even the motives that led many to denounce their companions, accusing them of such a dishonorable crime.

The fact that young pages and apprentice seamen were subject to the authority of boatswains, guardianes, or stewards was propitious for hiding a pederastic relationship. In many cases, the boys were placed by their parents under the tutelage of an officer, in order to have one less mouth to feed and to ensure that the youth could learn to be an officer. In such circumstances the dependency was even greater, and it was easier to camouflage affections that were purely sexual under the protective coloration of paternalistic effusions. Stories were told on ships in which the protagonists generally were boatswains who, beneath the ship's bridge, taught tender young pages the "secrets" of the sea.[125]

For an adult with homosexual tendencies and some authority on board, the young pages and apprentices could be a strong temptation. The lists of crewmen contained a whole series of human types marked by wounds and the passage of time. Alongside the majority of mariners with faces crisscrossed by scars and burns, who were bald, lame, or toothless, there were pages and apprentices like "Juanes de Jáuregui, son of Martín de Jáuregui, fifteen years old, with a beautiful face."[126] These young boys with beautiful faces were the most frequent objects of inflamed amorous passions. The importance of having a position of authority in this type of conduct is reflected in the fact that, among the six cases of homosexuality collected, the instigators included five officers (among them an old general of the fleet, plus a master, a boatswain, an ensign, and a steward) and only one sailor.

But when the matter came to light, not even the most noteworthy officers in the fleet could escape severe punishment. Thus, for example, one of the first victims of the Magellan-Elcano expedition was the master of the ship *Victoria*, the Sicilian Antonio Salomón, executed by order of Magellan upon being found guilty of committing the "nefarious crime" of homosexual conduct. Salomón was not the only one executed for this reason, because a Genoese apprentice on the same ship, Antonio Varesa, perished upon being thrown into the sea by persons unknown. This turbulent affair, which occurred on one of the greatest voyages of discovery in human history, highlights the fact that homosexuality on board was an evident fact, and those who were punished were much less numerous than those who participated in such conduct.[127]

Burning at the stake had been the punishment for these crimes since the Middle Ages, and at this time it was still being used to execute mariners guilty of sodomy. That was the unhappy fate that overtook a sailor on the galleon *San Tadeo*, called Juan Bautista Finocho, who was accused of homosexuality and burned in Havana on July 3, 1575.[128] As an alternative to such brutal punishment, there was another that was no less inhumane: to be taken on a shallop among the anchored ships in a fleet, while being beaten to death. This was the penalty decreed for Gaspar Caravallo, a mulatto steward in the crew under the master Pero Díaz, on a ship in the New Spain fleet of 1591.[129]

The case against the mulatto can serve as an example of the circumstances and the treatment that those accused of sodomy received. Caravallo was twenty-seven years old and had been born in Brazil. It seems that he had enjoyed the confidence of the master and the rest of the crew, but that did not prevent the eruption of a scandal involving a terrorized page, thirteen years old. The page, called Pedro Merino, had been thrown into the water half naked near the beach of San Juan de Ulúa, and he had been able to swim to the ship serving as almiranta. Between sobs, the boy told how he had been obliged to flee because "Caravallo, a mulatto on the said almiranta, had kissed him and tried to mount him."[130]

Caravallo was immediately arrested, and an investigation was begun among all the crew members of the ship. Their testimonies made clear that various pages had been subjected to harassment by Caravallo and that the situation had been going on for several months. According to the information gathered, the steward, who had various of these youths under his authority, had shut them into the food storeroom with him, trying to fulfill his desires. On other occasions, he had molested them during the night, taking advantage of the darkness. In fact, the testimony about Caravallo's adventures and misadventures seems to be taken from a pornographic novel, and they would be laughable if the destiny of the protagonists were not so cruel. By way of example, I am going to reproduce one of the descriptions, although not among the most lurid so as not to offend the sensibilities of any reader who might be upset by such things:

> And after that . . . this witness [the page Pedro Merino] finding himself alone, the accused kissed whatever part he could see; and in the food locker, this witness having gone to take out food for the men, the accused took the witness's hand in his and groped him, and at other times he touched

(172)

his buttocks . . . ; and suspecting that he was a sodomite, this witness always went to sleep with many knots in his pants for fear of the said Gaspar Caravallo, so that he could not mount him. . . . And it was a month ago, more or less, that this witness having gone to sleep, the said Gaspar Caravallo arrived and kissed him as he was accustomed to do and told him that he wanted to screw him, and this witness told him that he did not want to; and the accused forcefully untied his pants, and the witness grabbed them with his hand, and at that he went to sleep, and after a while he awoke and found his pants down and the said Gaspar Caravallo next to this witness and behind him, and throwing an arm around him, he had his member up against the anal opening of this witness and wanted to put it inside, and this witness turned toward him and did not say a word to him, and he stayed awake until morning.

The investigation also showed that a Vizcayan apprentice seventeen years old had a certain complicity with the mulatto, since the two of them had gone behind closed doors to see which of the two had the larger sexual attributes. The Vizcayan denied this and only acknowledged having received immodest proposals from Caravallo, which he rebuffed, responding that "if Caravallo wanted to vent his passion . . . there was a ram on the ship with which he could do it," which shows us that even bestiality was not too far removed from the habits of some crew members.

All the testimonies worked against the mulatto; although he declared that the pages were angry with him because he punished them when they did not fulfill their duties, nothing could save him from being interrogated while suffering one of the most sadly characteristic tortures used on ships of the time: the *garrucha*. The prisoner was tied with his wrists behind him, and a cord attached to his wrists ran up to a spar and back down to the capstan. When the capstan was turned, the unfortunate prisoner was raised over the deck, with the consequence of dislocating all the joints in his shoulders and arms. To augment the pain, increasingly heavier weights were tied to his feet, and this could eventually impede his breathing and bring about death by asphyxiation, in a process similar to that suffered by those who were crucified.

The scrivener of the fleet recorded the torture applied to Caravallo in riveting testimony. It demonstrates not only the physical brutality of the proceedings but also the psychological torture involved in telling the prisoner, before beginning the interrogation, that if he died or had his limbs damaged, all the responsibility would be his for not telling the truth. With great attention to detail the scrivener reported how the unfortunate mulatto was hoisted off the ground as many as seven times. First they tied his feet to the breech of a small piece of artillery; then to two pieces of artillery; later to a net containing

The Ship as a Place of Life and Death

eight cannon balls; and finally to a lead ingot weighing more than one hundred kilograms. Early in the torture, Caravallo had the strength to shout for all the saints to come to his aid: "He called out and said, Mother of God, assist me; Mother of God, protect me . . . and he shouted, calling to St. Francis and to Jesus." As the weights were increased he did not speak but "frothed at the mouth . . . and vomited." Finally, in a moment when he recovered consciousness, he only denied the accusations and said that he felt as if he were already dead.

The torture very nearly killed the mulatto Caravallo, and although he did not confess his guilt, he was condemned to receive three hundred blows in sight of the whole armada, which surely would have ended his life. Surprisingly, however, the steward was saved. In the first place, he appealed the sentence to the judges of the House of Trade; then, upon arriving in Spain, someone must have bribed the master of the ship on which Caravallo arrived as a prisoner, and he disappeared without leaving a trace. Who would have paid the bribe? Could it have been the officers of his ship, who had considered him an honorable man before the charges were brought? Were too many people fearful that Caravallo would not have the same fortitude under further torture and would finally testify? Despite those possibilities, I would like to think that there were tolerant people who were capable of helping him, so that the tremendous and unjust weight of the law would not fall upon him.

Another person accused of sodomy who temporarily succeeded in saving his life was a boatswain. Originally from somewhere in the eastern Mediterranean, he was accused and arrested on the galleass *San Pelayo*. Knowing that his destiny, if he arrived on land, was to fall into the hands of the executioner, he promoted a mutiny that took control of the ship. This did not allow him to escape death, however, as he was assassinated by his comrades in the revolt.[131]

One disquieting circumstance is that, in the cases reviewed thus far, one of the accused was a mulatto of Brazilian origin, and the rest either were foreigners or seem to be foreigners, given their last names. We are really dealing with too few examples to be able to arrive at firm conclusions, but the inevitable impression is that accusations of sodomy implied a certain ethnic or national rancor. However, in the next two cases that I could find, undoubted Spaniards of noble rank were implicated, one of whom was second-in-command of all the naval forces in the Indies. These last cases differ from the former ones, yet there is something in common between the detention of a Brazilian mulatto and a Spanish admiral: the likely existence of rancor and envy that precipitated the accusation of sodomy. In this regard, the moral intransigence that treated sexual deviance so brutally was little more than a cloak to hide other "pleasantries" of the human spirit, such as xenophobia, racism, or professional jealousy.

Early in the seventeenth century, Miguel Pérez de Amezquita, captain of an infantry company embarked on a small fleet anchored in Havana, denounced his ensign Ginés Caballero del Castillo for sodomy.[132] The case apparently had no great novelty. Various pages and apprentices between fifteen and seventeen years of age testified against the ensign, giving highly realistic testimonies about the officer's homosexual tendencies. He would acknowledge only that the boys were accustomed to helping him take his clothes off, and that they scratched his legs because he had an ailment in them. However, other witnesses began to make clear that the captain of the company, who was also the principal denouncer, was a mortal enemy of the ensign, because the latter had been nominated directly by the king, displacing a nephew of the captain from the post. We find this nephew among the witnesses against Ginés Caballero, which leads one to suspect the impartiality of the rest of the witnesses. Those suspicions are confirmed with the knowledge that some of the pages withdrew their declarations and admitted to having been pressured by Captain Amezquita to establish the ensign's guilt. Despite everything, the disgraced Ginés Caballero was sent to Seville under arrest, where he was subjected to a very harsh interrogation that included torture "of water and rope." After the torture, all documentary trace of the case ceases; this might be because the ensign was seriously injured or perhaps died shortly afterward as a consequence of the brutal interrogation.

Even more notable, because of the importance of the persons implicated, was the case brought against Don Nicolás Cardona, accused by the page Juan García of trying to commit the "nefarious sin." Cardona was a Sevillian hidalgo who had been general of the Tierra Firme fleet in 1569 and who in 1571 was named by the king as admiral of the Guard Squadron of the Carrera de Indias; that is, second-in-command of that squadron, whose captain general was Pedro Menéndez de Avilés.[133]

Nicolás Cardona was jailed in Santo Domingo, found guilty, and condemned to torture. Nonetheless, in a surprising development, the Court of Appeals in Santo Domingo reviewed his case and declared him innocent in a sentence issued August 28, 1573, while his denouncer, the page Juan García, was punished with one hundred lashes for perjury. Admiral Cardona could scarcely enjoy his liberty, as he became ill while in jail and died at the end of 1573, perhaps demoralized for having been subjected to such an infamous proceeding.

The most interesting thing about the incident is the knowledge that Pedro Menéndez de Avilés had openly opposed Cardona's accession to the post of admiral. Although Cardona arrived with a royal nomination, Menéndez refused to give him possession of the post. The reasons for Menéndez de Avilés' behavior are very clear. Besides being a formidable mariner, he was the leader of a large coterie of military men from the Cantabrian coast, bound to him by ties of friendship, family, and clientage. The most important posts in the armada were normally filled by the captain general from among the members of his clan. When presented with an alien, who had the additional effrontery to be an Andalusian, to occupy the second slot in the hierarchy of command, Menéndez was indignant and let the king know it, which caused him to receive these complaints in a royal order:

> At court we were made aware that the majority of men who sailed on that armada were Vizcayans, Guipuzcoans, and Asturians, and the most distinguished among them, for many years, had occupied themselves in our service in your company on other armadas and in this one [the Guard Squadron of the Carrera de Indias] from the time of its foundation; and for that reason they had the presumption to think that we had to grant the favor of the said post of admiral to someone among them.

Although the monarch understood the reasoning of his captain general, he imperiously ordered him to comply with his orders. Pedro Menéndez had no recourse but to name Cardona as his admiral in 1571. We already know that the career of that Andalusian mariner in the squadron of men from the north was very short: he died from an illness contracted in prison, although one could say that he perished because of a calumny. Are there not perhaps too many coincidences to avoid thinking that many trials for homosexuality were really weapons launched at an enemy or a competitor, who, perhaps, and only perhaps, might have had sexual inclinations distinct from those of the majority of mariners?

Life Hanging by a Thread

Diego García de Palacio, someone who was well acquainted with life at sea, affirmed that if it was risky to commend one's fortunes to something as voluble and difficult to control as the force of the wind and the waves, it could be considered complete madness to put one's life "three or four fingers from death, which was the thickness of a ship's planking."[134] The risks that a transoceanic voyage ran were high and varied: the sailors' lives were threatened by shipwrecks, work-related accidents, epidemics, bad food, and assaults by corsairs and pirates. Of course, if someone had trouble selecting a way to die, he would find a wealth of choices by embarking on a sea voyage.

As in almost all human activities, experience lessened the dangers; undoubtedly, the possibility of losing one's life was much greater for the sailors on the first voyages of discovery than for those in fleets during the second half of the sixteenth century. It is no wonder that many of the crews on the dangerous expeditions to the Moluccas, who knew the risk they ran, had testaments drawn up before leaving and made solemn declarations as if they already had one foot in the grave.[135] Later, based on sad experience, sailors were familiar with some of the most dangerous reefs, the times of the year when the weather produced hurricanes and epidemics in some ports, or the hidden places where corsairs waited to intercept Spanish ships. Nonetheless, knowing the dangers did not eliminate all of their consequences; some were inevitable, and, mimicking the old refrain, anyone who did not want to get wet should not go to sea.

Shipwreck seemed to be the most obvious risk and the most common way to die for a man of the sea. A ship could sink for many reasons. As Escalante de Mendoza said, a ship loaded to the mast tops was as fragile as a "flask filled with water, which a small blow could break into pieces."[136]   (177)

The ships of the Carrera de Indias normally sailed overloaded, and the blows capable of breaking them to bits were not inflicted only by colliding with a reef. In the middle of the ocean a wave of great size could strike a fierce blow on the keel capable of opening the hull to deadly waters. Other times the rolling of a ship during a storm made the masts, which normally rested on the keel, open great breaches in the hull. If very heavy cargo had been placed on the upper decks, the ship's stability was compromised, and a small tilt could cause a fatal somersault. Finally, the ships of the Carrera de Indias had shallow drafts to enable them to cross sandbars in ports such as Sanlúcar, San Juan de Ulúa, or Nombre de Dios, and this could turn into a great inconvenience if a storm caught the high prow of a ship between two waves and momentarily left part of the live work above the water, which could cause grave breaks in the structure of the hull.

Faced with so many disagreeable possibilities, when the master of a ship predicted an oncoming storm, he immediately sprang into action. The first task was to physically and psychologically prepare his mariners to confront the forces of nature. Taking into account that even death can be faced better on a full stomach than with empty guts, the first thing was to feed those who were going to expend greater-than-normal physical efforts for hours, or even days. Psychological support would come from the fortitude demonstrated by the officers, and especially the captain, master, and pilot. If any of these "commanders" preferred to go to bed in order "not to see death with his eyes open," as sometimes happened, the morale of the crew fell sharply, and the fate of the ship lay in the hands of Providence or destiny alone. Thus wrote Juan de Escalante de Mendoza about the period before a storm, when the crew received a meal that strongly recalled the last supper of a condemned man:

> When the good captain, master, or pilot sees that such a piece of bad luck
> is beginning, he ought to order his men called to the poop and have the
> best food and drink in the hold brought on deck and invite his officers and

---

The Ship as a Place of Life and Death

sailors and the other able people to share it, speaking to them in this way: "Well, then, brothers, eat and drink and behave like good people and do not be afraid, for this is nothing to fear, for God Our Lord is and will be with us; and now I want to see who the good sailors are." And as long as the crisis lasts the captain, master, or pilot should not sleep, nor go to bed, nor retire, nor go where he cannot be seen, but he should be ever watchful, speaking and calling out and giving orders with a show of much spirit and strength.[137]

Once the mariners had filled their stomachs, the master should begin clearing the decks of any object that would impede maneuvers. If the state of the sea worsened, he ought to remove burdens at the highest parts of the ship and throw them into the water. If this was not sufficient, he ought to cut down the superstructure; and, finally, the last recourse consisted in throwing the spars and even the masts into the sea. The openings where water flowed in could be fought with the pumps, and also by plugging with "palletes," that is, tarred canvas that worked like bandages on the entry points for water in the hull's exterior. If the damage was great and the entire ship began to break apart, one desperate solution consisted in binding the hull with the anchor cables to reinforce it. But if all these efforts failed, there remained no other remedy but to leave the ship.

If one was very lucky and sailed on frequented routes, perhaps some other ship would come to help. But one should not entertain the delusion that the help was free. That became obvious to the captain and pilot Juan Rodríguez de Noriega, who, after suffering through a tremendous storm, was left with his ship *Concepción* on the point of sinking, in the vicinity of the Bermuda Islands. By chance a Spanish caravel appeared, initiating negotiations as to how the crew and the silver on Noriega's ship could be transferred to the caravel. The problem was that in order to provide room for the survivors of the storm, their rescuers had to throw part of their own cargo into the sea, and they demanded that the survivors pay top market prices for any jettisoned items. When the accord seemed concluded, the men on the caravel complained that the provisions on the wrecked ship were unusable, which meant that everyone would have to share the caravel's food, and perhaps all of them might die of hunger. With this turn of events, the negotiations were broken off, and the desperate crew members of the ship *Concepción* were abandoned to their fate. Surprisingly, luck was on their side, since another ship appeared with which they finally reached an agreement. Noriega was able to reach Seville and see that the captain of the caravel was fined for refusing to provide help at sea.[138]

Within Spanish fleets, the abandonment of a ship would not be as dramatic, since the shipwrecked men would be distributed among various other ships in the convoy. Nonetheless, the possibility of an easy rescue was not good for business, in the opinion of shipowners, since it inspired the abandonment of many ships and the consequent ruin of their owners. Faced with the existence of a possible retreat from danger, the sailors did not defend themselves with the same zeal as if they were alone in the middle of the ocean. That is why a shipowner like Juan de Escalante de Mendoza referred admiringly to stratagems employed by some ship lords to avoid a rapid abandonment of the vessel.

There were shipowners who were the equal of Hernán Cortés himself, since, like Cortés, they cut off any possibility of escape to their men. Nonetheless, whereas the conqueror of Mexico grounded and sank his fleet, the shipowners tried to do just the opposite. That explains why some ships left the company of a convoy during the night, even with the vessel in serious straits; this way, the crew understood that only by saving the ship—that is, the fortune of the owner—could they also save their own lives. An even simpler maneuver consisted in untying the ship's boat, making it impossible to abandon ship with any hope of survival. And there was even the tale of a captain who, to keep his men from being alarmed at the appearance of leaks, secretly caused small leaks to familiarize his sailors with them, so that they would not panic at a critical moment.[139]

Despite what we might assume, shipwrecks most frequently occurred in the vicinity of the coast. Sailing at night in the proximity of the shore carried a very high risk. If the pilot was careless and the currents were too strong, the ship could find itself in peril. That happened to the ship serving as almiranta in the New Spain fleet of 1582. The pilot was ill, and the ship was commanded by an impulsive and imprudent master, who, contrary to the recommendations of the mariners, turned toward land in the middle of the night. He wanted to be the first to enter Veracruz, but in the darkness he was surprised by a strange brightness, first attributed to the light of the dawn but which finally proved to be the deadly whiteness of a reef, against which the ship crashed and broke into pieces. "And because for half an hour he saw the sea whitening, like the foam of waves breaking, the master asked the sailors to be on guard with this witness, to see what was making the sea lighten; and they all said that it was the light of day, and this witness, still looking carefully to see what it was, recognized it to be a shallow place, and many voices called out to the boatswain and the men to take a sounding."[140]

When storms pushed ships toward the rocks, every experienced sailor knew that, if there was not a good port nearby, their lives were more secure at sea than in approaching the land. Despite the fact that inexperienced passengers asked to be taken rapidly ashore, the good master was supposed to avoid the deadly songs of the sirens and head the prow out to sea to ride out the storm.

The Ship as a Place of Life and Death

Nonetheless, a sailing ship laden with heavy merchandise could not always avoid being dragged against the reefs. At times an error in recognizing a coast could place a ship in a trap from which it was very difficult to escape. Thus in 1570, the hulk *La Concepción* sailed in the vicinity of the extreme west of Cuba, approaching Cape Corrientes. Its pilot committed a grave error and mistook this jagged coastline for Cape San Antón, which was twelve leagues farther west. Before those on board could realize their mistake, the wind pushed them toward the coast, and they came upon Cape Antón, which they believed they had already passed and which then blocked their way. That was the start of nine long days and nights in which the crew did everything possible to avoid smashing against the coast. They threw out all the anchors, but one after another the anchor cables broke, and when a single anchor remained, the wind changed and they could finally leave their rattrap, towed by their own ship's boat: "Off the said sandy beach [of Corrientes] we spent nine days and nights suffering through great labors and every hour tending to the mooring ropes at the prow, wrapping them so that they would not wear through, and making all the other repairs . . . with great diligence and care, going without sleeping every night and without eating most of the days, forgetting everything else to save our lives."[141]

But not everyone had such luck. The wreck of the nao named *La Buitrona*, because its owner was Cosme Buitrón, won tragic fame for the number of victims who perished on her and because the wreck occurred in the vicinity of the coast, with Spanish beaches already in sight, after having completed a very long voyage. The ship sailed in the fleet of Cosme Rodríguez Farfán, and it was caught by a storm that dragged it into the proximity of Zahara, near Cape Trafalgar. The ship rode out the storm anchored near the coast, but the passengers, seeing their deceptive salvation so near, mutinied and cut the anchor cables so that the ship would run aground on the nearby sandy beach. Unfortunately, they chose a bad moment to mutiny, since the tide was high and beginning to recede. For that reason, the ship ran aground far enough from the shore, and with such a strong undertow from the tide, that it was pulled back into the sea, ending the lives of 180 persons, with their salvation just a few meters away.[142]

One of the greatest causes of shipwrecks was fire. On sixteenth-century ships, everything but the nails was combustible, and that is why carelessness with lighted candles on board constituted a very high risk. The cooking fire was the only light that was permitted on board without being enclosed in a metal or glass lantern. During storms, the cooking fire was put out after sunset. At night, the only light that remained was the one that illuminated the compass box and one lantern shared among those on guard. Despite these precautions, there were many disastrous fires, but perhaps none like that in September

1561, which destroyed twenty-three ships moored in the port of Seville. The origin of the fire was in the tomfoolery of a sailor, who eased his boredom by setting cats on fire; the bad luck was that one of these animals, running around terrified and with its fur alight, set fire to half the fleet.[143]

When a ship wrecked at sea, destroyed itself against the shore, or burned, everyone on board suffered the consequences. In addition, even without these dramatic moments, sailors were exposed to a large number of work-related accidents. To maneuver the ship's boat in midocean posed an obvious risk. These small auxiliary craft sank fairly easily and claimed many victims. Thus, the sinking of the boat from the nao *San Gabriel*, which belonged to Loaisa's expedition to the Moluccas, ended the lives of seventeen men, among them the ship's treasurer.[144] To work the masts during a storm carried the risk not only of plummeting to the deck but of being struck by lightning, a fairly frequent occurrence.[145] On other occasions, instead of the sailor falling from a spar, it was the spar that fell on the unfortunate sailor.[146] For all that, the most frequent working accident consisted of falling into the water. Even in cases where the event was observed by someone, the wretched victim did not have many possibilities of being recovered alive, due to the difficulties of handling a ship under sail. Nonetheless, Alonso de Chaves provided a whole gallery of useful advice for those who found themselves in such a perilous situation; at the same time, he launched his malediction against ships' masters who did not overly exert themselves to recover a crewman who had fallen into the sea:

> And the man should, as he falls to the water, let out a great yell so that someone will hear it, if the accident happens at night or at some other time when no one would have seen him fall, so that those on board can quickly go to whichever side it was, and also so that, the minute he strikes the water, sharks or other fish will not come to eat him, because they will be frightened of him and flee. . . . Besides yelling, he ought to strike the water and make noise so that the fish will stay away.[147]

But neither accidents nor shipwrecks produced as many victims among the mariners as the epidemics unleashed in tropical American ports, where the fleets were obliged to remain, at times, for many months. Illnesses for which they had no immunity, because the illnesses rarely occurred in Europe, together with the minimal hygienic conditions and the crowded conditions on board the ships, caused authentic catastrophes. The ships' masters tried to keep the crews on board the ships to prevent desertions and because at any moment a hurricane might loose its fury, and many hands would be needed to save the ship. It is no wonder that many reports complain about the shortage of Spanish mariners, "so many mariners who were natives of Spain having died in the Indies, especially in Veracruz and Nombre de Dios."[148]

The Ship as a Place of Life and Death

Perhaps the most dangerous place of all was the insalubrious northern coast of Panama, site of the port of Nombre de Dios, where commercial fairs were held to exchange European merchandise for the silver of Potosí. The months of July, August, and September were the worst, since the heat and the rains rotted the ships' rigging with the same rapidity and intensity with which they rotted the bodies and the morale of the crews. For that reason, the rhythm of the Tierra Firme fleets eventually adapted itself to this reality, leaving Spain at the end of summer in order to arrive at the Isthmus of Panama after these dangerous months had passed. Had this not been the case, "and if the fleets go in summer to Nombre de Dios, everyone will die, so that there will be no one to bring the ships back to Spain."[149]

(182)

The geographer Juan López de Velasco defined Nombre de Dios as "a very sickly town" and calculated that if a fleet had the bad fortune to arrive there between the months of May and November, it was condemned to pay a tribute of more than three hundred victims, which, taking into account that the total number of crew members would be between two thousand and three thousand, meant that the expedition would be literally decimated by epidemics.[150]

When the decision was taken in 1585 to move the fairs to the nearby locality of Portobelo, not a great deal was gained in the matter of healthfulness.[151] The new port had a beautiful and suggestive name, but it always was a miserable place where the houses were counted in the dozens and the graves in the thousands. This is how Antonio de Alcedo described the climate and the working conditions for mariners during the layovers in Portobelo:

> The climate of this city is very bad, because of the excessive heat, to which its location contributes, being surrounded by mountains on all sides so that no breeze can pass through . . . and from which vapors rise that condense into clouds and form copious rains; then, when the rains end, the sun comes out, but before its rays have dried the surface of the land . . . it rains again . . . ; this continuous bad weather, joined to the fatiguing work of the mariners, makes them sweat so much that it weakens them, and to recover their strength they resort to strong liquor, of which they consume an extraordinary amount; and the excessive work, the disorders caused by drinking, and the perversity of the climate damage even the best constitutions and produce the malign illnesses that are common there.[152]

If a sailor fell ill, his only hope of survival effectively rested in his own powers of resistance, which were customarily increased by the administration of a special diet for the sick. The only doctors in the fleets sailed on the capitana and the almiranta, and their science was as limited in effectiveness as that of their colleagues on land, with the added disadvantage of having fewer means at their disposal to treat the sick. On the rest of the ships, the person responsible for health care was often a barber-surgeon. Some of them even knew how to bleed a sick person, which did more harm than good to the poor patient, who became even more debilitated by the hemorrhage. But many others did not even know how to finish off a sick person efficiently, because they were simple sailors contracted to "serve in the post of surgeon."[153] Pity the crewman who fell into the hands of some of these apprentice bloodletters! It would have been better simply to let them eat the broth, chicken, and white biscuit (which was the diet destined for the sick) than to rely on the remedies of whoever on board was in charge of health care.

(183)

In America, if an illness worsened, the sailor was disembarked and interned in a hospital. In Veracruz as well as in Cartagena de Indias, there were functioning institutions run by religious orders, destined primarily for the care of the destitute, among whom sick crewmen would customarily be found. When officers or crewmen with some resources fell ill, they tried to avoid these hospitals. They preferred to contract for care with local women, who, for a sum of money, normally very inflated, would lodge sick persons in their homes and feed them until they either recovered or died. There they also received visits from local doctors, who did what little they could to save their lives.

The sailor also had the opportunity to take part in naval battles and to experience firsthand another type of death, even if such opportunities were few. During the first half of the century, and before the establishment of the convoy system, there were quite a few ships intercepted by corsairs and pirates. In these initial decades, naval battles had a strong medieval flavor, and almost all of the action consisted in boarding and defending against boarding by the enemy.

Merchant ships normally tried to avoid combat, but if there was no way to escape and a hostile encounter with a corsair was inevitable, the captain or the master had to prepare his sailors to face battle and death. Just as in the moments prior to a storm, the crew received a full ration of food and drink, although it was advisable to water the wine so that it would animate the men without clouding their judgment. Afterwards came psychological support in the form of a harangue by the captain, who surely would have referred to his men many times with such appellations as "drunkards" or "rogues" but who now would call them "brothers," so as not to remind them that they would be fighting for someone else's fortunes. He would also appeal in his discourse to their opportunity to show that sailors were men of "honor and shame." Given the likelihood that all this flattery would not count for much, he would also remind them that were they to retreat during the struggle, if the corsairs did not kill them, he would see to it himself.[154]

Before engaging in combat, it was wise to position oneself upwind from the enemy, so that all the smoke of the firearms would blind men on the opposing ship. Heavy artillery was still scarce during the first half of the century; if one had it, the first mission would be to fire solid cannon balls of metal or stone to open breaches near the water line of the enemy ship. When the distance between the ships was very short, one would fire twin cannonballs linked with chains, destined to break the rigging, the spars, and the masts, thus immobilizing the enemy. To achieve these ends, Alonso de Chaves recommended that the gunners remain calm and verify before firing that they had really put the ball in the gun, since fear and nervousness often led to the firing of harmless salvos instead of cannon balls.[155]

Meanwhile, on deck the men would have placed barrels of water and wet blankets to put out fires and would have protected the sides of the aftcastle and the forecastle with mattresses. From the castles, men would fire the smaller guns on board (*falconetes*, small culverins, or *versos*, and so on), harquebuses, muskets, and crossbows. But much smaller projectiles were not scorned either. From the tops of the foremast and mainmast the men threw whatever they had that might wound or incapacitate the enemy, from javelins to flaming arrows (called *alacranes*) down to the simple and prehistoric stone.[156] The thrown objects most commonly used were small ceramic or clay receptacles, called *alcancías*. There were incendiary types, filled with gunpowder and the tar and oil mixture called *alquitrán*, which were armed by lighting them with a match before throwing them. Others were filled with oil or soap, with the intention of shattering them on the enemy's deck and making the men slip and fall. Finally, there were some filled with lime to blind the enemy. This series of ingenious weapons was complemented with *abrojos*, pieces of iron with four sharp points projecting at equal angles, which were thrown on the enemy's decks as hazardous obstacles.

The minimal sophistication of these thrown weapons may perhaps bring a smile to a man of today, accustomed to napalm, surface-to-air missiles, and hydrogen bombs. But we should not deceive ourselves; although these weapons were less effective than weapons in use today, the intent was the same. When the intent succeeded and produced victims, the writers of treatises on naval warfare all advised immediately removing the dead or wounded from the battle, both to treat those still alive and to prevent the evidence of their tremendous wounds from sapping the morale of the rest of the combatants.

Once everything at hand had been launched, boarding was inevitable. The defensive position advised placing the men under the wooden grating between the forecastle and the aftcastle. This grating impeded direct access to the interior of the hull, and if the enemy jumped upon it they could not clearly see the defenders, who would be protected by the penumbra formed by the wooden grate. By contrast, the attackers would offer perfect targets, fully visible, to be shot at from below. In some cases the wooden grating was protected with a "false grating" of rope. If the enemy jumped upon it, the rope grating was suddenly removed, causing an attacker to fall on the wooden grating, where he was killed.

In the second half of the century, the protection that warships provided to the merchant convoys decreased the incidence of attacks and ensured that no fleet could be taken by an enemy. The techniques of warfare were also changing, and the use of artillery inexorably replaced boarding. In a memorandum directed to the king, Juan de Escalante de Mendoza advised adopting the tactics of the corsairs, who never attacked if they were not sure of winning, and when they did it was by "shooting from afar without approaching the enemy, nor boarding until after having forced the enemy to surrender by force of gunfire and balls"—of iron, of course.[157]

(185)

Thus, the causes of death at sea were many. Normally, the blame was divided among epidemics, storms, and corsairs; nonetheless, often one forgets the existence of a secret cause, common to almost all deaths at sea: human greed. In the case of piratical assaults, the presence of avarice as the ultimate cause seems evident and needs no clarification. But how could one establish human culpability in the sinking of a ship in the middle of a storm? Obviously, the men of the sixteenth century held very little dominion over the forces of nature, but they could decide to load a ship to the mast tops and to convert it into an unstable platform disposed to sink at the first roll. The reports and memorandums of the time point out that changes designed to augment the ships' cargo capacities and the ambition of shipowners to earn larger freight fees were the true causes of many tragedies.[158]

Work-related accidents, apparently attributable to the dangerous work on board ships, had at base an explanation rooted in an unbounded lust for gain. Thus, there were many sailors who drowned maneuvering the ship's boat, which would not be too strange if we did not know that some ships were so overloaded that they did not have a place on board to put the boat, and they had to tow it behind the ship. Because the auxiliary craft was too valuable to leave untended, two or three crewmen were assigned to it during the voyage. These unfortunate men were frequently battered by the waves and lost their lives so that the owner could collect more profit from freight charges.[159]

Plagues and illnesses were caused by pathogenic microorganisms, but how many mariners were not debilitated by rations that had been cut for the benefit of stewards and masters, who, moreover, would have bought provisions of the worst quality. And then, upon arriving in port, the crews found themselves prevented from disembarking, forced to maintain ships that were converted by the sun's rays into veritable ovens in which all types of infections stewed.

Well then, whatever the causes of death, how many crewmen who sailed toward the Indies left their poor bones interred in some American port or with

The Ship as a Place of Life and Death

the whole ocean as their shroud? I have carried out a small survey of 2,357 persons belonging to seven armada expeditions that left Spain between 1573 and 1593. Of those crewmen, 290 perished during voyages and did not return to their port of departure.[160] The dead men included the 140 crewmen of the galleons *Nuestra Señora de Begoña* and *Santa Catalina*, which were lost in 1579 during their return voyage and from which no one survived.[161]

These 290 victims constituted 12.3 percent of the crews, or, expressing it as demographers do, 123 per thousand. If we take into account that the average mortality in Mediterranean Europe in that century hovered around 40 per thousand,[162] we can conclude that mortality among the mariners was at least three times higher than the average for people on land.

But there were circumstances that made the figures for mortality among mariners even more grave. The general rate of 40 per thousand included the infantile population, which suffered the highest rates of mortality. By contrast, the crews of ships were made up of youths and mature men who were normally found among sectors of the population that were more resistant to illness.

I must also point out that, among the seven expeditions studied, I do not have information that they suffered any epidemic. We already know that the geographer López de Velasco calculated that, when a fleet was surprised by plague in Nombre de Dios, the victims customarily numbered more than three hundred. Fortunately, during the years in question the rhythm of transatlantic voyages was fluid and did not include the feared sojourns in tropical ports. This, together with the knowledge that had been gathered about American climatology, might have saved the crews from epidemics that, had they struck a single convoy, would have doubled the index of mortality.

But death did not mean the end of hope for the men of the sea. Their faith gave them confidence in a later life and for that reason made them worry about the destiny of their mortal remains and about ceremonies destined to assure a more rapid and sure access to heaven. Unfortunately, in this respect the physical conditions surrounding their deaths were as irregular as those that presided over their lives, and the men of the sea faced many difficulties in securing a dignified burial.

In the first place, arranging for the body to rest underground in a sacred place was not always possible. Whoever died at sea was assured of being thrown to the depths of the ocean, and this would produce a certain disquiet. One must take into account that, according to Christian beliefs in the resurrection of the flesh, when the Day of Judgment arrived the dead would leave their tombs in their mortal body to approach God. To have a definite tomb, if possible inside a church, was certainly a more secure and respectable form of awaiting the end of time than having one's bones scattered in the bottomless depths of the sea. Of course, everyone knew that the resurrection of the dead was a miraculous thing and that the worms on land had as little respect for human remains as the fishes in the sea. Nonetheless, if possible the sailors would have preferred to make things as easy as possible for the Creator, and they wanted a thousand times more to be buried on land than to be thrown overboard.

Moreover, ceremonies arranged for the dead during a voyage were limited and lacking in pomp and dignity. For ordinary sailors, a sack and a cannonball served as a coffin. Only the generals of armadas were done the honor of sending their body into the sea enclosed in a wooden box.[163] On the war galleons where there was a chaplain, the funeral service would include responses and prayers in Latin, but on the majority of merchant ships the only funerary honors consisted of words (rather unpolished ones, I fear) from the master of the watch.

Perhaps for that reason, when the guild association of mariners in the Carrera de Indias founded the Brotherhood of Our Lady of Fair Wind, they took special care to dignify the burials of their brothers. This custom of placing such significance on a dignified burial, though common for brotherhoods in other professions, was possibly even more important for men who ran a high risk of not having one.

The ordinances of the Brotherhood of Our Lady of Fair Wind specified that four brothers ought to keep vigil at the death agony of a moribund colleague, and, after his death, all of the others would be advised so that they could attend the burial. To communicate the bad news they named an officer called a *muñidor* (beadle). Wearing a bonete and a blue garment (the typical color of the men of the sea), carrying an image of the Virgin of Fair Wind, and sounding a small bell, he would go through the streets of the maritime neighborhood of Triana, announcing the ceremonies that would take place in the parish of Santa Ana.[164]

The brotherhood wanted to demonstrate the honor of the members of their profession, and for that there was nothing better than an ostentatious ceremony. According to their proposed ordinances, the deceased would enter the church carried on the shoulders of four sacristans, preceded by the orphans of the parish *(niños de la doctrina)* carrying large lighted candles and followed by the rest of the brothers with smaller candles. The number of large candles indicated the importance of the deceased. Ceremonies for brothers and their wives would use twelve large candles; for those who had been made brothers only to have a ceremonial burial, eight large candles would suffice, while the ceremonies for children and servants would use six long, thin candles. It is curious to note that when the authorities of the House of Trade reviewed these ordinances, one of the few points that they amended related to the funerary rites. The seafarers saw the luminous expenditure for their burials restricted to only six large candles for the titular brothers and their wives and two long, thin candles for everyone else.

The Ship as a Place of Life and Death

Even today, with some important differences, this type of brotherhood continues to render similar services, which assures the heirs that the last rites of their deceased relatives will be carried out with dignity and at moderate prices. At least the sailors who died on the high seas did not have a monetary problem, for they "enjoyed" a cheap ceremony, and their heirs could receive their wages almost in full. In spite of that, it never failed that someone was disposed to extract some benefit from the situation for himself. Because it was customary on ships to auction the goods of the deceased among his comrades, royal constables claimed the right to preside over the auctions and to charge a corresponding commission.[165] The sale itself aimed to keep the goods from being lost or damaged and to provide some additional money for the heirs. If a relative or countryman of the deceased also traveled on the ship, normally he took charge of the proceeds of the auction so that he could order some mass for the deceased upon arriving on land and thus provide him with a somewhat more dignified passage toward eternal life.[166]

But if the crewman became ill on land and did not want to go to a hospital for the poor, then he could be sure that the care, food, and medicines he received would take a tremendous bite out of his goods, which normally consisted of little more than the salary that the master owed him. Felipe Boquín, captain of the hulk *El Aguila Volante*, who declared that he had paid for the medicines, care, and burial of various of his sailors, discounted this from their wages in amounts between fourteen and thirty-four ducats, which represented between 20 and 25 percent of their wages.[167] In other words, to die in the sixteenth century, the same as in the twentieth, besides being uncomfortable was also very expensive.

As an example, I reproduce a list of the costs of the sickness and death of the master Nicolás de Rodas, who perished in Nombre de Dios in 1561. The total liquidation of his possessions, minus the debts, were valued at 124,294 maravedís, of which 34,931 were spent on his futile attempt to cheat death and in paying for his burial.[168]

- To the public scrivener in Nombre de Dios, for the testament, inventory, and auction of belongings: 4,950 maravedís
- Wax candles for the burial of the body of Nicolás de Rodas: 450 maravedís
- To the senior brother of the Brotherhood of the Most Holy Sacrament, for receiving Nicolás de Rodas as a brother after his death and burying him with the cloth and wax of the said brotherhood: 2,700 maravedís
- To the barber, for spending one night applying the cupping glass to bleed him: 843.75 maravedís
- To the canon precentor of the Holy Cathedral Church of Panama, vicar

of the city of Nombre de Dios, for the burial, masses, and vigils and those who accompanied the body, and the offerings and fees of the sacristan, and the tomb and the cross for the mass of the mortal remains of said Nicolás de Rodas: 9,225 maravedís

— For the alms of six thousand prayed masses: 2,025 maravedís
— To the vicar of Nombre de Dios for the tomb in which he was buried: 2,700 maravedís
— To Dr. Marín, a doctor in Nombre de Dios, for certain visits: 2,700 maravedís
— To the pharmacist, for medicines: 2,250 maravedís
— To Juana Corza, a married woman, for lodging and bed and services for the days in which the said Nicolás de Rodas was in her house: 2,250 maravedís
— To the same, for feeding him with food for the sick: chickens and hens, sugar, almonds, oranges, preserves, lettuce, bread, wine, saffron, and soap to wash his clothes: 4,837.25 maravedís
— Total: 34.931 maravedís

FIVE

Discipline and Conflict

From Colleagues to Proletarians

To understand the full gamut of conflicts that arose aboard ships, especially those that pitted the sailors against the men who exercised authority on the vessels, it is first necessary to understand that many experts in naval history see the sixteenth century as a transition between the late Middle Ages and the early modern age. The change centered on a difference in the general view of the sailor, who went from being a "comrade," in some ways a coparticipant in the business of maritime transport, to being treated as a simple proletarian, that is, someone who brought no more than a pair of hands and lots of muscle to the development of the enterprise.

During the late Middle Ages, the sailor was linked economically to the development of maritime enterprise, since he collected a part, however small, of the profits earned. If the profits were large, everyone on board benefited, from the master to the least apprentice. Ruin, whether it arrived in the form of a shipwreck, a pirate assault, or some other type of reversal, affected the owner as well as the crew. This—shall we say—complicity caused the simple sailor to be esteemed as a person to take into account in making important decisions. One could say that the risk that he ran in having his fortunes linked to those of the enterprise brought dividends in the form of "consideration," apart, of course, from the concrete economic considerations that accrued to him.

A number of late medieval law codes have been preserved, but one generally thinks of the famous Rôles d'Oléron, which were in effect on the Atlantic coasts, and the *Libro del Consulado del Mar*, which played a similar role in the Mediterranean.[1] Both of them mentioned the obligation of each master to ask the opinion of his crew in resolving delicate situations; although that opinion was not binding, if the master did not follow it, and some inconvenience resulted from his decision, the owners of the ship would consider him solely responsible, making him pay personally for the consequences.

For almost all important decisions, the agreement of the mariners was a necessary step, as much when jettisoning part of the cargo in the teeth of a storm as when the question centered on the dismissal of a sailor who had neglected his duties. One of the most typical and well-known expressions of the consideration accorded to the crew appeared in the second article of the Rôles d'Oléron, which made the timing of a ship's departure contingent on the agreement of the assembled crew: "The master ought to consult with his sailors and he ought to say to them: Sirs, what do you think of this weather? And some of them would tell him: this weather is not good; and some of them would say: the weather is good and fair. The master is obliged to conform with the majority; and if he does otherwise, he is bound to pay all the damages to the ship and to the merchandise that is carried thereon."[2]

By contrast, if we could make a great leap through time and place ourselves on the bridge of a ship in the second half of the eighteenth century, we would see sailors transformed into simple followers of orders, who earned no other benefit from the enterprise than their monthly salary; nor did they have anything to bring to it other than their own physical force. They had been transformed into proletarians, and their experience was not valued, nor was their knowledge taken into consideration; all that was needed were their muscles and their hands. That is why, when the master of an English ship called his crew to attend to some task, he normally employed the expression: "All hands on deck!"[3] It is clear what part of the sailor's body most interested the officers of that epoch. They did not need their brains or their common sense; they only wanted their hands!—that is, the force and sweat of their muscles. There is, without a doubt, a great distance between this expression and the denomination of "comrades" that medieval masters customarily used with their men.[4]

When it came time to mete out the discipline that supported authority, the situation was similar. Of course, transgressors in the late Middle Ages were punished with a harshness that one could easily call cruelty. It was common to apply punishments that might have been inspired by the ancient notion of "an eye for an eye," which held sway in the remote days of the Babylonian lawgiver Hammurabi. For striking an officer, a man had his hand or finger cut off; for attacking an officer with a knife, the aggressor had his hand nailed to a mast; and even more serious offenses merited such brutalities as being keelhauled. But despite all this, medieval laws did not leave a sailor totally defenseless.

No medieval law code permitted what became common during the eighteenth century: the unrestricted power of the captain to treat his men with extreme cruelty, without the possibility of defense or reciprocity.[5] The worst thing was not just the brutality of the discipline, in which authority sustained by the lash converted many decks into authentic slaughterhouses, but the arbitrariness and the treachery with which many officers administered their misnamed justice.[6]

The medieval sailor knew that if he really did something wrong, he would be punished harshly; but if the master unjustly vented his anger against him, showing himself to be implacable and unmerciful, the sailor could legally respond to the attack. Even when he was guilty of some infraction, the law recognized that the sailor's patience had a limit, as article 12 of the Rôles d'Oléron declared: "And if there is contention between the master and some sailor, the sailor ought to put up with the first blow or slap, and if the master wants to give him more, the sailor can well defend himself."[7]

The customs of the sea obliged the master to give the sailor time to reflect, ask forgiveness, and promise to make up for the harm done. This time customarily was three days, and if repentance occurred during that time, the master was not supposed to dismiss the sailor from the ship; if he did so anyway, he had to pay the sailor's full wages and take responsibility for the possible losses that the ship might suffer by being short one crew member.[8]

With all that, the most palpable demonstration of the existence of certain limitations on authority in the medieval law codes appeared in the *Libro del Consulado del Mar*. Those laws even designated a physical space on the ship that could be used as a sanctuary, where the sailor could not be pursued by a furious master bent on beating his brains out. Just as the right of asylum in churches was respected for centuries by the civil authorities, if a sailor stood beyond the anchor chain, he could consider himself safe from the fury of the pursuing officer, assuming of course that the latter did not decide to ignore both law and tradition. If that happened, the sailor would probably receive a beating, but the testimony of the rest of the crew would prove the officer guilty of aggression. "Also, every sailor is obliged to put up with the master when he says a harsh word. And if the master runs after him, the sailor can flee toward the prow and stand beside the anchor chain. And if the master follows him there, he can jump to the other side, and if he catches him there he can defend himself, calling witnesses to what has happened, because the master cannot go beyond the chain."[9]

What were the reasons for the transformation of the old medieval "comrades" into simple "proletarians" by the final years of the early modern period? Some explanations clearly come from economic theory: as maritime commerce grew and prospered, becoming a crucial part of the international movement of merchandise and riches, shipowners were increasingly less disposed to pay sailors with a part of the profits. They preferred to give them a fixed salary by the voyage or by the month.[10] At the same time, the need to lower costs meant that ships grew ever larger but were crewed by relatively fewer men. This meant that each person had to perform considerably more work, and only a rigid discipline could keep the sailor subjected to increasingly intense labor.[11]

One should recognize that many of the prerogatives granted to mariners in the old medieval law codes were not solely designed to protect the crews; they also offered certain guarantees to the owners of the cargo. Merchants had to risk leaving their goods in the hands of the men of the sea, and they felt more secure if the important decisions were agreed upon by all of the crew, instead of confiding in the exclusive judgment of the master. Besides, in a world such as medieval Europe, in which judicial and administrative structures were not very solid, the mariners' testimony was crucial in resolving many conflicts.

The progressive development of modern states, with their growing bureaucracies, increasingly displaced sailors from their erstwhile mission, in which they acted in a way as mediators between merchants and shipowners. Nonetheless, the thing that weakened their position most rapidly was the realization that the ultimate success of maritime enterprises depended less and less on the voluntary service of sailors.

At no time was the collaboration of the crew more necessary than during an accident at sea or in port. If the sailor was a coparticipant in the profits, he would struggle to the end, because at stake was not only his life but also the ruin or survival of his children. There was no better way to inspire their loyalty than to make them partners. Nonetheless, as time went on, dangerous and unknown maritime routes were transformed into well-known paths, traveled almost uneventfully by thousands of vessels each year. Ships were increasingly secure and accidents less frequent. In sum, maritime experience and advances in naval technology converted the solidarity of the sailor into a much less valuable commodity, from which shipowners could gradually divorce themselves. What they did not need they did not pay for. Thus, businessmen centuries ago acted exactly like their counterparts in the twentieth century, who foster the interest of the workers by making them coparticipants in the initial uncertain phase of a business but consider it madness to offer the same thing in a well-established business with predictable profits.

For those reasons, some authors have argued that the history of men of the sea from the thirteenth to the eighteenth century is a long, depressing road toward the loss of privileges[12] and that grim descriptions of the servitude or slavery of medieval sailors are fundamentally unsupported legends.[13] Nonetheless, one should not idealize the situation of sailors in the late Middle Ages too much. Certainly their rights were better defended legally, but they were nonetheless subjected to fierce discipline and paternalistic authority. Paternalism, although it mitigated the violence of authority, also mitigated the energy of enterprise. The conquests carried out by the maritime proletariat over the centuries might not have been achieved had the medieval system of dependence persisted.

Nowadays, in the final years of the twentieth century, there are still ships' crews that function as associates of shipowners, participating in the profits and the failures of the business. That is the case with many coastal fishermen, a sector of the men of the sea for whom mutual aid, solidarity, and cooperation continue being valuable commodities. They generally work on dangerous wooden-hulled vessels, and the sailor's eye is still indispensable to the enterprise as a whole in finding good fishing banks.

But without going so far forward in time, we can ask about the exact position of Spanish sailors on Indies fleets during the sixteenth century. To which definition were they closer: being considered comrades or being considered proletarians?

On the first maritime expeditions of discovery, and especially on those devoted to the search for the Spice Islands, which were the most risky, the old spirit of the Rôles d'Oléron still had great vitality. The sailors and officers were coparticipants in the business through their quintaladas, or shares, and they accepted having part of their salary invested in the global capital of the enterprise. Besides, once they had sailed beyond the traditional routes and sickness had decimated the original officers, important decisions began to be made by agreement of all the members of the expeditions. As a whole, they were defined in the documents not as "the crew" of the ship but as the ship's "company," and each one in particular was not a "sailor" or an "apprentice" but a comrade or *compañero*.

The testimonies from Loaisa's expedition to the Moluccas tell us how those in charge were selected through accords between the captain and the "company" of the ships[14] and that even the post of captain general was decided on various occasions by votes in which all the survivors participated.[15] Sebastian Cabot, on the small fleet that he commanded to the same destination, provided examples of supplication and homage in his relations with the crews that have a clearly medieval flavor. There are testimonies that Cabot used old devices of paternalistic authority, proclaiming that he had not subordinates but "sons" under his command, although that did not prevent him from abandoning three of his "sons" on the coast of Brazil.[16]

It is quite possible that the aforementioned speeches were impregnated with a good dose of populism, and even demagoguery, but that does not preclude considering them as part of a still vigorous tradition, at least when the established lines of authority and communication with the metropolis failed. Some ships' captains behaved like the conquistadores who skillfully manipulated their men in order to justify their own treasons and desertions. Like Hernán Cortés, who used his compañeros to legalize his rebellion in Veracruz shortly after disembarking, Rodrigo de Acuña, one of the captains on Loaisa's expedition, used his crew as an excuse to mask his desertion in returning to Spain.

Don Rodrigo de Acuña, once he left the company of the fleet, ordered all his crew to gather on deck, giving them a choice among the different routes to follow. Though it is not absolutely certain that he tallied the votes strictly as they were cast, the spectacle of a full captain asking the opinion of his subordinates is clearly interesting. This is how one of the ship's survivors described the event: "And so we came toward Río de Genero [Rio de Janeiro] and there Captain Acuña asked for the opinions of the master and the pilot and all the compañeros about what he ought to do, if they should go to the Moluccas by way of the Cape of Good Hope, or return to the Strait of Magellan along the coast to search for the head captain [Loaisa], or if we should go back to Spain."[17]

As the routes of navigation became better known and more secure, this communal spirit was rapidly falling apart. Even the collection of wages based on participation in the freight charges was giving way to the payment of fixed salaries. Nonetheless, at the end of the sixteenth century, although the sailor was no longer considered a comrade of his ship's master, he never lost his identity as a proud free man who was not obliged to render personal services and who could not, with impunity, be treated unjustly or cruelly.

The court of appeals in the House of Trade, the ordinary justices in American ports, and even the generals of the fleets judged the abuses of masters and captains; although inevitably vested interests came into play, there were a great many cases in which sailors' accusations were believed by these authorities, who had no qualms about throwing into jail masters who wronged their crews or failed to pay their salaries.

This attitude seems to contrast strongly, as some recent studies have shown, with the attitude maintained by British maritime tribunals in subsequent centuries. The courts of admiralty served fundamentally to sustain the authority of the captains and masters, giving preference to the rights of shipowners and, in the background, to British industry and commerce—to the detriment of the sailors.[18] On the Spanish routes of the sixteenth century one could not make the same claim. Analysis of the lawsuits filed by the sailors against their masters does not indicate that the owners of capital held a favored position, and one could even conclude that exactly the opposite was true. Spain was not a republic of merchants in the sixteenth century; for that reason, neither the shipowners nor the owners of merchandise succeeded in having their interests defended in total disregard for the rights of the ships' crews.

Spanish monarchs and their advisers probably thought that the dynastic policies of the Austrian Habsburgs coincided in large measure with the interests of the great shipowners in the Carrera de Indias. It is nonetheless certain that they believed their duty lay in protecting the rights of the weak, that is to say, of the sailors; it was not for nothing that governing meant imposing justice. This vision of the situation may have contributed to making Spain's navigational routes function less efficiently than they might otherwise, since shipowners never had total freedom to extract the maximum benefit from manual laborers who worked on their ships. Were some higher quotas of justice obtained in exchange for diminished efficiency? Could this help to explain the eventual failure of Spain's system of maritime communications, which was superseded by other laws and governments less scrupulous with the destiny of their ships' crews? This is, of course, a hypothesis that needs confirmation; to provide arguments in its favor we follow various conflicts that developed between sailors and the officers who represented the constituted authority.

The Struggle for a Salary

One of the most frequent conflicts in the Carrera de Indias occurred when masters and shipowners did not pay the salaries owed to their crews. Normally, the disagreements were resolved peacefully by way of petitions before the judicial tribunals; there are no references that I know of to mutinies or grave disturbances provoked by these situations. The lack of violence in resolving wage conflicts suggests either that punishments were expedited before attempted mutinies or that the judicial route was considered sufficiently effective. The existence of a good number of wage claims heard by the tribunals makes me think that sailors in the Carrera de Indias had a certain degree of confidence in the resolution of their economic problems by the legal system.

On the other hand, the king's justice, which generally forced private parties to conform to legal norms regarding salaries, appeared much more reluctant to act against the interests of the state, when the crown patronized military expeditions or voyages of discovery. This demonstrates once again that kings did not distinguish themselves from other mortals and showed the typical human defect of measuring their own acts and those of others with different yardsticks.

One observes proof of the state's parsimony in the way it treated the survivors and heirs of the great maritime expeditions sent to the Pacific during the first half of the century. Owing to the distance from the metropolis and to the lack of good intermediate bases during the long voyages, many ships were lost en route, and dozens of crewmen wandered for years on Pacific islands, from which only a few succeeded in returning to Spain.

The most significant case might be that of the small fleet sent to the Moluccas in 1525 under the command of García Jofre de Loaisa. On this armada some 450 men left Spain, plus another 110 on a rescue expedition sent from Mexico by Hernán Cortés under the command of Álvaro de Saavedra. Of the total, and excluding some 85 men on the *San Gabriel* and *Santiago* who succeeded in returning to Spain and Mexico, only a few more than half a dozen crewmen returned to the metropolis, after having spent between eleven and twelve years in faraway lands.[19] The petitions of the few survivors and of the heirs of sailors who died filled the offices of the House of Trade in Seville. The royal govern-

---

Discipline and Conflict

ment was not overly generous with subjects who had zealously defended the rights of the monarchy under very difficult conditions.

The Council of the Indies believed that the state's obligations were fulfilled by assigning the sailors a few years' salary, because that was the time considered normal for an armada to make a round-trip voyage to the other side of the world. The attorney of the council, the *licenciado* Villalobos, was charged with defending the interests of the crown against the heirs. He argued that all of the sailors had gone voluntarily and that they were coparticipants in the success or failure of the expedition through their quintaladas. Though they had all sailed with the intention of enriching themselves, the king had no intention of charging them for the costs if the venture had no profits; it was enough to accord them two years' salary![20]

The claims of survivors and heirs clashed again and again with the type of legalized shamelessness that politicians customarily call by the pompous name of "Reason of State." The licenciado Villalobos blamed the delay in the men's return on their propensity to "wander around" all of God's creation or on their "lack of perseverance" in the service of the king. That was precisely how the attorney answered Juan de Mazuelos, a sailor from Lepe, who had spent ten years in the Moluccas: "That although he had originally been in the said armada, he did not persevere in it, and later he went wandering around as he pleased, for which not a single thing is owed to him."[21]

The story of Mazuelos from Lepe is not unique. The cold state machinery did not even make an exception in the disgraceful case of Juan de Menchaca, who, almost twelve years after having left Spain, died worn out and half blind on a Portuguese ship at the latitude of the Azores, just a few days away from being reunited with his family. They received the aforementioned two-years' salary, after showing through witnesses that Menchaca had served faithfully for all the time he was absent.[22]

Heirs challenged this policy in every way possible. Some even employed a sarcastic irony, saying that their relatives "should not be blamed for dying" and arguing that the person responsible for their absence was the king for not having sent ships to bring them home.[23] In 1556, thirty years after Loaisa's expedition departed, legal cases continued between the crown and the descendants of the crew, who finally received a beggar's pittance to definitively quiet their protests. Perhaps the only case in which one feels a certain sympathy for the arguments of the royal attorney was that of the sailor Juan de Perea, a survivor of Loaisa's expedition, who named as his heir a priest in the hospital in Toledo where he had died burdened by debts and poverty. The licenciado Villalobos accused the priest of exemplifying "uncontrolled greed" for taking advantage of the debility of the dying sailor to try to gain his small inheritance and claim it from the king.[24]

Of all the veterans of the expeditions to the Pacific, the most intelligent defense was made by Gonzalo Gómez de Espinosa, a survivor of the first expedition to the Moluccas with Magellan. To the royal attorney's accusation that he had stayed in the islands to seek his own fortune, Gómez responded that the king of Spain had also profited greatly by selling his rights to the Moluccas to Portugal. Therefore, it was only fair that the king share some of those profits with the men who had helped to keep the royal coat of arms on those lands.[25]

In fact, royal stinginess in dealing with the sailors related to the sale of the Moluccas to Portugal by the Treaty of Zaragoza of 1529. When Juan Sebastián Elcano returned with the ship *Victoria* loaded with spices, the survivors were royally compensated, since the crown expected to exploit the Asian trade intensely. Then, once it became clear that the business would not be very easy to consolidate, the Moluccas lost importance for Spain and were handed over to Portugal as one more piece in the game of diplomacy.

When the crews of later Spanish expeditions to the Pacific began to return home, Spain's Oriental spice business had been liquidated; the House of Trade founded in La Coruña to direct it had been dismantled; and the deeds of the stragglers from the Moluccas counted for little. It is well known that collective memory is even more fragile than individual memory in showing gratitude for someone else's sacrifices. When it comes to gathering the fruits of victory, not even heroes can rest on their laurels. The survivors of Loaisa's expedition had exactly the same experience as one illustrious crewman of the galley *Marquesa*, Miguel de Cervantes. He also had the bad luck to arrive late in claiming the reward for his contribution to naval exploits that by then were almost forgotten.

Besides these cases, which related to early voyages of discovery in which the crown participated directly, the state continued wrangling over salaries with sailors on its warships. Like many other public employees, they suffered from the monetary afflictions and bankruptcies of the Royal Treasury, with delays in their payments that sometimes stretched out for several months.[26] Faced with this situation, the only possibility was to file claims through legal channels and to have patience. Although the bureaucratic machinery was slow, at least it could not slip away like some shipowners and masters could, leaving their crews without any hope of collecting their salary.

The causes of salary conflicts with the owners of private vessels could have very diverse origins. One of the most frequent arose when sailors remained in America because of illness. Because salaries were paid once the ship had passed through the Bahama Channel on the return voyage, the sick sailor who stayed behind had generally collected nothing more than a small advance received before departure. If he recuperated and succeeded in returning to Spain, he

Discipline and Conflict

could present a petition before the House of Trade asking that the master pay his wages. If the sailor had signed on for a share of the freight charges he had the right to his complete share, but if he had signed on for a fixed sum, he had a claim only to the salary corresponding to the time that he had worked.

In case of death, the situation was very similar. The master was obliged to send the belongings and wages of the deceased to the receivers "of the belongings of the dead" who functioned in American ports, and they took charge of sending them to Spain. But in that case, as in the case of the sick, full wages were due only if he had sailed for a share in the freight charges. Because the majority of the pilots sailed for a fixed salary, when one of them died the old maritime custom of "dead men do not earn wages" was applied; although the pilot's heirs might try to get the owner to pay them the full salary promised, the House of Trade generally did not endorse their demands, and they received wages only for the time sailed.[27]

The drafts, or levies, carried out for the king's ships among the crews of merchant ships also created conflict. When warships lacked crewmen, the generals had no qualms about extracting two or three sailors from each ship in the convoy in order to fill the gaps. These men were then placed in a somewhat ambiguous salary situation and risked having to sue the crown as well as their old bosses to collect their wages. Since both parties tried to avoid responsibility for paying, the sailors found themselves in the sad situation of being pawns in their financial game.[28]

But the majority of problems arose, plainly and simply, when masters and shipowners tried to cheat the sailor by paying him less than promised or even by not paying him at all. Sometimes they used the pretext that they had accepted the crewman only to keep him from dying of hunger and with the charitable intent of providing him at least somewhere to sleep and something to eat. On other occasions a conflict arose because a sailor had provisionally done the job of an officer, and the owner refused to pay him for this extra responsibility. Finally, and most commonly, the sailors thought the master had falsified the profits earned from the freight fees. There were a thousand ways of doing that: increasing the expenses fictitiously; not recording the collection of various fees; or reducing the value of each share by augmenting the number of crewmen with imaginary sailors who were really slaves, servants, or passengers and therefore not eligible to collect.

When a conflict arose about the value, or monto, of the freight fees, the custom was to have recourse to the tribunals, which immediately arranged for intermediaries or third parties (terceros) to sort things out. Each side selected one, and they met to analyze the accounts in the hospital that the Brotherhood and University of Seafarers maintained in Triana, on the banks of the

Guadalquivir.[29] Normally, the agreements of the terceros were respected and confirmed by the tribunal of the House of Trade.

From the mid-sixteenth century, the system of paying fixed sums for salaries became ever more frequent, and relations between masters and sailors were regulated by signed contracts, also called "concerts" or "accords." The formal contracts were simple documents. They did not occupy more than one side of a folio sheet, and the text recorded that a particular sailor "concerted" with a master for a specific voyage, in exchange for a specified salary. The signature of both parties, plus that of the ship's scrivener and two witnesses, completed the process.

(201)

These simple documents served the sailors as an indisputable instrument of their claims, and their effect in the Carrera de Indias was tremendous. It seems difficult to believe that a weapon apparently so weak could enable a simple sailor to put his old boss in a considerable squeeze. Yet if he presented it to the authorities of the House of Trade, once the voyage and the unloading had been completed, he set in motion a mechanism that warned the master in a few days of his obligation to pay. If the master made some excuse or tried maliciously to delay, he could be sure of ending up in the House of Trade's jail and of having some of his belongings seized and auctioned off in order to pay the crew. The constables of the House of Trade seem to have had a special predilection for requisitioning trays and other objects of silver, as this type of object was easy to sell at auction. The document bundles in the Archive of the Indies hold dozens of lamentations, some of them written in jail, from masters arrested for not having paid wages to their sailors.[30]

In a bureaucratic system that has always been famous for its slowness, the extraordinary rapidity of the judicial process in those cases is especially surprising. For example, within two days after various apprentices from the ship *Santa Ana* presented a wage claim against the captain and shipowner, Hernando Ramos Ortiz, he had suffered the seizure of a "silver platter," which was auctioned eighteen days later.[31] In other claims, such as those against the masters Pedro Sánchez, Cristóbal Martín, and Gaspar de Espinosa, the time from filing the complaint to jailing the master ranged from two to eight days.[32] In some cases, the process took around a month, but I have found few that exceeded that period. Once the sentence was handed down, the master not only was condemned to pay the wages, but he had to add two reales (in lieu of the daily ration) for each day that he had delayed paying what he owed his men.

The power of the contracts even created situations in which the boss was the wronged party, manipulated by a sailor who knew how to use the law to his advantage. This was the case with the caulker Pedro de Sepúlveda, who contracted with Juan Bautista Justiniani, owner of the ship *Santa Ana*, to sail from Santo Domingo to Seville in 1589. Sepúlveda possessed a legal contract, but he turned out to be a quarrelsome individual. No sooner had he begun work than he knifed a citizen of Santo Domingo, after which he remained hidden and did not reappear until some moments before the ship left for Havana. In Havana he absented himself for several days with the excuse of attending the burial of a relative, and the master had to hire another caulker in his place. Despite the fact that his violent tendencies and his dereliction of duty were confirmed by various witnesses, the House of Trade supported Sepúlveda's claim, based on the terms of the contract. The master was warned that either he comply with the payment or he would end up visiting one of the jail cells maintained by that institution.[33]

(202)

Such was the power that a contract wielded over a master that when Cristóbal Martín acknowledged his debt from jail and agreed to pay wages due to the Portuguese sailor Anton Jorge, he did so on one condition: "That I be given the original contract [conocimiento] that the other party has, in which I was obligated to do what he asks of me; because it would not be just that I pay once here, and because of the same conocimiento find myself bothered in the Indies and made to pay again."[34]

The employer had his hands tied once he signed the contract, and one has the impression that, because mariners were normally scarce in the labor force, it was not easy to get many of them to accept embarkation without first signing an agreement. Nonetheless, there are cases in which a sailor committed the sin of trusting too much and paid very dearly for it. Some agreed to sign a paper signaling the end of their employment without having received all of the pay due them; naturally, they were never able to collect the remainder.[35] Nor do we lack cases of guileless sailors who gave their contracts to a third party to hold for them, which is what happened to the apprentice Bartolomé Sánchez. He entrusted it to the boatswain of the ship, who, in collusion with the master, broke the original contract and left the poor apprentice unable to collect. Undoubtedly, the next time he would be much sharper.[36]

The most useful tool that the masters had in flouting contracts was their mobility. A ship is a vehicle, and its master could slip away and put oceans between himself and any claims. The Spanish authorities tried to avoid this by obliging the master to name guarantors (fiadores). Nonetheless, we have already seen that there were scams to name insolvent guarantors, and on some occasions it was not easy to find the guarantor when things went wrong.

In such cases, and with the master absent, the sailors had to initiate a long lawsuit to try to collect, and the majority of them did not have the financial resources to maintain a legal dispute that could last months or years. If, finally, the suit was resolved, the attorneys were always the winners. It is quite probable that some of them agreed to take on these nearly lost causes on condition of walking away with the lion's share if they finally succeeded in winning. This must have been one of the occupations of the licenciado Salvador Hagunde, attorney of the royal appeals court of the House of Trade. For defending the interests of the apprentice Gonzalo Pérez, he collected a fee worth about a third of the sum finally obtained in the judgment.[37] Surely Gonzalo Pérez would have subscribed to the old curse, "May you have lawsuits and win them!"

It is possible, in practice, that there were even more ways in which masters could mock the salary obligations that they had contracted with their crews. However, the bureaucratic machinery of the Carrera de Indias was an impor- (203) tant restraint on the shipowners' freedom to exploit manual labor. It is interesting to realize that, until the publication of the "Act for the Better Regulation and Government of the Seamen in the Merchants Service" in 1729, written contracts for maritime labor had not come into general use in England.[38] Even then, some authors affirmed that the admiralty courts gave more importance to the sailors' obligations, as reflected in those documents, than to their rights.[39]

Authority versus Lack of Discipline: Disrespect, Mutinies, and Desertions

"No one but a great lord can govern and punish a sailor." This phrase comes from someone very familiar with the maritime sociology of the British Isles during the Middle Ages. It reminds us that, for a long time, the men of the sea possessed an indomitable spirit that did not easily stoop to comply with the orders of the command structure.[40] In other words, submissiveness and servility did not form part of the character of ships' crews. Other authors have gone even further and have seen the sailor as one of the purest expressions of the spirit of rebellion inherent in human beings.[41] From this latter perspective, the men of the sea were considered especially predisposed to instigate strikes and labor conflicts, along with other groups of workers, such as miners, who also labored in difficult physical conditions that isolated them from the rest of society.[42]

This propensity for conflict has a curious proof in the English language, since the very word *strike,* which today means a work stoppage, evidently has nautical origins, as it also means to take down a sail. Its use to designate a work stoppage was generalized from 1768 on, when the sailors of an English merchant fleet decided to immobilize it by taking down the sails on all the ships.[43] British sailors were, in effect, famous for their riots and mutinies, in which they sometimes held entire cities under their absolute dominion, challenging military forces sent by the crown.[44]

Regarding the Spanish sailors of the sixteenth century, abundant testimonies establish their scant affection for humbling themselves before the powerful of the earth. Thus, for example, the authorities of the House of Trade once accused the masters and ship lords of the University of Seafarers of being too mild in imposing discipline on board ships, thus enabling many sailors to desert in American ports. In their defense, the representative of the Sevillian shipowners responded:

> The people I represent are not constables, and the sailors and officers on the ships are not slaves, nor can the masters hold them with prison bars. They are free persons, and even indomitable persons; and it is necessary for the masters to give them gifts and money in advance to keep them content, so that they want to make the voyages and sail and serve on the ships, without which navigation would not be possible.[45]

A ship lord such as Juan de Escalante de Mendoza, who had many Spanish sailors under his command in the sixteenth century, knew very well that he could not order them to do any work that was not directly related to their jobs, as they were not disposed to carry out the duties of servants. Though this was evident in the case of seasoned sailors, one could argue about it at times in the case of young apprentices, from whom officers often required personal services. But the apprentices sometimes also refused to do it, and more than one found himself beaten for trying to maintain his dignity as a free worker.[46] The position of the sailor with regard to his employer was very far from the typical image of the humble servant or the tenant farmer who listened respectfully, with his hat in his hand and his eyes downcast, to the orders of his lord. Escalante de Mendoza pointed out the lack of delicacy in the responses of many sailors to the orders of their officers. "And I have seen, and you, Sir, will also see on this voyage—God being served—that in ordering them to do anything that they do not like, they respond by saying that they will find someone else to do it, because they are not obliged to do what you have ordered, and things of this sort ordinarily cause wrangles, grudges, and outbursts."[47]

But the authority of the captains and masters had to be imposed in some fashion; given the times and the arrogance of the men of the sea, it is no wonder that the said authority made itself effective, in many cases, through force. The youngest on board, that is the pages and above all the apprentices, were the ones who most frequently received the "caresses" of the boatswain and the guardianes, who were the fierce executors of orders from the superior officers.

A curious sketch made in 1529 by the German traveler Christoph Weiditz shows the working tools of someone whom he calls "the patron" of the ship and who possibly corresponded to the master, or perhaps the boatswain. In one hand he carries the whistle used to direct the handling of the ship, and in the other he carries a piece of short, thick cable called a *rebenque*, used to punish lazy apprentices.[48]

For an apprentice to be treated to blows of the rebenque seemed the most

The boatswain with the instruments of his office: the whistle and the whip. Drawing by Christoph Weiditz, 1529. Biblioteca Nacional, Madrid.

normal thing in the world. After all, the officers were dealing with boys who had to be taught, and in those days people thought that there was nothing better for keeping a young tree straight than to give it a good whack. One curious proof that this custom existed was the case of an officer of the guard who did not respond to the shouts of the victim of an attack, because "he thought it was the boatswain punishing some apprentice."[49] Also significant is the case of a steward who, when he was observed hitting one of these boys, responded "that he wanted to do it, and that he also was an officer of the ship and thus able to administer punishment."[50]

But although normally the apprentices and pages bore no more than the occasional blow, at times the cruelty of an officer made them suffer sadistic beat-

Discipline and Conflict

ings. This was the case of Francisco Quintero, pilot of the ship acting as capitana of the New Spain fleet of 1582. Suspecting that two pages, of ten and fourteen years of age, had stolen a bit of thread destined to sew the sails, he ordered them tied up in the poop chamber and gave them three or four dozen blows with a rebenque "two fingers thick." According to the testimony of the surgeon on board, the boys had "on their bodies a large number of very dark discolorations . . . , and right after the beating they could have passed out and been in danger because the wounds were bleeding and there were so many of them."[51] This type of conduct was not normal, or at least it was considered wrongful, and the pilot was prosecuted for it.

(206)

To strike a sailor, that is to say, a mature man of the sea, was not very common. Nonetheless, there were violent masters who administered physical punishment to wayward sailors. In such cases, the sailor, if he wanted to have an opportunity to avenge the offense, had to either put up with it momentarily or flee, so that he could protest to the general of the fleet or to the authorities in a coastal city. If he took justice into his own hands, he would lose any right to bring a complaint, and he would expose himself to grave punishments. Needless to say, if the sailor was the aggressor or was found guilty of proven indiscipline, the corrective measures applied on the ships were rapid and cruel.

Judicial procedures were normally summary, since they were seen before the general as the military authority of each fleet, with the possibility of appealing to the House of Trade in the gravest cases. For the most minor faults such as insults, occasional blasphemies, or small breaches of discipline, it was normal to have to spend a month with one's feet in the stocks. Though this was not considered too rigorous a punishment, it left more than one sailor half crippled.

Thwarted attacks on officers (above all if they were done with deadly weapons), threats or defiance of the authorities on board, or initiating an uprising normally carried the fixed punishment of receiving "three treatments of the cord." The aggressor, with his hands behind him, was hoisted by the wrists to the end of a spar and allowed to fall precipitously until just above the surface of the water. Repeating this tremendous punishment several times could leave the offender an invalid for the rest of his life.[52]

Theft was generally punished with flogging, and if the quantity taken was important, the blows were no fewer than one hundred. As sailors customarily appealed to the House of Trade before receiving this harsh punishment, many public floggings were carried out in Seville. The sailors were sent under arrest to the prison of the House of Trade or to the so-called Admiral's Jail. This was located in the neighborhood of La Cestería, outside the city walls near the river, and it was used for housing the perpetrators of crimes related to maritime traffic. Clearly, "housing" was too mild a term, as simply obtaining a mat to

This is how thieving
sailors were taken to the
place of punishment.
Drawing by Christoph
Weiditz, 1529. Biblioteca
Nacional, Madrid.

sleep on or a ration of jailhouse food was an ordeal and even an impossibility
for someone who did not have sufficient money to bribe the guards. The lamentations of a Vizcayan sailor named San Juan, condemned for stealing four hundred pesos after the shipwreck of his vessel in 1536, provide testimony of the
harshness of life in Sevillian jails in the sixteenth century. After spending several months in prison, the sailor was told his sentence, which was phrased in
these terms:

> We judge that we should condemn, and we do condemn, the prisoner to
> be taken from the jail where he is imprisoned, on the back of an ass and
> with a noose around his neck and with the voice of the town crier an-
> nouncing his crime, and brought through the Arenal and riverbank dis-

Discipline and Conflict

trict of this city and given one hundred lashes publicly; and we condemn him also to exile from this city and its jurisdiction for five years, and that he spend the first three of them on His Majesty's galleys.[53]

More serious crimes, such as mutiny, automatically carried the death penalty, which in the early years of voyages to the Indies could be fulfilled by the traditional method of abandoning the miscreant in an inhospitable place. The instructions given to Sebastian Cabot included the possibility of punishing sailors by leaving them "in the lands of infidels or lands that were yet to be conquered," with the promise of giving them a pardon if they were still alive when another fleet of the king of Spain passed through, on condition that they had learned the language of the locality and could serve as interpreters for future voyages.[54] Clearly, our ancestors, besides being a bit sadistic, were masters in the art of providing incentives to learn foreign languages.

Despite the cruelty of punishments applied to maintain discipline, if the sailors stoically put up with the blows and later complained to the authorities, the officers stood a good chance of seeing themselves tried, jailed, and sentenced to give some sort of recompense to their victims. This was the case even when the officer had committed the aggression while exercising his authority but abusing it and employing violence in a disproportionate manner.

Thus, if an officer used a cudgeling to stop the protests of a sailor who complained about short rations, he could be sentenced to pay for treating the sailor's wounds and for the costs of the legal proceedings; the sailor retained the effects of the beating for having breached discipline.[55] But a much harsher sentence was received by Pero Díaz Machín, master and lord of the ship *La Magdalena*, for beating and assaulting one of his sailors named Juan de Altamira. The incident in question arose in the mid-sixteenth century, and concepts of honor figured in the judicial decision, which recalled medieval traditions and rights that protected sailors according to the old Rôles d'Oléron.[56]

Pero Díaz Machín had had certain reasons for attacking the sailor, who had not carried out his work with the necessary speed. Nonetheless, Díaz exceeded his authority when, with the help of a brother of his, he assailed Juan de Altamira "and they grabbed his beard and pulled out much of it, while insulting and affronting him."[57] It is well known that to pluck out a man's beard was considered a very grave affront in the Middle Ages. Thus, the sailor did not hesitate to go to the governor's assistant in the port of Nombre de Dios, who jailed Díaz Machín, sentenced him to two years of exile from the Indies, and suspended him from the office of ship's master.

This form of dealing with relations between sailors and shipowners would be unheard of in the eighteenth century, but it was perfectly possible in 1551. For Díaz Machín the decision could mean his ruin, since he could not exercise his office nor take his ship into that port for two years. Thus, he acknowledged that his anger had been excessive, he made peace with the sailor, and he respectfully allowed the sentence to be read publicly on board, "there being on the said vessel all the ship's company."[58]

This does not mean that the lord and master of the ship *La Magdalena* was weak or lacking in courage. Far from it! Upon arriving in Seville, he asked the House of Trade to lift the punishment imposed by the judge in Nombre de Dios in recompense for his valor. During the voyage, he had dived overboard in the middle of the ocean to nail sheets of lead beneath the water line of two ships that were about to sink. Díaz Machín must have been an expert in such work, and with his action he had saved two ships from almost certain calamity. This man who was capable of acts of almost imprudent valor still saw himself obliged by tradition and law to ask forgiveness from one of his sailors for having offended his honor. (209)

This was not a unique case. There are other testimonies of sailors who went to the authorities because of suffering insults, sometimes accompanied by a blow of little importance. One might think that an insult is not a very serious injury, but one should not forget that imprecations in the Castilian language offer brilliantly expressive and sonorous possibilities, which have survived even to our own times. The sailors argued, pained, that they were "honorable married men" who should not have to put up with being stigmatized as drunks, homosexuals, or complacent cuckolds.[59]

As we might imagine, these relatively polite terms were not the ones used on the ships of the Carrera de Indias. Francisco de Santiago, captain and owner of the ship *Santiago* in the New Spain fleet of 1571, was a violent man who treated his sailors with contempt and was denounced for that behavior to General Cristóbal de Eraso. When various of his men were stretching an awning over the ship, the captain was bothered by their lack of speed in the work; directing himself to the sailor Bernabé López, he told him he was "a sodomite and a cuckold and I'll have to tie you up by the horns." A witness provides some amusing details about how the dispute developed:

> This witness was on the ship and heard Francisco de Santiago say: "You're taking your own sweet time putting up this awning." And the said Bartolomé *[sic]* López said: "Sir captain, don't treat the men in that manner, because you have very honorable men on your ship," to which the said Francisco de Santiago responded: "You lie like an enormous rogue, you he-goat with a whore for a wife." To which, a while later, the said complainant told the said Francisco de Santiago that he lied, and the said Francisco de Santiago responded that he would cut off his cuckold's horns.[60]

The foul-mouthed captain had to spend several days in the jail on the galleon that served as flagship of the fleet. Then he was allowed to return to his ship, with the promise of treating it as his prison and not leaving it nor insulting his men, under penalty of five hundred ducats. Nonetheless, it seems that the warning did not have much effect; Francisco de Santiago continued provoking confrontations with his crew, and there is no proof that he ever had to pay the high fine. In other words, a sailor on the Carrera de Indias could have his captain thrown in jail for subjecting him to simple insults, although reality showed that the imprisonment did not last long, nor was it certain to prevent the repetition of such conduct.

When insults progressed into actions, fines were indeed imposed and collected, although in smaller quantities than the five hundred ducats with which Francisco Santiago was threatened. Thus, for example, a master was sentenced to pay eighty ducats for giving various "violent blows and kicks" to the ship's steward and calling him "an old cuckold."[61] The king's justice was truly brought to bear in such cases; otherwise, it would not be possible to explain why a caulker jumped into the ocean in San Juan de Ulúa when constables came to seize him for having given "an open-handed blow" to one of the apprentices who served as his assistant.[62]

The most important conclusion of everything said thus far is that neither the shipowners nor those who represented them had entirely free hands in exercising an arbitrary discipline on the sailors for their own economic interests. For me, the case that seems emblematic of this conclusion involved the "merchant" Bartolomé Rodríguez, owner of the cargo and the ship *Nuestra Señora de Belén*, incorporated into the New Spain fleet of 1583, under the command of General Álvaro Flores Quiñones.

Although Bartolomé Rodríguez sailed aboard his ship, he contracted with a master, a pilot, and a boatswain to direct the crew. These officers complied strictly with the orders given by the general of the fleet and unloaded some hides that had overloaded the ship. The owner became furious that his employees either had not wanted to hide the excess merchandise or did not know how to do so. Besides this, he had the bad judgment to insult the whole guild of men of the sea, from the general on down to the sailors. He said that General Álvaro Flores was a "lowly man" (referring of course to his social condition and not to his stature) and that his ensign, or insignia, instead of being a flag, was "a little tattered banner." And he branded all the masters and pilots of the Carrera de Indias as "thieves, rogues, and drunks."

Naturally, these affirmations made their way to the ears of the general, who jailed the angry shipowner and levied a small fine against him.[63] This might seem a simple anecdote, but it points out that the owners of capital were subject to the administrative system of the Carrera de Indias. This placed them under the jurisdiction of generals and admirals, who, though they also engaged in commercial ventures, thought of themselves fundamentally as military men and felt a certain disdain for those whose only interest was in enriching themselves in commerce.

A mutiny was the most characteristic expression of mass violence in the history of navigation. In the second half of the sixteenth century, the development of the administrative machinery of the Carrera de Indias evidently put an end to rebellions by entire crews; on the other hand, the long voyages of discovery to unknown regions, carried out in the first half of the century, provided ideal places for these collective eruptions to brew.

Many elements converted the voyages of discovery into propitious circumstances for opening Pandora's box. Desperation filtered through all the chinks in the decks, spreading the spirit of rebellion among crews lost in the middle of the ocean. The uncertainty was, of course, the worst of all evils. An expedition might be only a few miles from its objective, with the shore just on the other side of the horizon, and the crew could still feel themselves surrounded by an infinite sea. Something like that happened on Columbus's first voyage, when the future admiral of the Ocean Sea had to face down an attempted mutiny only a few leagues from the Bahamas.

The fear of the unknown, the terror of not ever returning home and of watching the provisions rapidly decreasing in the holds or rotting inside their barrels, generally provided the fuses that touched off an explosion of violence. The ambition to take over command and the hatreds and prejudices generated by regional, national, or racial differences also played important roles in the conflicts. An especially common motive was the existence of captains general of foreign nationality, who awakened the nationalistic zeal of their crews.

The Spanish expeditions to the Spice Islands had all the ingredients necessary for the appearance of mutinies: enormous distances, tremendous uncertainties, acute privations, and every sort of regional and national jealousy. The mutinies that occurred on the expeditions of Magellan (1519) and Sebastian Cabot (1526) had much in common. In both cases, the captains general were foreigners, and on both occasions the mutineers were Spaniards who occupied the second place in the chain of command. Juan de Cartagena was the overseer *(veedor)* on Magellan's expedition and had been placed administratively at practically the same level as the Portuguese captain general when it came to making important decisions. The case of Cabot was even more significant, as he abandoned in Brazil Francisco de Rojas, Miguel de Rodas, and Martín Méndez, the three persons directly beneath him in the expedition's chain of command.[64] To the legitimate interest of the captains general in defending their authority, together with their not-so-justifiable desire to place their relatives and friends in posts occupied by Castilians, these latter responded with their own ambitions and nationalistic prejudices.

In the event, these motives were not made explicit, and the reasons adduced by the mutineers to gain the support of part of the crew were much easier for the disheartened, hungry, and fearful sailors to understand: the captain general was lost and did not know the route, and above all, while the foreign commanders and their friends ate the best provisions, the rest of the crew went hungry. The right to obtain a proper ration has always been one of the most common causes of revolt at sea and the easiest weapon to use against the constituted authority by those who wanted to overthrow it.

The first reports that arrived in Spain about the mutiny against Magellan recounted how the rebels, captained by Juan de Cartagena and Gaspar de Quesada, opened the food lockers on the ships and distributed food to the crews without quotas or measures, in order to win them to their cause.[65] The importance of good food, like a balm to avoid erosions of morale, had already been mentioned in the instructions given to Magellan. The text tacitly recognized that a hungry man was not obliged to stay the course: "As long as the provisions are abundant, no one would dare to speak out on the said voyage, whether the discovery takes much time or little, but they do what they were brought along to do on the expedition."[66] Something very similar happened in the case of the armada of Sebastian Cabot, where complaints about deficient food were also a cause of generalized discontent.[67]

But on both expeditions, the captains general eventually succeeded in imposing their full authority, and the mutineers suffered the full brutality of discipline at sea. Those who, because they were such important persons, did not lose their heads were abandoned on inhospitable coasts filled with hostile local inhabitants, where very few managed to survive.

On the second great expedition to the Moluccas, commanded by García Jofre de Loaisa in 1525, the captain general was Spanish, but that did not prevent tensions and desertions; it was one of the most calamity-prone and unfortunate expeditions in the whole first half of the sixteenth century. One of Loaisa's captains, Don Rodrigo de Acuña, deserted with the ship San Gabriel. In turn, he suffered the rebellion of a large part of his crew, who jumped ship at the Río de la Plata and went to look for the riches that they had heard about from some Spanish survivors of the expedition of Juan Díaz de Solís.[68]

Much less well known was the revolt that occurred in the middle of the Pacific Ocean on another ship in Loaisa's small fleet, the caravel Santa María del Parral, commanded by Don Jorge Manrique de Nájera. By a real coincidence, Álvaro de Saavedra, whom Cortés sent to aid Loaisa, rescued some shipwrecked sailors from this caravel. One of them ended up confessing that the mutinous crew had thrown their captain into the water and then killed him with a barrage of lances. The head of the rebellion was taken prisoner, keelhauled until he died, and finished off by being quartered and left as food for wild beasts.[69]

But without doubt, the most novelistic mutiny on Spanish voyages in the sixteenth century was led by Lope Martínez de Lagos, a mulatto of Portuguese origin who, though he earned much less fame than the other great rebel of the sixteenth century, his namesake Lope de Aguirre, was not inferior to him in audacity, the magnitude of his voyage, or his absolute disregard for human life.[70]

Lope the mulatto traveled to the Philippines in 1564 with the expedition of Miguel López de Legazpi and Andrés de Urdaneta, serving as pilot on one of the dispatch boats in the fleet. Later he was ordered to return to Mexico, which he did, arriving two months before Andrés de Urdaneta on the ship *San Pedro*, the capitana of the expedition. This feat of nautical prowess earned him the congratulations of the Mexican authorities, who confided an important sum of money to him to buy another ship with which to return immediately to the Philippines. But Lope Martínez was not worthy of such confidence, and he showed it by spending all the money without ever acquiring a ship. The judges of the court of appeal in Mexico thought about hanging him immediately, but they preferred to pretend that they had pardoned him, in order to take advantage of his nautical skills one last time. In effect, the mulatto was "pardoned" and obliged to sign on as a pilot on a ship returning to the Philippines. On board, there was a secret letter for Governor Legazpi, which said: "Comes here Lope Martínez; in payment of his services, upon arriving you should hang him."[71]

It is not known exactly how, but the mulatto's lucky star allowed him to find out about his future death sentence, and he decided to take matters into his own hands. The sergeant of the infantry on the ship was ambitious, and Lope Martínez de Lagos filled his head with tales of fabulous islands where riches could be gathered by simply stretching out one's hand. Lope promised him, in exchange for help, entire ships loaded with gold that could carry him to Flanders or France. At last the sergeant succumbed to these strong temptations, and the two of them decided to kill the captain and the ensign in order to take control of the ship. The description of the assassination of the two officers might well belong in the pages of some adventure novel; in it, the audacity of the deed and the impudence with which they communicated their treason to the rest of the crew are stunning:

> Putting their plan into effect then, at night the sergeant stationed four sailors at the door where the captain was, and he entered and found him and the ensign sleeping, and he lay hands on a dagger and stabbed both of them, and then the sailors threw them into the water, and the sergeant said to the soldiers: "Don't be scandalized, your Graces, since you can say 'The Lord's Prayer' for the captain and the ensign, who were thrown into the sea tonight," at which the soldiers were shocked and didn't know what to do.[72]

But the sergeant and accomplice of Lope Martínez de Lagos was soon attacked by remorse. Before he could become an obstacle to the mulatto's plans,

Discipline and Conflict

Lope invited him to a banquet, in the course of which some sailors threw a cord around his neck and hanged him. As we can see, this Lope of the Pacific followed the same path as his contemporary on the Marañón River. He seemed to have more luck than Lope de Aguirre, since the king's justice never caught up with him. Months later, some of the members of the crew, who remained faithful to the king, succeeded in making off with the ship, taking advantage of the mulatto's absence on land. Thereafter, the memory and recognition of this very interesting personage were lost among the thousands of islands in the great ocean, without the slightest notice remaining of him or of the accomplices who remained with him.

Mutinies became much less frequent from midcentury, when the Carrera de Indias became a fixed trajectory of annual expeditions that were almost monotonous for crews who knew the routes, the timetable, and the distances perfectly well. Perhaps the most interesting mutiny occurred on the galleass *San Pelayo*, flagship of the armada of Pedro Menéndez de Avilés for his attack on the French Huguenots in Florida. Once the Spanish infantry disembarked, the ship fell into the hands of the crew, most of them foreigners, stirred up by three men who were returning to Santo Domingo as prisoners: two for pretending to be Catalans, though they were French, and the other for having committed the "nefarious sin" of sodomy.[73] Apart from this episode, discipline on the majority of other ships was disturbed only by minor incidents provoked by the rivalry between sailors and soldiers.[74]

Nonetheless, in moments of grave danger, when the ship was on the point of capsizing in the midst of a storm, many captains and masters lost the capacity to keep the crew under their orders. These cases, however, rather than being premeditated attacks on authority, were simply examples of "Save yourself if you can!" which like a torrent swept away any barrier that tried to impose discipline. These situations were very frequent; the documents tell us about masters who, sword in hand, were still unable to stop the terrified crew from abandoning ship and seeking safety on the remaining vessels in the fleet.[75]

Juan de Escalante de Mendoza, shipowner that he was, complained about the pressures to which the "poor owner" was subjected to give the order to abandon ship.[76] According to Escalante de Mendoza, the masters who succeeded in overcoming the terror of their crews acted as "very Christian men, and as skilled and spirited mariners." But this was not easy, since the sailors were not disposed to gamble with their lives merely to save the shipowner's fortunes. In any case, if there was no choice but to leap into the dinghies, Juan de Escalante de Mendoza proposed a very strict order for quitting the ship, demonstrating that the familiar cry of "Women and children first!" is something more modern and related to the moral victories of our times—theoretical victories, of course![77]

> And when it becomes necessary to abandon the ship, the first things that ought to be thrown into the ship's boats are the coins of gold and silver and the pearls, and all the other things of little volume and much value. Second, all the women and children, people who are old, sick, or impaired, and priests and religious found on the ship. Third, all the passengers and slaves. Fourth, the youngest pages on the ship and the oldest and weakest sailors. And when only the captain, master, pilot, boatswain and other officers, sailors, and apprentices remain, then you can transfer to the other ships valuable merchandise such as silks, dyestuffs such as grana and cochineal, and all the rest, according to the space and time available.[78]

(215)

Perhaps some alert reader has thought, "What a great example of self-abnegation and moral victory: the slaves were saved before the mariners!" Unfortunately, that reader ought not ring the victory bells just yet. A slave was a valuable piece of merchandise that had cost its owners many ducats; that is why he had to be saved before an unhappy sailor, whose death interested only his family, and not always them.

One last way that sailors avoided the harsh discipline to which they were subject consisted in abandoning their posts permanently. There were many reasons to desert. Some fled before an expedition had even departed, carrying off the several months' salary that had been paid in advance. Others enlisted as sailors in order to emigrate to the Indies, and the fact of their disappearance was independent of the treatment they received during the voyage. In any case, the mass flight of sailors represented a serious threat to the functioning of seaborne communications. It also constituted an important collective weapon in the struggle to obtain better pay and working conditions.[79]

A muster carried out among 2,357 crew members pertaining to the armadas that protected the American convoys during the last quarter of the century demonstrates that 9.42 percent of the sailors deserted before leaving Spain, while 21.9 percent fled in one American port or another.[80] The crown lost considerable money because of deserters who left the fleets before the anchors were raised in the port of departure. A report in 1587 regarding men signed up in the southwestern county of Niebla calculated that deserters made off with six thousand ducats;[81] in an armada outfitted in Lisbon in 1595 to escort the Indies fleets, the sum was more than fourteen thousand ducats, and the number of deserters amounted to 707 persons.[82] Regarding the men who disappeared in America, the proportion was even higher, which helps to explain the continual search for new crew members by generals and authorities in the House of Trade.

It seems evident that this continual turnover of new sailors, together with a high rate of absenteeism, meant that crews might be totally replaced in a few years. Nonetheless, it is reasonable to assume that the urge to desert would not have affected all the men of the sea in a uniform manner and that a nucleus of sailors reenlisted year after year, making service on the ships an almost permanent profession.

Although the proportions of deserters mentioned pertained to the escort squadrons, I do not believe that the figures would be very different on merchant ships. Desertions were generally much more abundant when sailors were recruited for an exclusively military expedition destined for the Channel or the Netherlands. Nonetheless, the galleons of the Carrera de Indias always mixed cargo and passengers, and their crews were not exposed to a higher level of danger than those of merchant ships on the same route. Even with these qualifications, however, there is no doubt that the phenomenon of desertions by sailors, as much on merchant ships as on warships, reached significant proportions, at least if we measure it by the continual complaints by generals in the armadas and masters of merchant ships in the fleets.

The new lands and their possibilities for enrichment constituted an irresistible attraction for the sailors. The generals worked hard to issue proclamations threatening deserters with severe penalties, including beatings, the loss of salary, several years' service without pay, or pulling oars on the king's galleys. But neither the most inflamed oratory nor the most severe warnings had any effect.[83] Nor was it very useful to put guards under the command of the officers to prevent flight; as General Álvaro Flores Quiñones commented in a letter to the king: Who would be in charge of watching the guards, who were often the first to flee, led by their officers?[84]

Many times generals had to take up collections among all the ships' masters of a fleet, in order to hire constables to pursue the deserters. The success of these efforts was generally very limited. For example, of the fifty-nine fugitives from the galleon *Santa Isabel* in 1578, only six were caught, and three of them escaped again.[85] Somewhat luckier were the efforts of Nicolás Cardona, general of the Tierra Firme fleet of 1569. Of twenty-six deserters, thirteen were found and returned to the ship. According to the report on the men taken, some of them were recognized because of physical defects that made them unmistakable. Being too fat, one-eyed, or lame was unfortunate for men who, besides having to put up with these physical defects, were trying to fashion a future for themselves as illegal immigrants in the Indies.[86]

Delinquency and Personal Conflicts

In the past, the present, and possibly in the future as well, the ambience of seaports is not the most appropriate venue to educate anyone in "good habits." No father would send his sons and daughters to graduate from such a university, unless he wanted them to be turned into professionals of dubious distinction. The world of the sailor, on shipboard and in the ports, with people always passing through, has been considered an extraordinary breeding ground for the most varied sorts of delinquency. Moreover, men of the sea have had a bad reputation for centuries, and they have been viewed with a certain prejudice by the "orderly people" who lived inland and distrusted the social and personal instability of sailors.

Friar Antonio de Guevara said that the "denizens" of a galley were "falsifying, unfaithful, piratical, thieving, traitorous, brawling, knife-scarred, assault prone, adulterous, homicidal, and blasphemous."[87] In the matter of picaresque characters, the galleys provided almost everything. We might think that Friar Antonio was referring exclusively to men sentenced to the oar for their crimes; they were simple prisoners whose inclination toward crime far preceded their enforced maritime "vocation." Nonetheless, the sailing friar did not restrict his descriptions to the oarsmen; he also accused sailors of being consummate thieves, ending with a generalization that left little room for doubt: "The sea is the cloak of sinners and the refuge of malefactors."[88]

Moreover, this unfavorable opinion of mariners was not restricted to Spain. An English writer at the beginning of the eighteenth century had a similar way of summing up the teachings that any young man could hope to acquire on board ship. These were grounded in his apprenticeship in the "seven liberal sciences": to swear, to drink, to steal, to fornicate, to murder, to deceive, and to defame—which is not unimpressive as a course of study.[89]

One should ask if these generalizations corresponded to reality or if they were only the fruit of a certain prejudice. Cervantes, a man of equanimity and a great observer and expert of the underworld, considered that the promised land of the picaresque, that is to say, the *non plus ultra* of all the "jailable" arts, was located in the coastal fisheries of southern Spain. There the seafaring world and all nautical activities were linked to an abundance of criminal activities.[90] However, it would be unjust to think that pícaros existed only on the decks of ships. Cervantes himself recognized that the district called the Ventillas in Toledo and the area around the city walls in Seville also gathered together the most notorious elements of the Spanish underworld[91] and that the region around Seville, and the Indies themselves, served as a refuge for a whole panoply of murderers, gamblers, and thieves.[92]

Among all the criminal activities on board ships, robbery was the most frequent. For that reason, it is no wonder that one of the best authors of navigational books advised people always to be as quiet as possible on board ship, so that one could hear the blows produced by someone trying to break open a barrel or unlock a strongbox.[93] Of course, if passengers were careless in watching their money, they might as well have left it behind in the port of departure,

Discipline and Conflict

because they would lose it in no time on board.[94] Still, what occurred most frequently were small thefts of food to compensate for the monotony and scarcity of the rations or pilferings of rigging and reserve equipment on the ship that could be sold upon arrival in port. Some passengers with a sweet tooth carried boxes of sweets with them, and this was too powerful a temptation for many. Juan Núñez Suárez, a passenger on the New Spain fleet of 1572, tried to safeguard his tasty jugs of preserves by using more than a dozen nails to fasten the box in which they traveled. But the expertise of the "Society of Friends of Bad Behavior" was accustomed to overcoming this type of difficulty. The hungry passenger was left with only two jugs from his store, which tells us that the thief did not lack some Christian charity toward his victim.[95]

(218)

In all fairness, we should recognize that a crew might contain abundant pilferers, petty criminals, or cutpurses without their having the right to be called thieves in the full sense of that term. In fact, the greatest delinquents did not work as sailors on the ships but lived on land and held positions of responsibility and importance. In the sixteenth century, as in our own times, in order to rob, engage in contraband, or defraud the public treasury of great sums, one must be rich and powerful, and the sailors were not. The protagonists of the greatest crimes against property committed in the Carrera de Indias were customarily bureaucrats with few scruples rather than light-fingered apprentices. In those days the specialty of appropriating public goods was already well developed, as it was understood that, because they belonged to everybody but really to nobody, the crime would probably go unpunished. One can well understand how a pilot such as Alonso de Zapata would use a very old refrain to point out that the most dangerous defrauders of the royal treasury were not the sailors but the functionaries who accepted kickbacks and bribes. "There is a saying," Zapata said, "that the ass that belongs to everybody the wolves devour, and thus they devour the king's royal treasury."[96]

The conflicts caused by the criminal activities of the sailors had their explanation in the poverty and marginalization to which they were normally subjected; they formed part of the ample group of the disinherited of the earth. Besides, one found on board ships a level of personal violence that originated in the oppressive conditions in which life on board developed, which was capable of affecting even those who were comrades and colleagues.

The lack of the least private living space was probably one of the most important factors in fostering the aggressiveness that many of the sailors relished. Common daily occurrences included disputes about finding a good place to sleep that was level and dry, which was not very easy on a ship, and knife fights over a place to put one's few personal belongings.[97] At the same time, work on the ships alternated between phases of extreme agitation and long periods of boredom. Moreover, in port the masters tried to keep the sailors enclosed in their wooden jails in order to avoid desertions, and this enforced inactivity provoked an irritability that translated into physical violence.

Apart from these general explanations, the particular circumstances that created a spark capable of inflaming the passions were quite varied. Gambling and drink were perhaps the two most common propitious elements. The rage of the loser, the excessive pride of the winner, or the peevish insistence of the onlooker in demanding his barato, or tip, were frequent causes of conflict.[98] Hard drinking also complicated everything. In the words of a witness to a fight on the armada flagship of General Sancho de Arciniega, "such drinking bouts cause all these arguments, because there is good wine on this ship."[99]

In addition, regional or national rivalries were specific causes of friction. We hear, for example, how a Castilian called the sailors of another ship "roguish Vizcayans," at which everyone commenced to hit one another with sticks and the flat part of their broadswords.[100] At times the insults acquired hints of racial prejudice, and to call a freed man a "black dog" generally led to a fight.[101] That said, one of the most constant motives for strife related to the professional rivalry that separated the sailors from the soldiers embarked on escort vessels. The two groups mixed as badly as oil and water.[102] The soldiers, swaggering and quarrelsome, tried to lord it over the sailors, who, taking advantage of their knowledge of the sea, challenged them for the best places to sleep. The troops, for their part, unwittingly got in the way of the maneuvers and the work of the mariners; thus, if a sailor went to stow a cable and found that a soldier had hung his clothes on it to dry, a conflict was assured.[103]

There was a time and a place that seemed especially propitious for the unleashing of all these antagonisms. Both were related to the basic and elemental need to feed oneself daily. The time for distribution of the rations and for eating meals not only occasioned annoyance with the officers for the scarcity of rations or meals but also caused strife among the ship's company over a particularly tasty morsel or one biscuit more or less. Sometimes a knife was taken out of its sheath and found a fatal place between the ribs of an erstwhile friend, all over a matter of very little importance. This is what happened between two apprentices on the flagship of the armada of Don Cristóbal de Eraso:

> About four days ago the said Juan Pérez and Amador de Ante were eating together, and the said Juan Pérez, having tossed a piece of biscuit into the common stew *[mojo]* to soften it for eating, the said Amador de Ante took a bit of it to eat, and the said Juan Pérez said to him: "Leave that alone, don't take it"; and the said Amador de Ante said: "I will if I want to; . . . since you tossed it into the pot, you tossed it to everybody"; and with that he took a piece of the said biscuit, and then the said Juan Pérez . . . grabbed his knife and stabbed him in the left shoulder blade, which began to bleed.[104]

Discipline and Conflict

Precisely because of the bad humor that an empty stomach can awaken, the hearth or cookstove of the ship was also a place where words led to deeds very quickly. On top of the narrow grill placed over the fire, dozens of frying pans, crocks, and roasters accumulated, all of them put there almost at the same time by their hungry owners to satisfy their appetites. Searching for an ember or raking away a red-hot coal toward your own sardine could leave your neighbor frustrated, with his own fritter uncooked, and totally predisposed to come to blows, or, in the worst cases, to knife points. There were those who, angry enough to treat a comrade like a chicken prepared for the fire, tried to skewer the offending competitor with the cooking spit itself.[105]

Normally, violent confrontations between sailors followed the same trajectory. First they launched a barrage of insults at one another; then the dispute escalated from words to actions. The imagination with which the crewmen laid into one another verbally was so impressive that we can barely begin to define some of the pathways they followed. A first group of slurs made reference to the sexual comportment of the man himself or of his wife, which led to qualifying one's adversary as a "sodomite," someone "screwed over" (jodido), or a cuckold. In the next category came religious or political characteristics that were considered denigrating. Thus, to call a person "French" was taken as an insult, just like accusing them of being a "Jew," a "heretic," or a "proven Lutheran." In third place were adjectives that made reference to some small personal defect such as being a "drunken monkey lover," a "thief," a "rogue," a "sponger," or a long list of et ceteras. But there were some verbal artists who added sarcasm to the insult, preceding it with a contemptuous honorific title, thus, for example, calling their neighbor "Sir Rogue." Others combined various of the groups we have just defined, achieving syntheses as pointed as a "roguish cuckold" or a "Jewish sponger."

The familiar stereotype of Spanish disdain for mechanical labor was not really represented among the insults heard on board ship, perhaps because all the sailors were conscious of their humble condition as workers and lowly members of society. There is only one exception, and those are the references—certainly abundant enough—to the "smoke of the cookstove." It was tremendously offensive to tell someone that his beard was impregnated with the odors of cooking. Moreover, if a comrade or a petty officer tried to impose his authority, it was very easy to answer back that he should "go order the cookstove around." It was also common to mock and scorn someone by threatening to do him the honor of "being perfumed with smoke from the cookstove."

After this "battle of flowers" came the real battle. Any object that came to hand could be an offensive weapon. Jugs, jars, clay plates, sticks—they all constituted the first projectiles launched at an opponent. But unfortunately, all the sailors carried knives in their waistbands as an essential instrument in their work; in the majority of fights, these weapons eventually came to light. That is why the consequences of many fights remained engraved on the faces of the crewmen in the form of scars that were sometimes horrendous.

Antonio López, a sailor in the armada of Sancho de Arciniega, "had his nose cut off" in a fight that occurred in 1566.[106] Pedro Enríquez, a sailor on the flagship of the 1583 fleet, received "a knife slash on his face from the neck to near the eye."[107] Such wounds marked a sailor forever; some of them, like the unhappy Sebastián Salgado, a sailor in the 1582 fleet, "remained so ugly and abominable that this witness would not want to be in his place for all the money in the world."[108]

Offensive weapons were used with the intention of wounding not only one's neighbor's body but also his honor. Our ancestors thought that a cut produced by a fine Toledo sword, although it could hurt a lot and might even be fatal, was honorable. On the other hand, to receive a stab wound with a knife used to flay pigs could infect not only one's body but also one's honor. That is why the steward Juan Gallego, in his attempt to humiliate the sailor Domingo Hernández, chose to attack him with a cow's horn. This is how a witness described this singular "bullfight":

> This witness saw the said Juan Gallego appear on the gangway of the said ship and tell the said complainant: "You drunken rogue, for the love of me you are going to leave this ship. I swear to God that I'm going ashore and I'll stab you with a horn and not with a dagger nor with a stick." And then this witness saw . . . the said Juan Gallego take a horn that was on the ship and use it to stab the sailor in the back.[109]

It is difficult to know how many violent incidents occurred each year, although we do have proof that about half of the sailors bore the marks of wounds on their hands and faces that in many cases were the consequences of old brawls. By way of example, we know about the cases adjudicated by General Juan de Alcega in the New Spain fleet of 1572–73. From a total of a dozen cases that included cudgelings, blasphemies, and fights, half produced wounds made by offensive weapons. These data make reference to only one of the two fleets that sailed annually. Moreover, they correspond only to conflicts that came before the highest authority in the convoy for resolution, which allows us to suspect that the real number of incidents would have been much higher.[110]

Those who inflicted knife wounds, if the wounds were not fatal, were customarily punished by being hoisted by a pulley and dropped, but in many cases the comrades of the adversaries tried to patch things up between them and get the victim to reconcile with and pardon the aggressor. Then both of them acknowledged that they had been friends before the conflict and had been blinded by sudden rage. Clearly—although this is not easy to prove—it is quite possible that such gestures of generosity and Christian charity were accompanied by a monetary inducement for the victim to withdraw his complaint. Because many sailors did not have any belongings, it was common to cede part of one's pay to the wounded man, for medical treatment and to provide recompense for his trouble. If the aggressor fled, his salary was handed over to the victim by order of the general of the fleet.[111]

(222) But there have always been clever people capable of escaping punishment through trickery. That is what was done by Juan Bautista, a young apprentice on the flagship of General Cristóbal de Eraso's fleet. The apprentice was caught in the act of stealing some pinches of white biscuit that were kept in the dispensary for the general's table. The sailor who discovered him struck him a few blows, but he had the imprudence to accompany them with curses in the presence of witnesses. This allowed the thieving little apprentice to accuse the sailor of blasphemy, a much graver sin, which made the authorities forget his own transgression. The impassioned declarations of the sailor that he had acted in defense of the general's biscuit did him no good. Nor did it help him to play phonetic games, claiming that he had not said "For the life of God [Dios]" but rather "For the life of ten [diez]". Thirty days in the stocks were his punishment for having taken the name of God in vain.[112]

SIX

The Mental Horizons of the Men of the Sea

A Culture Forged in Contradiction

Persons who spent many months away from their homes, and who sometimes had no home for entire years, necessarily had a perception of family and neighborly ties different from that of ordinary people. It was impossible for a farmer from central Castile to interact with his countrymen in the same way that a sailor in the Indies fleets did. The sailor's eyes would carry engraved on their retinas images of a diverse and exotic world, which made the events and landscapes of daily life on land seem insufferably monotonous. Possibly also, their ears would long retain echoes of the voices of their comrades during the interminable months at sea, many of which they would know better than the voice of a son whose existence they only learned about after disembarking.

The warnings that the local priest dictated from the pulpit, the authority represented by the mayor of the town with his rod of justice, the comments of the local matrons, always vigilant in the maintenance of good behavior, would have much less importance for those who could go to sea again and escape the rules and norms of that little world on land. On board ship there were other authorities, other companions, and other circumstances that determined their particular vision of relations with others. The possibility of a way to escape, the fact of being able to swim between two bodies of water, made them apparently freer. However, because every advantage must be paid for in this life, fleeing the narrow social control of their hometowns placed them between the narrow bulkheads of a ship, where the distances that separated men from one another were not measured in meters or kilometers but in centimeters.

The life of mariners, like that of all human beings, was filled with paradoxes and contradictions. In the specific case of the men of the sea, there were only two fundamental paradoxes: to live crammed together with other people and yet be subject to a collective isolation from the rest of human society; and to travel all over the face of the earth while enclosed in a wooden prison. Said in another way: A sailor could feel himself separated from the world and at the same time physically crushed by the presence of his few comrades; and he could watch thousands of landscapes pass before his eyes and scarcely have occasion

to experience any of them. These circumstances constituted, and still consti-
tute today, the character and the burden of a life at sea, providing the keys to
understanding the mentality of those who lived it.[1]

We might ask how conscious the men who sailed on the Indies routes were
of their isolation. One can suspect, besides, that such a sense would have
evolved at the same time as the maritime routes were constructed. It is evident
that in the first years of the century, when expeditions departed toward unknown horizons and without knowing exactly how long the voyage would

last, the sensation of solitude would have been much greater than when the
Carrera de Indias constituted a well-organized trajectory with relatively predictable times of departure and arrival.

The documentation generally does not provide much information about
such intimate themes, but sometimes one can find a document where a crew
member was unusually open in revealing the hidden recesses of his soul to outsiders. Last wills and testaments are good places to look for this type of declaration. Many testaments followed preconceived formulas and are of little use
for our purposes. Others were exemplars of expressiveness, such as the will of
Francisco del Campo, who sailed as head of an infantry unit on the ship *Santa
María del Parral*, which belonged to Loaisa's armada to the Moluccas.[2]

After the experience of the first expedition to the Far East, all the crew
members who enrolled on the second armada to those faraway lands must have
known perfectly well the risks to which they would be exposed. They would
remain separated from their family and friends for many a year, and they might
never return. Nonetheless, except for the pessimists, no one could have imagined the grim destiny of those 450 men. The only ones who returned after almost ten years of hardship can be counted on the fingers of one's hands! Francisco del Campo seems to have had a presentiment of what his destiny would
be, and fifteen days before leaving from La Coruña he dictated his last will to
a scrivener in the city.

This man was fully conscious of the high probability that he would die in
the enterprise. For that reason, in reviewing his outstanding accounts, he distinguished between those mandated by law and those fixed by conscience.
Thus, in referring to one of his debtors, who it seems had never paid him anything, he commented: "Regarding the debt of Juan del Castillo, I say that on
the passage where I am going, however much he owes me would not be much
good, no matter how many IOUs I might show."[3]

Francisco del Campo was certain he would be in imminent peril. The
phrase "on the passage where I am going" is repeated several times in the course
of the document, used to indicate that a man on the verge of dying could not
do less than be sincere. Even in matters as delicate as blaming his father for hav-

ing wasted his inheritance, he took refuge in the freedom that comes from knowing oneself to be close to rendering accounts before God. How many mariners leaving on one of the numerous expeditions of discovery would not have had similar sentiments? If their fears have not come down to us, it must be because they did not have the opportunity, or the sincerity, to express them in writing.

Even if Francisco del Campo were to return alive, the voyage still represented for him a wrenching break that separated him from his former life. He felt himself to be an exile, which is essentially what all mariners were: "To the aforesaid my children, I commend them to my brother Antonio del Campo and to their mother, so that for my sake, or for everyone's sake, they love them and set them up well, so that if God keeps them alive they will not find themselves exiled from their lands as their father was."[4] Not every departing sailor would have such a dark vision of his future life. Some were inspired by a desire to seek their fortunes; to emigrate to lands where life would be easier; or simply to alleviate family pressures by leaving home. In any case, departure signified separating oneself and isolating oneself from the rest of society.

(225)

One way of measuring and defining the degree of separation of men of the sea from their contemporaries can be gained through language. Of course, each group of mariners used language from the territory where they had their habitual residences on land, but their forms of expression were marked by terms that were incomprehensible to people who lived inland. This was originally a matter of having a professional language, but it was extrapolated to many activities in ordinary life, constituting a true sign of a person's identity. If there is nothing more distinctive than language for measuring the singularity of a human group, the maritime language showed through its specific terms the dual identities of the mariners, who lived straddling the land and the sea.

All marginal groups end up developing their own language, but in the case of mariners, it was less a matter of distinguishing themselves than of defining a reality of life and work that was radically different from its counterpart on land. The ship was, in principle, a very complicated machine filled with hundreds of cables, levers, pulleys, wheels, spikes, and sails. The fact that each thing had its characteristic denomination and that each action was clearly defined and separated from its opposite was not a matter of capriciousness but a vital necessity. Maneuvering a vessel in moments of peril, when the rocks on the coast were nearby or when one had to change direction in the middle of a storm, made such precision necessary. If each action and each piece of the ship's equipment had not had its own name, the lives of everyone on board would not have been worth a maravedí.[5]

The tremendous danger represented by the unleashed forces of nature also

The maritime experiences
of the sixteenth century
put an end to
medieval monsters.

obliged these men, who felt isolated from the rest of society, to collaborate intensely among themselves. Mutual aid was not only the crystallization of a
good instinct but a compelling necessity. Even people on land, when they want
to express a spirit of collaboration, often indicate it by saying, "In the end, we
are all in the same boat."

Even if they were in different boats, mariners generally came to the aid of
their comrades in peril. They did so following an instinct that governs the existence of every nomad who inhabits the deserts on earth and which is summed
up in the old phrase, "Today for you, tomorrow for me."[6] The harshness of the
medium in which they work equalizes the behavior of a camel driver in the Sa-
hara with that of a sailor. One should not forget that the men of the sea tra-

versed the most extensive deserts on earth, though they were not made of sand, as one might assume at first, but of salt water.

The mariners had not only to collaborate with their working companions but also to live alongside them in very reduced living quarters. In moments of danger all the crew had to act as a single man, but once calm was restored, there were too many differences among the crew members not to establish smaller living units. Moreover, only by establishing a certain distance from others could one have a clear sense of one's own identity.

On Spanish ships of the Carrera de Indias, these smaller units were called *camaradas*. One should not forget that this word, which today means "comrades," has a strong nautical flavor and corresponded then to men who shared a chamber, which is what the lodgings on a ship were called. *Camarada* ended up designating the space itself as much as the collection of persons who lived in it. Many mariners and soldiers sailing on the fleets spoke of their "camarada" in this double spatial-personal sense.[7] The camaradas slept and ate together; they shared their leisure time; they delimited their own space with the chests in which they stored their few personal effects; and they distinguished themselves from outsiders during the conflicts and fights that affirmed the personality of their little group.

The term *rancho* was also used frequently to define a place where a group of crew members resided together. Because the main meal was one of the moments in which better ties of communication were established, the word was losing its spatial significance; in modern times it came to designate the soldiers' mess.

The components of each camarada or each rancho generally had a geographic identity. Since the ties of the nuclear family could not be reproduced on board, at least one could establish ties based on geographic and cultural proximity. To associate with "people of your homeland" was the norm in the Carrera de Indias. With the agreement of your countrymen you could even initiate a mutiny, as a matter of personal vengeance; and, at the end of life, there were some who left something in their will to ransom countrymen who had been captured by the Moors.[8] As we see, although the sea distanced the individual from his roots, it was not capable of eliminating them completely.

Mariners were people in continual movement. In a world where communications by land were extraordinarily slow, and each mountain range, or some few hundred kilometers, signified barriers that were only occasionally breached, ships covered thousands of miles and united the continents by the most rapid means of transport known.

Going from one country to another, from the Orient to the Occident, and from north to south meant acquiring a global vision of the world and of the plurality of its peoples and cultures. The difference between the vision of the

---

world held by a peasant in the interior and that of a sailor on the high seas was as wide as an abyss. The horizons of the peasant were limited by the height of the church steeple in his village, which he might never get to leave. The sailor could learn how the firmament changed on the other side of the equator, he could visit the lands that produced cinnamon, he could see rivers as deep as seas, and he could admire the golden-roofed cities that Marco Polo had spoken of in his *Book of Marvels.*

(228) This mobility must have produced the first visions of the world that can truly be called cosmopolitan. Unfortunately, the average level of education of the men of the sea allowed them to be only oral transmitters of these novelties, leaving more cultured individuals the honor of relating them in writing for future generations. At the same time, the Renaissance mariner, like a modern-day St. George, put an end to many of the monsters with which the medieval imagination had filled the seas. He accomplished that task not with lances or shields but with his direct experience of visiting the most distant regions on the planet.

But one should point out that the mariner's cultural horizons began expanding long before he arrived at his destination. Generally, each ship and each port was a small version of the Tower of Babel, where people of different ethnic and geographic origins lived together. Mariners in Seville, Amsterdam, London, or Genoa had a vision of the world with a vast range of common denominators, and each one of them knew the peculiarities of the wage scale, discipline, or rations that held sway among their colleagues. The long and the short of it is that mariners spearheaded the process that destroyed the barriers separating peoples from one another. It is no wonder that the first signs of a really international culture appeared in the maritime community.

The ceaseless mobility of men of the sea fostered one last characteristic of their personality. After a long voyage, the mariner spent months of accumulated salary in explosions of unbridled sensuality, which frequently ended in disputes with the peaceable burghers of the port towns, who reproached sailors for the way they openly trampled traditional morals.[9] As a result, the man of the sea, accustomed to constant movement, did not have much taste for the accumulation of property and preferred to happily spend the money he earned, only to sign up again when he had spent it all. As the old marine proverb put it, "A rolling stone gathers no moss."[10]

These men covered thousands of miles inside very reduced spaces, much narrower and more inescapable than the strongest of prisons. To add insult to injury, once they arrived in port the shipowners tried to keep them on board and to limit their freedom of movement. In those circumstances, the men of the sea were disposed to assert their rights as free men. On the Spanish routes of the sixteenth century, the sailors defended those rights by mass desertions and by demonstrating their highly developed ability to flout the norms dictated by the economic interests that ruled society in their times.

Experience as a Source of Knowledge

A mariner developed his professional skills in a struggle against the forces of nature in a milieu that was often hostile. To survive, entire generations of men of the sea had to learn to respect and, above all, to know the enemy. To know how to determine atmospheric changes by the color of the water or the quality of dawn and dusk, to smell and sense imminent storms, to find islands in the middle of the ocean by following the flight of birds, or to learn how the winds and currents circulated to create highways in the middle of the ocean were part of the basic baggage of knowledge carried by any mariner. This was a very ancient sort of knowledge that was learned not from books but from living on the sea and listening carefully to old sailors loaded with experience. But even when the sea and the wind were calm, the vast spaces of the ocean with no points of reference presented the risk of mistaking the course and getting lost. That is why mariners also relied on a knowledge of nature, learning how to guide themselves by the stars.

(229)

It was not too long ago, more or less from the thirteenth century onward, that certain improvements were made to the knowledge of navigation learned by experience, which were the fruit of reflection by intellectuals far from the world of the sea. Instruments were appearing that measured the angle of stars from the horizon with greater precision. Above all, sailors learned to use the magnetic properties of the lodestone to follow a fixed course. This eruption of science and technology in the world of navigation required a minimum amount of precision in calculations, since the height of the sun at midday did not correspond exactly to the ship's latitude, nor did the indication of north on a compass coincide exactly with the geographic north of the earth. The world of science is a world of exactitude, and these deviations between reality and the marks on the instruments, which today are known as the *solar declination* and the *magnetic declination,* were available in tables that were corrected by introducing simple mathematical formulas.

But solving these rudimentary theoretical problems required a certain schooling. To use the tables, one had to know how to read, and to apply the formulas one had to possess an elementary education in arithmetic. Navigation began to be a skilled art *(arte)* and ceased being only an occupation *(oficio)*. These two terms were employed in the sixteenth century and were differentiated with great clarity. An art was something that "no one could learn by himself, and thus it was fitting to have a teacher instruct you," whereas an occupation "a man could learn by himself with practice."[11]

In mastering the art of navigation, the men of the sea had an inconvenient disadvantage: their high degree of illiteracy. The world of the sea was fundamentally unlettered, and its culture was transmitted almost exclusively by oral means. It is not that this set the men of the sea much apart from other laboring groups at the same social and economic level. The problem was that in the development of oceanic communications, they needed to master knowledge that required a certain degree of theoretical abstraction, which was very difficult to acquire without at least minimal schooling.

Knowing with precision the levels of illiteracy of the men of the sea is not easy. One can attempt an estimate through measuring the incapacity of sailors to sign documents in lawsuits heard by the tribunals of the House of Trade and the Council of the Indies. Nonetheless, signatures that were perfectly written could hide many functional illiterates who were simply artists reproducing a scrawl but were incapable of understanding writing in the pages of a book.

With this warning, and insisting that the results provide only a minimal indication of illiteracy, I have carried out a study of about 800 crewmen over the course of the century (798 persons, to be exact), measuring their capacity to sign documents. The data are presented in table 6.1.[12]

As we see by these data, all the generals, admirals, overseers, and captains of the war galleons knew how to sign; they generally belonged to the lower nobility or other social sectors that were fairly well educated. A broad majority of shipbuilders, shipowners, and masters were also people with a certain degree of schooling. Even the humble administrator of a frigate, that is, a master, needed at least to know how to figure accounts and to keep in touch with the owner through correspondence sent to the destination ports.

The technicians in artillery and the marine officers represent the frontier between those who needed some instruction and the majority of illiterates. These latter reached very high proportions in the broad base of mariners, in which at least eight out of ten sailors, apprentices, and pages did not even know how to write their own name.

The most significant group, nonetheless, was that of the pilots. They had to be the most expert on board in the art of navigation, but we see that somewhat more than one-fourth of them were still totally illiterate. The existence of unlettered pilots clearly contrasted with the advance of modern nautical techniques and shows how knowledge based on personal experience continued having capital importance for many centuries. This happened not only in Spain and Portugal, countries that possessed the best navigational techniques in western Europe at the time, but also elsewhere, such as England, where the situation lasted through the following century.[13]

The problem was aggravated when the mid-sixteenth century produced a notable increase in commercial traffic, which consequently demanded hundreds of new pilots. There were not enough experienced mariners to meet the

6.1 Ability of Sixteenth-Century Mariners to Sign Their Name

	Knew How to Sign (%)	Did Not Know How to Sign (%)
Officers in the high command of the armadas	100	0
Owners and master of ships	83	17
Pilots	74	26
Marine officers (boatswains, guardianes, stewards, etc.)	44	56
Gunners	55	45
Sailors, apprentices, and pages	21	79

(231)

demand, and a frantic race began to train new pilots in modern methods of the art of navigation.[14] Even so, the supply of navigational technicians was always lower than the demand, and it was necessary to accept mariners as pilots who had some experience but no education.

Contemporaries were the first to make fun of the vacillations and lack of precision in the calculations made by pilots on the Carrera de Indias. One satirical piece in circulation related with poisonous irony what transpired when pilots gathered to compare data that they could never get to coincide:

> There was a ship coming from the Indies and in it were three pilots, all of whom brought their charts and other instruments. . . . And all of them together took the angle of the sun and each marked the ship's position on his chart. Based on those marks, one thought they were one hundred leagues from land, another put them forty-five leagues away, and the other said that, according to his mark, they were sailing on land.[15]

Thus, there existed a clear sense that the most sophisticated system of navigation (calculating latitude by measuring the angle of the sun with the horizon at midday) was more a question of luck than of science. No wonder that in the relation of the merits and services of Captain Esteban de las Alas "the Younger," his maritime knowledge was praised in this curious manner: "Esteban de las Alas . . . is also a very excellent mariner . . . and he is a man who knows much about it, having studied this calling, and this he knows for having seen and having been seen conjecturing correctly about many things in going and coming to the Indies, making bets with the pilots about the day they were going to sight land, and many times the said Esteban de las Alas won those bets."[16]

Among passengers who had a certain level of education, the belief existed that the pretended "science" of the pilots was easily achievable by simply applying oneself and observing the pilots as they worked. Thus, for example, the

Dominican friar Tomás de la Torre affirmed that Father Bartolomé de las Casas, with his experience of having crossed the Atlantic sixteen times, was already as good a pilot as the best; and that Father Pedro Calvo, another friar of that order, simply by having paid attention to how the angle of the sun was measured, was expert enough by the end of the voyage to be consulted respectfully by the pilots themselves.[17]

Nonetheless, despite the scorn of many, the labor of the pilots was not simple, nor was it learned so easily. The problem was rooted in the fact that, with respect to the development of nautical science, the sixteenth century marked the transition between ancient mariners and modern navigators. The first depended only on their personal knowledge about the coasts, winds, and currents, while the second had to know besides how to calculate a position with precision. In sum, in the sixteenth century science had to be added to experience, which was not simple for men who for centuries, and one could even say millennia, were accustomed to strictly following tradition.

Juan de Escalante de Mendoza, general of Indies fleets and a cultured man who knew much about nautical subjects, summarized the question well. It was "almost impossible" that a skilled pilot would also be a man "graduated as a master in the arts either of a cosmographer or of a great astrologer." But, at the same time, however much theory he knew, no one who had not begun sailing from his tenderest youth would ever be a great mariner;[18] theory, when it was not accompanied by practical knowledge, had caused the loss of many ships.[19]

The need to join science and experience was another of the paradoxes of which we have been speaking that help us to comprehend the mental horizons of men who had to assimilate the rapid changes at the beginning of the early modern age. Perhaps the best place to appreciate this type of intellectual schizophrenia is in a notable lawsuit between the years 1544 and 1545, which pitted cosmographers against pilots within the House of Trade in Seville.[20]

A cosmographer was an intellectual, normally a graduate of the Faculty of Arts, in which he was taught diverse matters that ran from geometry to mathematics and ended with a study of the cosmos. The House of Trade had various of these men in its service, either paying them fixed salaries or conceding special payments to them for specific work they had carried out. They formed the band of pure scientists, partisans of teaching pilots the art of navigation as a discipline capable of resolving problems anywhere and any time—that is, with the universal validity held by any scientific knowledge. Their "art" was based on the application of the study of the stars to the practical concerns of navigation, above all through the calculation of latitude from the observation of the height *(altura)* or angle of the sun with the horizon at noon. To navigate by alturas, that is, through calculating latitude by the sun, was the latest word in scientific navigation of the epoch. The determination of longitude remained, for the moment, subject to estimates based on the course and the distance traveled, and it would not be solved in a scientific manner until the second half of the eighteenth century.

Cosmographers were the authors of the principal books of navigation published in Spain during the sixteenth century, which served as manuals from which a good part of the non-Iberian mariners in that century learned the art of navigation.[21] In these books one can clearly appreciate the Olympian superiority, and even the poorly disguised scorn, that cosmographers held for pilots, despite the fact that these latter were the principal audience for their books. After all, the pilots were little more than sailors with somewhat greater experience; for that reason, the cosmographers characterized them as "coarse men," "of little understanding," and "ignorant."[22]

Some of these cosmographers, more or less linked to the House of Trade, such as Alonso de Chaves, Pedro de Medina, and Pero Mexía, in 1544 presented a formal accusation against Sebastian Cabot, the visible head of the pilots of the Carrera de Indias as pilot major of the House of Trade, and against his colleague Diego Gutiérrez, the House of Trade's maker of nautical instruments.

The charges were quite diverse, but they were similar in attacking irregularities committed in the pilots' examinations; in demonstrating imperfections in the maps, tables, and nautical instruments approved by the House of Trade; and, above all, in denouncing the accused as promoting among the rest of the pilots navigational procedures that were barely scientific and dominated by routine. The principal target of the cosmographers' attack was new nautical charts that Diego Gutiérrez had invented and that were employed in the Carrera de Indias with the blessing of the pilot major. These were the famous "double-scaled charts."

This type of chart tried to solve for the pilots a fairly serious problem of sailing "by the altitudes." Following a compass course was a simple procedure within reach of any man of the sea, which did not entail the complications of calculating latitude by the sun. Nonetheless, compasses had to be corrected so that they would point exactly north. The angle of difference between magnetic north and true north is called today "magnetic declination," a variable that depends upon where one is on the face of the earth and that also changes with the passage of time. A good pilot, one who knew the most elementary secrets of astronomical navigation, could periodically compensate for the error in his compass by comparing it with the direction of the polestar, which also marked true north fairly accurately. Nonetheless, sometimes clouds, or the pilot's ignorance, impeded an accurate observation of the star.

To avoid such trouble for the pilot and to make his work simpler, Diego Gutiérrez calculated the declinations that existed on the most frequent routes and made charts that resolved the problem, but at the cost of producing alterations in the location of American coasts with respect to European coasts. On this type of chart, the Old World was presented with an equator that was not in line with the equator on the American coasts but with a variation of some three degrees. In other words, the charts used two distinct scales for the two hemispheres.

If a pilot did not diverge from the most common routes, the procedure was convenient, as he had only to follow his compass on the course marked by the chart. However, if for some reason he deviated from the habitual routes, the chart was of no use.

The cosmographers decried this type of development, which converted the work of the pilot into a purely mechanical knowledge, ignorant of the fundamentals of celestial navigation, and which totally invalidated all the charts designed for use with latitude sailing. The pilots who used the new charts did no more than follow the compass, and they did not even fully know how that instrument functioned. The cosmographer Alonso de Chaves summed up the question this way:

> If many of these pilots know how to sail to the Indies, it is because of their great experience and the attention they have paid to this route; but it seems to me that if they were forced to navigate along other coasts, in seas and to lands unknown to them, and in many other parts of the world where they have not been, they would not know how to do it, because they lack the general science and doctrine that they ought to have in navigation.[23]

But Diego Gutiérrez, supported by the pilot major, counterattacked, accusing the cosmographers of not having been on a ship in their lives and of being responsible for many shipwrecks by making maps filled with latitude graduations but imprecise in their description of the shallows and hidden rocks along the coasts. According to Gutiérrez, he made his maps following the advice of the "oldest and most experienced" pilots, taking into consideration the data that had been transmitted to him by those who had seen the coasts of the Indies "with their own eyes" rather than by those who only burned the midnight oil writing about them. This is how Gutiérrez answered the attacks of his accusers:

> And that is why I make the charts conform to the reports that pilots who go to and from the Indies give me, and, as they have so much experience and they use it continually and see things with their own eyes, they succeed better than the cosmographers, or any others, who through their astrology and cosmography cannot know nor achieve the same thing, not possessing, as they do, the art of navigation.[24]

We can ask ourselves what the majority opinion was among those for whom the "double-scaled" charts were designed, that is, the pilots of the Carrera de Indias. The response is very clear: they supported to a man everything that could make their daily tasks easier, without complicating matters with declinations, compensations, formulas, and other imbroglios thought up by people whom

Pilots calculated latitude
by measuring the angle of
the sun over the horizon
at noon. Pedro de Medina,
Regimiento de navegación
(Seville, 1561). Biblioteca
del Palacio Real de Madrid.

they considered freshwater sailors and armchair navigators. A document signed
by fifty-five pilots of the Carrera de Indias supported the production of "double-
scaled" charts with these arguments: "And there is experience that in this manner the ships go and come safely and are not lost, and there should be no other
novelty that would be the cause of losing all the ships. . . . We ask and implore
your graces not to make us depart from our customs, which we use and know
and follow and find certain and sure, and not to introduce anything new."[25]

The development of this lawsuit is extremely instructive in two very different ways. In the first place it points out some of the positive and negative
values in the mentality of the men of the sea. Experience, generally linked to
age, was a supreme good. In an oral culture in which knowledge is transmitted

from fathers to sons and in which each person learns from the experiences of his life, the oldest is always the wisest. Alonso de Zapata, another pilot of the Carrera de Indias, in a very interesting memorandum to the king, said that old people are generally good and even-handed governors, as opposed to the "tyranny of the young."[26] Many things have changed from the sixteenth century to the present; in a society like ours, where collective memory is stored on computer disks, recognition for an experienced old person is limited, and the values of the fullness and physical power of youth are in fashion.

(236)   By contrast, for the majority of men of the sea in the sixteenth century, "the new" was something dangerous and untrustworthy. Thus, when the House of Trade tried to carry out specific modifications in the relations between merchants and shipbuilders, the masters and ship lords resident in Seville asked that things remain as they were, since "all the others say this is to introduce novelties and things that have not been seen nor used . . . nor ought your graces to consent, nor allow these novelties, nor oppressions, nor indispositions, since what His Majesty has provided and ordered is sufficient."[27] A novelty, in the eyes of the mariners, seemed akin to an oppression, which was a natural feeling for those who based the major part of their knowledge on a centuries-old tradition.

But those who might think that the lawsuit between the Sevillian cosmographers and pilots was an exclusively technical confrontation in which all the contenders sought the common good would be mistaken. Both sides fought primarily for their own personal interests, and more concretely for their economic interests, which are the most personal of all. This is the second great lesson of that inflamed confrontation.

It seems that Diego Gutiérrez had garnered the exclusive right to make official charts and nautical instruments, for which there was an enormous and lucrative demand in Seville in that epoch. Gutiérrez himself, helped by his sons Luis and Sancho, for twenty-five years had made all the charts, compasses, astrolabes, cross-staffs, and nautical tables that were sold in Seville. They had so much work that they contracted with tinsmiths to make the astrolabes and with carpenters to make the cross-staffs, which were then sold in a shop that Luis Gutiérrez opened to the public in Seville. Their monopoly had no legal endorsement; any cosmographer with royal permission could try to sell instruments that he knew how to make. Nonetheless, what he could never achieve was for the said instruments to pass the prior inspection of the House of Trade. The final permission had to be given by the pilot major, Sebastian Cabot, and this he bestowed only on the instruments that carried the signature of his friend and colleague Diego Gutiérrez. This was a simple business, effective and carried out according to the oldest commercial technique in the world.[28]

When the cosmographer Pedro de Medina arrived in Seville with the ingenuous pretension of obtaining a shipment of woad, he ran up against the wall constructed by the Gutiérrez family, and that is where the whole conflict started. Medina dragged into his faction other cosmographers who felt themselves frozen out, such as Chaves and Mexía, and together they initiated hostilities against Cabot and Gutiérrez. One thing stands out in all this. It seems that none of the protagonists tried to hide his fondness for wealth. Were our ancestors more forthcoming than we are? Would cosmographers and pilots really have shown their plebeian spirit by nakedly exposing their monetary ambitions? Perhaps the explanation is simpler: profits from the sale of nautical instruments were so large that to attempt to deny their importance in the dispute would have been tantamount to insulting the intelligence of the judges of the House of Trade.

Religiosity and Superstition

Analyzing the testimonies of passengers who had the opportunity to live among mariners in the sixteenth century, some authors have detected on board ships a strange mixture of religiosity and disinterest in complying with the precepts of the Catholic Church.[29] To sum this up in a graphic though partial manner, blasphemies were as frequent on board as prayers. It seems, then, that we are faced with one more of the contradictions that defined the way that men of the sea viewed the world.

If we wanted to marshal proof that ships in the Carrera de Indias inhabited a world of intense religiosity, there would be a wide range of evidence to choose from. Perhaps we would begin with the names of the ships, among which it is almost impossible to find one that was not placed under the protection of a saint, one of the incarnations of the Virgin, or the plurality of blessed souls. Of course, we know that many of the ships had aliases, or nicknames, beginning with the very famous ship of Columbus, the *Santa María*, called *La Gallega*. Nonetheless, the presence of the saintly among the names is so overwhelming that it leaves no room for doubt. And if perchance a doubt remains, one has only to realize that the first great series of galleons built to defend the Carrera de Indias was a group of twelve, each of which was given the name of one of the apostles. When, in addition to the galleons, armadas began to be formed with Flemish hulks and fluyts, one could distinguish them from their names alone. Contrasted with the denominations of the Spanish ships, which recalled the whole celestial court, the Flemish ships tended to have such evocative names as the *Unicorn*, the *Flying Stag*, the *Red Lion*, and so on.[30]

The authorities worried about procuring the benediction of heaven, as much in putting ships under the protection of the saints as in ordering generals and admirals not to let any sailor on board who had not confessed his sins and received communion.[31] As Juan de Escalante said, the obligations of the good general included keeping the souls of the sailors empty of sins as well as keeping the ships well filled with provisions.[32]

Life on board was marked by a large number of invocations and recitations of prayers. Upon departure, the ship was commended to its celestial protectors. Once the voyage began, and each time the sand clocks were turned, the pages recited psalms and prayers. At nightfall, these same pages filled the ears of all present with the principal prayers of the Christian faith, repeating them monotonously until everyone finally would have committed them to memory. The celebration of the Mass was not common on ships; only the great war galleons carried a chaplain, and it does not seem that the friars who traveled as passengers were accustomed to saying Mass during the voyage. The religious function of greatest importance occurred on Saturdays, in a ceremony presided over by the master which consisted in a solemn singing of the "Salve Regina" followed by litanies attended by all the passengers and the crew. If a storm placed the ship on the verge of sinking, the sailors made vows and said special prayers, which interrupted the normal rhythm of religious observance on board. Finally, when the ship arrived at its destination, prayers were said to express gratitude for the happy conclusion of the voyage.

Another custom, followed at least on the expeditions of discovery in the first half of the century, was to include some saints on the crew lists, so that, when the moment came to distribute wages, they would receive their share. Thus, for example, on the Magellan-Elcano voyage, the lists include "El señor Santiago," "Santo Lesmes," "San Antonio de Padua," "Santa Bárbara," "Nuestra Señora de Montserrat," and so on. Each of them received a portion of cloves from the Moluccas, although it is true that the total quantity was inferior to the amount assigned to a boatswain.[33]

As the alert reader will already have surmised, these sums were not given directly to the saints but to the priests and friars charged with caring for their cult. Unfortunately, on board ships not even the work of the saints was well paid, and that is why it was common for religious orders to fill the ships with almoners and poor boxes. The friars appeared shortly before departure and confided the money box to a pious sailor, with the commission that he look after it during the voyage. Because this practice was so lucrative, poor boxes proliferated in such a way that the authorities had to prohibit them. In spite of everything, money boxes continued to find their way on board; in an inspection of the frigate Santa Catalina in 1579, the authorities confiscated an "alms box," nailed shut and with a slit for accepting coins, that contained the not-contemptible sum of 1,144 reales.[34]

Finally, when a sailor found himself approaching the hour of his death, he always had an economic remembrance for Mother Church. In their testaments, although their only possessions were the clothes on their backs and their forthcoming wages, sailors tried to leave some small amount for charity so that a few masses would be said for their souls.

Nonetheless, in contrast with all these details (and one could find many more) that showed how religion played a role in the daily life of men of the sea, there are other, contradictory, testimonies that seem to minimize the importance of that role. In the first place, the totality of their contemporaries considered sailors to be the worst observers of the church's commandments. They did not observe holy days, fasts, confessions, and Easter communions, nor were they involved in all the full and varied gamut of rites and liturgical celebrations of the time. Such was their indolence in these matters that Alonso de Chaves, upon editing his manual of navigation, dedicated the first chapter to constructing a liturgical calendar on which one could locate all the movable religious feasts in perpetuity. With this calendar, the devout cosmographer tried to ensure that "the aforesaid mariners cannot pretend ignorance, nor will they have room for excuses."[35]

In fact, however much Alonso Chaves pushed the mariners, the unsettled life at sea was a good excuse for not attending church; but the real problem was the impudence with which some sailors bragged about their irreligion. Friar Antonio de Guevara gave one of the most direct testimonies of the lack of respect the men of the sea flaunted in neglecting their religious duties: "Sometimes the oarsmen and sailors on the galley make fun of me when I ask them for their certificates of confession; they show me a deck of cards, saying that in their holy confraternity, they learned not how to confess their sins but to gamble."[36]

When this same friar reproached the men for eating meat on the most holy fast days of the year without showing any shame for it, they responded that if the people on land did not stop eating fish on those designated days, there was no reason for them to stop eating meat. We do not know what Friar Antonio de Guevara replied to them, but his argument cannot have had the devastating logic displayed by the sailors.

One might think that the galleys, with their contingents of oarsmen formed from the dregs of society, would not be a perfect example and that on other kinds of ships, and among people of a higher social level, more devotion might exist. Nonetheless, the case of the admiral Álvaro de Valdés, an Asturian hidalgo who fell ill on a journey from Nombre de Dios to Panama, shows that the failure to attend church also reached into the high command of the armadas. Thinking that he would die in an inn in the middle of the countryside, he included in his testament a petition to his executors, which was at the same time an expression of faith and a confession of his lack of attention to the precepts of the church: "I ask the executors, for the love of God, to care for my soul and note that I die in the countryside without confession, it being about a year that I have not confessed, and with this I entrust them as Christians."[37]

Mariners seemed to show the most intense devotion in the midst of a storm.

Then came shouted declarations of faith, public repentance of past sins, and, of course, promises to change one's life in the future and to make pious offerings and pilgrimages, if God was kind enough to bring them through that critical moment. Of course, some of the promises made were not worth much, like that of the Portuguese sailor who solemnly promised, in the full fury of a storm, to quit his occupation forever if he was saved; despite the reigning panic of the moment, his pledge still provoked a general guffaw among those who heard him.[38] Other vows were more serious; nonetheless, once the danger passed, the sailors forgot their good intentions easily and returned to their habitual disinterest in religious matters: "In a dangerous storm the sailors set themselves to praying, they occupy themselves in groaning, they take to crying, and once it is over, they slowly settle down to eat, talk, gamble, fish, and even to blaspheme, telling one another of the dangers that they witnessed and the promises that they made."[39]

(240)

In general one could say that religion was a last resort for the men of the sea. Mariners, seemingly in greater measure than people on land, only believed in Santa Bárbara—who protected believers from sudden explosions—and in the rest of the celestial court when it thundered. Even in the midst of a storm, if the mariners continued to curse, the passengers could know that things were not too bad, but if the curses turned to prayers, then the situation was really desperate.[40] Something like this happened, for example, on the hulk *Nuestra Señora de la Concepción*, trapped by a storm in a cove off the southwestern coast of Cuba. The winds pushed the ship toward the rocks, and the crew struggled fearlessly trying to prevent the storm from breaking the anchor cables. After a week of effort, when they had used up every human recourse to save themselves and only one frayed anchor cable remained, they decided that the moment had come to solicit outside help:

> Having lost confidence and hope of being able to get the hulk to leave the cove, the said master, considering the grave danger in which they found themselves, ordered an altar made in which he put an image of Nuestra Señora de Consolación [Our Lady of Consolation] with two blessed wax candles; and he convoked all the men on board the said hulk, exhorting them all to commend themselves to Our Lady and ask her for succor and help, so that by her intercession, Our Lord would be pleased to free them from the agony in which they found themselves; and all of this was done with great clamor and much devotion, with everyone on their knees and some flagellating themselves and praying to Our Lord to help them; and with their prayers the blessed San Telmo appeared, and with the dawning, the storm let up a little.[41]

Regarding the religious devotion shown by men of the sea in their testaments, one cannot deny that all of them contain solemn declarations of their identity as fervent Catholics and that they bequeathed sums of money, more or less large, for pious works. Nonetheless, a detailed study of several dozen testaments pertaining to crew members on Spanish expeditions to the Pacific permits us to introduce some very interesting shadings to this general picture.[42]

The crew members of the said expeditions were, of course, men of religious faith, despite their not respecting many of the commandments, especially the sixth precept about not committing adultery, since many of them consigned legacies to bastard children and pensions to women to whom they were indebted (not necessarily in money).[43] When it came time to distribute the material goods that they had possessed on this earth, old lovers and natural children received larger quantities than churches and monasteries, which says much about the humanity of the crewmen.[44] But perhaps the most curious thing to realize is that, in one out of three testaments, the legacies for religious activities would have had to come from the wages that the king owed them, that is, from something that they did not really have and that it was very doubtful they were going to possess. These were really empty gestures and not thoughtless gestures or products of confidence in the punctuality of payment by the Royal Treasury, but just the opposite. The landed property owned in Spain, or the merchandise, clothing, and other belongings that the mariner had with him, were expressly divided among his nearest relatives, leaving the compliance of the pious bequests dependent upon whether the king decided to pay his debts. One clear example of this type of conduct appears in a paragraph from the testament of Juan Sebastián Elcano, in which he specified the form of paying his religious bequests: "They should be paid from the money that His Majesty owes me, and until then, my other goods are not obligated to pay nor comply with any of the said bequests."[45]

Finally, there is no doubt that various prayers were said on the ships all during the day. But what were these prayers? The Inquisition in Mexico was very preoccupied with the purity of customs of the mariners and sent commissioners to Veracruz to inspect the ships arriving in San Juan de Ulúa. At times the investigations followed paths and themes that were quite amusing, as when the austere inquisitors searched the ships looking for paintings in which male and female saints appeared "not with their due decency and honesty, but as figures of dashing men and very beautiful and worldly women."[46] Then there was the grotesque inquiry into a supposed miracle that happened on board the almiranta of the 1582 fleet. On that occasion a sailor leaped into the water when he believed that the ship was about to sink and was rescued thanks to the miraculous intercession of a painting of the Virgin. Of course the matter should not have been taken seriously, since the sailor jumped into the water while hanging onto the painting, and probably the wood of the frame and the stretcher bars for the canvas accomplished the miracle, rather than Our Lady. But those

(241)

were different times, and the inquisitors investigated the matter.[47] Much more serious was the analysis made by the visitors from the Holy Office of the Inquisition regarding vows made during the voyage.

It is of great interest that a letter sent in 1586 by the inquisitor general of Mexico urged the commissioner in Veracruz to continue inspecting the ships, since "the images, relics, and prayers of these men of the sea . . . for the most part are all superstition, such as the contents of the prayer that you sent us, and thus similar prayers will be burned."[48] Some of these prayers, collected on an inspection by the Inquisition, have come down to us. I am not sure if they were clearly considered superstitious, but there is no doubt that they were on the borderline between official dogma and a popular religiosity charged with propitiatory imprecations of an intense pagan flavor:[49]

Prayer to St. Elmo

Holy Body, true friend of mariners, we want you to help us, and always to appear at night before us.

Prayer to St. Nicholas

Saint Nicholas, be pleased to guard our keel, our tiller, our bridge, and the rigging that extends beyond the rail and inside the ship; on this voyage and many other better ones . . . with fair seas and constant wind and a good and safe voyage.

Prayer to the Four Evangelists

To the four saints, to the four holy bodies, Luke and Mark, John and Matthew, commend us to Our Lord Jesus Christ, if something bad befalls this ship, so that it departs and we are placed out of harm's way.

Prayer to Our Lady of Fair Seas

That she succors us and gives us fair seas, with bright days and a good breeze.

Prayer to Our Lady of Barrameda

Now that we have passed your sandbar, be pleased to have us return and pass over it again, with a good and safe voyage.

Prayer to St. Clare

That she be pleased to give us clear skies night and day and bring us good weather and keep us from bad shoals, and bad fleets, and bad company, and that she be pleased to bring us safely to good harbor, Our Father, Ave Maria.

I believe one can clearly detect in this type of prayer the religious symbiosis that shaped Christianity in southern Europe, in which the recalcitrant monotheism of Judaic tradition was not capable of eliminating the plurality of gods in the Greco-Roman world. The ancient maleficent and beneficent spirits were converted into devils, saints, and variations on the Virgin, disposed to harm or to protect human beings. The case of St. Elmo, with his phantasmal apparitions enveloped in fire, is the best known, but there are many more.

The desired protection could be spatial, and thus, the "four holy bodies" of the Evangelists were invoked so that they would guard the four corners of the ship; or all the components of the ship that needed attention were detailed, from the keel to the rigging. Equally, natural hazards such as the sandbar of Sanlúcar de Barrameda, responsible for a thousand shipwrecks, had its protective "genie," now transformed into an appellation of the Virgin. According to the beliefs of the sailors, one ought to take care not to forget to salute, with gun salvos, these celestial guardians, since they were rancorous enough and capable of sending a monstrous storm against the forgetful and inconsiderate. Also, the visibility necessary for navigation, or the fair seas that made some voyages as pleasant as a stroll, were the object of advocacy, personalized as saints and Virgins (St. Clare and Our Lady of Fair Seas) to whom one prayed so that they would send the benefits that their names represented.

The superstitions of the men of the sea were not expressed through prayers alone. The ships also underwent a process of personalization that saw them as good or bad, lucky or unlucky, honorable or dishonorable. On many occasions, the crews developed such an identification with the attributes of their ship that they got into fights to defend, for example, the "honor" of an almiranta, by which I am referring, of course, to the ship that flew the insignia of the admiral and not to the latter's spouse.[50]

There were also cursed islands and places where it was believed that devils raised up great storms. In this sense, the Bermuda Islands had a very bad reputation in the sixteenth century, and mariners tried to avoid them, arguing heatedly about whether the evil omen was conjured up by passing to the north or to the south of the islands.[51] To avoid the evil eye, the crew members wore around their necks the well-known "figs," that is, small amulets shaped like hands with the thumb placed between the index finger and the middle finger, which have been found in abundance in the remains of shipwrecks.[52]

On some occasions, the belief in spectral apparitions paralyzed the mariners to the extent that it put at risk the lives of everyone on board. Juan de Escalante commented on what happened when, on a storm-tossed ship, the lights called St. Elmo's fire appeared on the masts. The credulous sailors took this to be a manifestation of the spirit of the protector saint of the men of the sea:

It was thus at the same moment that someone said: "Look at San Telmo" in some part of the ship; and everybody stopped what they were doing to look where it had appeared. And in seeing those lights, they all began to say: "Save us, save us, San Telmo, holy body"; and they were stunned and stupefied and left off for the moment doing even the most necessary tasks; and as long as these instances continued, they could not stop watching nor move to do what was necessary and what they were obliged to do, confiding in the virtue of that light to liberate them from the affliction and peril in which they found themselves. They did not even act in accord with the common refrain that says: "Pray to God and hammer the enemy" [a Dios rogando y con el mazo dando]. And when the ignorance of the pilot or of his chief is equal to that of the sailors, the harm worsens, so that when the men return to their senses, the ship has rolled over and sits keel up in the water.[53]

Now, in the sixteenth century not only the men of the sea were superstitious. Even respectable friars with their feet firmly planted on the ground believed more than one tall tale. Thus, for example, a man of the intellectual caliber of the Carmelite Antonio Vázquez de Espinosa, author of one of the most monumental books written on American geography, was capable of attributing the misfortunes of a voyage between Veracruz and Seville to the fact that the ship had not fired salvos to salute Nuestra Señora de la Concepción, the patroness of one of the ports that they visited on the voyage.[54]

The real problem consists in determining whether the sailors were more superstitious than the majority of their contemporaries. This is a very difficult question to answer, but I will dare to do so affirmatively. I believe that there are two arguments in support of this hypothesis. In the first place is the enormous intensity of the danger at sea. The energy unleashed by nature frequently fell on the ships with the terrible and indiscriminate violence of a gigantic sledgehammer. Mariners were continually witnessing the cruelty of these natural forces that, according to the purest Catholic orthodoxy, were sent directly by God. Of course it was possible to hold God responsible for all these evils, but official religious doctrine had shifted the blame toward the Devil and the sins of man. Nonetheless, despite the efforts of theologians, believing fully in a merciful God, capable of caring for his creatures and attuned to their sufferings, was much more difficult at sea than on land. One can easily comprehend how and why the sailors shifted their beliefs toward a world of maleficent and beneficent spirits (though they were called demons and saints), responsible for good and evil deeds, whom one had to appease in order to find good fortune. In this way they could understand much better the variety of situations that they lived through at sea; the demons with their wickedness, and the saints with their intercession, which could be more or less effective, took a bit of the responsibility away from Almighty God for permitting such misfortunes.

But the superstitious character of the men of the sea is supported by a second argument: despite the efforts deployed by the Inquisition in some ports, the life of the men of the sea was always much more hidden from the gaze of the ecclesiastical hierarchy than the lives of people on land. Distance, as the jurist Solórzano Pereira said, made the mandates of princes arrive weakened; in this regard, there was nothing to distinguish between the princes of the secular authority and the princes of the church. In the mariners' favor as well was their status as a separate and marginal group, to whom, for that reason, certain liberties could be permitted, since there was not as much risk of their contaminating the nucleus of society.   (245)

In summary, considering the consistent lack of interest in liturgical celebrations among the mariners of diverse countries and considering also the scant attention they paid to messages from the clergy and their belief in numerous superstitions, it is understandable for a historian to affirm that the men of the sea were one of the most irreligious groups in early modern Europe.[55] Whether one accepts this affirmation or not depends on the concept that each person has about what constitutes religion. There are many people who think there is not much difference between superstition and religion in general. From this point of view, if religious belief is not much more than a collection of well-structured superstitions that use universal explanations and aspirations to regulate human societies, perhaps we ought not qualify the mariners of the sixteenth century as irreligious. They simply held a system of beliefs somewhat different from the precepts of official dogma, and they counted, thanks to the peculiarities of their work, on the possibility of maintaining those beliefs outside the supervision of many of the established powers on earth.

Mental Horizons

Notes

Chapter 1: The Land Environment of the Men of the Sea

1. Mateo Alemán, *Vida del pícaro Guzmán de Alfarache* (Barcelona, 1963), bk. 1, p. 40.

2. Studies dealing with the population of Seville are as abundant as they are contradictory. Some of the best known are cited here: Antonio Collantes de Terán, *Sevilla en la Baja Edad Media: La ciudad y sus hombres* (Seville, 1984); Miguel Angel Ladero Quesada, *Historia de Sevilla: La ciudad medieval* (Seville, 1980); Francisco Morales Padrón, *Historia de Sevilla: La ciudad del Quinientos* (Seville, 1983); Antonio Domínguez Ortiz, *Orto y ocaso de Sevilla* (Seville, 1974); Jean Sentaurens, "Séville dans la seconde moitié du XVI siècle: Population et structures sociales. Le rencensements de 1561," *Bulletin Hispanique* (Bordeaux) 77, nos. 3–4 (July–Dec. 1975): 321–90.

3. Ladero Quesada, *Historia de Sevilla*, p. 73.

4. Collantes de Terán, *Sevilla en la Baja Edad Media*, p. 156; Sentaurens, "Séville dans la seconde moitié du XVI siècle," p. 354.

5. Fernand Braudel, *El Mediterráneo y el mundo mediterráneo en la época de Felipe II*, 2 vols. (Madrid, 1976), 1:395–413. This seminal work, originally published in French, is also available in English as *The Mediterranean and the Mediterranean World in the Age of Philip II*, trans. Siân Reynolds (New York, 1976).

6. Florentino Pérez Embid, "Navegación y comercio en el puerto de Sevilla durante la Baja Edad Media," in *Estudios de Historia Marítima* (Seville, 1979), p. 159.

7. See the images of European ports collected in the famous atlas called *Civitates Orbis Terrarum, 1572–1618* (Amsterdam, 1965).

8. Ibid.

9. Luis Navarro García, "El puerto de Sevilla a fines del siglo XVI," *Archivo Hispalense* (Seville) (1966): 27–28.

10. Ibid., pp. 6–7.

11. Archivo General de Indias (hereafter, AGI), Contratación 72, an accusation against the gunner Bonifacio Morales for damages done to a chandler's shop, Seville, 1606.

12. AGI, Contratación 717, an incident that occurred on the Arenal, "near the place where the rope makers work," Seville, 1578.

13. See AGI, Indiferente General 2007, a disturbance on the Arenal, Seville, January 22, 1604.

14. Ibid.

15. AGI, Contratación 72, case against the gunner Hernando de Estrada, Seville, February 15, 1606.

16. AGI, Justicia 823, sentence against the sailor Sanjuán, Seville, November 14, 1536.

17. Juan López de Velasco, *Geografía y descripción universal de las Indias* (1574; Madrid, 1971), p. 35.

18. AGI, Indiferente General 2495, royal order, dated at San Lorenzo el Real, Oct. 12, 1577. This document details a project to construct various galleons and carefully records their measurements and characteristics.

19. For the organization of the fleets of the Carrera de Indias, see the following works: José Veitia Linage, *Norte de la contratación de las Indias Occidentales* (Seville, 1672); Clarence H. Haring, *Comercio y navegación entre España y las Indias en la época de los Habsburgos* (Mexico, 1934), originally published in English as *Trade and Navigation between Spain and the Indies in the Time of the Hapsburgs* (Cambridge, Mass., 1918); Guillermo Céspedes del Castillo, "La avería en el comercio de Indias," *Anuario de Estudios Hispanoamericanos* (Seville) 9 (1954): 617–703.

20. López de Velasco, *Geografía*, p. 110.

21. AGI, Mapas y planos, Mexico and Florida, no. 36.

22. López de Velasco, *Geografía*, p. 109. Antonio Vázquez de Espinosa, *Compendio y descripción de las Indias Occidentales* [c. 1628] (Madrid, 1969), pp. 92–93.

23. Vázquez de Espinosa, *Compendio y descripción*, p. 220. See also AGI, Mapas y Planos, Panamá, Santa Fe y Quito, no. 45, city plan of Cartagena de Indias in 1628.

24. Pablo Emilio Pérez-Mallaína Bueno and Bibiano Torres Ramírez, *La Armada del Mar del Sur* (Seville, 1987).

25. López de Velasco, *Geografía*, p. 174.

26. Haring, *Comercio y navegación*, p. 233.

27. AGI, Mapas y Planos, Santo Domingo, nos. 4 and 12, city plans of Havana in 1567 and 1591.

28. López de Velasco, *Geografía*, p. 59; Vázquez de Espinosa, *Compendio y descripción*, p. 73.

29. Collantes de Terán, *Sevilla en la Baja Edad Media*, p. 244.

30. Sentaurens, "Séville dans la seconde moitié du XVI siècle," pp. 363, 387–88.

31. Juan de Mal Lara, *Recibimiento que hizo la muy noble y muy leal ciudad de Sevilla a la Católica Real Majestad del rey Don Felipe, nuestro señor* (Seville, 1570).

32. AGI, Justicia 903, undated, ca. May of 1570.

33. Ibid.

34. AGI, Justicia 957. In the inspection *(visita)* carried out in the fleet of General Juan de Alcega, the mariners who testified gave much detail about their places of residence, Seville, September 25, 1573.

35. Sentaurens, "Séville dans la seconde moitié du XVI siècle," pp. 340–41; Morales Padrón, *Historia de Sevilla*, p. 60.

36. AGI, Contratación 719, lawsuit between Juan de Arrieta and the heirs of various crewmen in the fleets, Seville, November 21, 1580.

37. AGI, Indiferente General 2005, "Ordenanzas y reglas de los hombres de la mar cofrades del hospital de Nuestra Señora del Buen Aire," Seville, March 13, 1561; "Regla segunda de la Universidad de los maestres y pilotos de Sevilla,"

Seville, December 28, 1562. See also *Actas de la Universidad de Mareantes de Sevilla*, preliminary study by Luis Navarro García and María del Carmen Borrego Plá (Seville, 1972).

38. AGI, Indiferente General 2005. Chapter 7 of the rules of the brotherhood stated: "Moreover, we order and find it good that if any sailor becomes ill from fevers or is injured handling the ship or working on it, that he be cared for, and that he be given a bed in the said hospital."

39. Andrés Navagero, *Viaje por España, 1524–26* (Madrid, 1983).

40. Sentaurens, "Séville dans la seconde moitié du XVI siècle," pp. 343–44.

41. AGI, Patronato 41, ramo 3, documents regarding the collection of the wages of Miguel de Rodas, Medina del Campo, December 22, 1531.

42. AGI, Patronato 38, ramo 15, sentence of the Council of the Indies, Madrid, Oct. 13, 1539.

43. AGI, Contratación 136, "Letter regarding the dowry given Ana Gómez, householder of Seville," Seville, April 28, 1554.

44. AGI, Patronato 35, ramo 7. Madrid, December 11, 1533.

45. AGI, Patronato 36, ramo 4, sentence of the Council of the Indies, Aranda de Duero, July 11, 1547.

46. AGI, Patronato 36, ramo 6, allegation of the royal attorney, April 29, 1549. See also the case of Catalina López in AGI, Patronato 36, ramo 1, sentence of the Council of the Indies, Valladolid, May 24, 1538.

47. AGI, Patronato 255, no. 4, general 5, ramo 1, Seville, October 10, 1614.

Chapter 2: The Origin and Social Condition of the Men of the Sea

1. Diego García de Palacio, *Instrucción náutica para navegar* (Mexico City, 1587; Madrid, 1944), fol. 2.

2. Friar Antonio de Guevara, "De muchos trabajos que se pasan en las galeras, 1539," in *Pasajeros a Indias*, ed. José Luis Martínez (Mexico, 1984), p. 229.

3. Marcus Rediker, *Between the Devil and the Deep Blue Sea: Merchant Seamen, Pirates, and the Anglo-American Maritime World, 1700–1750* (New York, 1987), p. 13.

4. García de Palacio, *Instrucción náutica*, fol. 2.

5. Ralph Davis, *The Rise of the English Shipping Industry in the Seventeenth and Eighteenth Centuries* (London, 1962), p. 158.

6. Ibid., p. 153.

7. Juan de Escalante de Mendoza, *Itinerario de navegación de los mares y tierras occidentales* (1575; reprint, Madrid, 1985), pp. 115–16.

8. Miguel de Cervantes Saavedra, "El celoso extremeño," in *Novelas ejemplares* (Madrid, 1986), 2:99.

9. AGI, Indiferente General 2005, testimony of witnesses regarding the petition of Francisco Manuel to take the pilot's examination, dated Seville, August 21, 1593.

10. Ibid.

11. AGI, Indiferente General 2006, petition of Pero Hernández to the House of Trade, dated Seville, January 21, 1587.

12. AGI, Contratación 2936, petition of Alonso Sánchez, dated Seville, September 4, 1577.

13. AGI, Justicia 886, declaration of Jorge Griego in the prison at Cádiz, dated Cádiz, February 22, 1567.

14. AGI, Contratación 59, charges against Marco Antonio, ship's boy, dated Cádiz, July 11, 1582.

15. This would have been the case with three veteran sailors who had been pilots, masters, and shipowners and who testified that they began to sail between the ages of fifteen and twenty-three years. AGI, Patronato 38, ramo 18, document dated Zumaya, August 14, 1537. A further example is the case of another old sea wolf, General Bartolomé Carreño, who sailed from the age of twenty in ships that he owned. AGI, Justicia 869, testimony given in Seville, November 24, 1563.

16. Cristóbal de Eraso and Diego de Flores Valdés were members of the Knights of the Order of Santiago. Pedro Menéndez held the title of *comendador* of Santa Cruz de la Zarza, and Álvaro de Bazán, senior, was a nobleman of Basque origin whose son rose to the high nobility with the title of first marquis of Santa Cruz. See AGI, Contaduría 473, nominations of officers in the Guard Squadron of the Carrera de Indias.

17. AGI, Patronato 258, no. 8, general 2, ramo 1, testament of the admiral Álvaro de Valdés, dated Chagre, September 22, 1578.

18. AGI, Patronato 254, no. 1, general 2, ramo 3, report on the merits and service of Esteban de las Alas, dated Seville, January 30, 1558.

19. AGI, Contaduría 468 and 473.

20. AGI, Justicia 969, draft of the charges against General Don Cristóbal de Eraso, dated Seville, September 8, 1581.

21. AGI, Contaduria 509, royal order, dated El Pardo, February 2, 1579.

22. AGI, Patronato 255, no. 3, general 2, ramo 2. In the armada of 1574, the general was Diego de Flores Valdés and the admiral was Álvaro de Flores Valdés. In the Tierra Firme fleet of 1582, the general was Don Diego Maldonado and the admiral was Don Francisco Maldonado. See AGI, Contratación 59.

23. B. R. Burg, *Sodomy and the Perception of Evil: English Sea Rovers in the Seventeenth-Century Caribbean* (New York, 1983), p. 54.

24. Ibid., p. 57.

25. AGI, Contratación 72, privileges that His Majesty has conceded to the men of the sea, Ventosilla, November 4, 1606.

26. García de Palacio, *Instrucción náutica*, fols. 3v–5.

27. AGI, Patronato 35, ramo 1, the attorney of the king regarding Captain Gonzalo Gómez de Espinosa, Burgos, January 14, 1528.

28. AGI, Contratación 4792, Seville, May 27, 1588.

29. AGI, Indiferente General 2673, report of Captain Iñigo de Lecoya, undated, but ca. 1575.

30. AGI, Contaduría 503, "A list of sailors and soldiers who went on eight ships in this armada," Sanlúcar de Barrameda, October 8, 1579.

31. AGI, Contaduría 526, "Contracts and agreements of the galleon *San Martín*," October 8, 1579.

32. AGI, Contratación 59, on the flagship, sailing on the return voyage to Spain, July 8, 1583.

33. Pablo Emilio Pérez-Mallaína Bueno, "Los libros de náutica españoles del siglo XVI y su influencia en el descubrimiento y conquista de los océanos," *Ciencia, vida y espacio en Iberoamérica* (Madrid) 3 (1989): 457–84.

34. AGI, Contratación 200, testament of the pilot Luis Sánchez, native of Seville, and son of the river carpenter Bartolomé Sánchez, householder of La Cestería in Seville, "Document made on the ship *Santiago*, on what is called the Ocean Sea," July 22, 1561.

35. AGI, Indiferente General 2673, memorandum of the pilot Alonso de Zapata, Seville, October 10, 1551.

36. AGI, Patronato 46, ramo 8, "Report of an armada that was refitted in New Spain to go to the said Moluccas in 1565."

37. AGI, Contaduría 468, "Roster, muster rolls, and payments... of the galleon *San Pedro*." In the Gulf of the Mares, April 18, 1575.

38. AGI, Indiferente General 2673, ordinances issued by the Council of the Indies and directed to the House of Trade (Palencia, September 28, 1534); and instructions from the officials of the House of Trade to the masters of the Carrera de Indias (ca. 1535).

39. Ibid., supplication of the masters and ship lords in response to the ordinances and instructions of 1534 and 1535.

40. *Actas de la Universidad de Mareantes de Sevilla*, analysis and transcription by Luis Navarro García and María del Carmen Borrego Plá (Seville, 1972), p. 39, acts of the session of January 26, 1582.

41. Luis Navarro García, "La gente de mar en Sevilla en el siglo XVI," *Revista de Historia de América* (Mexico) 67–68 (1969): 44–46.

42. AGI, Indiferente General 2673, memorandum of Captain Cosme Buitrón, Seville, January 8, 1566.

43. AGI, Indiferente General 2005, memorandum to the Council of the Indies from Juan Rodríguez de Noriega, undated, but ca. 1561.

44. Ibid., proposed ordinances of the University of Seafarers, Seville, December 28, 1662.

45. Ibid., proposed ordinances of the Brotherhood of Our Lady of Fair Wind, Seville, March 13, 1561, article 27.

46. Ibid., commentary of the House of Trade on the statutes of the Brotherhood and University of Seafarers, Seville, November 11, 1568.

47. Regarding the privileges of the gunners, see AGI, Indiferente General 2007, memorandum of Andrés Muñoz, head gunner of the House of Trade, undated, but ca. 1604. A royal order issued in Madrid on May 6, 1595, gave the gunners of the Carrera de Indias the same privileges as those of Burgos.

48. AGI, Contratación 72, "Privileges, exemptions, and liberties that His Majesty concedes to the men of the sea," Ventosilla, November 4, 1606.

(251)

49. AGI, Contaduría 473, nomination of officers, cosmographers, pilots, and other employees of the Guard Squadron of the Carrera de Indias, 1568–77.

50. AGI, Patronato 39, ramo 10, the royal attorney against the heirs of Toribio Alonso de Salazar, Valladolid, July 20, 1543.

51. AGI, Patronato 258, no. 8, general 2, ramo 1, will of Admiral Álvaro de Valdés, Chagre, September 22, 1578.

52. AGI, Patronato 256, general 3, ramo 1, Madrid, November 6, 1600.

53. AGI, Justicia 869, testimony of the canon Alonso de Nomparte, Seville, November 24, 1563.

54. AGI, Indiferente General 2495, instructions to Sebastian Cabot, Seville, March 24, 1526; and a royal order issued in El Pardo, March 18, 1576.

55. AGI, Patronato 255, no. 3, general 1, ramo 6, Havana, June 25, 1574.

56. AGI, Indiferente General 2495, royal order addressed to Captain General Don Cristóbal de Eraso, Madrid, March 27, 1576.

57. This was what happened on an expedition sent to Florida in aid of Pedro Menéndez de Avilés. AGI, Contratación 58, attempted mutiny in sight of Lanzarote, April 23, 1566.

58. AGI, Justicia 914, sentence condemning the captain Gregorio de Polanco to a year's suspension from his duties, Seville, September 5, 1573.

59. I prefer to use the figure of average crewmen per ship, rather than crew members per ton, taking into account the problems that exist in determining the precise value of a ton. The Cantabrian area used a system of measure different from that in Andalusia, and there was also a difference in figuring the tonnage of merchant ships and warships. One of the latest studies that reflects the complexity of the problem is José Luis Casado Soto, *Los barcos españoles del siglo XVI y la Gran Armada de 1588* (Madrid, 1988).

60. Pierre Chaunu and Huguette Chaunu, *Séville et l'Atlantique,* 8 vols. in 12 (Paris, 1955–59), 6:329.

61. First, I calculated that each of the armadas contained an average of fourteen ships. Then, I considered that some fourteen warships and 188 merchant ships would have departed in 1608 and applied the corresponding average number of crewmen, yielding a result of 9,050 men.

62. AGI, Justicia 1146, testimony of the cosmographer Pedro de Medina, Seville, September 3, 1544.

63. AGI, Justicia 884, power of attorney authorized in the name of the University of Masters, Pilots, and Shipowners for the Indies fleets in the Ocean Sea, Seville, January 3, 1563.

64. Juan de Mal Lara, *Recibimiento que hizo la muy noble y muy leal ciudad de Sevilla a la Católica Real Majestad del rey Don Felipe, nuestro señor* (Seville, 1570), fols. 38v–39v.

65. Navarro García, "Gente de mar en Sevilla," p. 38.

66. AGI, Patronato 260, no. 2, ramo 30, "Memoria de los capitanes y maestres y señores de naos y pilotos y marineros señalados," undated, but ca. 1572. The number that the document gives is fifty-one captains of sea and war and 2,650 sailors,

but it does not include some important maritime towns such as Castro Urdiales and Pasajes.

67. Christopher Lloyd, *The British Seamen, 1200–1860: A Social Survey* (London, 1968), p. 34. The total number of sailors in the whole country was estimated at 17,157.

68. W. Laird Clowes, *The Royal Navy: A History from the Earliest Times to the Present* (New York, 1966), p. 425.

69. Colin Martin and Geoffrey Parker, *La Gran Armada, 1588* (Madrid, 1988), p. 62. The book was also published in English as *The Spanish Armada* (London, 1988).

70. *Historia primitiva y exacta del monasterio del Escorial, escrita en el siglo XVI por el padre Fray José de Sigüenza, bibliotecario del monastero y primer historiador de Felipe II* (Madrid, 1891), p. 92.

71. The following table presents the regional origin of crews on Spanish armadas.

Regional Origin of Seamen on Armadas, 1573–1593

	Officers	Gunners and Sailors
Cantabrians	81 (49.09%)	271 (50.19%)
Andalusians	68 (41.21%)	226 (41.85%)
Canary Islanders	0	5 (0.93%)
Other Castilians	13 (7.88%)	21 (3.89%)
From Kingdom of Aragón	3 (1.82%)	17 (3.15%)
Total	165 (100.00%)	540 (100.01%)

Source: Data from AGI, Contratación 468 and 4792; Justicia 961.

72. The following table presents the regional origin of crews on Spanish merchant fleets.

Regional Origin of Seamen on Merchant Fleets to New Spain and Tierra Firme, 1593–1594

	Officers	Gunners and Sailors
Andalusians	309 (80.47%)	1,310 (78.02%)
Cantabrians	36 (9.38%)	202 (12.03%)
Canary Islanders	11 (2.86%)	16 (0.95%)
Other Castilians	12 (3.13%)	68 (4.05%)
From Kingdom of Aragón	16 (4.17%)	83 (4.94%)
Total	384 (100.01%)	1,679 (99.99%)

Source: Data from AGI, Contratación 1099–1108.

73. Memorandum of the Franciscans of Hispaniola to Cardinal Cisneros, October 12, 1500, in *Cartas particulares a Colón y relaciones coetáneas*, ed. Juan Gil (Madrid, 1984), p. 289.

74. Martín Fernández Navarrete, *Colección de los viajes y descubrimientos que hicieron por mar los españoles desde finales del siglo XV* (Madrid, 1964), 2:421–29.

75. AGI, Patronato 34, ramo 4, "Relación del sueldo que se debe a los que fueron a Maluco en la Armada que fué por capitán Hernando de Magallanes," undated.

76. AGI, Patronato 34, ramo 6, Seville, August 9, 1519.

77. AGI, Indiferente General 2495, Council of the Indies to Sebastian Cabot, Toledo, November 12, 1525.

78. AGI, Patronato 42, ramo 1.

79. AGI, Contratación 3253. Of 255 mariners with known origin, 37 were foreigners, which was 14.5 percent.

80. AGI, Justicia 886. The mutiny took place in October 1565.

81. AGI, Indiferente General 2005, instruction to the masters of the Carrera de Indias, Seville, March 26, 1568.

82. AGI, Contaduría 468, 503, and 526; Contratación 1099–1108, 2936, and 4792; Justicia 961.

83. The exact proportion of foreigners in one sample made among eight hundred infantrymen was 3.8 percent. AGI, Contaduría 468, muster lists and payments made to sailors and soldiers in the armada of 1573–74.

84. AGI, Indiferente General 2673, report by Alonso de Zapata, Seville, October 10, 1551.

85. Ibid., memorandum of Juan de Melgarejo titled "Reformación de la carrera de Indias de Su Majestad del Mar Océano, de muchas cosas y malas costumbres que hay que quitar y de otras que tienen necesitad de enmendar," Seville, December 13, 1568.

86. Ibid.

87. Ibid.

88. AGI, Contaduría 468, muster lists and payments made in different ports. The first three names appeared among the crew of the galleon *San Tadeo* during the muster made off the Canaries on April 23, 1575. Pero Díaz was a steward who was listed on the nao *Santiago*. AGI, Contratación 138-A, Seville, September 9, 1580.

89. Rediker, *Between the Devil and the Deep Blue Sea*, p. 80.

90. AGI, Indiferente General 2673, memorandum of Captain Iñigo de Lecoya, undated, ca. 1575.

91. Ibid.

Chapter 3: The Ship as a Place of Work

1. Diego García de Palacio, *Instrucción náutica para navegar* (Mexico City, 1587; Madrid, 1944), fol. 87.

2. Ibid., fol. 90v.

3. To calculate the provisions, I used the data from Alonso de Chaves's sixteenth-century treatise *Espejo de navegantes* (Madrid, 1983), pp. 225–26. To de-

termine the tonnage for various items of merchandise, I relied on the size of containers listed in José Veitia Linage, *Norte de la contratación de las Indias Occidentales* (Seville, 1672), bk. 2, chap. 16. On the question of weights and measures, I followed the data in Miguel Angel Ladero Quesada, *La hacienda real de Castilla en el siglo XV* (La Laguna, Canary Islands, 1973).

4. The principal anchor of a *nao* of four hundred toneladas weighed sixteen *quintales* (736 kilograms), and the cable that sustained it weighed between fourteen and eighteen quintales (from 644 to 828 kilograms). See García de Palacio, *Instrucción náutica*, fol. 109v. According to Chaves, *Espejo de navegantes*, p. 219, the largest of the anchors of a nao of three hundred toneles weighed eleven quintales (506 kilograms). (255)

5. Juan de Escalante de Mendoza, *Itinerario de navegación de los mares y tierras occidentales* (1575; reprint, Madrid, 1985), p. 63.

6. García de Palacio, *Instrucción náutica*, fol. 90v.

7. The custom of putting out fires with sails dampened in urine was the system used in the English navy in the Tudor epoch. See Christopher Lloyd, *The British Seamen, 1200–1860: A Social Survey* (London, 1968), p. 33.

8. Chaves, *Espejo de navegantes*, p. 231.

9. Escalante de Mendoza, *Itinerario*, p. 54.

10. I am referring to the diary of Edward Barlow, who described the force of a storm at sea in a form very similar to what I have used in the text. See Marcus Rediker, *Between the Devil and the Deep Blue Sea: Merchant Seamen, Pirates, and the Anglo-American Maritime World, 1700–1750* (New York, 1987), pp. 88–89.

11. Ibid., p. 94.

12. AGI, Patronato 43, ramo 11.

13. AGI, Patronato 37, ramo 36.

14. AGI, Justicia 853, lawsuit over the salvage of the nao *Concepción*, Toledo, September 25, 1551.

15. AGI, Indiferente General 2673, lawsuit between Pero Díaz and Juan de Altamira, Seville, September 17, 1551.

16. Of a total of 1,953 sailors, 919 (47 percent) showed signs of wounds on the face and hands. This count excluded any other type of mark and natural physical characteristics such as moles, discolorations of the skin, and so on. AGI, Contaduría 471, 503, and 526.

17. In the armada of 1575, the crew was dismissed on August 21, and the enlistment of sailors for the new expedition began on December 24. AGI, Contaduría 503.

18. Escalante de Mendoza, *Itinerario*, p. 169.

19. The data referring to age were taken from the wills of 626 men of the sea, from pages to generals, revealed in cases heard before the House of Trade and the Council of the Indies and preserved in the sections called Contratación and Justicia in the AGI. These data coincide in general terms with those that appear in Escalante de Mendoza, *Itinerario*, pp. 46–50.

20. AGI, Contratación 72, a legal process against the ensign Ginés Caballero del Castillo, Havana, October 24, 1606.

21. Escalante de Mendoza, *Itinerario*, p. 192. It seems that one had to be over seventeen years of age to be considered a sailor. See AGI, Justicia 886, legal process for mutiny against Jorge Griego, Cádiz, March 22, 1567.

22. AGI, Contratación 58. One such was Ruy Díaz, an illiterate sailor and a native of Ribadeo, who appeared as a witness in a judgment for a disturbance over a game.

23. AGI, Indiferente General 2007, report of the chief gunner of the House of Trade, 1604.

24. AGI, Indiferente General 2495, royal order, signed at El Pardo, March 11, 1578.

25. Lloyd, *British Seamen*; also Ralph Davis, *The Rise of the English Shipping Industry in the Seventeenth and Eighteenth Centuries* (London, 1962), p. 145.

26. Luis Navarro García, "Pilotos, maestres y señores de naos en la Carrera de Indias," *Archivo Hispalense* (Seville) 46–47, nos. 141–46 (1967): 241–95.

27. Davis, *Rise of the English Shipping Industry*, p. 123.

28. AGI, Patronato 255, no. 2, general 1, ramo 12, Cristóbal de Eraso to the Council of the Indies, undated, ca. 1578.

29. AGI, Patronato 254, no. 1, general 2, ramo 3, relation of the merits and services of Esteban de las Alas "The Younger," Seville, January 30, 1585.

30. Eugenio de Salazar, *La mar descrita por los mareados* (1573), in *Pasajeros a Indias*, ed. José Luis Martínez (Mexico City, 1984), p. 294. This is available in English as "Life at Sea in the Sixteenth Century: The Landlubber's Lament of Eugenio de Salazar," translated by Carla Rahn Phillips, no. 24 of the James Ford Bell Lectures (Minneapolis, 1987).

31. AGI, Contratación 59, investigation of the loss of the *almiranta* (the admiral's ship, second-in-command) of the New Spain fleet, which happened near Veracruz, September 19, 1582.

32. García de Palacio, *Instrucción náutica*, fol. 112.

33. AGI, Contratación 200, will of Captain Pedro de Mata, Cartagena de Indias, April 17, 1562.

34. In the instructions issued by the House of Trade in 1535, interpreting ordinances from the previous year, whipping was also foreseen as a punishment for masters who broke the law. AGI, Indiferente General 2673.

35. AGI, Contratación 138–46.

36. AGI, Indiferente General 2673. The ship was owned by Hernando Pizarro, and the event took place in 1537.

37. About the form of carrying out this type of fraud and many others, see the report of Juan de Melgarejo, entitled "Reformación de la Carrera de Indias," AGI, Indiferente General 2673, Seville, December 13, 1568.

38. AGI, Contratación 4792. Here is the wording of the clause from the owner Francisco Correa to the master Alonso Rodríguez in the master's contract, edited in Seville on January 23, 1589: "Moreover, we obligate ourselves to exclude, in peace and safety, you, the said master, regarding the salaries and wages of the sailors, men, and company of the said vessel on the outbound and return voyages, because

(256)

you, the aforesaid, know everything about the contracts made . . . and it remains in our charge to comply with them and to pay them, and to exclude you in peace and safety from them."

39. AGI, Justicia 853, Toledo, September 25, 1560, sentence regarding the rescue of the nao *Concepción*.

40. AGI, Justicia 957 and 958. Cristóbal de Monte Bernardo and Andrés de Paz were two of the four great Sevillian shipowners who, in a letter sent to King Philip II in 1584, ostentatiously made reference to the fact that they each possessed riches of between twenty thousand and thirty thousand ducats. See Luis Navarro García, "La gente de mar en Sevilla en el siglo XVI," *Revista de Historia de America* (Mexico) 67–68 (1969): 44–46. 〔 257 〕

41. AGI, Indiferente General 2673, report of the Captain Cosme Buitrón, Seville, January 8, 1566.

42. Fernand Braudel, *El Mediterráneo y el mundo mediterráneo en la época de Felipe II*, 2 vols. (Madrid, 1976), 1:413.

43. AGI, Indiferente General 2673, testimony of Alonso Martín in the lawsuit filed by Captain Cosme Buitrón, Seville, 1566.

44. This was the case with the masters Lorenzo Martín Montoya and Hernán García, householders of Triana, who wanted to buy a ship of 140 toneladas that cost fourteen hundred ducats; the king paid them one thousand ducats to sail it as a dispatch ship to Cartagena de Indias. AGI, Patronato 257, no. 1, general 7, ramo 4, Seville, April 3, 1583.

45. Of the 154 "ship lords," 119 went as masters, 28 as captains, 6 as pilots, and 1 as chief scrivener. On another nine ships, a son or brother of the owners traveled on the voyage. Francisco Fernández del Castillo, comp., *Libros y libreros en el siglo XVI* (Mexico City, 1982), pp. 351–511.

46. AGI, Indiferente General 2005, power of attorney authorized before the scrivener Benito Luis, Seville, January 3, 1563.

47. *Actas de la Universidad de Mareantes* (Seville, 1972).

48. Davis, *Rise of the English Shipping Industry*, p. 81.

49. Ruth Pike, *Aristócratas y comerciantes en la sociedad sevillana del siglo XVI* (Barcelona, 1978), originally published in English as *Aristocrats and Traders: Sevillian Society in the Sixteenth Century* (Ithaca, N.Y., 1972).

50. AGI, Patronato 255, no. 1, general 3, ramo 6, report about the good service and personal qualities of various generals, January 4, 1574.

51. In order to prove the multifaceted character of these military men, it is sufficient to read the relations of their merits and services. As examples, see the reports on Esteban de las Alas, "The Elder" and "The Younger," in AGI, Patronato 254, no. 1, general 2, ramo 3; Antonio de Osorio, in AGI, Patronato 258, no. 2, general 3, ramo 5; Sancho Pardo Osorio, in AGI, Patronato 258, no. 3, general 1, ramo 1; and, finally, Hernando de Liermo y Agüero, AGI, Patronato 256, no. 2, general 3, ramo 1.

52. AGI, Justicia 869. Pedro Menéndez de Avilés indicated that the officials of the House of Trade had always felt an antipathy toward him because he was the

first general of a fleet named directly by the king and that, because of this, they had forced his incarceration.

53. AGI, Patronato 254, no. 1, general 5, ramo 4, information about the conduct and ability of General Juan de Alcega, Madrid, January 2, 1572.

54. AGI, Justicia 957, inspection and judicial inquiry into the fleet of General Diego de Flores Valdés, Seville, October 27, 1573.

55. Archivo General de Simancas (hereafter, AGS), Guerra y marina 1, investigation carried out in Santander by Juan Rodríguez de Salamanca against Gonzalo Pérez de Herrera, owner of a galley, Santander, 1388.

56. AGI, Patronato 261, ramo 7, contract between the pilot Ginés Pinzón (grandson of Martín Alonso Pinzón, who accompanied Columbus in 1492) and the master Manuel de Fonseca, Gran Canaria, December 16, 1583.

57. A Spanish version of the Rôles d'Oléron (possibly from the fourteenth century) can be consulted in the Biblioteca Nacional in Madrid, Ms. 716, fols. 90v–94. A comparative edition of the principal maritime-mercantile law codes of antiquity and the Middle Ages was published by Jean Marie Pardessus in his now-classic work, *Us et coutumes de la mer, ou collection des usages maritimes des peuples de l'Antiquité et du Moyen Age* (Paris, 1847). For medieval legislation about the Mediterranean, one can consult a modern edition of the *Libro del Consulado del Mar*, such as the one published in 1965 by the Barcelona Chamber of Commerce.

58. Bernal Díaz del Castillo, *Historia verdadera de la conquista de la Nueva España* (Mexico City, 1955), chap. 105.

59. This quantity supposes 3 percent of the profits. See AGI, Contratación 3251, relation and account of the expenses made on a caravel of seventy-five toneles for the voyage made to Hispaniola, 1507. The name given to the fee collected by the owner of the ship was the *avería*, which should not be confused with the contribution collected for the maintenance of the warships that escorted the fleets.

60. Jean Merrien, *La Vie quotidienne des marins au Moyen Age des Vikings aux galères* (Paris, 1969), p. 119.

61. See, for example, AGI, Contratación 4792, value of the freight charges for the ship *Santiago* that traveled between 1583 and 1584 from Garachico (Tenerife, Canary Islands) to Margarita Island in the Caribbean. A detailed description of how the freight fees were divided also appears in Escalante de Mendoza, *Itinerario*, pp. 188–91.

62. AGI, Contaduría 425, relation of the cloves that came in the ship *Victoria*; and the relation of the wages that were owing to the captain, officers, and crew of the ship *Victoria*.

63. AGI, Indiferente General 2495, correspondence between the deputies charged with the dispatch of the armada of Sebastian Cabot and the Council of the Indies, 1525.

64. AGI, Patronato 42, ramo 1, petition of Antonio Ponce, constable of the armada of Sebastian Cabot, 1531.

65. AGI, Patronato 37, ramo 1, undated memo on what is best for the good of the business arrangements of an armada going to the Spice Islands.

66. AGI, Patronato 255, no. 2, general 1, ramo 8, the Council of the Indies to the *corregidor* of the Lordship of Vizcaya, Madrid, August 8, 1581.

67. AGI, Escribanía de Cámara 1077-A, Seville, December 18, 1612.

68. Davis, *Rise of the English Shipping Industry*, p. 140.

69. AGI, Contratación 200, testament of the pilot Luis Sánchez, at sea, July 22, 1561.

70. AGI, Justicia 914, Seville, September 7, 1573.

71. AGI, Justicia 884, 1567.

72. AGI, Contratación 200. The testament of Juan de Arango (Havana, July 7, 1562) shows that this sailor devoted himself to such undertakings in collaboration with the master of his ship.

《 259 》

73. AGI, Contratación 59, report by General Álvaro Flores Quiñones. At sea, off the coast of Alvarado, October 21, 1582.

74. Rediker, *Between the Devil and the Deep Blue Sea*, p. 130.

75. AGI, Justicia 958, inspection and official inquiry of the officers of the New Spain fleet in the year 1574, Seville, October 5, 1574.

76. Miguel de Cervantes Saavedra, "El coloquio de los perros," in *Novelas ejemplares* (Madrid, 1986), 2:327.

77. Merrien, *Vie quotidienne*, pp. 146–47.

78. AGI, Indiferente General, reform of the king's Carrera de Indias of the Ocean Sea, proposed by Juan de Melgarejo, Seville, December 13, 1568.

79. AGI, Justicia 958.

80. Ibid.

81. Ibid.

82. Ibid.

83. AGI, Patronato, no. 2, general 3, ramo 5. Although the majority of the data collected from this document pertain to the relation of merits and services written by Osorio himself, there are also marginal notes written by functionaries of the Council of the Indies, which inspire greater credibility than the text by the general.

84. AGI, Justicia 1147.

85. AGI, Indiferente General 2673. The ship was the galleon *San Pelayo* of over one thousand toneladas. See the memorandum of Pedro Menéndez de Avilés, Madrid, January 30, 1566.

86. AGI, Justicia 970, definitive sentence of the Council of the Indies against Pedro Menéndez de Avilés, Madrid, January 24, 1565.

87. AGI, Justicia 959, royal order, Madrid, November 12, 1578.

88. AGI, Justicia 959–69.

89. AGI, Justicia 959.

90. Cesáreo Fernández Duro, *Armada española desde la unión de los reinos de Castilla y León* (Madrid, 1972), 2:314.

91. Ibid., p. 224.

92. AGI, Indiferente General 2006, Don Álvaro de Bazán to the king, Lisbon, November 26, 1582.

93. AGI, Justicia 956, response of Don Cristóbal de Eraso to the charges brought against him, Seville, September 17, 1581.

94. AGI, Indiferente General 2495, royal order, in the forest of Segovia, June 3, 1578. For galleons built for the crown, see Carla Rahn Phillips, *Six Galleons for the King of Spain* (Baltimore, 1986), especially chaps. 2–3.

95. The data summarized in the table come from Earl J. Hamilton, "Wages and Subsistence on Spanish Treasure Ships, 1503–1660," *Journal of Political Economy* 37 (Feb.–Dec. 1929): 430–50; and *El tesoro americano y la revolución de los precios en España, 1500–1650* (Barcelona, 1983), app. 7. This classic work was originally published in English as *American Treasure and the Price Revolution in Spain, 1501–1650* (Cambridge, Mass., 1934). The research I have done in different sections of the Archive of the Indies has generally corroborated the figures offered by Hamilton, and for that reason I have decided to use them.

96. Klaus Wagner, "Apuntes para el coste de la vida en Sevilla, agosto 1544–febrero 1545," *Archivo Hispalense* (Seville) 55, no. 170 (1972): 119–30.

97. AGI, Contratación 4792, Cádiz, February 23, 1543.

98. AGI, Patronato, no. 38, ramo 3, inventory and auction of the goods of accountant Iñigo Cortés Perea. At sea, sailing on the flagship, August 3, 1526.

99. AGI, Indiferente General 2495, royal order, Madrid, March 26, 1576.

100. Contratación 4792–98, legal documents filed by mariners and soldiers for the collection of their wages, 1543–1650. Because the documentation begins to be abundant from the last quarter of the sixteenth century, I have restricted myself to these years. Besides these sources, I have used a hundred or so legal cases about the payment of salaries, dispersed among various bundles *(ramos)* in the Contratación and Justicia sections of the AGI.

101. AGI, Contratación 138, payment at sea upon leaving the Bahama Channel, August 14, 1581.

102. AGI, Contratación 4792, agreement reached by Pedro Ortiz to be a sailor on the flyboat *La Esperanza*, San Juan de Ulúa, November 15, 1597.

103. Ibid., petition of Gonzalo Pérez, Seville, January 10, 1592.

104. Braudel, *Mediterráneo*, 1:607.

105. Ibid., 1:05.

106. AGI, Contratación 200, testament of Pedro Rabí, sailor on the ship *San Salvador*, San Juan de Ulúa, January 21, 1562.

107. AGI, Indiferente General 2005, report of the maravedís proceeding from the goods and wages of masters, pilots, and sailors who died in service on the Carrera de Indias, 1569–76, Seville, December 19, 1576.

108. The average value of the personal objects of the sailors was 10.5 ducats. See AGI, Contaduría 485, accounts of the goods of deceased dependents of the armada from 1574 to 1580.

109. Ibid., testament of Pedro Roboredo, native of Vivero, June 30, 1576.

110. AGI, Contratación 2674, testament of Antonio Núñez, Veracruz, December 8, 1701. [Translator's note: The correct date is presumably 1601.]

111. AGI, Contaduría 485, accounts of goods of deceased dependents of the armadas, 1576.

112. Davis, *Rise of the English Shipping Industry*, p. 151.

113. Ibid., p. 177, citing the diary of Edward Barlow.

114. AGI, Patronato 260, no. 2, ramo 5, memorandum of the pilots in the House of Trade in Seville and the salaries they earned, undated.

115. AGI, Patronato 41, ramo 3, testament of Miguel de Rodas, Seville, January 29, 1526.

116. Pike, *Aristócratas y comerciantes*, pp. 100, 152.

117. AGI, Patronato 42, ramo 2, document filed by Sebastian Cabot in the name of the pilots of the Carrera de Indias. Undated, ca. 1548.

118. Pike, *Aristócratas y comerciantes*, p. 80.

119. AGI, Patronato 42, ramo 2.

120. Ibid., testament of Diego Gutiérrez.

121. AGI, Contratación 4792.

122. AGI, Justicia 958, inspection of the fleet of 1576–77, Seville, October 17, 1577.

123. AGI, Contratación 200, testament of the captain Pedro de Mata, Cartagena de Indias, April 17, 1562.

124. *Actas de la Universidad de Mareantes*, proceedings of February 1, 1598.

125. Davis, *Rise of the English Shipping Industry*, p. 84.

126. A caravel of 70 toneles bought in 1507 cost 575 ducats. See AGI, Contratación 3251. In 1513, a new caravel, bought for the expedition to Darien, cost 412 ducats. See AGI, Contratación 3253.

127. The flagship of the armada sent to Darien under the command of Pedrarías Dávila, with a carrying capacity of 130 toneles, cost 672 ducats, including repairs. See AGI, Contratación 3253.

128. AGI, Indiferente General 2495, report of the ships present in the river at Seville, 1578. On April 3, 1583, a *nao* of 140 toneladas was sold in Seville for the sum of fourteen hundred ducats. AGI, Patronato 257, no. 1, general 7, ramo 4.

129. Navarro García, "Gente de mar en Sevilla," p. 44.

130. AGI, Indiferente General 2673, memorandum of Captain Cosme Buitrón, Seville, January 8, 1566.

131. AGI, Contratación 5730.

132. Pike, *Aristócratas y comerciantes*, p. 118.

133. Sancho Pardo Osorio, general of the New Spain fleet of 1594, was paid two hundred ducats per month. See AGI, Contratación 4792.

134. AGI, Indiferente General 2673; Contaduría 503, and Patronato 255, no. 3, general 13, ramo 10. The salaries of captains general and admirals had risen considerably by the early seventeenth century, and those on armadas earned far more than those on merchant fleets. See Phillips, *Six Galleons*, p. 239.

135. AGI, Justicia 869.

136. AGI, Patronato 258, no. 1, general 3, ramo 5.

137. Ibid.

138. AGI, Patronato 254, no. 1, general 2, ramo 3, relation of the merits and services of Captain Esteban de las Alas, "The Younger," Seville, January 20, 1585. Another case of the same type can be seen in AGI, Patronato 256, no. 2, general 3, ramo 1, relation of the merits and services of Captain Hernando de Liermo y Agüero, Madrid, November 6, 1600.

139. Pike, *Aristócratas y comerciantes*, p. 215.

140. AGI, Contratación 72, legal case against the ensign Ginés Caballero del Castillo, Havana, October 24, 1606.

Chapter 4: The Ship as a Place of Life and Death

1. AGI, Contratación 58, petition from Diego and Cristóbal de Saavedra to General Don Cristóbal de Eraso, at sea, October 30, 1571. Emphasis added.

2. Friar Tomás de la Torre, "Diario del viaje de Salamanca a Ciudad Real (Chiapas), 1544–1545," in *Pasajeros a Indias*, ed. José Luis Martínez (Mexico, 1984), app. 2, p. 248.

3. "No man will be a sailor who has contrivance enough to get himself into a jail; for being in a ship is being in jail with the chance of being drowned. . . . A man in jail has more room, better food, and commonly better company." From the diary of Dr. Johnson (1759), cited by Ralph Davis in *The Rise of the English Shipping Industry in the Seventeenth and Eighteenth Centuries* (London, 1962), p. 154.

4. *Recopilación de las leyes de los Reinos de Indias* (Madrid, 1680), lib. 9, título 28, ley 21.

5. AGI, Contratación 3253, "Relación de lo que se ha cargado en la carabela de Juan López Vizcochero . . . y la nao de Alonso Hernández," 1513.

6. AGI, Indiferente General 2673, ordinances directed to the House of Trade, Palencia, September 28, 1534.

7. Philippe Ariès and Georges Duby, eds., *Historia de la vida privada* (Madrid, 1988), 2: 447. This is also available in English as *A History of Private Life*, 5 vols. (Cambridge, Mass., 1987–91).

8. AGI, Contratación 3251, "Relación y cuenta del gasto que se hizo con la carabela de sesenta y cinco toneles para el viaje que se hizo a la isla Española con ropa de mercadería de que fué por maestre Cristóbal Vizcaíno, vecino de Sevilla," 1507.

9. AGI, Contratación 58, testimony of the passenger Juan Núñez Suárez, resident of Seville, sailing toward Havana on the *capitana* of the fleet of Don Cristóbal de Eraso, June 5, 1572.

10. AGI, Contratación 200, testament of the captain and master Pedro de Mata, Cartagena de Indias, April 17, 1562.

11. Cited by Marcus Rediker, *Between the Devil and the Deep Blue Sea: Merchant Seamen, Pirates, and the Anglo-American Maritime World, 1700–1750* (New York, 1987), p. 161.

12. José Luis Martínez, ed., *Pasajeros a Indias* (Mexico City, 1984), p. 143.

13. Friar Antonio de Guevara, "De muchos trabajos que se pasan en las galeras, 1539," in Martínez, *Pasajeros a Indias*, app. 1, p. 222.

14. Eugenio de Salazar, *La mar descrita por los mareados* (1573), in Martínez, *Pasajeros a Indias*, app. 3, pp. 283–84.

15. Miguel de Cervantes Saavedra, "El licenciado Vidriera," in *Novelas ejemplares* (Madrid, 1986), 2:47–61.

16. AGI, Indiferente General 2498, royal order, San Lorenzo el Real, October 12, 1577. A report written in 1535 by the masters of the Carrera de Indias noted: "In the old days the ships customarily did not have more than one deck . . . and now we make them with two planked decks." AGI, Indiferente General 2673. The Spanish galleon can be considered a multipurpose vessel throughout its history. See Carla Rahn Phillips, *Six Galleons for the King of Spain* (Baltimore, 1986), pp. 40–46.

17. Juan de Escalante de Mendoza, *Itinerario de navegación de los mares y tierras occidentales* (1575; reprint, Madrid, 1985), p. 70.

18. Torre, "Diario del viaje," p. 247.

19. Guevara, "Muchos trabajos," pp. 231–32.

20. AGI, Patronato 39, ramo 1, Madrid, July 30, 1526.

21. An apprentice on the capitana of one fleet was questioned about his participation in the beating of a companion: "Asked where he slept that night . . . he said on top of the grating in the middle of the ship, with Juan Vivas, sailor, until almost midnight, when they wanted to lower the mainsail, so he moved to the top of the poop deck." AGI, Contratación, sailing toward Bermuda, August 28, 1572.

22. The reference comes from a lawsuit among various gentlemen belonging to the complement of a capitana, one of whom was found "reclining in a hammock" when an argument began, followed by a duel. AGI, Contratación 58, Ocoa, October 13, 1571.

23. AGI, Contratación 72. This bundle of documents contains various passage contracts signed by the master of the ship *San Francisco*, which went to New Spain in the fleet of General Don Lope Díaz de Armendáriz in 1606.

24. AGI, Indiferente General 2673, memorandum of Juan de Melgarejo, December 13, 1568.

25. AGI, Contratación 59, declaration of Arias Maldonado, Sanlúcar de Barrameda, April 5, 1582.

26. AGI, Indiferente General 2673, memorandum of Captain Iñigo de Lecoya, undated, but from the last quarter of the sixteenth century.

27. "Ces cièges percés places tout à l'avant, ou l'on passe chacun son tour, sans aucun privilège." Jean Merrien, *La Vie quotidienne des marins au Moyen Age des Vikings aux galères* (Paris, 1969), p. 150.

28. Salazar, *Mar descrita por los mareados*, p. 283.

29. Ibid., p. 283.

30. More than one conflict was occasioned on the ships when soldiers and passengers hung their clothes on rigging that the sailors had to maneuver. AGI, Contratación 58, complaint on the armada of Sancho de Arciniega, sailing "in the Golfo Largo," May 14, 1566.

31. Guevara, "Muchos trabajos," p. 221.

32. AGI, Indiferente General 2673, "Traslado de un capítulo de la instrucción

... que Su Majestad mandó dar ... sobre el buen gobierno de la Armada de que es capitán Pedro Menéndez de Avilés," Madrid, May 8, 1568. The data coincide substantially with those of other scholars who have treated these questions, as, for example, Earl J. Hamilton, "Wages and Subsistence on Spanish Treasure Ships, 1503–1660," *Journal of Political Economy* 37 (Feb.–Dec. 1929): 430–50; Martínez, *Pasajeros a Indias*, p. 63; Phillips, *Six Galleons*, pp. 167–72, 241–42; Fernando López-Ríos Fernández, "La alimentación en las navegaciones colombinas," *Revista General al de Marina* (Madrid) (Aug–Sept. 1990): 261–67.

(264) 33. The quantities corresponding to the consumption of oil and vinegar did not figure in the instruction given to Pedro Menéndez de Avilés, and I have taken them from Alonso de Chaves's sixteenth-century treatise, *Espejo de navegantes* (Madrid, 1983), pp. 225–26.

34. "One notes that the river pilot, if he drinks wine, should drink little that day, and very watered down, because, as some of them always travel by water, they like wine more than is useful for the quickness and memory needed to execute their offices." Escalante de Mendoza, *Itinerario*, pp. 27–28.

35. The relation of provisions on the armada of Pedrarías Dávila contained sardines, *pargo* (red snapper), and "fish from Ireland." AGI, Contratación 3253.

36. Escalante de Mendoza, *Itinerario*, p. 42.

37. This is also the opinion of Merrien, *Vie quotidienne*, p. 117.

38. According to Friar Antonio de Guevara, they ate "on the ground like Moors or on their knees like women." "Muchos trabajos," p. 220.

39. For a crew of forty-seven men, experts advised carrying only two dozen soup plates. Chaves, *Espejo de navegantes*, p. 226.

40. Salazar, *Mar descrita por los mareados*, pp. 287–88.

41. On the hours and composition of each of the meals, see Escalante de Mendoza, *Itinerario*, pp. 61, 212; and Diego García de Palacio, *Instrucción náutica para navegar* (Mexico, 1587; Madrid, 1944), fol. 116.

42. Hamilton, "Wages and Subsistence," pp. 434–39; López-Ríos Fernández, "Alimentación," p. 265.

43. Enrique Rojas Hidalgo, *Regímenes dietéticos: Introducción a la dietética hospitalaria* (Madrid, 1968), p. 35; López-Ríos Fernández, "Alimentación," p. 265. See Phillips, *Six Galleons*, pp. 163–77, for an extended discussion of shipboard diets and their nutritional content.

44. Christopher Lloyd, *The British Seamen, 1200–1860: A Social Survey* (London, 1968), p. 46.

45. Rojas Hidalgo, *Regímenes dietéticos*, p. 36.

46. AGI, Contratación 58, case against Juan Caballero, soldier on the ship *San Juan*, at sea, sailing near Florida, June 3, 1566.

47. Pablo Emilio Pérez-Mallaína Bueno and Bibiano Torres Ramírez, *La Armada del Mar del Sur* (Seville, 1987), p. 58. The existence of these procedures in the British navy is noted by Rediker, *Between the Devil and the Deep Blue Sea*, p. 143.

48. Rediker, *Between the Devil and the Deep Blue Sea*, p. 126.

49. AGI, Contratación 58, on Escalante's ship, at sea, June 12, 1566.

50. Escalante de Mendoza, *Itinerario*, p. 160; Torre, "Diario del viaje," p. 256.

51. Rediker, *Between the Devil and the Deep Blue Sea*, p. 128.

52. See Carmen Bernis, *Indumentaria española en tiempos de Carlos V* (Madrid, 1962). From the same author, "La moda en la España de Felipe II a través del retrato de Corte," in *Alonso Sánchez Coello y el retrato en la Corte de Felipe II* (Madrid, 1990), pp. 65–111.

53. Ibid. The name *medias* (stockings; literally, "halves") is used today to describe hose, because, in the sixteenth century, hose were made in two pieces, with the ones that covered only the lower extremities called *medias calzas*, or half-stockings.

54. The zaragüelles, or long, loose pants, were another ancient article of clothing that was retained by the most humble social classes, especially fishermen and men of the sea. It descended directly from the loose leg covering *(tubrucos)* worn by the Germans who entered the ancient Roman Empire. Because zaragüelles had a status inferior to stockings, they appear in historical texts as part of the outfits of shepherds, farmers, sailors, and so on. Bernis, *Indumentaria española*, pp. 70–80.

(265)

55. Miguel de Cervantes Saavedra, "El celoso extremeño," in *Novelas ejemplares* (Madrid, 1986), 2:117.

56. Escalante de Mendoza, *Itinerario*, p. 53.

57. "From another cape came another small dugout with one man. . . . And I, who was on the poop deck of the ship and saw all this, sent for him and gave him a red bonnet and some small green glass beads." *Cristóbal Colón: Textos y documentos completos, relaciones de viajes, cartas y memoriales*, ed. Consuelo Varela (Madrid, 1984), p. 34. Translated in Oliver Dunn and James E. Kelley Jr., eds., *The "Diario" of Christopher Columbus's First Voyage to America, 1492–1493*, Abstracted by Fray Bartolomé de las Casas (Norman, Okla., 1989), p. 81.

58. Escalante de Mendoza, *Itinerario*, p. 24.

59. AGI, Justicia 884, Seville, August 9, 1567.

60. Paulino Iradiel Murugarren, *Evolución de la industria textil castellana en los siglos XIII–XVI: Factores de desarrollo, organización y costes de la producción manufacturera en Cuenca* (Salamanca, 1974), pp. 179–86.

61. The use of dishware as instruments of attack and defense can be seen in a document in AGI, Contratación 58, sailing toward New Spain on the armada of Don Cristóbal de Eraso, October 22, 1571. See also AGI, Contratación 59, document written on the fleet of Álvaro de Flores Valdés, in San Juan de Ulúa, November 23, 1571.

62. AGI, Contratación 58, inspection of the sea chest of the sailor Antonio González, ordered by General Don Cristóbal de Eraso, San Juan de Ulúa, December 31, 1571.

63. *Das Trachtenbuch des Christoph Weiditz von seinem Reisen nach Spanien (1529) und den Niederlanden (1531–1532)* (Berlin-Leipzig, 1927).

64. AGI, Contratación 200, testament and inventory of the goods of Pedro de Mata, Cartagena de Indias, April 17, 1562.

65. Bernis, *Indumentaria española*, p. 16.

66. Juan de Mal Lara, *Recibimiento que hizo la muy noble y muy leal ciudad de Sevilla a la Católica Real Majestad de Don Felipe, nuestro señor* (Seville, 1570).

67. See the inventories conserved in AGI, Patronato, of goods of various personages pertaining to the armada sent to the Moluccas. Miguel de Cervantes also pointed out the "gallantry" of these soldiers dressed like "parrots." See "El licenciado Vidriera," 2:44–47.

68. AGI, Indiferente General 739, advice to the king from the Council of the Indies, Madrid, October 6, 1580. In the documents, the officials ordered that some of the jewels taken from the accused be returned to him, as they were considered to be for his personal use. See also, AGI, Justicia 959, objects confiscated from General Francisco Maldonado, Seville, 1579.

69. María Helena Mendes Pinto, *Biombos nambam* (Lisbon, 1988).

70. AGI, Patronato 39, ramo 10, auction of the goods of Toribio Alonso de Salazar, accountant on the caravel *Santa María del Parral*, in Loaisa's expedition, written at sea on September 20, 1526. See also AGI, Patronato 38, ramo 13, inventory and auction of the goods of the accountant Iñigo Cortés Perea, sailing, August 3, 1526.

71. AGI, Contratación 200, testament and inventory of goods, Cartagena de Indias, April 17, 1562.

72. AGI, Patronato 38, ramo 1, testament of Juan Sebastián Elcano, on the ship *Victoria*, in the Pacific Ocean one degree from the equinoctial line, July 26, 1526.

73. AGI, Indiferente General 739, advice to the king from the Council of the Indies, Madrid, October 6, 1580. The document lists the personal effects taken from, and then returned to, Don Francisco de Eraso.

74. Guevara, "Muchos trabajos," p. 233.

75. Torre, "Diario del viaje," p. 255.

76. AGI, Indiferente General 2673.

77. Escalante de Mendoza, *Itinerario*, p. 116.

78. AGI, Justicia 958, testimony of Juan Felipe, captain and master of the ship *Trinidad*, Seville, October 5, 1574.

79. AGI, Justicia 957, inspection and investigation of the captain, admiral, and other officers on the fleet that came from New Spain in the year 1573.

80. Ibid., declaration of the royal constable Juan Vázquez de Olivera.

81. AGI, Contratación 58, sailing toward Florida, May 17, 1566.

82. Ibid., on the capitana of the armada of Don Cristóbal de Eraso, San Juan de Ulúa, March 3, 1572.

83. AGI, Justicia 823, sentence of the Council of the Indies, Valladolid, November 29, 1543.

84. The game of "veintiuna" (twenty-one) was a variant of "treinta por fuerza" but whose optimal point total was twenty-one rather than thirty. Miguel de Cervantes Saavedra, "Rinconete y Cortadillo," in *Novelas ejemplares* (Madrid, 1986), 1:196.

85. Ibid., p. 197. See also Guevara, "Muchos trabajos," p. 232.

86. Merrien, *Vie quotidienne*, p. 118.

87. A full description of the games played on the galleys is provided by Guevara, "Muchos trabajos," p. 232.

88. Ibid.

89. AGI, Contratación 58, declaration of Salvador Morales, sailing in sight of Lanzarote island in the Canaries, April 23, 1566.

90. These data are known, thanks to the work of Francisco Fernández del Castillo. He compiled the information from documents in the Archivo General de la Nación de México about inspections by the Inquisition on ships arriving in San Juan de Ulúa between 1572 and 1600. See Fernández del Castillo, comp., *Libros y libreros en el siglo XVI* (Mexico, 1982).

91. Ibid., p. 422.

92. Ibid., p. 389.

93. A study of contemporary maritime ethnography shows that, even in recent times, books are not common instruments of entertainment for the men of the sea, who possess a fundamentally oral culture. In the nineteenth century, many Scandinavian mariners used the pages of books to roll their cigarettes, and even for much less dignified purposes. See Knut Weibust, *Deep Sea Sailors: A Study in Maritime Ethnology* (Stockholm, 1969), p. 115.

94. Fernández del Castillo, *Libros y libreros*, pp. 351–511.

95. Ibid., p. 434.

96. Ibid., p. 442.

97. The data come from Fernández del Castillo, *Libros y libreros*, pp. 351–511. It is appropriate, however, to make some corrections to this list. In the first place, I have not considered the books of hours as a single work, since there is documentary proof that there were manuals of prayer written by diverse authors in diverse languages: Latin, Greek, and *romance* (Castilian Spanish). Otherwise, these books would have been in first place, as they were cited for 105 ships. There was also a devotional book called *Spiritual Prayer*, and it is possible that there was more than one work with the same title. Not being certain of this latter point, however, I kept it as a single work. Finally, although the most-read author was Friar Luis de Granada, in many cases a list indicated only that the ship carried "a work by Friar Luis de Granada," without specifying anything more. For that reason I have judged his book the most frequently carried on board, while indicating that it was not the only one pertaining to this author that appeared to be included on the list.

98. Carlos Alberto González Sánchez, "El libro en la Carrera de Indias: Registro de ida de los navíos," *Archivo Hispalense* (Seville), no. 220 (1989): 93–103. Two classic works on this particular theme are Irving A. Leonard, *Books of the Brave* (Cambridge, Mass., 1949), and Marcel Bataillon, *Erasmo y España* (Mexico, 1966).

99. Ludovico Ariosto, *Orlando furioso* (Mexico, 1955), canto 1, pp. 1–2.

100. Ibid., canto 9, pp. 130–31.

101. Ibid., canto 10, pp. 152–53.

102. Cervantes, "Rinconete y Cortadillo," 1:209.

103. AGI, Indiferente General 2005, sentence against the ship's master, Felipe Boquín, Seville, July 4, 1555.

104. AGI, Indiferente General 2673, memorandum from Alonso de Zapata to Dr. Hernán Pérez, inspector *(visitador)* of the Court of Appeal of Seville, October 10, 1551.

105. AGI, Indiferente General 2495.

106. Chaves, *Espejo de navegantes*, pp. 229–30.

107. AGI, Justicia 957, inspection and investigation of the officers of the armada and fleet of Tierra Firme, Seville, October 27, 1573.

108. AGI, Justicia 958, sentence issued in Seville, October 17, 1577.

109. AGI, Contratación 138-A, accusation made against the master of the ship *Nuestra Señora de Begoña*, Seville, September 20, 1580.

110. Guevara, "Muchos trabajos," p. 223.

111. Cervantes, "El celoso extremeño," 2:99.

112. AGI, Indiferente General 2673, memorandum of Captain Iñigo de Lecoya, undated, but from the last quarter of the sixteenth century.

113. AGI, Contratación 58, legal case against Francisco Espínola, at sea, sailing toward Havana, June 5, 1572.

114. Ibid., legal case against Cristóbal de Maldonado, declaration of Juan Treviño, October 4, 1571.

115. Ibid., declaration of Cristóbal de Maldonado. [Translator's note: The declarant used the verb *cabalgar*, which has a range of meanings and connotations, from engaging in a mounted cavalcade to fornicating.]

116. Ibid., declaration of Cristóbal Gallego. [Translator's note: The phrase used was *hacer arrimadillas*, which may refer to a game in which the object was to toss a token as close as possible to a wall, without actually touching it.]

117. B. R. Burg, *Sodomy and the Perception of Evil: English Sea Rovers in the Seventeenth-Century Caribbean* (New York, 1983), p. 109.

118. AGI, Indiferente General 1105, "Sumario de las personas de todas suertes y edades que fueron por pasajeros en la flota de este año de 1594."

119. Michel Mollat, *La Vie quotidienne des gens de mer en Atlantique, IX–XVIe siècle* (Paris, 1983), p. 223.

120. AGI, Contratación 58, legal case against the boatswain and other officers and sailors on the nao almiranta, San Juan de Ulúa, January 18, 1572.

121. "The presence of sodomites among those who make their livings from the sea is not a startling revelation. Sexual encounters involving sailors are a part of maritime lore." Burg, *Sodomy*, p. xvii.

122. "I have never encountered anything quite like it. Time and again it has happened that big, powerful men have suddenly blurted: 'You know, there is no one like a mother!' and then have dissolved in tears." Weibust, *Deep Sea Sailors*, p. 425.

123. Burg, *Sodomy*, pp. 107–9.

124. Francisco Morales Padrón, *Historia de Sevilla: La ciudad del Quinientos* (Seville, 1983), p. 121. The author cites the "Apéndice de Ajusticiados" of Father Pedro de León.

125. Burg, *Sodomy*, p. xvii.

126. AGI, Contratación 468, muster list and payments to the sailors and soldiers of the ships that composed the armada of Lieutenant General Álvaro de Flores Valdés; crew of the galleon *San Pedro*, April 23, 1575.

127. AGI, Patronato 34, ramo 11, report of the persons who have died on the armada that the Emperor our lord sent to discover the source of spices, of which the captain general was Ferdinand Magellan. See also AGI, Contaduría 425, report of the salary owing to those who went to the Moluccas.

128. AGI, Contaduría 468, muster list and payments to the sailors and soldiers of the ships that composed the armada of Lieutenant General Álvaro de Flores Valdés, 1575.

129. AGI, Contratación 5730, sentence handed down by General Antonio Navarro del Prado against Gaspar Caravallo, San Juan de Ulúa, March 16, 1591.

130. Ibid. All the references to this case are found in the same set of documents in the bundle cited in n. 129.

131. AGI, Justicia 886.

132. AGI, Contratación 72, Havana, October 24, 1606.

133. See the whole of the document in AGI, Patronato 254, no. 3, general 2, ramo 2.

134. García de Palacio, *Instrucción náutica*, fol. 2v.

135. AGI, Patronato 40, no. 1, ramo 1. See the testament of Francisco del Campo, who traveled in Loaisa's armada, made in La Coruña, July 9, 1525.

136. Escalante de Mendoza, *Itinerario*, p. 248.

137. Ibid., p. 142.

138. AGI, Justicia 853. The sentence of the Council of the Indies (Toledo, September 25, 1560) was not too harsh, since the judges took into account the reasons expressed by the caravel's captain regarding the risk that his small ship would have taken in picking up all the crew of the larger ship.

139. Escalante de Mendoza, *Itinerario*, pp. 251, 259, 262.

140. AGI, Contratación 59, dossier about the loss of the almiranta of New Spain, September 19, 1582.

141. AGI, Justicia 903.

142. AGI, Indiferente General 2005, report of those drowned on two shipwrecks, undated, but ca. 1555. See also Escalante de Mendoza, *Itinerario*, p. 246.

143. Escalante de Mendoza, *Itinerario*, p. 246.

144. AGI, Patronato 39, ramo 8.

145. AGI, Contratación 138-A. The caulker Pedro Camargo, a native of Triana embarked on the ship *San Salvador*, was killed by a bolt of lightning off the coast of Cuba in 1580.

146. Ibid. "Regarding the sailor Pedro Agustín de Santana, a native of Triana . . . the master says that, sailing on this ship . . . a spar fell from the main topsail and hit him on the head, and while being carried to Seville for treatment, he died near Coria."

147. Chaves, *Espejo de navegantes*, pp. 233–34.

(269)

148. AGI, Indiferente General 2673, memorandum of Juan de Melgarejo about the "Reform of the Carrera de Indias," December 13, 1568.

149. Ibid., memorandum of Captain Iñigo de Lecoya, undated, around the last quarter of the sixteenth century.

150. Juan López de Velasco, *Geografía e descripción universal de las Indias* (1574; Madrid, 1971), p. 174.

151. Antonio Alcedo, *Diccionario geográfico histórico de las Indias Occidentales o América* (1786–89; Madrid, 1967), 3:36.

152. Ibid., p. 230.

153. AGI, Contratación 4792, legal case against Gaspar Rodríguez, a sailor who was serving as ship's surgeon, and the ship's master, 1581.

154. Escalante de Mendoza, *Itinerario*, p. 256.

155. Chaves, *Espejo de navegantes*, p. 240.

156. Ibid., and García de Palacio, *Instrucción náutica*, fol. 127v.

157. AGI, Patronato 260, no. 2, ramo 45.

158. AGI, Indiferente General 2673, memorandum of Juan de Melgarejo about the "Reform of the Carrera de Indias," December 13, 1568.

159. Ibid.

160. AGI, Contaduría 468, 471, 503, and 526, Contratación 2936 and 4792.

161. AGI, Justicia 961, "Relación de las personas . . . que salieron de la Habana en los galeones y fragatas de la armada de Su Majestad . . . y de los que de ellos llegaron a España por noviembre de 79." See also AGI, Indiferente General 1095, report on the cost of the armada of General Cristóbal de Eraso.

162. Fernand Braudel, *El Mediterráneo y el mundo mediterráneo en la época de Felipe II*, 2 vols. (Madrid, 1976), 1:54748. [Translator's note: The mortality rate in Europe was forty per thousand per year in the total population, which was not directly comparable to the mortality in a series of fleets.]

163. Toribio Alonso de Salazar, who commanded the expedition of Commander Loaisa for a month and a half, "was shrouded and thrown into the sea in a chest." AGI, Patronato 39, ramo 10.

164. AGI, Indiferente General 2005, "Ordenanzas y reglas de los hombres de mar."

165. AGI, Indiferente General 2495, royal order issued on petition of the constable Pedro Martínez de Oñate, which respected his right "to conduct the auction of the goods of those who died on the said armadas and to exact fees for his work," Madrid, March 19, 1576.

166. "Juan de Morán, a soldier and a native of Oviedo. He died in Veragua. They threw him into the sea. The ensign Juan de Argüelles, his countryman, took what he had, which was a sword and his clothing, to pay for arranging a good turn for his soul." AGI, Contaduría 485, accounts of the goods of the dead who were dependents of the armada from 1574 to 1580.

167. AGI, Contratación 200, act of the Court of Appeals of Mexico, ordering that the persons who had possession of the goods of sailors who died without a testament had to declare them.

168. Ibid., lawsuit against the heirs of Nicolás de Rodas and Cosme Buitrón, owner of the galleon *Los Tres Reyes*, Seville, February 25, 1562.

Chapter 5: Discipline and Conflict

1. Although the date of the collection called the Rôles d'Oléron is uncertain, the rules are generally thought to have been produced during the thirteenth century, based on very old traditions that linked them with the laws current under the Roman Empire. In this respect, see Jean Marie Pardessus, *Us et coutumes de la mer, ou collection des usages maritimes des peuples de l'Antiquité et du Moyen Age* (Paris, 1847).

A manuscript from the fourteenth century containing the Rôles d'Oléron is conserved in the Biblioteca Nacional in Madrid, inside a volume called "Privilegios y Ordenanzas de Sevilla," MS 716, fols. 91–93.

The legislation specific to the Mediterranean is found in the Catalan *Libro del Consulado del Mar: Edición y texto original catalán y traducción al castellano de Antonio Capmany* (Barcelona, 1965).

2. Biblioteca Nacional, Madrid (hereafter, BN), MS 716, fol. 91.

3. Marcus Rediker, *Between the Devil and the Deep Blue Sea: Merchant Seamen, Pirates, and the Anglo-American Maritime World, 1700–1750* (New York, 1987).

4. Jean Merrien, *La Vie quotidienne des marins au Moyen Age des Vikings aux galères* (Paris, 1969), p. 145.

5. Rediker, *Between the Devil and the Deep Blue Sea*, p. 212.

6. Ibid., p. 213.

7. BN, MS 716, fol. 92v.

8. Ibid., article 14 of the Rôles d'Oléron.

9. *Libro del Consulado del Mar*, chap. 164, p. 144.

10. Juan de Escalante de Mendoza himself seemed conscious of the relationship that existed between an increment in the profits of the shipowners and the end of concessions mentioned in medieval law codes:

Although it is true that in the business of bonuses for stockings *[calzas]* and bonuses on the weight charges *[quintalada]*, we take into account the specific orders, freedoms, liberties, and laws of the sea, which the sailors call the Law of Leilón (Oléron), these were made in olden times . . . when there were not, nor were there carried so many thousands of ducats or quantities of freight as today are carried and brought to the Indies.

Juan de Escalante de Mendoza, *Itinerario de navegación de los mares y tierras occidentales* (1575; reprint, Madrid, 1985), p. 190.

11. Rediker, *Between the Devil and the Deep Blue Sea*, pp. 112–209.

12. Christopher Lloyd, *The British Seamen, 1200–1860: A Social Survey* (London, 1968), p. 22.

13. Merrien, *Vie quotidienne*, p. 143.

14. AGI, Patronato 37, ramo 23. The testimony of Domingo de Ubillos stated: "Given that the said Gonzalo de Salmerón, treasurer of the said ship *[San Gabriel]*

drowned, after the drowning, the said captain and company chose the said Francisco de Ávila as treasurer." La Coruña, February 19, 1528.

15. AGI, Patronato 37, ramo 36, "Relación que Andrés de Urdaneta hace a V.S.M. de la Armada que V.M. mando para la Especiería," Valladolid, February 26, 1537.

16. AGI, Patronato 41, ramo 4, testimony of the accountant Antón Montoya, undated, but ca. 1534: "And this witness solemnly swore to God that what was understood from the said lord Captain General [Sebastian Cabot] was that he regarded us all as his sons, and that nothing else should be considered."

17. AGI, Patronato 38, ramo 7, document made in Pernambuco with the testimony of various survivors, October 26, 1528.

18. Rediker, *Between the Devil and the Deep Blue Sea*, pp. 120, 141, 210.

19. AGI, Patronato 37, ramo 36, "Relación que Andrés de Urdaneta hace a V.S.M.," Valladolid, February 26, 1537.

20. See, for example, the arguments of the licenciado Villalobos in response to the claims of Diego Solier, an infantry officer on Loaisa's expedition, in AGI, Patronato 38, ramo 4, October 1534.

21. AGI, Patronato 38. ramo 2, Dueñas, September 26, 1534.

22. AGI, Patronato 38, ramo 15.

23. AGI, Patronato 38, ramo 13, claims of the heirs of Iñigo Cortés Perea, accountant of the flagship on Loaisa's expedition, Valladolid, October 5, 1538.

24. The case of Juan de Perea is in AGI, Patronato 39, ramo 2, Toledo, November 11, 1538. Various petitions from the heirs are conserved in AGI, Patronato 40, no. 1, ramo 5.

25. AGI, Patronato 35, ramo 2, petition of Gonzalo Gómez de Espinosa to the king, Madrid, September 21, 1529.

26. AGI, Indiferente General 2495. This document bundle includes numerous claims from sailors and soldiers on the armadas.

27. AGI, Contratación 200, lawsuit between the heirs of master Nicolás de Rodas and Cosme Buitrón, owner of the ship *Los Tres Reyes*, Seville, February 25, 1562.

28. AGI, Contratación 724, claim of three mariners taken by force to serve on the flagship of the fleet and armada of Tierra Firme, under the command of general Diego Maldonado, Seville, October 15, 1583.

29. See, for example, the claim of the sailor Gaspar Rodríguez against his master Gerónimo Bello. In this lawsuit the question was resolved "in the said hospital of seafarers, where the payments are customarily made." AGI, Contratación 4792, Seville, undated, but ca. 1581.

30. AGI, Contratación 4792, efforts made by the sailors and soldiers for collecting their salaries. For the period between 1584 and 1596, I have found in this bundle a dozen owners and masters who were jailed and detained for not paying their sailors.

31. Ibid., lawsuit against Hernando Ramos, Seville, June 6, 1590.

32. Ibid. The dates of these lawsuits are September 22, 1584; September 9, 1588; and December 5, 1596.

33. Ibid., Seville, January 30, 1590.

34. Ibid., Seville, December 5, 1596.

35. Ibid., lawsuit between the sailor Pedro Gaya and Diego Rodríguez, owner of the ship *San Antonio*, Seville, March 18, 1586.

36. Ibid., lawsuit between Bartolomé Sánchez and the master Manuel Ortiz, Seville, January 13, 1590.

37. Ibid., lawsuit between the apprentice Gonzalo Pérez and the master Bartolomé Liñán, Seville, January 10, 1592.

38. Ralph Davis, *The Rise of the English Shipping Industry in the Seventeenth and Eighteenth Centuries* (London, 1962), p. 142.

39. Rediker, *Between the Devil and the Deep Blue Sea*, pp. 137–38.

40. Lloyd, *British Seamen*, p. 24.

41. Rediker, *Between the Devil and the Deep Blue Sea*. The title of chapter 5 is "The Seaman as the 'Spirit of Rebellion.'"

42. Knut Weibust, *Deep Sea Sailors: A Study in Maritime Ethnology* (Stockholm, 1969), p. 453.

43. Rediker, *Between the Devil and the Deep Blue Sea*, p. 110.

44. One recalls, for example, the mutiny of armed sailors who took over Liverpool for three days in 1775. Davis, *Rise of the English Shipping Industry*, p. 155.

45. AGI, Contratación 5728, petition of Juan Bautista in the name of the University of Seafarers, Seville, October 8, 1567. One also finds this petition in AGI, Justicia 884.

46. AGI, Patronato 41, ramo 4. The testimony of the overseer Octaviano Briñe, given against Captain Francisco de Rojas, who commanded a ship on the expedition of Sebastian Cabot to the Moluccas, stated: "One day this witness saw him beat an apprentice because he did not want to serve someone . . . who was the boss [*abad*; literally, "abbot"] of the ship *Trinidad*; the apprentice told him that he did not want to serve him in his capacity as an apprentice of the ship." Regarding the refusal of men of the sea to carry out personal services, see also Escalante de Mendoza, *Itinerario*, pp. 48–49.

47. Escalante de Mendoza, *Itinerario*, p. 46.

48. *Das Trachtenbuch des Christoph Weiditz von seinim Reisen nach Spanien (1529) und den Niederlanden (1531–1533)* (Berlin-Leipzig, 1927), plate 2. The Castilian translation of the text to this plate says: "This is the patron of the ship, who directs and governs the vessel; he is found calmly looking at the winds to see how the vessel sails; when he blows his whistle, the sailor knows what to do; when they make mistakes he takes the cord and hits them."

49. AGI, Contratación 58, legal case against Alonso Hernández. On the flagship of the New Spain fleet, sailing toward Bermuda, August 28, 1572.

50. Ibid., legal case against Agustín Genovés. At sea, September 11, 1571.

51. AGI, Contratación 59, legal case against the pilot Francisco Quintero, San Juan de Ulúa, December 31, 1582.

52. Ibid., legal case against the sailor Juan Gutiérrez, San Juan de Ulúa, September 9, 1581; legal case against the sailor Asensio Hernández, Havana, April 23, 1582.

53. AGI, Justicia 823, sentence of the Council of the Indies, Valladolid, March 7, 1537.

54. AGI, Indiferente General 2495, instructions to Sebastian Cabot, Toledo, September 20, 1525.

55. AGI, Contratación 58, legal case against the pilot Gonzalo Poldero, sailing between Dominica and Puerto Rico, June 5, 1566.

56. AGI, Indiferente General 2673, petition of Pero Díaz Machín to the House of Trade, Seville, November 17, 1551.

57. Ibid., sentence handed down by the governor's assistant in Nombre de Dios, July 2, 1551.

58. Ibid., testimony of the sailor Antonio de Arévalo.

59. AGI, Contratación 59, testimony of various sailors against the master Pedro Alonso Conquero, Veracruz, September 19, 1582.

60. AGI, Contratación 58, legal case against the shipowner and master Francisco de Santiago, testimony of the sailor Hernán Ramírez, Las Palmas, Gran Canaria, September 3, 1571.

61. Ibid., accusation of the steward Leonardo Pérez against the master Alonso Díaz, San Agustín, Florida, April 28, 1566.

62. Ibid., accusation of the steward Pero Alonso against the caulker Juan de Saldaña, San Juan de Ulúa, March 24, 1572.

63. AGI, Contratación 59, accusation against Bartolomé Rodríguez, Havana, June 25, 1583.

64. AGI, Indiferente General 2495, royal order issued in Toledo, October 25, 1525, ordering that, if Sebastian Cabot died, these three persons were destined to take his place.

65. AGI, Patronato 34, ramo 14, San Julián, April 19, 1520. The testimony of the steward Juan Ortiz is the most significant: "I saw how the provisions were being used up without being weighed or measured, and everything was given openly to whoever wanted to take it; and the said Gaspar de Quesada threatened this witness, who had charge of the storeroom of the said ship, telling him not to apply the official measures but to hand over everything he was asked for."

66. Martín Fernández Navarrete, *Colección de los viajes y descubrimientos que hicieron por mar los españoles desde finales del siglo XV* (Madrid, 1964), 2:490.

67. AGI, Patronato 41, ramo 4, testimony of Nicolao de Nápoles, boatswain of the flagship, undated, but ca. 1530. This document records a conversation between the witness and Manuel de Rodas, one of the men abandoned by Cabot: "And the said Manuel de Rodas told him that the sailors would die because their half *cuartillo* of wine had been taken away, and this witness said again that all the sailors were in good shape and content . . . and the said Manuel de Rodas told the witness who is testifying: 'You! May you eat and be treated like the slaves *(nocheles)* in the Levant!'"

68. AGI, Patronato 38, ramo 7, report of Don Rodrigo de Acuña, Valladolid, September 5, 1537.

69. AGI, Patronato 37, ramo 36, "Relación que Andrés de Urdaneta hace a V.S.M.," Valladolid, February 26, 1537.

70. AGI, Patronato 46, ramo 8, "Relación de una armada que se aprestó en la Nueva España para ir a dicho Maluco el año de 1565."

71. Ibid.

72. Ibid.

73. AGI, Justicia 886, undated, but ca. October 1565.

74. AGI, Contratación 58, attempted mutiny on the ship *San Felipe*, in sight of Lanzarote, September 23, 1566.

75. AGI, Justicia 958. The judicial inquiry carried out by the officials of the Tierra Firme fleet of 1576 revealed that the crew of Cristóbal Galindo's ship abandoned the vessel and Galindo could do nothing to stop them.

(275)

76. Escalante de Mendoza, *Itinerario*, p. 251.

77. Remember that in the wreck of the *Titanic* in 1912, the women and children saved were mostly those from first class.

78. Escalante de Mendoza, *Itinerario*, p. 280.

79. Rediker, *Between the Devil and the Deep Blue Sea*, p. 104.

80. AGI, Contaduría 468, 471, 503, and 526; AGI, Contratación 2936 and 4792.

81. AGI, Indiferente General 2006, the officers of the House of Trade to the king, Seville, January 22, 1587.

82. AGI, Indiferente General 1106, report about the men absent from the armada under the command of General Antonio de Urquiola, Lisbon, 1595.

83. AGI, Justicia 958, inspection and judicial inquiry of the New Spain fleet of 1574.

84. AGI, Patronato 255, no. 3, general 3, ramo 5, General Álvaro Flores Quiñones to the king, Cartagena, November 4, 1586.

85. AGI, Contaduría 526, Cartagena de Indias, October 28, 1578.

86. AGI, Indiferente General 2673, General Nicolás Cardona to the viceroy Don Francisco de Toledo, Nombre de Dios, July 10, 1569.

87. Friar Antonio de Guevara, "De los muchos trabajos que se pasan en las galeras, 1539," in *Pasajeros a Indias,* ed. José Luis Martínez (Mexico, 1984), app. 1, p. 223.

88. Ibid., p. 229.

89. Rediker, *Between the Devil and the Deep Blue Sea*, p. 165.

90. Miguel de Cervantes Saavedra, "La ilustre fregona," in *Novelas ejemplares* (Madrid, 1986), 2:140–41.

91. Ibid.

92. Ibid.; and Miguel de Cervantes Saavedra, "El celoso extremeño," in *Novelas ejemplares* (Madrid, 1986), 2:99.

93. Alonso Chaves, *Espejo de navegantes* (Madrid, 1983), p. 231.

94. Guevara, "Muchos trabajos," p. 224.

95. AGI, Contratación 58, investigation carried out on board the flagship of the New Spain fleet, sailing toward Havana, June 5, 1572. The testimony of the passenger Juan Núñez Suárez stated: "This witness had . . . a box nailed shut with twelve nails, which they took away from this witness and removed

eleven containers of preserves and left only two, which accounted for all the preserves."

96. AGI, Indiferente General 2673, memorandum of Alonso de Zapata, Seville, October 10, 1551.

97. AGI, Contratación 58; concerning a dispute between two sailors of the ship *San Juan* who were at daggers drawn in a disagreement about the placement of their respective boxes of clothing; San Juan de Ulúa, December 31, 1571.

98. Ibid., knife fight on the flagship of the New Spain fleet, when a sailor watching a game of cards asked for a tip *(barato)* from the winner of the game.

99. Ibid., at sea, sailing toward New Spain, October 17, 1571.

100. Ibid., on board the hulk *El Negro*, sailing in sight of the Canaries, April 26, 1566.

101. AGI, Contratación 59, on the ship of master Pedro Dasco, sailing after passing through the Bahama Channel, August 8, 1583.

102. AGI, Contratación 5728, incident on the armada of General Sancho de Arciniega, at sea, April 23, 1566.

103. AGI, Contratación 58, on the flagship of General Sancho de Arciniega, sailing in the Golfo Largo, May 14, 1566.

104. Ibid., on the flagship of General Cristóbal de Eraso, sailing off Las Palmas, Gran Canaria, August 30, 1571.

105. Ibid., sailing toward the Bermudas, August 28, 1572.

106. Ibid., on the armada of General Sancho de Arciniega, at sea, in sight of Lanzarote, April 23, 1566.

107. AGI, Contratación 2936, on the flagship of General Don Diego Maldonado, sailing toward Havana, June 1583.

108. AGI, Contratación 59, on the ship *San Nicolás*, Havana, June 17, 1582.

109. AGI, Contratación 2936, San Juan de Ulúa, January 22, 1583.

110. AGI, Justicia 957, inspection of the fleet of General Juan de Alcega, Seville, November 5, 1573.

111. AGI, Contratación 59, on board the ship *San Nicolás*, Havana, June 17, 1582.

112. AGI, Contratación 58, on the flagship of General Cristóbal de Eraso, sailing toward Havana, May 29, 1572.

Chapter 6: The Mental Horizons of the Men of the Sea

1. For all these themes, see chapter 4 of Marcus Rediker, *Between the Devil and the Deep Blue Sea: Merchant Seamen, Pirates, and the Anglo-American Maritime World, 1700–1750* (New York, 1987).

See also the works of Jacques Bernard, *Navires et gens de mer à Bordeaux (vers 1400–vers 1500)* (Paris, 1968); Knut Weibust, *Deep Sea Sailors: A Study in Maritime Ethnology* (Stockholm, 1969); Michel Mollat, *La Vie quotidienne des gens de mer en Atlantique, IX–XVIe siècle* (Paris, 1983); and Alain Carbantous, *Le Ciel dans la mer: Christianisme et civilisation maritime, XVI–XIX siècles* (Paris, 1990).

2. AGI, Patronato 40, no. 1, ramo 1, testament dated in La Coruña, shortly before the departure of the expedition, on July 9, 1525.

3. Ibid.

4. Ibid.

5. Rediker, *Between the Devil and the Deep Blue Sea*, pp. 162–68.

6. Ibid., p. 248. "Hoy por ti, mañana por mí."

7. AGI, Contratación 58. In a legal case for robbery that happened on the armada of General Cristóbal de Eraso in 1572, one of the witnesses declared: "This witness knows that the said Diego de Palermo took three hens from the cookstove, where they were roasting, . . . and he took them to his camarada and ate them with his camarada."

8. AGI, Patronato 37, ramo 20, testament of Bartolomé Domínguez, made on the ship *Victoria* (Loaisa's expedition), July 13, 1526. Bartolomé Domínguez, who was from La Coruña, left a part of his goods to free Galicians held captive in North Africa, and if there were none, he willed that the funds be used to rescue Asturians, who at least were neighbors.

9. Mollat, *Vie quotidienne*, p. 222.

10. Rediker, *Between the Devil and the Deep Blue Sea*, p. 147.

11. Real Academia de la Historia, Colección de don Juan Bautista Muñoz, A-71, no. 304, "Coloquio sobre las dos graduaciones diferentes que las cartas de Indias tienen," attributed to Hernando Colón, undated.

12. The data were obtained from dozens of document bundles pertaining, above all, to the Contratación section in the Archive of the Indies, which holds legal cases from the House of Trade. The breakdown by rank of the individuals studied follows:

Officers of the highest ranks in the Armadas	47
Owners and masters of ships	161
Pilots	82
Marine officers	143
Gunners	20
Sailors, apprentices, and pages	345
Total	798

13. Ralph Davis, *The Rise of the English Shipping Industry in the Seventeenth and Eighteenth Centuries* (London, 1962), pp. 122–23. In the Spanish case, as late as 1574 Gonzalo Gayón, pilot major of the New Spain fleet, signed documents by sketching a mark in the form of a star.

14. Luis Navarro García, "La gente de mar en Sevilla en el siglo XVI," *Revista de Historia de América* (Mexico) 67–68 (1969): 1–64. From the same author, "Pilotos, maestres y señores de naos de la Carrera de Indias," *Archivo Hispalense* (Seville) 46–47, nos. 141–46 (1967): 241–95.

15. Real Academia de la Historia, "Coloquio sobre las dos graduaciones," fol. 3v.

16. AGI, Patronato 254, no. 1, general 2, ramo 3, Seville, January 30, 1585.

17. Friar Tomás de la Torre, "Diario del viaje de Salamanca a Ciudad Real (Chiapas), 1544–1545," in *Pasajeros a Indias,* ed. José Luis Martínez (Mexico, 1984), app. 2, pp. 264–66.

18. Juan de Escalante de Mendoza, *Itinerario de navegación de los mares y tierras occidentales* (1575; reprint, Madrid, 1985), p. 116.

19. AGI, Patronato 255, no. 2, general 1, ramo 12, dossier on the loss of four ships in the armada of New Spain, commanded by Captain General Don Cristóbal de Eraso, undated, possibly October 1578. Cristóbal de Eraso also wrote to the king to explain the disaster: "I found myself very confused on this voyage [despite the fact that] the pilot whom I brought is the oldest and most experienced on this course; and although in matters pertaining to marking charts and measuring the angle of the sun he is very skilled, he and all the other pilots are not experienced on this coast, which is the most useful thing."

20. AGI, Justicia 1146, Seville, 1544–45. See also José Pulido Rubio, *El piloto mayor, pilotos mayores, catedráticos de cosmografía y cosmógrafos de la Casa de la Contratación de Sevilla* (Seville, 1950).

21. José María López Piñero, *El arte de navegar en la España del Renacimiento* (Barcelona, 1979).

22. Pablo Emilio Pérez-Mallaína Bueno, "Los libros de náutica españoles del siglo XVI y su influencia en el descubrimiento y conquista de los océanos," *Ciencia, vida y espacio en Iberoamérica* (Madrid) 3 (1990): 457–84.

23. AGI, Justicia 1146, pieza 3, August 1544.

24. Ibid., pieza 2, August 1544.

25. Ibid.

26. AGI, Indiferente General 2673, memorandum of the pilot Alonso de Zapata, Seville, September 16, 1551.

27. AGI, Indiferente General 2005, Seville, undated, toward the middle of the sixteenth century.

28. AGI, Justicia 1146.

29. Martínez, *Pasajeros a Indias,* p. 97.

30. AGI, Patronato 254, no. 3, ramo 6, relation of the sailors and soldiers on seventeen galleons, flyboats, and other ships of the armada of General Francisco de Coloma, Puerto Rico, 1599.

31. AGI, Patronato 44, ramo 1, instructions to Diego García, captain of a caravel and a dispatch boat sent toward the Indies in 1526.

32. Escalante de Mendoza, *Itinerario,* pp. 52–56.

33. AGI, Contaduría 425, "Relación del clavo que vino en la nao *Victoria.*"

34. AGI, Justicia 959.

35. Alonso Chaves, *Espejo de navegantes* (Madrid, 1983), p. 79.

36. Friar Antonio de Guevara, "De muchos trabajos que se pasan en las galeras, 1539," in Martínez, *Pasajeros a Indias,* app. 1, p. 226.

37. AGI, Patronato 258, no. 8, general 2, ramo 1, testament of Álvaro de Valdés, Chagre, September 22, 1578.

38. Torre, "Diario del viaje," pp. 266–67.

39. Guevara, "Muchos trabajos," p. 226.

40. Rediker, *Between the Devil and the Deep Blue Sea*, p. 169.

41. AGI, Justicia 903, declaration of a witness, Cádiz, September 8, 1570. "St. Elmo's fire" was the arcing of lightning in the rigging, which sometimes occurred in storms and which was considered good luck by mariners.

42. Most of this documentation is found in AGI, Patronato 34–46.

43. See, for example, the case of Martín García de Carquizano, who willed thirty-five ducats to two young women "inasmuch as I am in their debt." AGI, Patronato 39, ramo 3. A relative of the aforementioned, Martín Iñíguez Carquizano, who ended up leading the second expedition to the Moluccas, mentioned his "poor bastards" in his testament; AGI, Patronato 40, no. 1, ramo 4. To avoid being tiresome, it is enough to add that Juan Sebastián Elcano also had extramarital lovers and natural children; AGI, Patronato 38, ramo 1.

44. Besides the cases referred to in the previous note, see also the case of Toribio Alonso de Salazar; AGI, Patronato 39, ramo 10.

45. AGI, Patronato 38, ramo 1, on the ship *Victoria*, in the Pacific Ocean, one degree from the equinoctial line, July 26, 1526. See also other cases such as that of Juan de Menchaca, AGI, Patronato 38, ramo 15; Martín García de Carquizano, AGI, Patronato 39, ramo 3; Luis de Luzón, AGI, Patronato 39, ramo 7; Toribio Alonso de Salazar, AGI, Patronato 39, ramo 10.

46. "Orden que se ha de tener en la visita de los navíos," in Francisco Fernández del Castillo, comp., *Libros y libreros en el siglo XVI* (Mexico, 1982), pp. 424–25.

47. Ibid., inspection of the 1582 fleet.

48. Ibid., pp. 424–25.

49. All of the prayers that follow were collected from the ship *Nuestra Señora de Begonia*, captained by Juan Palomares de Vargas, a native of Cádiz, who arrived in San Juan de Ulúa in 1575. Ibid., pp. 369–70.

50. AGI, Justicia 914. In an argument between Gregorio Polanco, captain of a frigate in the armada, and Álvaro de Espinosa, sergeant on the ship serving as almiranta, the latter defended the honor and the prerogatives of his vessel; Seville, September 5, 1573.

51. Escalante de Mendoza, *Itinerario*, pp. 201–11.

52. Specifically, the Museo de las Cases Reales de Santo Domingo (Dominican Republic) houses various amulets of this type, which came from shipwrecks that occurred on the coasts of that island.

53. Escalante de Mendoza, *Itinerario*, p. 214.

54. Martínez, *Pasajeros a Indias*, p. 143.

55. Rediker, *Between the Devil and the Deep Blue Sea*, p. 169.

(279)

Index

abacus, 84
abrojos (iron projectiles), 184
accidents at sea, 74, 181, 185, 194
Acuña, Rodrigo de, 195–96, 212
admirals, 126–28, 166, 250n22; supplements
  to income of, 108–12. *See also* generals;
  military personnel; officers
Admiral's jail, 206
El Aguila Volante (ship), 187
Aguirre, Lope de, 213
alacranes (flaming arrows), 184
Alas, Esteban de las, 32
Alas, Esteban de las (the younger), 86,
  127–28, 231
Alas, Gregorio de las, 32
alcancias (incendiaries), 184
alcázar (aft-castle), 130, 134
Alcázar palace, 5
Alcedo, Antonio de, 182
Alcega, Juan de, 97, 155, 221
Alfonso X (the Wise), 3, 5
alguacil (constable of fleet), 37, 95
almadiamiento (seasickness), 10, 135–36
Almaraz, Alonso, 158
almiranta (second-ranked ship in fleet), 87,
  106, 114, 159, 172, 179, 182, 243, 256n31
alms, 100, 103–4, 238
alquitrán (mixture of tar and oil), 137
Altamira, Juan de, 208
Altozano area of Triana, 88
ampolletas (sand clocks), 76–77
anchors, 69, 178, 180, 255n4
animals on ships, 132–34
Ante, Amador de, 219
Antonelli, Bautista, 12
apprentices, 28, 29, 219; homosexual activity
  and, 173; punishment of, 77–78, 204–5;
  salaries of, 119, 202–3; as servants, 77, 204,
  273n46
La Araucana (literary work; Ercilla), 159
Arciniega, Sancho de, 144, 155, 157, 221

Arenal (sandy beach) area, 4, 6–8, 88
Arenal Gate, 5
Ariès, Philippe, 131
Ariosto, Ludovico, 162
Armada of the Southern Sea, 13
armadas, 13, 50–53, 95–98, 102, 118, 186,
  224; composition of, 51; royal, 125,
  260n95. *See also* military expeditions
Arrieta, Juan de, 17
Arrieta, Sancha de, 18
artillery. *See* cannons; gunners
astrolabe, 65, 84, 85, 86, 236
avería (owner's fee), 258n59
awning (part of ship; *tolda*), 130, 134
Ayamonte (port), 2
Azores, 14, 111, 112, 113, 153

ballast, 68, 72, 111
barato (tip), 155, 156, 276n98
barber-surgeons, 80, 159, 183
Barbeto, Gonzalo, 38
Barlow, Edward, 255n10
Basques (Vizcayans), 54, 59, 61
"battle of flowers," 220
Bautista, Juan, 222
Bautista Finocho, Juan, 172
Bazán, Álvaro de, 96, 97, 125
Bazán, Álvaro de, Sr., 31, 110, 112
bilge pumps, 65, 71–72, 80, 140
blacks, 11–12, 16, 38–39, 40
blasphemy, 129, 154, 155–56, 220
boarding during combat, 184–85
boatswains, 56, 70, 81–82, 88, 122, 143, 202;
  homosexual activity and, 171, 174; instruments of, 205; punishment by, 204–5
boatswain's helper (*guardián*), 78, 82–83
books on ships, 158–61, 267nn93&97
Boquín, Felipe, 164, 187
Braudel, Fernand, 93, 120
bribery, 57–58, 88, 98, 100, 101, 105–14, 165,
  265n53

252nn61&66, 253n71; age ranges of, 75, 77, 78, 83, 87, 250n15, 256n21; buying power of, 114–22; conflict among, 191–222; division of labor among, 75–98; economic stature of, 114–26; foreigners as, 55–62, 214, 253n72, 254n83; funerals of, 186–87; on galleons, 135, 252n59; identities of, 58, 74, 216, 221, 255n16; morale during storms of, 177; motivations of, 23–35; origins of, 49–62; and prestige, 39–49, 84, 142–43; sexual activity of, 164–76. *See also* clothing; families of crew members; salaries; *particular occupations*
cross-staff, 65, 84, 236
crowding on ships, 130–34, 181
cudgeling, 208
cursing, 220

Dávila, Pedrarías, 130, 264n35
Davis, Ralph, 26, 124
deserters, 90–91, 212, 215–16; emigrants as, 25, 27
Díaz, Pedro, 73
Díaz del Castillo, Bernal, 99
Díaz de Solís, Juan, 212
Díaz Machín, Pero, 208–9
diet. *See* mealtimes; rations, daily
discipline, 191–222. *See also* punishment
dispensero (steward), 81
divers, 72–73, 80, 209
diversions on ships, 153–64
division of labor, 75–98
doctors, 182–83. *See also* barber-surgeons
Dominica Island (Lesser Antilles), 10
Drake, Francis, 102, 113
Durango, Juana de, 19

Elcano, Juan Sebastián, 37, 101, 122, 152, 199, 241
Enríquez, Don Martín, 11
Enríquez, Pedro, 221
ensigns, 109, 210
entertainment on ships, 153–64
epidemics, 9–10, 11, 14, 18, 181–82. *See also* illness
Eraso, Alonso de, 32, 113
Eraso, Cristóbal de, 45, 96, 126, 129, 153, 169, 209, 222, 250n16; and contraband scandal, 111–14; nepotism of, 31–33; and salaries, 118; and sunken ships, 86, 278n19; on violence at sea, 219

Eraso, Francisco de, 31, 32, 153
Eraso, Gonzalo de, 32–33, 113
Eraso, Miguel de, 32, 113
Escalante de Mendoza, Juan de, 69, 185, 204, 271n10; on clothing, 147, 149; on gaming, 154; on mealtimes, 142; on night at sea, 71; on officers, 81, 88, 237–38; on seasickness, 135–36; on storms at sea, 177, 214–15; on types of seafarers, 26, 30; on work at sea, 75
Escorial palace, 53
Espinola, Francisco de, 168
Espinosa, Gaspar de, 201
Espinosa, Martín de, 111
Estrada, Francisco de, 106
Estrada, Hernando de, 8, 247n15

families of crew members, 24, 30, 38, 55, 194, 223–24; and salaries, 18–19, 102, 117, 120–21, 197–200
Fernández, Alejo, 60
Fernández, Diego, 38
Fernández de Córdoba, Gonzalo (Great Captain), 46, 114
fiadores (guarantors), 202
finances, 3, 87–88, 95, 108. *See also* bribery; contraband trade; salaries
fire, 70, 158, 180–81, 184; from cookstoves, 134, 142
flagships, 109
Flandes, Martín Alonso de, 106
Flemish ships, 237
flogging. *See under* punishment
Flores Quiñones, Álvaro, 106, 210, 216
Flores Valdés, Diego de, 31, 32, 45, 47–48, 97–98, 166, 250n16
fluyts (ships), 237
fogones (cookstoves), 81, 134, 142, 180, 220
Fonseca, Juan Rodríguez de, 54
foreigners as crew members, 55–60, 214, 253n72
Fortunate Isles. *See* Canary Islands
freight charges, 118, 196, 200–201, 258n61. See also *quintalada;* salaries

galleass, 56, 111, 125, 174
Gallego, Juan, 221
galleons, 12, 45, 97, 216, 237; described, 8, 30, 134–35, 209; in royal armadas, 125, 260n95
galleta (biscuit), 141
games and gambling, 135, 153–57, 266n84, 267n87

(283)

Index

Virgin of Fair Wind, 187
visitas, 4, 88, 97–98, 108, 166, 248n34. *See also* inspections
vizcaínos, 54
Vizcayans (Basques), 54, 59, 61

wages. *See* salaries
warships, 30, 45, 187; described, 64, 134; protection by, 9, 13, 50, 95, 185; and salaries, 101, 103, 114, 118, 199
water constable, 95

weather conditions, 10, 11, 14, 182; and life on ships, 136–37. *See also* storms
Weiditz, Christoph, 204, 205
"the well" (part of ship), 134
whipping, 41, 192, 204, 206, 256n34
whipstaff (*pinzote*), 64
whistle, 82, 204
women, 18–21, 128, 169; on ships, 35, 164–71

Zapata, Alonso de, 57–58, 165, 218, 236

Index

Library of Congress Cataloging-in-Publication Data

Pérez-Mallaína Buena, Pablo Emilio.
[Hombres del océano. English]
Spain's men of the sea : daily life on the Indies fleets in the sixteenth
century / Pablo E. Pérez-Mallaína ; translated by Carla Rahn Phillips.
p.   cm.
Includes bibliographical references and index.
ISBN 0-8018-5746-5 (alk. paper)
1. Navigation—Spain—History—16th century.   2. Seafaring life—
Spain—History—16th century.   I. Phillips, Carla Rahn, 1943–
II. Title.
VK87.P47   1998
387.5'0946'09031—dc21   97-42172 CIP